THE ETHNIC HISTORY
OF
TRANSYLVANIA

THE ETHNIC HISTORY
OF
TRANSYLVANIA

BY

ENDRE HARASZTI
B.A., Cert. Educ., B.Ed., M.A.

Published by the Danubian Press, Inc. Astor Park, Florida, 32002
With the approval of the
Danubian Research and Information Center

Library of Congress Catalog Card Number 69—19410
International Standard Book Number 0—87934—004—5
Copyright 1971. Danubian Press, Inc. Astor Park, Florida, 32002

This book was published with the cooperation of
The Frigyes Balázs Thardy Memorial Foundation.

Lectured by Zsolt Györffy

Printed by The Sovereign Press, Toronto, Canada

PREFACE

What does the average western person know about Transylvania? Usually, he knows absolutely nothing.

Now, let me ask the same question this way: What does the average but supposedly enthusiastic geography — or history — student know about Transylvania, spending many years in various high schools and universities of the North American Continent?

The answer is the same again, in most cases: he knows absolutely nothing. Being a schoolteacher in Canada, but being a person of East-Central European origin, and still having basically European historical and political interests, I felt that it was a very interesting experiment, when I asked senior high school students, university students, postgraduate students, even members of history or geography faculties: "What do you know about Tranylvania?"

I received various answers. In most of the cases, the answer was very frank: "I know nothing." In many cases the answer was associated with a question: "Where is this Transylvania, after all?" I had a very intelligent student, who remembered that he had heard mention of this world already, and he also remembered that "Count Dracula was born there." Most of the high school students were not sure that Transylvania was a European, Asian or African country, and one of them, — a very "self-conscious" boy and proud of his origin, — even expressed his personal feeling, according which: "I do not know where this mysterious place is, but I do not care. It is probably an unimportant country. It was never a member of the British Commonwealth." Students of American origin, surprisingly, showed much more interest about Eastern Europe than Canadians, but their actual knowledge in most cases did not go farther and one of my disappointments was that I found that some of the encyclopedias, published in America know only one "Transylvania", which is "a colonizing enterprise and separate government in the Kentucky country just preceding and during the Revolutionary war." (Thus, the editors and the highly respected academic contributors knew only about the American Transylvania (the so-called Louisa Co.), which was organized at Hillsborough, North Carolina, in Aug. 1774 by Richard Henderson and his five associates.) Other Transylvania simply "did not exist", and I suppose most of the contributing academic personalities imagined that "the other Transylvania, the mysterious birth place of Count Dracula, exists only in the fictious world of the fables and horror stories." These simple, and actually very uneducated, western academic personalities did not even suspect that Transylvania is a real country somewhere in Eastern Europe, and Count Dracula was also a real person, though historically not an important one, whose castle still represents some sort of touristic spectacle among the "fearful" Transylvanian mountains.

Knowing that the average East-Central European student often knows much more about the West than the western student himself, I was shocked by my very first experiences. Later I found many excuses for the West. I realized that psychologically it is very hard to build, to look the future, and simultaneously to dream, looking only the past. We are meditating and dreaming often, when the West looked the future practically, and built the future, becoming more and more ignorant about the "melancholy" of the past. European student-life was filled with the atmosphere of "historia magistra vitae est", and now, witnessing the fantastic trips of the Astronauts, I am wondering: does this sentence represent reality anymore?

A

Yes, perhaps, it does. Only the World was transformed around us, only our environment was recreated by the human technological genius, but we, mankind, we actually did not change our physical and emotional nature in these, quite well known, few thousand years. We conquered Mesopotamia and Egypt and we fought bloody wars among us. We conquered "Mother Earth", fighting cruel, imperialistic wars among us, often concluding those wars with unjust treaties, ignoring natural ethnic and cultural frontiers, ignoring the suffering and crying claims of "non-important" minority groups. Yes, we did not, and we are not going to change ourselves. We will conquer this Galaxy system, sooner or later, step by tep. We will fight for certain planets and we will kill other claimants from our mother-planet, or from other planets. We will arrange inhuman, idiotic treaties in the future too, and we will ignore any knowledge about another "Transylvania" in the future, — perhaps another "Transylvania" of the planet Mars.

I confess, my feeling is that "historia est magistra vitae" stands very well even in the stormy atmosphere of our technological revolution. Even if we have "internationalist" ideas, we are still living in the age of nations, nationalities and nationalism. Many helpless orphans are around us without any real aid and understanding and there are many multinational states where certain minority groups are without any real aid and understanding. Superficial treaties pushed them into the arms of totalitarian dictatorships, or "imperial-minded" political bureaucracies. They are under the pressure of linguicide, which represents genocide for them. A nation or a nationality is able to preserve its identity only by the preservation of her native language and culture.

I know that Transylvania is "a very hard topic", because it is similar to Czechoslovakia, which was, according to many British politicians "only" a distant, little country, "and we know nothing about it." (1938). I know that it was not easy to know Transylvania, because this country has many faces and many names too. For the student of Ancient History it was Dacia, for the student of Medieval History it did not even exist, because it was simply the land of the "Seklers" and an integral part of the Hungarian Kingdom. For the student of Modern History it could be Transylvania, but could be Ardeal or Siebenburgen too.

However, it does not make any difference, what the "right" name of this country is. The main fact is that Transylvania is — similarly to Switzerland — the ancient home of three nationalities, speaking three very dissimilar languages. The other main fact is, that Transylvania, — very dissimilarly from Switzerland, — is one of the poorest and unhappiest countries of the world today. The third fact is that Transylvania's unhappiness is the direct and logical result of two factors: (1) Totalitarianism and consequently, minority-discrimination, and (2) the historical irresponsibility of the West concluding the First World War, and the historico-educational ignorance since then.

"Oh, well! Transylvania is only a distant little country and we do not know anything about it" — you may say. No, my dear reader. I will not give you opportunity for a cheap excuse this time. I am going to introduce this country in detail. I will discuss its geography, its history, its very unique position on the crossroads of many different cultures and its unique minority problems. The three nationality-situation was always an obstacle in the way of solutions, but this situation could also represent the key to the solution.

And now, let us ask, — not with the usual western naivity, but with real interest and enthusiasm: — "Where is Transylvania?"

B

TABLE OF CONTENT

I. *Introduction. The Transylvanian Problem* **1**
(The various names of Transylvania. (1), The Transylvanian problem. (2).

II. *The Geographical Unity of Transylvania* **5**
(Transylvanian phisiography (5), Transylvanian ethnography (7).

III. *Transylvanian Prehistory* **8**
(The "Danubian Phases", The Bronze Age (8), The Iron Age (9), The Scythians (9), The Thracians and the Daks (10).

IV. *Ancient Transylvania* **11**
(The political effort of Bucharest (11), Dacians and Getans (11), Burebista and the Roman threat (12), Decebal's freedomfight against Trajanus (13), Roman Dacia and the "Dako-Roman Theory" (14), Dacia from 117 to 271 (16), Visigoths and Ostrogoths (18), The Hun Conquest (20), The Hun origin of the Székelys (22), Gothia (23), The failure of Attila. The revolt of the Gepidas (24), Archeological evidences 24).

V. *The Ethno-Linguistic History of Medieval Transylvania Before the Hungarian Conquest* **26**
(Gepidas, Lombards, Herulians (26), Hun, Bulgarian and Slav elements, (27), The Avar origin and conquest (28), The ethno-linguistic similarity of Huns, Avars and Magyars (30), The Avar decline, The rise of the Bulgars (31), The possibility of Avar effects in the European ethnicum (32), Bulgarian domination in Transylvania (33), The political alliances of the coming Magyars. The Conquest. (33).

VI. *The Problem of Wallachian Origin and Early Migration* **35**
(A brief review of Transylvanian ethno-linguistic history until the Hungarian Conquest. (35), Historical evidences versus "Big Power interest" (36), The Wallachians. (Race or linguistic group?), (36), The origin of the Rumanian language (37), The Wallachian ancestors: the "Megleno-Rumuns", the "Aurumuns", and the "Istro-Rumuns" (38), The early migration of the Wallachians (39).

VII. *The Effects of the Hungarian Conquest on the Ethnic Transformation of Transylvania* **40**
(Ethno-linguistic situation in the time of the Conquest (40), The trine lines of the Conquest. The early settlement. (41), "Septem Castra" (42).

VIII. *Transylvania as an Integral Part of the Medieval Hungarian Kingdom.*
Part I: The Arpád Dynasty and Erdöelve **44**
(The attitude of Turanian conquerors on subjected minorities (44), Székely warriors and Vlach shepherds (46), The external and internal role of Transylvania (48), Transylvania and the western "adventures" (49), Christianization (49), Transylvania as the citadel of the "pagan" and Byzantine resistances (50), Cuman-Wallachian amalgamation and infiltration (52), The "Golden Bull" (53), "Silva Vlachorum" (54), The Mongol invasion (54), Székely settlement and privileges. (56).

IX. *Transylvania an an Integral Part of the Medieval Hungarian Kingdom.*
    Part II: The Transylvanian Saxons 57
    (Saxons from the Moselle region and from Lower Rhine. (57), The Teutonic Knights (58), The Saxon privileges (58).

X. *Transylvania an an Integral Part of the Medieval Hungarian Kingdom.*
    Part III: The Zenith of the Hungarian Power 60
    (The Anjou kings and Transylvania. (60), Sigismund of Luxemburg. (64), The real Dracula (65), The peasant revolt of 1437 and "The Union of Three Nations" (66), Jagellos, Habsburgs and Hunyadis (67), Mohács (69).

XI. *The Independent Principality of Transylvania* 70
    (Transylvania as one of the three fragments of Hungary (70), The essence of the Transylvanian Constitution (72), The agreement of the Three Nation at Torda (72), Rumanian opinions about the Transylvanian Principality. (73), Transylvania, citadel of Protestantism (74), The freedom of religion in Transylvania (74), The ethno-linguistic freedom in press and education in Transylvania. (75), The growing Wallachian population (76), The international respect of Transylvania. Stephen Báthory as King of Poland (76). Christopher and Sigismund Báthory. The terror of Michael, the Wallachian (77), The terror of Básta. The Counterreformation. The Bocskay-revolution. (78), The "Golden Age of Transylvania." The Transylvanian Constitution. (79), The position of the Wallachians. (80), Sigismund Rákoczi and Gabriel Báthory. Gabriel Bethlen. (81), The Thirty Years' War and Transylvania. George Rákoczi I. and the Wallachians. (82), The time of troubles. The end of the "Golden Age." The "liberation" of Hungary (83), The fall of Transylvania, as an independent Principality. (84).

XII. *Transylvania as the Province of the Habsburg Empire (Part I)* 85
    (The Thököly-revolution. The "Diploma Leopoldium." (85), "Gubernium". The Wallachians became a majority. The "Uniate Church," (86), "Divide et Impera". (87), Ethno-linguistic transformation in the 18th century. The Rákoczi Revolution; "Patria et Libertate." (88), "Enlightened Absolutism" and Transylvania. The problem of feudalism associated with the problem of minorities. (89), "Pragmatica Sanctio." Innocentius Micu-Klein, and the Wallachian demand. (91), Austrian minority policy. Transylvania the "Grand Pricipality." (92), Germanization. "Supplex Libellum Vallachorum". (93), "Edict of Tolerance", The Horia rebellion. (94), Transylvania tourched by the French Revolution. Napoleon and the Magyars. (96), The War of "Liberation". Metternich and Transylvania. (97), Liberal-nationalism. (98), The "Reform Age" as road to Revolution. (99).

XIII. *Transylvania as the Province of the Habsburg Empire (Part II: Revolution — Reaction — Compromise)* 102
    (The great year of 1848. Demand for the union of Hungary with Transylvania. (102), Wallachian nationalism in Transylvania, Moldavia and Wallachia Proper. (103), The Freedomfight of 1848/49, and Transylvania. (105), Russian invasion. (106), The bloody assizes of Arad, the "Bach Regime". (108), The semi-constitutional system and the minorities. Moldavia and Wallachia. (109), Birth of "Rumania", Growing Wallachian nationalism in Transylvania, The "Ausgleich" and Transylvania. (110).

D

XIV. *The Dual Monarchy and Transylvania*
    (Part I: "Magyarization") 112
    (The "Ausgleich, the booming economy, and their reaction among the
    Wallachians (112), Wallachian emotionalism and Wallachia Proper
    (113), The "Nationality Act" of 1868, and the Wallachian demand for
    automony (114), Rumanian "pro-Catholicism" and "anti-Semitism"
    (115), Centralization (116), "Magyarization": natural assimilation or
    aggressive activity — or both? (117).

XV. *The Dual Monarchy and Transylvania*
    (Part II: From the Millennium to Trianon) 121
    (Hungarian reasons refusing to grant autonomy for Wallachians. The
    Millenium. (121), The Saxons at the end of the 19th century (122),
    Wallachian demands (123), The School-question (124), The develop-
    ment of ethnic population (125), The political development of Rumania
    Proper (127), Bucharest "changed sides" in the War. (128), The Na-
    tional Council in Gyulafehérvár (129), Revolution, Rumanian con-
    quest, Counterrevolution. The Treaty of Trianon. (130), The Tran-
    sylvanian minorities. (131).

XVI. *Transylvania, As Province of the Rumanian Kingdom* 134
    (Minority situation after the War (134), Organization of Greater
    Rumania, Revisionism (136), Is it possible to solve minority problems
    by "political democracy" in a multinational country? (137), The "Land
    Reform". (138), Centralisation, Economic minority discrimination,
    educational discrimination. (139), The new Rumanian "science".
    Rumanian party-struggles. (140), The Paris peace-treaties as main
    sources of fascism both in revisionist, and statusquo-states. (141),
    Revisionism in Hungary (142), The census of 1930 in Rumania (143),
    The Rumanian road to fascism. (144), Situation in Transylvania in
    the late 1930-es. "To the Magyars in Transylvania." (145), The ex-
    treme anti-Hungarian feeling in Rumania. (146), Regicide at Mar-
    seilles, Hungarian "feudalcapitalism". (147), The road to fascism
    in Hungary. (148), The "Anschluss" as a turning point (149), Slow
    "linguicide" in Transylvania. (150), Carol and Hitler. The Csáky-
    proposal. (151).

XVII. *The Dismemberment of Transylvania* 152
    (Transylvania in 1939. Bucharest changed its side again (152), The
    "Vienna Award" (153), Hungarian re-incorporation of Northern Tran-
    sylvania (154), The Antonescu Dictatorship (155), Stalin's manipula-
    tions with Transylvania. (156), The suicide of Count Teleki (157),
    The hopes of the Rumanian Fascism (157), Ethno-linguistic situation
    in 1941. (158), Bucharest speculating to change sides again (159),
    The Bánffy mission (159), Surrender of Rumania. How did became
    Rumania "a faithful ally" again? (160), The tragic ghost of Trianon
    reappears. (161).

XVIII. *Transylvania in the Shadow of Stalin* 163
    (Russian occupation (163), Bucharest transforms itself from Fascism
    to Communism (164), The Stalinist National Policy (164), The
    "Magyar Delegation" in Paris (165), Bucharest "Stalinizes", Buda-
    pest tries to resist (166), "Salami-policy" (16E), The "new ethnic
    policy" in Transylvania (168), Ethnic situation in 1948, (169), Educa-
    tion (170), Terror both in Hungary and Rumania (171), The "Auto-
    nomous Magyar Province" (171), The new "Status Catholicus (172),
    The death of Stalin. (173).

XIX. The Hungarian Revolution and Transylvania *174*

(Hopes and anxieties after the death of Stalin. (174), The feeling of
togetherness in Transylvania (174), Malenkov and Khruschev (175),
The "Dilemma of Khruschev" (176), "Melting" in Budapest, (177),
Transylvanian ethnography in 1956. (178), The Hungarian Revolution
and Transylvania. (181), Effect on Rumania Proper. (183), Call for
a "democratic Danubian Confederation". (183), The "preventive
measures" of Moscow and Bucharest. (184), Gheorghiu-Dei's ways of
"consolidation". (185).

XX. The Rumanian "National Communism" and Transylvania *186*

(Persecutions in Transylvania after 1956, (186), The role of Bucharest
in the "Nagy-case". (187), Ceausescu and the experiment of "national
communism" (187), Persecutions on the fields of education, economics,
and religion (188), The "Autonom Hungarian-Mures Territory." (188),
The manipulation of Khrushchev with Transylvania; the Russian
"Divide et Impera" policy. (189), The Hungarian political emigration
as an international political force. (191), The Western press and Transylvania (191), The "International Commission of Jurists" and Transylvania. (192), The Rumanian "national communism", and its attempts to exterminate the national minorities of Transylvania. (193).

XXI. CONCLUSION *195*

(Problems in "chronological sense" and in "geopolitical sense." (195),
Transylvania, a small figure on the chessboard of international forces
(197), Transylvanian "interest" and Big Power "interests" (197),
Repetition of the main thesis, mentioned in the Introduction (198),
Political democracy and minority problems, (198), The confusion of
"Nation" with "State" (199), General problem of ethnic minorities
in the framework of the State, (200), "Regional autonomy" as a
proposed solution. (200), "Exchange of population, as another pro-
posed solution (201), "Territorial partition" (202), The failure of the
United Nations. (203), The precondition of the European integration.
(204), The possibility of the Danubian Federation, as a precondition
(204), Liberation and multiliteral guarantees, as precondition (205),
Independent and federativ Transylvania as a precondition. (205),
The Transylvanian spirit and togetherness (206), Hungarian-Rumanian
similarities and common aims. (207), The modernized version of the
"Three Nation"-tradition in the new "Switzerland" of the Carpathian
Alps. (208), Pacifism as supporter of any aggression. (209), Historical
"race" between genocide and natural development of history. (209),
Our "friend", Count Dracula ends the series of speculations. (209).

BIBLIOGRAPHY *212*

F

LIST OF MAPS

I. Transylvania   117 A.D. 15
(Dacia under Roman Conquest)

II. Transylvania Cca   350-400 19
(Germanic Migrations. Goths and Gepids)

III. Transylvania   430-453 21
(Part of the Hun Empire)

IV. Transylvania Cca   600-800 29
(Part of the Avar Empire)

V. Transylvania   894-895 34
(In the time of the Hungarian Conquest)

VI. Transylvania Cca   896-900 43
(Following the Hungarian Conquest)

VII. Transylvania Cca 1000-1200 47
(Part of the early Hungarian Kingdom)

VIII. Transylvania Cca 1360 63
(Part of the Anjou Kingdom of Hungary)

IX. Transylvania Cca 1560 71
(The Principality of Transylvania)

X. Transylvania   1740-1760 90
(Part of the Habsburg Empire)

XI. Transylvania   1847 101
(A general map of Hungary and Transylvania)

XII. Transylvania   1849 107
(The 2nd year of the Hungarian Freedomfight)

XIII. Transylvania   1910 133
(Ethnographic Map)

XIV. Transylvania   1919-1940 162
(Hungarian Revisionism. 1938-1941.)

XV. Transylvania   1968 182
(The most important cities and towns)

Sources for the Maps:

I.-XI.: See "Bibliography" Nos. 17, 20, 36, 51, 62, 64, 67, 69, 82.
XII.: See "Bibliography" No. 66.
XIII.: See "Bibliography" Nos. 8, 57, 102.
XIV.: See "Bibliography" Nos. 45, 61, 75, 106.
XV.: See "Bibliography" No. 80.

I. INTRODUCTION

THE TRANSYLVANIAN PROBLEM

Today, when we talk of Transylvania, we understand the entire territory of 103,903 square kilometers, which was taken from Hungary and annexed by Rumania after World War I.

The historical Transylvania, east of the Bihar Mountains and enclosed on the South and East by the bend of the Carpathian Mountains, was much smaller, no more than 57,804 square kilometers, and it was called for centuries in the Hungarian and literary language: "Erdély" or the "Land of Transylvania."

At this point, we meet with our first linguistic question.

The internationally used name "Transylvania" is nothing else, but the latin translation of the Hungarian name "Erdély", or "Erdöelve". This name was used and spelled by the Hungarian population in the 10th, 11th, and 12th centuries. The Wallachians, crossing the Carpathians from the South-East, and representing a growing minority, were not able to follow the Magyar pronounciation very well. They changed the original name of the country from "Erdély" to "Ardeal".

Let me introduce the linguistic origin of this country's name:

	Hungarian	English
a).	erdö	forest
b).	Erdély, or Erdöelve	beyond the forest
	(with original spelling: "Erdelew")	

The word "Transylvania", which is, of course, the Latinized form of the "Beyond the Forest" title, appeared first in the 17th century, when the official language of the Hungarian public and administration was already Latin. The Wallachians, gradually referring to themselves as "Rumanians" and claiming that they were the late descendants of the Romans, — did not use the word "Transylvania" before the 17th century. As they adopted the name "Erdély" ("Ardeal") from the Magyars, they also adopted the Latinized name "Transylvania" from the Latinized Hungarian political administration.

The name "Transylvania" did not appear on any of the original Rumanian documents before the 18th century.

Did the Rumanians have any reason to use the name "Transylvania" before this time? Has this word any connection with the claimed Roman origin?

The answer is: no. it has not. The Romans never called this territory Transylvania. The Romans called this territory the "Province of Dacia" after the previous inhabitants, the Daks, who were not of any raical or linguistic connection with the conquering Romans, and who were almost completely exterminated by the Roman Legions.

Officially, the Rumanians have been using the name "Transylvania" since 1920, when Bucharest received this country from the victorious powers by the Treaty of Trianon. However, it might be interesting to mention, that in their own native tongue, they still refer it as "Ardeal" which word derives, phonetically from the thousand year old Hungarian word: "Erdély". Why do they do this? Would it not be much more logical if these "late Romans" would call this territory "Dacia"? Or would it not be much more reasonable if they would use the name "Transylvania" — not only on "official" documents, but in their every days' conversations, and correspondences too? After all, "Transylvania" is a Latin word, and we may have every reason to expect its natural, conversational use from "Romans", even if they learned this word from the Hungarian administration in the 17th century.

But, let us leave this question for a while. We are going to detail this problem in this essay anyway. Let us take a look at the German name of this very complex country.

The Germans, who were settled here during the 13th century by Hungarian kings, call it "Siebenburgen". The linguistic explanation is the following:

	German	English
a.)	sieben	seven
b.)	burg	fort, fortress, (later: fortified town)
c.)	"Siebenburgen"	"Seven fortresses."

Thus, the name "Siebenburgen" was due to the seven administrative districts with fortifications, "Burg", in each.

We see now, that Transylvania has many names. The Hungarians have two names for this territory, one of them an original Magyar name, which was born probably in the 9th century, the other one is its Latinized form, which was born in the 17th century, and adopted by both international historiography and Rumanian administration. The Transylvanian Saxons also have a name for this country. This name originated in the 13th century, and it is still the name used for this territory by the local German-speaking population and by some history books written in Germany. The Rumanians do not have a term for this territory in their native language. Strangely enough they never used the ancient "Dacia" nomination, and the only thing they did was, that they adopted the "Transylvania" term from the Hungarian parliamentary language and the "Erdély" ("Ardeal") expression from the Magyar conversational language.

Leaving the world of languages, let us take a look at the actual Transylvanian problem.

"If you had been born in Transylvania, — wrote one of the native Transylvanians, who is one of the historians today, — you would not yet have to be fifty years of age and your citizenship status would have already been changed three times, without you ever leaving the town or village of your birth. You have been 'liberated' under different flags, or different party slogans, five times and each time under the pressure of an outside power which knew nothing about your problems and could not care less."(#1).

This quotation introduces an extremely strange situation but still does not mention one of the most extreme problems of Transylvania today. The problem is this:

If an individual happens to belong by birth to the Hungarian minority group of almost two million people, he finds himself in an even stranger situation than which was described — as a basic atmoshpere — in the quotation above. He will experience that he is forbidden to use his own

---

#1: Zathureczky: **"Transylvania, Citadel of the West."** Anderson Hall Research Center, University of Florida, "Problems Behind the Iron Curtain Series No. 1." 1963. P:V.

native language in publis places. He is discriminated against in every phase of his life. He is treated by government agencies as some sort of inferior type of human being, with no rights, only duties to the "Rumanian People's Republic." The time of elections usually does not represent any extraordinary excitement in a Communist dictatorship, because the citizen could vote for only one party, but probably our Hungarian individual represents a special danger even in these circumstances, because he is intimidated by gendarme brutality and perhaps kept away from the polls with bayonets.

"Constitutional rights" are usually slogans without practice in a dictatorship, but minority groups which are (well known) against the dictatorial rule of the dominating nation have a double load of suffering compared to the "major" nationality, which is actually represented by the government.

Liberal-democratic minded Rumanians probably feel that a Communist dictatorship could never represent their ideas about political and social life, but they will probably acknowledge that the government continues the Rumanian nationalistic traditions quite often in external policy and always in the treatment of those"rebellious" minority groups.

For in addition to the over-all communist terror and domination, Hungarians, and in a lesser extent, Saxons are facing the organized efforts of the Rumanian government to eliminate the so-called "Transylvanian Problem", through the total extermination of ethnic groups, which according to Rumanian doctrine, are the causes of this problem.

Before dealing with geographical and distorical background, hopefully it is clear to the readers of this essay, that the extermination of minority groups, whether Jews, Frenchmen, Hungarians or any other, is not the way problems should be solved on this earth. Other ways can and must be found through the use of good will.

The minority problems are not isolated cases, involving only a few million peoples here and there. We are all involved in them. Injustice obviously creates bitterness and hate. Every hate creates new injustices. These always returning facts must be regarded as a universal problem of the entire human society. Minority problems are usually danger spots not only in the national system, but in the international system too. History already produced many examples of minority problems which became danger spots, and in a certain moment became the sparks which disrupted the international system.

Therefore, it is not only our ethical and moral obligation to search for just solutions to these minority problems, but wisdom also dictates its necessity. After all, we should try to make the world a better place, not only for ourselves, but for all of mankind.

Returning to our main topic, the Transylvanian problem, we have to precede historical details with the expression of our feeling that it was always very unfortunate that in a postwar situation the Big Powers (the victorious powers) regarded the surface of our earth only as an area to share among themselves. After the First World War "the people's right to self-determination" appeared as a democratic principle, but it became practice only in certain cases when it could be associated with the interests of a victorious Big Power. In most of the cases this principle was ignored, creating a restless, bitter atmosphere in the Interwar Years and producing one important, provocative factor for the Second World War. The Big Powers did not seem to learn after the Second World War. Dividing the World into "spheres of interest", they regarded the problems of smaller nations as unimportant, best solved by dictatorial measures. The ethnic map of the earth was handled in a very superficial way again.

National selfdetermination and solution of minority problems represented even less importance in Yalta and Potsdam than in Versailles and in Trianon twenty five years ago. The Big Powers, representatives of large multinational empires just did not seem to care that history has proved again and again that dictatorial solutions are only of temporary nature and unsolved minority problems are political danger-spots for new world conflagrations.

"For almost a half-entury the Western World regarded the Transylvanian problem as a mere border dispute between Hungary and Rumania. From this view-point, it was settled and re-settled three times, without success." (#2).

First of all, let us express the idea, before we end this introductory chapter, that Transylvanian problem represents much more than a border dispute between two neighbouring nations, and the failure of the "solutions" was associated with the unfortunate fact, that this problem was misinterpreted as a border dispute: Secondly: each "solutions" were troubled by the fact that there were foreign "Big Power-interests" in the background.

My two assumptions are the following:

a.) The Transylvanian problem represents not a border-dispute, but mainly the problem of co-existence among three ethno-linguistic groups in the frame of a geopolitical unit, which is Transylvania itself.

b.) A just solution could be imagined only in a case where outside power-interests are not involved and the approach to a final settlement is by advancing only the interests of the three Transylvanian nationalities.

The Transylvanian problem — as we already mentioned — is not a theoretical minority problem. This problem is extreme. The discrimination against minorities in Transylvania during the 1960's reached the level of intellectual and economic genocide. The Rumanians in Transylvania, after fifty years of domination, represent still not more than 60% of the total Transylvanian population, but this "majority" enjoys the "protection" of Bucharest against the "rebellious" Hungarians and Saxons. The forefathers of the Hungarians came to Transylvania about eleven hundred years ago. The foferathers of the Saxons came to Transylvania seven hundred years ago. The "ruling nation" produced even earlier "evidence", simply associating itself with the Roman legions which conquered and ruled Davia between A.D. 98-271, — for 173 years.

We will deal with this quite stormy Roman conquest later in this essay. However our main goal is not to attack the very special Rumanian history-interpretations, but to find peaceful solution for the Transylvanian problem, which is unquestionably one of the most difficult minority problems in history.

My thesis question is this:

"How can the undisturbed and productive co-existence of the three Transylvanian nationalities best be achieved?"

Hoping that I will be able to answer this question, I have to introduce Transylvania as a "living unit" in its own right. It will be a geopolitical approach. It will be followed by a historical approach. History should provide us with evidence about the origin and evolution of the ethnic settlements, leading us to the functions of Transylvania within the European community.

#2: Zathureczky: **"Transylvania, Citadel of the West."** p. 4.

4

II.

THE GEOGRAPHICAL UNITY OF TRANSYLVANIA

Zathureczky, one of the experts of the Transylvanian problem, feels that geographical units are living units all over the world, having their own individuality in space and time.

> "In space, because they are different from all other regions. In time, because their inhabitants adapt themselves to the land and natural endowments of the geographical locations and create thereby the historical individuality of the region. The limitations and possibilities of th elocation determine the way of life and all its manifestations, and these manifestations build up into tradition under the influence of time." (#3).

It was always unquestionably true that the economy and structural development of society was determined by the unchangeable laws of nature, by the environment created by the climate, flora and fauna. People inhabiting the prairies have a different way of life than those who are settled in mountain regions or on the seashore. Consequently history witnessed many-many cases, when the borderlines of geographical units automatically turned into cultural frontiers, and later even to political frontiers.

One of the most delimited and firmly outlined living units of Europe is the Carpathian (Danubian) Basin, with its particular and specific historical individuality. Surrounded on the North, East and South-East by the chain of the Carpathian Mountains, this Basin stands leaning with its Western elbow on the Alps like a fortress facing the vast plains and steppes of the East, highways of barbaric invasions through all history. The Basin is separated from the Balkan Peninsula by the lower course of the Danube and by the bare, rocky ridges of the Karst.

The deep humus of the Hungarian Plan served for centuries as the granary of Europe. The natural water system is centralized: — all the rivers (#4) run toward the central plain. The Basin is a closed, compact living unit, not only geographically, but economically as well. Its separate regions cannot survive without one another, but as one living unit, the entire Danubian Basin fits into a perfect economic balance. Consequently all through history, it was a firm cultural, spiritual and political unit.

However, this geoplitical unit appeared often as a battleground, mosaic, sometimes as melting pot of extreme diversities. As the Basin was the meeting place of different climatic zones of Europe, here was where nomadic traditions and the Western way of life first mixed. Roman Catholicism, Protestantism and Oriental Orthodoxism challenged one another, or joined hands during consolidated times. Various races could find home and happiness in this living unit, — if the "interest" of certain outside powers did not disturb life here, if they did not interfere using the old "divide et impera" system (#5), or appearing as a "good, great uncle" of certain minority groups. (#6).

#3: Zathureczky: "Transylvania." p: 8.

#4: Except the Olt, which is crossing the Transylvania Alps and flowing south, reaching the Danube in Wallachia.

#5: The Austrian Empire was able to dominate in the Carpathian Basin only by the intensive use of this system.

#6: "Panslavism" could serve Russian imperialistic ambitions, which attempted to reach the "warm Sea" (the Mediterranean).

None of the nationalities living in the special atmosphere of this geographical and living unit was able to withdraw itself from the influences of the Danubian Basin. The Danubian German is different both from the Austrian and from the Prussian. The Serbian, settled on the Southern plain is different from the Serbs on the Balkans, and rather similar, in his lifestyle and philosophy, to the Croats. The Transylvanian Rumanian has an entirely different cultural background and mentality than those from Moldova, and Wallachia, across the Carpathians, and even the Transylvanian Hungarian (the Sekler) seems different from the other Hungarians who inhabit the Central Plain or Transdanubia.

Within the Danubian Basin, Transylvania is the region with the most individuality. It is an easily recognizable geographical unit.

White, high mountain ranges separate it from its neighbours, and on each side these mountains form the border of a basin composed of rolling country. Mountains, as natural frontiers of a cultural unit, are usually very important factors; the more clearly defined a basin is by the mountains on its borders, the stronger is the tendency of its inhabitants to live a life of heir own, to rely on themselves and constitute a separate political body.

The basin of Transylvania is separated by very high mountains from the territory surrounding it, especially in the east and in the south. The Southern Carpathians (The "Transylvanian Alps") form a most impressive frontier, separating Transylvania from Wallachia. (#7).

"Although both slopes of the chain are inhabited by Rumanian shepherds there is practically no intercourse between them ... The shepherds on the southern slope are shepherds of the migrating type. They spend the summers in the mountains, and in winters they drive the cattle down to the plains ... The shepherds of the northern slope ... drive their charges down to the Carpathian Basin. Here ... they feed their animal with hay." (#8).

The Eastern Carpathians differ markedly from the Southern Carpathians. They are irregular and not so high, but are even wider as a chain. West of this chain, the beautiful, little basins of high altitude are populated by the Seklers, people, whose language is almost identical with Hungarian, but who claim that they are late descendants of the Huns, people of the legendary king Attila. (#9).

On the western side, the side facing Hungary, Transylvania is not nearly so well separated from her neighbour by natural frontiers. The Transylvanian Basin and the Central Hungarian Basin are in close contact. The hills there are very populated, the rivers represent natural bridges for communication and transportation. It was the special geopolitical position of Transylvania which enforced its historical connection with Hungary, — rather than with Wallachia or Moldavia, — in Roman, Hun, Avar, and in Hungarian times, for about two thousand years. (#10).

The Transylvanian Basin itself is a high plateau of some 2,000 feet, which is moulded into a hilly country by rivers. The Basin is remarkably uniform in character, with a considerable economic wealth, with its salt mines, gold mines, a well developed agriculture, fisheries, a good stock of animals.

#7: Most of the range rises above 6500 feet.

#8: Eugene Cholnoky: "The Geographical Unity of Transylvania." (The Hungarian Quarterly, 1940/41, p. 660). The migrating type of shepherd can be found everywhere around the Mediterranean. The Transylvanian type is similar to the Tirolian and Swiss shepherd in his customs.

#9: Some historians feel that they are the descendants of the Avars.

#10: On the western side is the 'old "Great Forest", whence Transylvania took its Magyar and Latin names.

The Transylvanian rivers offer hydro-electric power. The plentiful quarries in the mountains facilitate the construction and maintenance of roads. The forests are the foundation of a thriving lumber industry and supply the needs of building.

In this country, which is approximately the size of Portugal and which is about two and one-half times as large as Switzerland (to which it is similar in geography), the visitor could study the diversity of population. According to the last prewar census its people declared themselves to be Rumanians (53.8%), Hungarians (31.6%), and Germans (10.7%), with the rest being Serbians, Ruthenians, Slovaks, Bulgarians, and others. (3.9%). (#11).

The three main nationalities, Rumanians, Hungarians, and the Transylvanian Saxons live in settlements that can not be easily divided inasmuch as most of the territory is dotted by mixed communities of verying ethnic proportions. (#12).

The religious composition closely follows the ethnic divisions. Hungarians are Roman Catholic, Calvinist, and Unitarian; the Transylvanian Saxons are Lutherans, the Swabians of the Bánát are Roman Catholics. The Rumanians belonged to the Greek Orthodox and Greek Catholic churches until after the Second World War when the latter was forcibly integrated into the Greek Orthodox Church. (#13).

"A single glance at the map of Transylvania — feels Zathureczky — gives the feeling of an advanced fortress nesting in the bed of the Carpathians, guarding the Danubian Basin from the East. In such a frontier position, everything happens under heat and pressure." (#14).

We may accept the concept, that Transylvania could be viewed and could serve as the eastern borderland of Western culture. Some Rumanian, Moldavian or Ukrainian historians would probably attack this sentence, but I suppose even they must agree that Transylvania is one of the main bridges between the East and the West by its specific geopolotical position and by its three nationalities from which two represent the Western — and the remaining one represents rather the Eastern-Byzantine historical and cultural traditions. We can also say, that Transylvania has been and still should be, the transmitting antenna of Western culture toward the East.

Such is the location, the geographical framework which determines the European functions of Transylvania, as an integral part of East-Central Europe, and also as an integral part of the Carpathian Basin.

Realizing the fact that the geographical unity of this land strangely coincides with the national disunity of its population, will lead us now from he geopolitical approach to the necessary historical investigation. It was the fate of many unjust treaties in history, that some dominating powers usually used the "might is right" theory revising political frontiers, almost completely ignoring enthno-linguistic history, as background and decisive evidence. To take a look at the Past is necessary here, and we do not feel it as an exaggeration to begin the investigation of the Transylvanian minority problem with the prehistoric times.

#11: Of course, we are going to analyze many similar statistics touching every stages of Transylvanian history.

#12: See the details of those settlements in the coming chapters.

#13: Details also in the coming chapters.

#14: Zathureczky: "Transylvania." p. 9.

III.

TRANSYLVANIAN PREHISTORY

We do not have certain evidence about the racial origin of the pre-historic men who populated the Danubian Basin in Mesolithic times. (#15). We know from archeological evidence that a full-fledged Neolithic culture (the so-called Danubian I, #16) appeared in the Danubian area about 2700 B.C., having come presumably from the east and south. If it came from the east, it could be of Scythan origin, which is suspected to be an early Ural-Altaic ethno-linguistic culture, and it could be interesting to mention that the Hungarian language of today belongs to he same linguistic group. If it came from the south, than it could be a norther branch of the ancient Minoan civilization, or the Hittite civilization. or even the Etruscan civilization. (#17).

This Neolithic culture was succeeded by the so-called Danubian II phase (2400-2200 B.C.). Contemparary Neolithic cultures, characterized by painted pottery, have been found at Erösd (Hungary) and some places in the Balkans, which fact seems to prove the Minoan-Mycenean origin, and reminds us that both the pre-Hellen Minoan ethno-linguistic culture, and its suspected origin the Mesopotamian-Sumerian culture were non-Indo-European cultures. Following this assumption, we may suppose that the Carpathian Basin was some sort of prehistoric stronghold of non-Indo-European peoples, and it is quite interesting, that this territory has the same characteristic even today. (#18).

With the Bronze Age (about 200-1000 B.C. or later) there were distinctive local developments in the Carpathian Basin, including of course Transylvania too, which seemed to be not only geographically but culturally an integral part of the main Basin, as early as these prehistoric times. The archeological findings represent proofs that the Etruscans, Mycenaean and Scythian influences were almost equally strong. These three (supposedly all) Ural Altaic ethno-lingual waves were quite similar in characteristics, although the Etruscan and Mycenean cultures (of Mediterranean origin) were stlightly different from the Central-Altaic Originated Scythan findings.

The civilization of Transylvania in the Bronze Age was relitively high. It had a dense population. There are a large number of finds from that age; funeral urns, bronze foundries, workshops, and so on. (#19). The man of the Bronze Age practised terrace-cultivation on the hill-sides. Thus he prevented landslides and made bette use of the rain-water, which was very necessary in Transylvania with its dry climate. Traces of the terraces can still be found in parts of Transylvania, the population of which is Hungarian or Saxon. (#20).

#15: The Mesolithic Period was the Middle Stone Age, the period of transition between the Old Stone Age (when men were hunters), and the New Stone Age, (when they learned to domesticate animals, to practice primitive agriculture, and to make pottery.)

#16: Herodotos mentioned Neolithic (New Stone Age) dwellings on the Balkans.

#17: The newest archeological findings seem to prove that the Etruscans were non-Indo-European, but Turanian, or Ural-Altaic peoples.

#18: The Hungarian language is a branch of the Ural-Altaic "family", representing the "Finno-Ugrian" group with the Finns and Estonians.

#19: From the country around Marosvasarhely (Rum.: Targu-Mures) alone over a ton of bronze was sent to the Transylvanian Museum.

#20: The Wallachian shepherds usually destroyed the terraces, because they were not land-cultivators and the slopes were easier to graze.

The man of the Bronze Age had also other means of economizing with water.

"In practically every side-valley of the main rivers they made fishponds by building dams. We know of more than 1,000 of such dams... Finds even show that the spill-water was utilized for turning small water-wheels which drove small mills." (#21).

The Iron Age began shortly after 1000 B.C. in Transylvania, with the development of the so-called "Hallstatt culture", followed by the La Téne (#22), which continued to Roman times.

It is mentionable that the two great Mediterranean cultures, which probably influenced the Carpathian Basin, disappeared after 1000 B.C. The Mycenaean assimilated into the Hellen culture, the Etruscan assimilated into the Roman culture. (#23). What did remain there? Of course, the Scythian influence, which gradually took advantage of the cultural and political vacuum. Taking any historical map, we will see that at about the time of Alexander the Great the Scythians occupied a large territory between the Theiss (Hung: Tisza) and the Dnieper (Greek: Borysthenes) and Transylvania was the western part of this Scythian conquest.

Who were the Scythians?

We may find some descriptions and speculations about them in the writings of Herodotos (#24), but of course we are still not certain about their ethno-linguistic origin. In almost every probability they were not Indo-Europeans. Judging after the archeological findings they could be a nordic, nomadic branch of the ancient Sumerian-Mesopotamians, who crossed the Caucausus after the Babylonian Conquest. (#25), and intermingling with the Mongoloid migrating tribes, they became the first ancient Turco-Tatar tribe-organization. The formation in the opposite way is possible too. They could be basically Mongols, receiving "blood transfusions" from the Caucasians, generation after generation. They were unquestionably nomadic people, cruel and filthy in their habbits. (#26). Their territory later comprised European Sarmatia too and roughly after 300 A.D. most of the western historians were confusing them with the "Sarmatians". (#27).

The newest archeological investigations around the Kaspian "Mediterranean", and north of the Black Sea led to rather surprising consequences. Certain totem-animal jewels, found in Scythian graves, are the exact illustrations of the Hun-Avar Magyar mythology! (#28). If we know, that on both the southern and northern slopes of the Caucasus, many towns and villages have the Maxera, Mazara, Matsar, Madzar, Madzsar names, then we may understand that the Magyar conquerors even in the IX-XIII centuries called themselves "Szittya"-s,, which term is nothing else, but the slightly transformed version of the term: Scytha!

#21: Eugene Cholnoky: **"The Geographical Unity of Transylvania."** p. 663.

#22: Hallstatt culture in Europe is traceable over an extensive territory from Spain and Portugal to Hungary. The cemetery of Hallstatt, is situated in the Austrian Salzkammergut. The La Téne period corresponds to a well-defined evolution of the sword, and the fibula. (safety pin).

#23: The Mycenaeans "disappeared" in about 900 B.C., the Etruscans in about 350 B.C.

#24: (c. 484-424 B.C.) He visited the Scythians around 440 B.C.

#25: Around 2000 B.C. (Speculation in Victor Padányi's **"Dentumagyaria."** (Editorial Transylvania, Buenos Aires, 1956.)

#26: King Darius learned this when he tried to bring them under Persian yoke in 507 B.C.

#27: The Sarmatians were probably early Indo-European tribe-organizations.

#28: The "wondrous, regal stag" was a central, respected symbol of Hungarian (and also of Hun and Avar) mythology.

Discussing "prehistoric" peoples appearing in Transylvania for a relatively long time, we must mention the Thracians too.

The Thracians appeared in the works of Homeros using the same sort of weapons as the Hellen Achaeans. (#29). Herodotos regarded them as the largest of all nations after the people of India. The early Thracians inhabited an area, (north from the Hellens and the Macedonians) from the Adriatic to the Pontus Euxinus (Black Sea). They were pushed off from the Adriatic towards East by the ancient Illyrians, (#30), around 1300 B.C. and their political-cultural influence was limited by the growing Macedonian power (5th cent. B.C.). In the time of Alexander the Great they populated the territory between the Ister (the ancient name of the Danube), the Pontus Euxinus and the Aegean Sea, roughly on the territory of Bulgaria of today. Although Hellen colonies were founded on the coasts of the Black Sea, Thrace did not absorb Greek culture.

Distributed by the military powers of Philip the Macedon and later by Alexander, the Thracians tended to move northwards, crossing the Danube. Certain tribes settled down in Moesia (which is Wallachia of today) and in about 300 B.C. a new great migration forced them to cross even the Transylvanian Alps. What happened?

During the third century B.C. the Macedonian rulers in Thrace were challenged by a wave of Celtic invaders. We really do not know their original home, but they came to Thrace from the direction of Illyria (#31). These Celts established a short-lived state in what is now central Bulgaria.

Following these Celtic conquests other disturbed Thracians crossed the Danube and joined the earlier settlements in Moesia. Following the routes of earlier Thracian tribes, many of them crossed the Carpathians to find security in the Transylvanian valley. (#32).

Historians do not describe the relatives of the Thracians in Transylvania as Thracians anymore. Supposing, that they used some sort of Thracian dialect, (or it was actually a "vulgarized" Thracian language), we call them "Dacians", or "Daks". (They were perhaps a Thracian-Scythian mixture.)

Some of the early Dacians were already in Transylvania in the time of Alexander the Great, but their migration into this great mountainous natural fortress was probably very slow, because in the third century B.C. Transylvania was still dominated by the Scythian horsemen. According to most of the historians.

"In the first century A.D. the Dacians, under their leader Burebista, formed a substantial state in Transylvania." (#33).

Burebista formed his Dacian kingdom only a few years before the Roman Conquest in Dacia. He did not find opposition in the north. Most Scythians disappeared (probably in a north eastern direction, #34), and the Daks could push their northern frontiers into the territory which is Slovakia of today. In the south they dominated both sides of the Danube. (Moesia).

In about 85 A.D. a new ruler, Decebal emerged as a leader. In the very same year the Roman legions began their invasions of Dacia.

We are not in "prehistory" anymore. With 85 A.D. the "recorded history" of Transylvania begun.

#29: N. Peloponesos was the ancient home of the Achaeans, powerful in 1300 B.C.

#30: Prehistoric Indo-European tribes on the Balkans. They were conquered by the Romans in 167 B.C.

#31: They came probably from S. Germany, carrying the Hallstatt culture.

#32: The Romans conquered Macedonia (and Thrace with it) in 148 B.C.

#33: Robert Lee Wolff: "The Balkan in Our Time." Harvard Uvin. Press, Cambridge, Massachussetts, 1956. p. 32. (Note: Transylvania is, of course, geographically not part of the Balkans, but the author discusses it as part of modern Rumania.)

#34: They were probably identical with the "mysterious" Bastarnae tribes.

IV.

ANCIENT TRANSYLVANIA

Rumanian historians investigated the Pre-Hungarian history of Transylvania with great enthusiasm and they concentrated very much on the Roman conquest of Dacia. Their great interest was associated not so much with the natural enthusiasm of historical science to find more and more details about the ancient Classical World. After 1920, when Rumania occupied Transylvania for the first time in her history, the historians of Bucharest approached the history of Roman Dacia not necessarily with historical objectivity. They adapted a rather subjective motive. They had to find — following the instructions of the Rumanian government — evidence, according to which Transylvanian history was nothing else but a continuous Roman history, and the one thousand year long (#35) Hungarian conquest represented only an "episode" aggressively interfering into this historical continuity.

We will return to this politico-historical effort later, when we will discuss Transylvanian history after the Treaty of Trianon. (1920). However, accepting the fact that Rumanian historians participated very actively in the investigations about the history of ancient Dacia, historical objectivity enforces us to use not only English. German and Hungarian, but also Rumanian reference books to this subtopic.

Our result, studying the references of those Rumanian historians, (paid by the Rumanian Government after 1920), is, that the leaders of the postwar Rumanian nationalism were "justly" dissatisfied with most of the "specially instructed" historians. N. Iorga, Professor of the University of Bucharest, Matila Ghyka, and others, having a real struggle with their own historical conscience, finally, were not able to satisfy fully their "employers". The Rumanian historians were able to produce suppositions, and assumptions. Using these, the Rumanian delegation could easily "convince" the "revancheist" Clemenceau and the careless, and ignorant Lloyd George in Paris. But historiography and the "sceptical" world of historians were not so easy to convince. When we are going to take a look at Dacian history now, we will see that even the most "enthusiastic" Rumanian historians were not able to produce evidence about Roman-Rumanian Transylvania.

In our previous chapter we arrived to 85 A.D., but — using the work of the famous Professor Iorga (#36), — we will take a look at Dacia in the time of King Burebista.

Iorga describes how the Romans called the Dacians "Davi" or "Daii". The name must. doubtless, be traced to the word "davae", which indicated their villages. We may have the assumption now, that the terms Daks, or Dacians were derived at by the amalgamation of the terms "Thracian" with the terms "Davi" or "Daii," and it could mean the identification of certain (Thracian originated) population in this Basin, who inhabited the villages. They were shepherds and peasants, distinguished from the "Getae". who had settlements resembling, though inferior to, the "cities" of the Gauls. (The "Getae" were probably Dacians of Scythian origin.)

There were kings among the Dacians, and the most important Dacian center was Sarmisagethusa, situated in the southern Carpathians. It became their capital in the time of King Burebista.

#35: Transylvania was part of the Magyar domination from 895 A.D. to 1920.

#36: N. Iorga: "A History of Roumania. Land, People, Civilisation." Translated by Joseph McCabe. Dodd, Mead & Company Publishers, New York.)

Iorga found with great triumph that the caps of the ancient Dacian commanders, the "pileus" was quite similar to the skin-cap of the Rumanian peasant of today, but with this he actually stopped to produce more evidence about the Dacian — modern-Rumanian relationship throughout many pages. We could learn from his well organized book, that Burebista was the greatest of the Dacian kings, who was able to push the Getan forces out from Dacia. The Getae probably left towards the northeast joining the Scythians, or Bastarnae. Burebista "received the inheritance of the Scythian king," wrote Iorga, (causing extreme dissatisfaction in political circles, because his sentence actually recognized, that some early forefathers of those "evil" Magyars were there even before the appearance of the Dacian tribe.). (#37). "Burebista seemed to promise the Carpatho-Danubian world a long and prosperous stability under the spectre of his vigorous dynasty." (#38).

However, the Dacians met a higher civilization, "more fortunate imitators of the imperialism of Alexander the Great: the Roman people and the victorious activity of the Caesars." (#39). Iorga recognises the fact that the recorded history of the Danubian Basin begins with the continental conquests of the Roman Empire. Augustus consolidated his rule on Achaia, Epirus, Macedonia on the Balkans and conquered Rhetia (#40), Noricum (#41), Pannonia (#42) and Moesia. His great successors continued his imperialistic policy, and the Roman ring of legions represented a deadly threat west, south and east of Dacia.

Iorga underlines the significance of the linguistic infiltration of the Romans. He confesses that "the historical sources, it is true, do not mention this expansion, ... hence it must have been a slow but steady infiltration that turned into a Roman population, speaking the vulgar Latin tongue, the Illyrians and Thracians." (#43). (Iorga uses these sentences as careful, preparatory arguments for his later assumptions, supposing a possible Dako-Roman intermarriage, — after the Roman Conquest of Dacia.)

After the annexation of Thrace. (#44), the legions of Tiberius Claudius Drusus (#45) appeared on the southern frontiers of Dacia, but the Dacians probably saw Romans already from Pannonia, and communicated with some of the Romans, who used the great road, built by Tiberius (#46), and connected the middle Danube with the lands on its lower course. The Dacians knew probably very well the great Roman political-military center of Aquincum too, which, in the time of Domitianus, became one of the preparatory bases for the Dacian invasion. (#47).

#37: N. Iorga: **"A History of Roumania."** (Ch. II: "The Creation of the Roumanian People." p: 23.

#38: **Ibid.**

#39: **Ibid.**

#40: It is on the territory which is Switzerland of today.

#41: This area could be associated with Austria of today.

#42: This is the Transdanubian region, w. Hungary, between Austria and the Middle-Danube.

#43: N. Iorga: **A History of Roumania."** p. 24.

#44. A.D. 46.

#45: (41-54), son of Germanicus, uncle of Caligula.

#46: (14-37). The road was built probably between 14-16, after the suppresion of the revolt of the Pannonian legions.

#47: Aquincum's ruins are on the northern part of Buda(pest). Titus Flavius Domitianus (81-96) succeeded upon the death of his older brother, Titus.

"Under Domitian, the imperial armies, under the command of Oppius Sabinus, Cornelius Fuscus and Julianus," — wrote Iorga, "were defeated by a king of superior ability, Decebalus." (#48).

The author seems to forget to mention the important fact, that the Dacian War of Domitianus began not with the invasion of Romans, but with the invasion of the Dacians across the lower Danube into Moesia. (Iorga probably does not like to mention this, because the Thraco-Moesians, — according to his theory — were already "Romanized", and the author dislikes the fact that the Dacians invaded their "fellow" Thracians.) This Dacian attack was repulsed by Domitian in person in 85. In 89, however, the complete reduction of Dacia appeared among the military plans of Domitian.

Iorga also fails to mention that the defeat of the Roman legions by the heroic Decebal (in 89) was associated not so much with the military genius of the Dacians, but rather with the fact that the Romans had trouble with the restless Marcomanni and Quadi (#49) at the very same time. The German tribes had occupied all the frontiers of the northern Danube, and they even appeared on the northwestern side of Dacia too. The Dacians did not have serious clash with the Roman legions, because Domitian concentrated the best troops on northern Noricum, Pannonia and Illyria. It was true that the Emperor made a somewhat humiliating peace with Decebal, who retained his independence. (#50.).

Marcus Ulpius Traianus (#51), this great Roman Emperor proved to be much more successful than Domitianus. He exceeded the limits set to the Empire by Augustus. In two Dacian Wars (101-107), the Romans were victorious and Dacia became a Roman province.

Iorga is right mentioning that "the stake was something more than the possession of Dacia itself." (#52). It had its gold and silver mines, it had its large salt mines with their indispensable product, but the main motive war rather strategic than economic. Iorga underlines the fact that Traianus realized that Dacia, surrounded by the high Carpathians, represents a natural, giant fortress against any invasion, coming from north, east, or from any other direction!

Did Traian need Dacia as a natural fortress?

Yes, he did need it very much! North-east of the Carpathians the Romans observed the appearance of Sarmata and Gothic tribes, and from the north, Alans, Suevi and especially Vandal tribes moved in the direction of the Carpathian Basin. To defeat and dominate the Dacians seemed to be the first and most important military step.

He prepared his first campaign in Upper Moesia (in A.D. 101). They conquered the Banat and tried to reach Sarmisagethusa from the west. The Roman legions captured the capital, but they were forced to withdraw by the strong counter-attack of Decebal, allied with Sarmatian and Teuton bands. In 105, Traian advanced by way of the valleys of the Jiiu and the Olt. The Dacians resisted in the mountains "with an incomparable fury, in which all the people shared. Even the women joined in." (#53). Sarmisagethusa was burned down this time. The Dacian chiefs, including Decebal, had drunk poison at a final banquet.

#48: N. Iorga: "A History of Roumania." p. 25.
#49: Germanic tribes, probably the very first waves of the German migration to Europe. They were followed by the more powerful Goths.
#50: Decebal was defeated but not crushed. The peace-treaty gave an opportunity to push the Quads, Marcomanni, and the Sarmatian (?) Yazigs away from the northern frontiers of the Empire.
#51: (98-117), successor of Emperor Nerva.
#52: Iorga: "A History of Roumania." p. 25.
#53: Ibid. p. 27.

"The conqueror, Trajan, raised at Rome a triumphal column higher and finer than that of Marcus Aurelius (#54) in memory of this difficult campaign, and he 'colonised' conquered Dacia."
— wrote Iorga. (#55).

The eminent Rumanian historian who tries to find some evidence about "Rumanian origin" in Transylvania in Roman times, and who — being unsuccessful in this effort, — attempts so hardly to produce "assumptions" at least, — seems to be quite absent minded in connection with Traian's mentioned column. He supposed that the Dacians used to wear a cap, which was very similar to the skin-cap of the Rumanian peasant, (#56), and he unfortunately forgot even to mention that Traian's column in Rome is almost our only source for the costume and appearance of the Dacians. What was interesting on the column?

"On the column we can see the Dacian nobles wearing brimless felt hats much like those of the Scythians, and the bare-headed Dacian peasantry." (#57).

Thus, Iorga, — and other Rumanian historians with him, — who tries so hard to limit, to underestimate Scythian influence on Dacia, who discusses the Dak warriors as some type forerunners of the skin-capped, long-haired Wallachian shepherds, — really could not do anything else, but to remain very silent about the archeological evidence of the Traian column, with its Scythian-type-nobility and with its bareheaded Dacian peasantry. Thus, they did not mention it at all.

Dacia became a Roman province, including not only what is Transylvania of today, but Western Wallachia too (#58). The Romans divided Dacia into three provinces under a single authority of an imperial legate. They bult roads which followed the courses of Transylvanian rivers, they built temples, basilicas, amphitheatres for the imperial officers, for their families, for the centurio's and for the legions, stationed in the newly built fortresses. A new capital, Ulpia Traiana replaced Sarmisagethusa. (See MAP I. on p. 15).

We know from the history of Roman colonisation, than is most of the colonised territories the officers and soldiers did not have much communication with the defeated and conquered local population. It was more than simply a custom: it was a military regulation. This regulation was accepted especially seriously on the frontier-provinces, which faced week after week, month after month, the danger of a possible Germanic invasion from the north or from north-east, and where the imperial officers could also face a rebellious uprising at any time. In Dacia the rules were, in every probability, very similar to the rules of Rhétia, Noricum, Pannonia and Moesia.

Rumanian historiography, in the unfortunate lack of historical evidence, could not do anything else, but suppose, that the "two civilizations co-existed, the language forming a link between them." (#59). Following this assumption, the Rumanian historians were all supposing that the Roman officials and soldiers communicated with the local population so warmly, that from the intermarriages of the "two peoples" was born the "Rumanian nation", as original population of Transylvania.

Thus, we know from the general philosophy and practice of Roman colonization that intermarriages (even sexual intercourses with the natives)

#54: (161-180). We just can not say that Iorga is very "historical-minded", when he compares Traian's column, (saying, that it is "higher and finer") to another one which was built many years later.
#55: N. Iorga: "A History of Roumania." p. 27.
#56: See our p. 12. Quotation from Iorga, p. 22.
#57: Robert Lee Wolff: "The Balkans of Our Time." p. 32.
#58: Wallachia east of the Olt and all of Moldavia remained outside the Roman Empire.

14

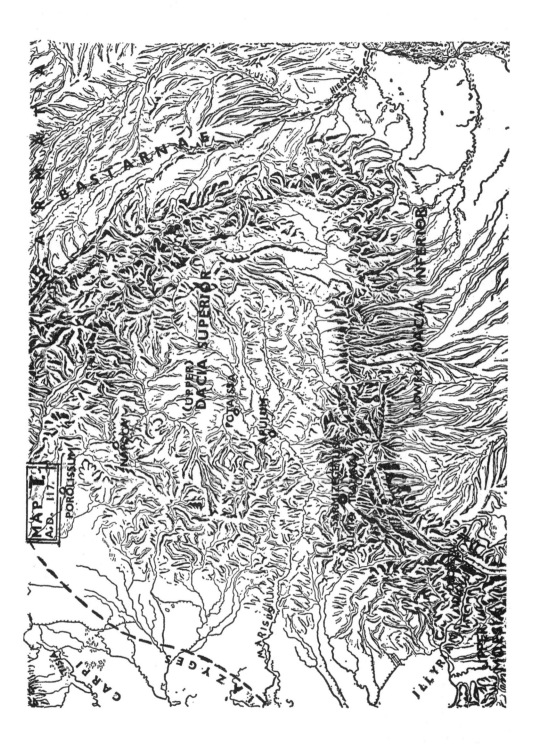

I. Transylvania   117 A.D. 15

were against colonial regulations; we know that the conquest of Dacia was about identical with the complete genocide of the Dacians, because males, fighting females, even elders and children were annihilated; we know that part of the survivors committed suicide, the other part was transported to Rome, and to other areas of the Empire to become slaves. Some of the historians adopted the Dako-Roman intermarriage-theory, without speculating about its contrasting nature towards historical proofs, but most of the historians did not accept this theory.

After the death of Traian (#59) the Roman military might left Dacia. Only the very strong fortifications, and some frontier legions guarded on the North-Eastern Carpathians, at the Pontus Euxinus (#60), and in the provincial capital Ilpia Traiana. The withdrawal was logical. The Dacian population almost completely disappeared, the Quads, and the Bastarnae were relatively quiet on the North, but, on the other hand the Parthian War (#61) made the transportation of some Dacian troops to Asia Minor necessary. The next Emperor, Hadrianus (#62) did not appear to be interested in Eastern European affairs. He concentrated his interest, (and his forces) in Britain and in North Africa. When the Jews in Judea revolted (#63), Hadrian probably limited even more the relative strength of the Roman military post in Dacia, because the movement of the fanatic Simon Bar-Cocheba could easily result in the partial disintegration of the Roman Empire in the Orient.

Antoninus Pius, the next ruler of Rome did not make any positive movement enywhere in the Empire and we have good reason to believe that in his time Dacia was rather a formal province of Rome, appearing only on the map. The Western Goths were quite close to the Eastern Carpathians, the first tribes of the Ostrogoths appeared on the North-East. It seemed that it would be a clever strategical step to withdraw the legions behind the Danube. The great river represented a much better military frontier against the coming horsement. The Roman legions did not like the high Carpathian mountains; they could not adapt them to their military system. Roman generals worried about the fact that some invaders from the Caucasus were much more "familiar" in the Carpathians than the Roman defenders. When Marcus Aurelius became Emperor, (#64), he had to concentrate on Parthia again. (#65). After this the Pannonian legions needed reinforcement from Dalmatia, from Dacia and from Rome, because the Marcomanni crossed the upper Danube north of Noricum. (#66).

Many of the contemporary Roman historians mentioned that the Carpathian Basin was quite depopulated. If any descendants of the (supposed) Dako-Roman intermarriages remained, they were annihilated by a terrible plague, which touched Dacia about 172 A.D. (#67).

The Empire faced the powerful pressure of the Great Migration. When the Sarmatians attacked the lower Danube frontier, it was clear to the Roman generals that their move towards a southwest direction was hap-

---

#59: A.D. 117. (See MAP I. on p. 15 again)

#60: The territory which extended north from the Danube-delta, and which is Bessarabia of today, was part of Roman Dacia. Here heavy forfitications faced the migratory tribes coming from the endless steppes of Central Asia.

#61: 113-117. (The Parthian revolt was led by Chosroes, Parthian monarch.)

#62: Publius Aelius Hadrianus (117)-138).

#63: 132-135.

#64: Marcus Aurelius Antoninus (161-180), following the death of Antoninus Pius (138-161).

#65: 162-165. Verus was the leader of this campaign.

#66: 166-175. The great general, Verus, died in this campaign.

#67: The Emperor introduced a precedent by importing considerable numbers of Marcomanni into the depopulated areas of the Empire.

pening under the pressure of much stronger tribe-organizations behind them. (#68).

However, the great Gothic migration somehow stopped north of the Caspian region. (#69). The withdrawal from the Dacian outpost behind the Danube could be postponed. The legions could relatively easily defend Noricum and Pannonia from the repeated attacks of the Marcomanni (#70). The weak emperors after the death of Marcus Aurelius (#71) were fortunate enough to have a temporary breath before the final, dark storms of the Great Migration. Contemporary historians noted that Septimius Severus was the first Roman emperor who recognized military marriages. (#72). This historical fact does not help, of course, the Dako-Roman theory.

Emperor Caracalla was the first who faced the problem of the great invasion of the Goths. The tribes of the Alemanni and the first tribes of the Western Goths attacked the Empire from the North and from the Lower Danube at the same time. Caracalla was successful, he still left strong troops in Dacia, but the land itself was depopulated, a real "No-mensland", appearing as a Roman province for a long time only on military maps. (#73).

We have to support the assumptions of Rumanian historians, as far as the Romanization of the Balkan is concerned. Since the Imperial permission of Septimus Severus, the Balkanic legions actually "Romanized" Moesia, and especially Thracia. (#74). (But it was still not the case in Dacia!)

The Great Migration came at this time, and the Empire was not able to stop these first powerful waves. Decius, one of the emperors (#75) sacrificed his life fighting against the Goths, who appeared in Dacia. His successors could not find the means against the barbarians. (#76).

The Roman Empire was forced to retrench, and the earliest retrenchment naturally took place at just the point where the most advanced conquest had been scored: Dacia. In 271, the Emperor Aurelian (#77) withdrew the final Roman legions from Dacia and "its seems fairly certain that at the same time he withdrew with them a substantial portion of the population. settling them in he province of Moesia, south of the Danube." (#78). Thus, if some brave family or individuals still hid themselves in the caves of the Dacian mountains, if they still survived the series of massacres and plagues, now they had to leave Dacia, finding relative security in Mocsia. "The towns were abandoned" — confesses even Iorga, one of the respected founder of Rumanian historiography, (#79), supposing that some of the villages remained populated.

#68: It happened in 172 or 173. The Sarmatians were pushed by the Goths.

#69: The migratory movements slowed down. The probable reason was that the great Hiung-Nu tribe organization (called Huns in Europe later) found a temporary home on the Kirghiz steppes and did not push the Goths westward for a while.

#70: 178-180. The emperor himself died at Vindobona (Vienna) in this campaign.

#71: Commodus (180-192), Pertinax (193), L. Septimius Severus (193-211).

#72: Since the immobilization of the legions had made these usual.

#73: Caracalla ruled from 211 to 217.

#74: Following Macrinus (217-18), Elagabalus (218-222), Secerus Alexander (222-235) the Rhine legions elevated a Thracian peasant, Julius Verus Maximinus (235-238), who was probably a quite good example of the Balcanic "Romanization", Rumanian historians did not even mention him, probably because he was famous about his lack of any culture.

#75: He followed Gordianus III (238-244) and Philippus (244-49). Ruled: 249-51.

#76: Gallus (251-53), Valerianus (253-59), Gallienue (259-68), Claudius II (268-70).

#77: L. Domitius Aurelianus (270-275).

#78: R. L. Wolff: "The Balkans of Our Time." p. 33.

#79: N. Iorga: "A History of Roumania." p. 29.

The Visigoths represented a growing pressure on the north-eastern provinces and it was hard to estimate that this pressure was an actual invasion, or it was nothing else, but a flight from the Huns. I suggest the second possibility. Claudius II was able to stop the frontal wawe of the Goths at Nish, (Upper Moesia), and settled them in Pannonia, where large groups of Quadi, Marcomanni and Vandals represented the main population. To the historians of today these Goths seemed to be refugees from the Hun menace, but of course the contemporary Roman historians did not even suspect the coming of even greater waves of destructive migratory tribes, — or they underestimated the military power of the Huns.

After the evacuation of Dacia (271), the Goths gradually occupied this territory. This Gothic conquest ended in about 375 A.D., and we have good reason to believe that if any Roman, or Romanized element still settled there, ignoring the order of the Emperor for evacuation, he became the victim of the barbarians. (The "assumptions" of the Rumanians goes far beyond any creditibility.) With the Goths other Germanic tribes found home in Dacia, for example Gepids in Northwestern Dacia and a tribe of Vandals in Western Dacia.

No Roman army could stop the entering great storm! After a series of weak rulers (#80), Aurelius Valerius Diocletianus (#81) could not help even with the most radical administrative reforms. (#82). After his approach of "divided responsibility", Constantinus I, the Great (#83) reunited the Empire (#84), which hopelessly disintegrated under the "rule" of his successors. (#85).

Beginning with A.D. 271 Dacia was not part of the Roman Empire anymore, so we do not have to associate its ethnic history with Rome, and we use its commonly used name, Transylvania from now on.

We mentioned already that the Visigoths, (with some Vandal and Gepida tribes) were the sole rulers of Transylvania until 375. Their relative peace was seriously disturbed by the arrival of the great Hun migration. The Huns crossed the Volga in 372, and pushing the Ostrogoths before them (#86) attacked the Visigoths. Athanaric, the king concentrated his forces east of the Carpathians, at the Dniester River, but realizing the Hun military might, withdrew to Transylvania. According to most of the sources, the Huns crossed the North-eastern Carpathians only by vanguard-troops, but it was enough to provoke a serious ethnic transformation in the Carpathian Basin. The Visigoths took refuge first; they crossed the southern Transylvanian Alps and they began their great adventure on the Balkans, later in Italy, and finaly on the Iberian peninsula The Ostrogoths crossed the Theiss (Tisza) River, also crossed the Danube and in a slow migration, tribe, after tribe, they settled down in Pannonia. (#87). (See MAP II. p. 19).

The great Hun tribe-organization, under the leadership of King Rugilas crossed the North-Eastern Carpathians only around 433. They conquered the Carpathian Basin completely, concentrating the military power on the Upper Theiss.

#80: Claudius Tacitus (275-76), Probus (276-81), Carus (281-283).

#81: (284-305).

#82: Division of the Empire into two areas, with two coequal emperors (Augusti), and with two chosen assistants and successors (Caesar).

#83: (306-337).

#84: Between 324 and 337. It is mentionable that Christianization did not make the invading Barbarians more "pious", but only made the Roman Army more decadent.

#85: No reason to note here the names of all the emperors, since Transylvania did not belong to Rome anymore.

#86: Defeating Hermanrich, (king of the Ostrogoths) in the same year.

#87: The disintegrating Roman legions could not stop them this time.

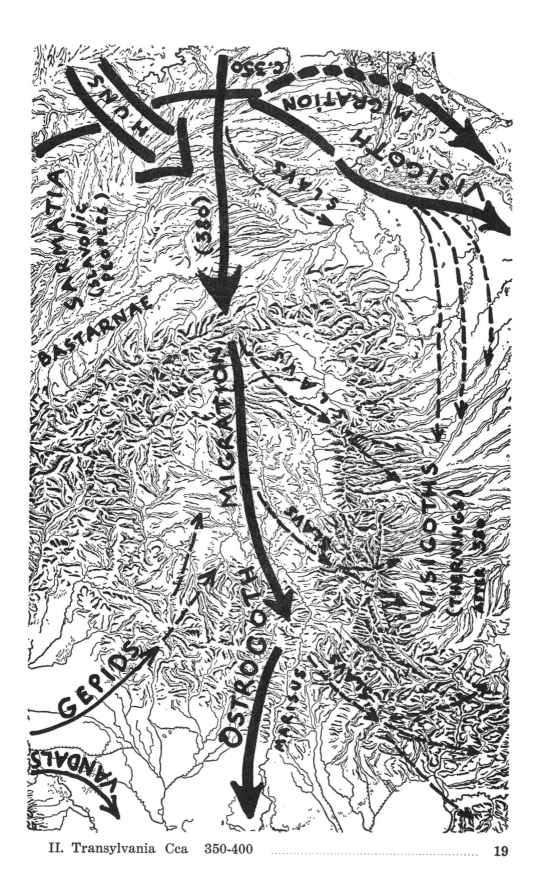

Transylvania became a — not too favoured — province of the great Hun Empire, which dominated the European Continent north of the Roman frontiers. It was not too favoured, because the Hun horsement liked the Great Hungarian Plain much more than the mountains and hills of the Eastern and Southern Carpathians. The Empire of King Attila, the "Scourge of God", as he was called in Rome, stretched his Empire from the Lake Aral to the Rhone, (which was the territory of the Franks already), and from the Alps to the Baltic Sea. The great King of the Huns, Attila, ruled together with his older brother, King Buda (#88) between 433 and 445. After the death of Buda, Attila dominated alone his giant Empire, overruling Gepids, Ostrogoths, Rugians, Scirians, Heruls, Thuringians, Alans, Burgundians and Ripurian Franks. (See MAP III. p. 21).

Who were the Huns?

Was this wild tribe organization the same which was known as Hiung-Nu, or Hsiung-Nu, representing a danger in the history of Ancient China, and formed a dynasty in China between 304- and 581? Was this the same people, which entered into Central Asia and later into Europe under the pressure of the Zhu-Zhu Empire in Asia? Did their appearance represent nothing else, but the return of the Scythians under a different name? Were they Mongols, as some of the references were mentioning them? Were they Turko-Tatars, as other references are trying to identify them?

I do not think that any of these references were telling the complete truth. All these references are naive. Western oversimplifications. However, all these references do contain some truth.

Unquestionably, the Huns were people of Ural-Altaic origin, just as the Scythians were before them, and just as the Avars and later the Magyars were members of this large ethno-linguistic family after them. Being a giant migratory nation, which swept westward from the Chinese Walls, they admitted into their tribal organization-system all the tribes whose language was similar o the Hun dialect. It was possible that the main body was idenical to the Hiung-Nu Mongols, but in their journey they were mingled with other Ural-Altaic (Scythian, or Turanian) tribes, which, (north of the Aral, of the Kaspian) were rather Turkish in their language, customs and appearance, than Mongoloid. (#89). The invasion of Europe was not an aimless adventure, but a considered political and military action. In every probability, they knew very well, that they were marching in the footsteps of the Scythian forefathers. The occupation of the Carpathian Basin could be considered as a reconquest, — at least from the Hun point of view, and as a step to find satisfactory pasturages for their horses and cattle. Were they really "barbarians"? Well, they were definitely wild and fearful in their appearance, but we must keep in mind that, being fearful, was a generally accepted military tactic both in the Ancient and Medieval Ages and we have many reasons and evidence to believe that the "Christianized" Romans (#90), Visigoths (#91), and Franks (#92) were not at all less cruel and "barbaric" in their military actions.

#88: The capital city of Hungary, Budapest represents one of the historical declarations, that the early Magyars remembered the Huns as forefathers.

#89: The "Turko-Tatar"-term, used by many Western historians, represents only a historical, and linguistic confusion. The "Tatars" were already the mixture of Mongols and Turks.

#90: Gradualy converted to Christianity from the 1st Century, but in large masses since Constantinus the Great's rule.

#91: The people of Alaric performed their destructive migration after their "Christianization" by the Gothic Bishop, Ulfilas (311-381).

#92: The Franks did not change their cruel system of warfare after the conversion of Clovis to Roman Catholicism. (496).

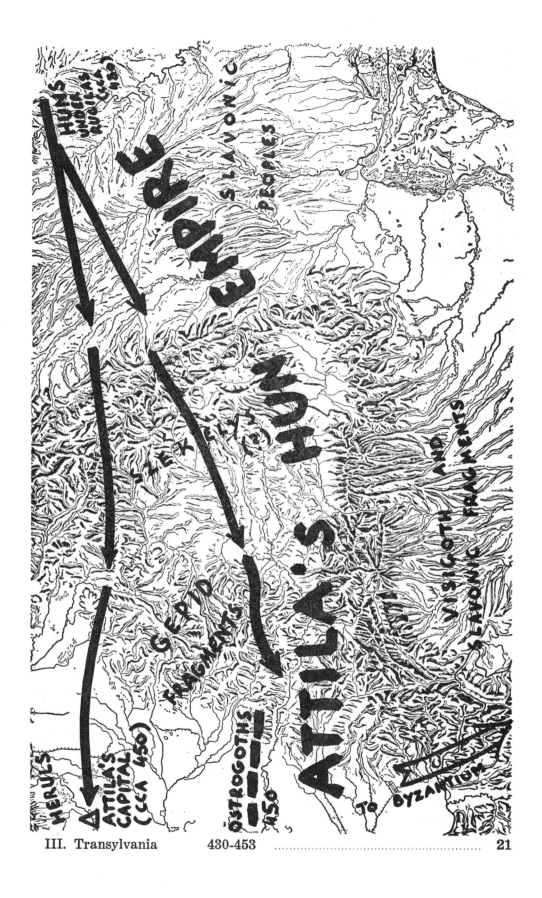

HUNS
(ODGAR)
RULERS?

EMPIRE

SLAVONIC

PEOPLES

HUN'S

SZEKELY(?)

ATTILA'S

GEPID

FRAGMENTS

OSTROGOTHS
450

VISIGOTH AND

SLAVONIC FRAGMENTS

HERULS

ATTILA'S
CAPITAL
(CCA 450)

TO BYZANTIUM

Reading the chronicles of alarmed monks, we have to take into consideration, that the authors were mortally frightened, they hated the Huns not only as invaders, but as "pagans" first of all, because the newcomers stubbornly refused to accept Christianity, and remained faithful to their own ancient, oriental religion. Studying the contemporary chronicles, it is interesting to note, that the authors of these rancorous works, were usually not disgusted by massacres, if they were managed by "Christianized" tribes, or military units, "for the sacred aims of the Cross". I feel, that it was a quite subjective attitude from these monks, and the adaptation of their chronicles from modern historians without any critimism, or careful reconsideration, reflects some sort of naivity.

The ambitious Attila faced Rome and the Frank territory with the plans of expansion. Transylvania was part of his conquest, but he did not estimate this mountainous country very highly. He realized the strategic value of the Carpathians, but he did not need too much military concentration there, because he ruled over the area east to Transylvania too, north of the Black Sea and the Kaspian. However, he stationed a Hun tribe in the Eastern Carpathians. The Szeklers (Székelys) of Transylvania are very proud to believe that they are the descendants of this Hun tribe of the fifth century.

All their legends, all their tales from their colorful mythology are the representatives of this tradition, reappearing in the life of the Transylvanian Székelys since many-many generations. One of these myths is especially very well known everywhere in the Carpathian Basin. The Székelys were the eastern frontier-tribe of the great Attila and their ruling Prince was Chaba, the younger son of the King. The great Hun Empire disintegrated, but the Székelys are still awaiting Prince Chaba and his army — from Heaven. The Milky-Way is still called the "Way of Armies" in Transylvania, the "Way" on which Prince Chaba and his glorious horsemen will reappear to bring protection for the poor Székely people.

Should we deny the factual content of this legend? It is true, that the contemporary Chronicles did not mention any son of Attila, named Chaba. (#93). Some of the Gothic sources were mentioning Irnac, or Hernac as son of Attila, and this son did not rule in Transylvania at all. Some of the historians were supposing that the Székelys were descendants of the Avars, who ruled the Danubian Basin in the Medieval Ages, and their imagined Hun tradition was only the romantic illusion of the peasant mind.

However, we have to take into consideration, that many myths and legends, which were denied by early historians, proved to be historical facts later, and archeology or new documents proved that they represented reality at least to some extent. It is also true, that he origin of many Ural-Altaic names was associated with a certain national service, or personal characteristics. "Caba" in Turkish means "the wanderer." We really do not know the number of Attila's sons, and it is quite interesting that the traditions of the Székelys gave reference even about the mother of Prince Chaba; she was a Byzantine Princess, whose intermarriage with Attila represented a temporary political agreement between the Hun Empire and Constantinople. We know that Marcian was the emperor of the East at this time. (#94). If Chaba ever existed, it is quite probable that he ruled Transylvania, which was the country connecting Attila's Empire with the Eastern Roman World.

We have even documentary evidence about the Székelys as direct Hun descendants. "Anonymus", the anonymous Chronicler of Bela III, who

---

#93: Following his ancient customs, of course, Attila had many wives and many children. According to the Székely legend, Chaba had a brother, named Aladár.
#94: (450-457). He, — just as Attila — used the Ostrogoths as warriors, in inferior status.

represents one of the most authentic historical sources from the twelfth century (#95), mentioned the Székelys as "Populi Atthyle regis" (#96). In his chronicle, which was written of course in Latin, he was nominating them as "Siculi", which term means "Frontier Guards" (#97). We do not have any reason to believe that the term "Székely" originated from the Latin "Siculi", because the word "Székely", or "Szekler", means "frontiersmen" in Turkish too! Supposing that the Huns were Turko-Mongol peoples, — and even the Rumanian historians could not deny this assumption, — it could be very possible that the government of Attila appointed them as frontier-tribe, using the ancient Turkish expression, that is:: "Székelys" (#98).

However, even if the Székelys were already in Transylvania in the fifth century, they were not the only people populating the territory between the Theiss and the high mountains. The Visigoths did not leave Transylvania completely. "Dacia was called Gothia throughout the fourth century. It is known that Alaric, the great King of the Visigoths, was born on the Danubian isle of Peuce," — noted Matila Ghyka, another well known Rumanian historian besides N. Iorga. (#99). Many of these Goths were still among the Transylvanian Mountains in Attila's time. They did not even need to hide themselves, because the main tribe of Attila did not care about Transylvania too much. The Goth warriors used the opportunity forming free troops, and participating in the western adventures of King Attila, together with the other subjected tribes of Germanic origin. "There is not a single word of Gothic origin in Roumanian" — declares Iorga, very proudly. (#100). Thus, the Rumanian historians did not "cooperate" very well, trying to prove the "Dako-Roman continuity" in Transylvania. Iorga confesses the complete evacuation of the "Dako-Roman" towns in the earlier part of his book, and now, the two prominent historians of Bucharest were producing collective evidence, that the Rumanian language did not adopt even a single term in the land which was called by many inhabiting benerations: "Gothia", because of its main population! (#101).

The main topic of this essay has no connection with Attila's western invasions, so I see no reason to detail them. Transylvania received a traditional importance as a strategic basis after 440. According to some sources, after 440, according to other sources, only around 450, the Eastern Roman Emperor refused to pay the "Hun Money" (#102), and Attila devastated Moesia, Macedonia, Thessalia, Epirus, Thrace, threatening even Constantinople with occupation.

At this point I have a mentionable remark.

#95: "Anonymus Belae Regis Gloriosissimi Notarius" ("The Anonym notary of the glorius King Bela") was the most important chronicler of 12th C. Hungary. He wrote the famous "Gesta Hungarorum." According to the newest historical evidence, his real name was Posa, and he was the Bishop of Diakovár. If this is true, than Anonymus was not the notary of Béla III (1172-96), but of Béla IV (1235-70), because Posa became Bishop of Diakovár only after 1238.

#96: C. A. Macartney: "Studies on the Early Hungarian Sources." Sárkány Printing Co. Budapest, 1940. Vol. III. p. 217.

#97: C. A. Macartney: "The Magyars in the Ninth Century." Cambridge, Univ. Press, 1930. "The Oldest report on the Countries of the North." p. 27.

#98: Count P. Teleki: "The Evolution of Hungary and Its Place In European History." The Macmillan Co., New York, 1923. "Making of the State". p. 39.

#99: Matila Ghyka: "A Documented Chronology of Roumanian History." B. H. Blackwell, Ltd. Oxford., 1941. "Pre-Sistory" p. 20.

#100: N. Iorga: "A History of Roumania." p. 32.

#101: The exaggarated ambitions led here to a blind alley.

#102: The war tax paid to the Huns by subjected or threatened States.

In the beginning of this invasion, Attila crossed an area between Upper Moesia and the lower Danube. This area is identical with Serbia of today. It appeared as part of Upper Moesia on the Roman maps of the 2nd century, but as "Dacia" on contemporary political-military maps at the end of the 4th century already. Noticing this interesting change, we may found another historical evidence, that after the evacuation of Roman-Dacia in Transylvania, the Romans concentrated most of the survived population here, south of the lower Danube, around the cities of Nassius and Serdica. The mountaneous territory presented quite good hiding places for the refugees, (whose ethno-linguistic origin and status is still very uncertain), against the Visigoths, (because the people of Alaric did not touch this area when they invaded the Balkans), but the Huns devastated this "Dacia No. 2", and probably they met with Romanized elements for the very first time. (#103). (See MAPs II. and III., p. 19 & 21).

The events of Hun history came with the dramatic speed of a storm. Attila began his great adventure against the West in 451 (#104) and after the decisive battle of Chalons (#105), he returned to the Carpathian Basin. One year later, he turned against Italy, razed Aquileia, ravaged the countryside (#106) and opened the road to Rome. According to the Catholic legend Pope Leo (#107) stopped him, but the fact is that plague, the shortage of food supply, and the arrival of the Roman reinforcement forced his return.

Attila's death (#108) was followed by a revolt of his German vassals led by the Gepids of Transylvania. (#109). They defeated the Huns on the Nedao (in Pannonia). The remaints of the Huns left in part on the lower Danube, others crossing the north-eastern Carpathians. The Ostrogoths settled in Pannonia, in Lower and in Upper Moeasia, the Gepidas dominated Transylvania. (#110). This was the situation in the Carpathian Basin, when on Sept. 4, 476, the Herulian Odovacar deposed Romulus Augustulus, the last emperor of the West, at Ravenna. It was the traditional end of the Roman Empire, and also the end of Ancient History.

We may mention, as a final conclusion to the history of Ancient Transylvania, that all the peoples, the Scythians, the Daks, the Romans, the Vandals, the Goths, the Huns and the Gepidas, who ruled over Transylvania for a shorter, or longer time, left the archeological evidences of their former existence. Only one people did not leave any traces of their life. They were the so-called Dako-Romans, the imagined mixture of the Roman conquerors with the subjected Daks.

Roman archeological findings are clearly, and typically Roman in their character. (#111). It was not possible to find any Dak influences in them. This is very understandable. The conquerors would not let themselves be influenced by a subjected, barbarian people, — who were almost completely annihilated before the foundation of Roman Dacia. After the eva-

---

#103: After 271 A.D. the Romans were able to manage a relatively secured situation for the peoples here. They were Illyrian and partly Germanic elements, with some Slav population. Their "Romanization" began at the end of the 3rd century.

#104: With his Gepids, Repuarian Franks and other subjected Germanic tribes.

#105: "Lacus Mauriacus" was the ancient name of this place, at the fields of "Catalaunum.'"

#106: Foundation of Venice.

#107: Leo the Great (440-461), the first great Pope.

#108: 453.

#109: 454.

#110: Around A.D. 480, a tribe of the Huns merged into the Bulgarian-Turk tribal federation. (The Bulgars were still Turko-Mongols this time.)

#111: The "limes" (fortifications), "castellum" (smaller forts), roads, etc. of Emperor Traianus and his successors.

cuation of Transylvanian Dacia, the Romans (as I mentioned already) managed the foundation of a Moesian "Dacia". In this second Dacia the archeologists were not able to find neither original Dak, nor Dako-Roman findings, consequently, the name "Dacia" represented nothing else (after 271), but the fact that the Legions of the evacuated Transylvanian Dacia were stationed here, behind the Lower Danube, facing the invasions from the North.

The latest, original Dak findings in Transylvania were from the 2nd and 3rd century B.C., (and not A.D.!) The findings have a very strong Scythian character. They are very similar to the Scythian ornaments from the 6th century B.C. (#112). These findings seem to support the opinions of some of the historians, who believed the Sumerian-Scythian origin of the prehistoric Daks. (#113). Among the findings it is possible to see Thracian elements (#114).

Just as the archeological findings of Roman origin did not show any Dak influence, the prehistoric Dak findings did not show any Roman influence. The Rumanian historians were not able to support their assumption with any single document or with any archeological evidence. (#115).

— — — — — — — — — — — — — — —

In the following chapters, we are going to discuss the ethnic history of Medieval Transylvania, trying to put the focus on the Transylvanian Basin itself. Only one of the sub-topics will lead us south of the Carpathians; opposing the Dako-Roman imaginations, we have to investigate the origins of the pre-Rumanians (the Vlachs, or Wallachians) on the Balkans. (At this point, let me note, that the Székely-problem has nothing to do with the Balkans. The origin of this ethno-linguistic group is definitely Asiatic.) (#116).

#112: Found north of the Pontus Euxinus.

#113: For example Viktor Padányi, who, in his **"Dentumagyaria."** used a large amount of linguistic speculations, trying to prove that the Transylvanian Getae were nothing else but the Hellenic version of the Daks. Herodotos found that the "Tisza-Getae" and the "Massza-Getae" were Scythians. Padányi believes that the Daks were the descendants of the "Dah" people, originated in Ancient Mesopotamia and left the valleys of the Tigris and Euphrates after the Babylonian Conquest. (c. 2000 B.C.) (Inf. **"Dentumagyaria."** ("Datas to the History of the Kaspian-Mediterraneum." p. 191).

#114: Mostly oval-shaped horsemen, with a bird and a dog.

#115: The archeological findings: 1934 (Szércse), 1953 (Csikszentkirály). (Both of these findings were found in Székelyland; inf.: Csiknémasági: **"Dak Archeological Findings on Székelyland."** ("Canadian Hungarian News", Winnipeg, Dec. 10 and 14., 1965.)

#116: The problem of the origin of the Székelys does not have any real significance. They were perhaps Huns, or perhaps Avars. In either case, they populated Transylvania before the Vlach migration.

V.

THE ETHNO-LINGUESTIC HISTORY OF MEDIEVAL TRANSYLVANIA BEFORE THE HUNGARIAN CONQUEST

After the fall of the Roman Empire, the Danubian Basin became the bridgehead of Eastern invaders for several centuries.

If we take a look at the political map of Europe in 476 (many of the historical-cartographers like to associate a certain political position of the Continent with the very year when the Roman Empire had fallen into pieces), we will realize that the Eastern Roman Empire represented still a considerable power. West of the Eastern Empire, the Ostrogoths owned actually two, politically separated territories. One of them was the Kingdom of Odoacer (#117), the other one was Ostrogoth Pannonia, with an additional territory on the south, which is Croatia of today.

Transylvania was still ruled by the Gepidas, people speaking a dialect of ancient German. Liberating themselves from the Hun domination, they enjoyed their political freedom, but they did not seem to show any tendency to form a permanent, organized state.

Missing the opportunity to fortificate the line behind the upper Theiss, they faced the consequence of it already around A.D. 520. Lombards and Heruls crossed the Theiss and penetrated into Transylvania. The Gepidas were forced to move south and they were able to represent some resistance in an area between the Theiss, Maros (Mures) and the Lower Danube. On the northern part of the Transylvanian Basin first the Heruls seemed to be stronger, but around 508 the Lombards destroyed them.

The movement of all these tribe-organization was definitely toward south-west. The main reason was probably the appearance of a new, great Ural-Altaic (Turanian) tribe-organization east of the Carpathians, similar to the fearful Huns, the Avars!

The Lombards and the Gepids could not move to the Balkans. The Eastern Roman Empire was strong enough now to stop these uninvited visitors. Emperor Justinianus (#118) concerned mostly with his Persian wars, and with North Africa, later with the reconquest of Italy (#119), but the lower Danube, (and the imperial mercennaires behind it) represented a strong wall — for a while. The Lombards and Gepids penetrated into the Ostrogothic Empire. After the reconquest of Italy (553), Justinian gave land to them in Noricum and Pannonia. (#120).

Transylvania was almost completely unpopulated for a few years. The terrible reputation, with all the usual exaggerations of the distubed imaginations, preceded the coming Avar tribes.

The Avars crossed the Eastern Carpathians around 550. Similarly to their relatives, the Huns, the newcomers pushed various weaker tribe-fragments before them. They were Bulgars and Slavs. Before dealing with the Avars, we have to mention certain informations about these new ethnic elements appearing in Transylvania and on both sides of the lower Danube.

#117: Mentioned on page 24 already. Odoacer (Odovacar) was a Herulian. He became the ruler of Italy by the revolt of the Heruls against the Romans. The successful revolt deposed Romulus Augustulus (476). He was killed by Theodoric the Great in 493.

#118: (527-565).

$119: Under the leadership of the great Belisarius, Justinian was able to unite the Roman Empire again.

#120: Justinian used their aid to defeat Theodoric and his Ostrogoths. The emperor's gratitude revealed in this patronage.

The first Bulgarian tribe, which appeared in the Transylvanian Basin and in the valley of the lower Danube was not identical with the great migration of the Volga-Bulgars from their ancient home to Europe. Pushed by the Avars, first only a relatively small Bulgarian tribe appeared at the Carpathians. In 540, — with some Hun elements with them — they crossed the Danube and raided the Balkan area as far south as the Isthmus of Corinth. (Other sources were mentioning another Bulgarian raid in 559. The Hun and even Slav elements seemed to dominate them. They advanced to the very gate of Constantinople, and only the great Belisarius was able to stop them. (#121).

These events, of course did not happen in Transylvania, but the appearance of Hun and Slav elements in these Bulgarian raids was so significant (form the aspect of the Transylvanian ethnic problem too), that we have to deal with it.

Let us take a look at the Slavs.

These Slav elements, pushed by the great Avar migration, seemed to be much more warlike than their northern relatives beyond the Vistula. (#122). Thse "Sclaveni" fought shoulder to shoulder with the Huns, Bulgars, and other Ural-Altaic elements against the soldiers of Belisarius. It took about 100 years until the Eastern Roman emperors were able to "civilize" them and arrange the first Slavic settlements on the Balkans. (#123).

We may comment the reappearance of the Huns this way: the Huns, Avars and Bulgars were all Ural-Altaic tribe-organizations, speaking only slightly different dialects. It was quite understandable, that the Eastern Roman soldiers, diplomats and historian confused them. (#124).

Generally speaking, it could be quite safe to say, that these Hun, Bulgar, Slav elements, and tribe-fragments, pushed by the Avars to the Balkans, were rather confused refugees, trying to find a new home, than a centralized organization, considering political conquest. They found themselves between two fires, the Avars and the Byzantine power. Their confusion "exploded" in senseless, savage activity.

#121: A D. 559 Belisar, the great general, and military genius served mostly in the Persian wars (beginning with 527), in the conquest of North Africa (533-43), and of course in the reconquest of Italy (535-554). The Hun-Bolgar attack began in 540, and Constantinople was able to defeat them only when Belisarius returned from Italy.

#122: The Greek and Roman writers called the northern Slavs as "Venedi." Their (historically known) first "home" was the territory between the Vistula and Dniester. The Gothic and Byzantine writers nominated them as "Sclaveni." According to our sources, they were peaceful hunters, and in the early Medieval Age, mostly farmers. The southern Slavs, probably under the influence of Hun, Bulgar, Avar elements, seemed to be much more warlike.

#123: Tiberius, Eastern Roman emperor (578-582) was troubled many times by Slav restlessness. The Slavs advanced into Thrace and Greece. They settled in large numbers, thus changing profoundly the ethnographic composition of the Balkans' populations. In 626, the Slavs (already with some Avar aid), attacked Constantinople by land and sea, but were unable to storm the walls. Some of these warlike Slavs were settled down on the northern Balkans, intermingling with the Illyrian population. heir descendants were the Serbs and Croats.

#124: László Tápay Szabó mentions a case in his **"Az Emberiség Története."** (The History of Mankind; Athenaeum, Budapest.) The first Avar ambassador appeared in Constantinople in the time of Justinian. His name was Kandik. His speech was translated to Greek by the Hun interpreter. The Hun and Avar languages were only dialects of the same tongue!

After these first tribe-fragments, — which brought the rumor of a terrible invasion coming from the East, — the Avars appeared at the gates of Europe, north of the Caucasian region, in 558. They soon became a serious threat to the Eastern Empire. They conquered Transylvania in 560 and the rest of the Carpathian Basin in 561. They entered into Thuringia in the next year. One of their tribes was defeated by the Franks (#125), but this affair did not stop them. They rode on their little Tatar horses with extraordinary speed and skill. Their system in attack reminded the Franks and Eastern Romans of their earlier relatives, the fearful Huns. They came to occupy "the inheritance of the legendary Attila," they conquered almost exactly the same territory; they felt that the center of their Empire — which reached from the Black Sea to the Baltic Sea, and from the Enns (#126) to the Don River, — should be the Carpathian Basin. They concentrated their main settlements exactly on the former Hun settlements and we have many reasons to believe, that they felt, that they are actually Huns.

The Lombards were the first who realized that the Avars could represent a useful means, — as military allies. With the help of the Avars, the Lombards could easily annihilate their old enemy, the Gepids. Than the Avars allied themselves with the Eastern Empire and from their Transylvanian bases they crossed the lower Danube keeping the restless Bulgaro-Slav peoples under control for a while in agreement with Constantinople (#127), though the ruler of the Eastern Empire did not like the idea that the Avars took all the fortresses, and did not wish to leave them in their hands (#128). Between 580—796 the Avar Empire was unquestionably one of the most powerful empires of Europe. Its power was more-less equal to the political and military powers of the Frankish Kingdom and Byzantium. They concentrated much more of their population in central fortifications (the famous "Avar Rings") than the Huns, but the political frontiers were almost identical to the Empire of the great Attila. The Avar Conquest seemed to be rather a "reconquest", — at least from the point of view of the Avars, but it also seemed to be that both the Franks and Byzantium recognized the Avar claim for the "inheritance of Attila." (See MAP IV. p. 29).

The ethnic history of Transylvania leads us very often outside of the Carpathians. This is necessary if we wish to trace the origin of certain peoples who settled the Transylvanian Basin for a longer or shorter period. This system forces us to ask the question: who were the Avars?

The answer is not easy, because these Ural-Altaic tribe-organizations represented actually a mixture of various Mongol and Turkish elements.

Some historians believe that the Avars were identical to the Juan-Juan tribe-organization, which founded the first Mongol Empire throughout Mongolia. (#129). It is only partly true. The Mongol elements in the Danubian Avars were probably from the Juan-Juan, but we have to keep in mind that this Mongol Empire split into many small kingdoms, and the western parts were almost completely "Türkicized". (#130). The Avars migrated westward and in their migration they were called by various names by various peoples and historians. (#131). They settled on the shores of the Caspian Sea and (some of their tribes) at the Aral Sea,

---

#125: (563). In every probability Sigibert I (son of Chlothar; 561-575) of the Merovingian Dynasty was successful against the Avars.

#126: Small river. Almost identical to the Austro-Hungarian frontier.

#127: (578). It was in the first year of Emperor Tiberius. (578-582).

#128: (583).

#129: (407-553). It was destroyed by the revolt of the subjected peoples.

#130: The revolting elements were all Turkish. Shortly the Avars were under complete Turkish domination.

#131: Obors, Vars, Pars, probably the Parthians (Latin term) were Avars too.

between Amu Daria and Sir Daria. (#132). They united themselves with various Scythian elements. Among these Scythian elements the Huns were the most important ones.

Studying the sources, we have several reasons to believe that the name of Attila was very famous, not only in Europe, but in Central Asia too. The main difference between the two Continents was, that in Europe Attila's name was associated with fear and horror, — of course especially in the chronicles of horrified monks, — but in Asia King Attila became a glorious legend. Even the fugitives of the disintegrated Hun Empire were received with extraordinary respect by the various Ural-Altaic tribes. Certain Hun chieftains, who declared themselves members of Attila's family, became the glorified leaders of these tribes, and tribe-organizations. The Avars and Bulgars identified themselves with the Huns, having a ruling dynasty above them from the descendants of Attila, the legendary King of Hunnia.

But, do we really know how far the Hun ethnic element was represented in the tribal-organization of the Avars, Bulgars and later the Magyars, these powerful "Scythian" peoples, who entered into Transylvania and appeared in the valleys of the Danube and the Theiss? Do we really know, that the Huns were only a leading aristocracy among them, or (with some difference,) the newcomers were the returning Huns themselves? Do we have enough historical evidence to prove, (or disprove), that the Hun language was only very similar, — or it was identical with the Avar and later, with the Magyar language? (See again #124).

"We have no precise knowledge of the origin of all the tribes which constituted the Magyar people at the time they entered their future home." — wrote Count Paul Teleki (#133). But we see that in a moment of great danger, in one of those moments of hot struggle which have a great impulse to migration, there arises *the man*, the man whom Asia's races needed to form peoples from the related but scattered ranks and to lead them to new conquests. The great peoples of Asia, — Huns, Hiungnus, Mongols and others — were all more or less collected from the same or related tribes. It was the will of the great chiefs, of the Attilas, Kublai Khans, and Tamerlanes, who raided the plains and put the stamp of the chief's own clan on all the peoples they touched ... All these peoples together made a conglomerate mass, rolling continuously westward, some-times as a coherent people governed by a warrior-prince, sometimes as a disintegrated mass of quarreling tribes. It is my opinion that Magyars, and Bulgars, Avars and Huns, Scythians and others were composed of similar elements, only the percentage of the various elements in each tribe being different." (#134).

Understanding this, it seemed to be quite logical that the Avars claimed the "inheritance of Attila", they spoke a dialect of the Hun, and they occupied almost exactly the same territory as Attila did. They reached probably the hight of their power when (in 591) they raided the very gates of Constantinople. (#135).

#132: Oxus and Jaxartes in some ancient, classical writings.

#133: (1879-1941). Hung. statesman and scholar. His ethnic map of the Carpathian Basin is one of the best of its kind. He committed suicide because attack on Yugoslavia (1941) proved to him that Hungary hopelessly became Hitler's satellite.

#134: This quotation is from Teleki's **"The Evolution of Hungary and its Place in European History."** The Macmillan Co. New York, 1923. "Making of the State." pp. 28, and 30.

#135: In 591 Maurice was the Emperor (582-602). His general, Priscus was able to defeat the Avars two years later, but in 619 (in the time of Emp. Heraclius I 610-41), the Avars raided Constantinople again, which was threatened on the Asiatic side too by the Persians.

The decline of the Avar power began in the first part of the seventh century. Two important political changes marked the relative weakness of the Avars. One on their west, one on their east. The eastern change represented a significant ethnic transformation in Transylvania many years later.

The Frank power used the opportunity when the greatest king of the Avars, Baján died. (#136). In 623, Dagobert I (#137) was able to build quite a strong "buffer-state" between the Franks and the Avars. Co-operating with Samo, a Frankish tradesman, and taking advance on the fact that the Avars concentrated mostly on the Balkans, the Frank diplo-macy managed to unite the Czechs, some of the Wends, and other Slav elements. The artificial "kingdom" was able to exist until 658 in the dangerous neighbourhood. (#138).

Ethnic transformation on the east represented much more danger for the Avars.

The Bulgars, — basically one of the Ural-Altaic ethno-linguestic branch-es, — who at the beginning of the seventh century had created a Great Bulgarian Empire in the Don region, established a state in the middle Volga area after the fall of that empire. Both of the Don-, and the Volga Bulgars were ruled over by Hun chieftains. The Huns used a slightly different dialect as the common Bulgars, and were respected as descendants of the great Attila. Thus the Huns, — just as in the case of the Avars, — appeared as some sort of high nobility among their ethno-linguistic relatives. (#139).

Their first authenticated ruler, Kurt (or Kubrat) (#140) freed them from the Avar yoke around 619, cooperating with Constantinople. His son (or grandson) Isperikh (or Asperuch) (#141) led his people westward. In the shadow of the great Khazarian Khaganate (#142) the Bulgars did not have any real security. Isperikh chose to move closer to the Avar center. The disintegrating Avar power did not represent danger anymore. Isperikh did not cross the Carpathians (#143). He turned south, crossed the lower Danube between 650 and 670, and established a new Bulgarian capital at Pliska. According to most of the historical maps, the Bulgars represented only part of the Avar Empire, but the real fact was that Isperikh's people were almost absolutely independent. The Avars could not control them anymore. Some of his Bulgars crossed the Carpathians from the south and settled in the Transylvanian Basin. The warlike Bul-gars defeated even the Byzantine Army in 680, and after it, they became respected conquerors of the Balkans, holding not only Wallachia, but Moldavia and Bessarabia as well. The amalgamation with Slavic inhabit-ants was probably very fast, but the upper, military class, the Huns re-mained strictly Ural-Altaic for a long time, and awaited the opportunity to take over "the inheritance of Attila" from the declining Avars. Under Isperikh's successors (#144) the ethnic map of Transylvania gradually changed. The Maros (Mures) River was the frontier. North of it Avars, south of it the Bulgars populated the Basin. (See MAP IV. again, p. 29).

However, the Avars still represented respect in Europe. Their military

---

#136: "Baján" is a Turkish term, which means "wealthy", "powerful". He ruled the Avar Empire from 562 to 602.
#137: King of Neustria (630-636), earlier King of Austrasia (623-628).
#138: Samo's attempt (c. 623-658) was the earliest construction of a Slavic state. After the death of Samo, his "kingdom" disintegrated.
#139: The Bulgarian "Dulo" dynasty declared itself as Attila's successors.
#140: (584-642). His dominion included the area from the Don to the Caucasus.
#141: (643-701).
#142: Another Ural-Altaic powerful kingdom, north of the Caspian Sea.
#143: Some Bulgar fragments entered into the Danubian valley, even to Italy.
#144: Tervel (701-18), Sevar (724-39), Kormisosh (739-56), Vinekh (756-61), etc.

power slowly declined, but their intermarriages with other European peoples strongly influenced the ethnic structure of the Continent. Interestingly enough the contemporary western chronicles were very quiet about these intermarriages, thus we do not have enough information. The chroniclers, — almost all of them priests and monks, — did not wish to note these "shameful" connections with "those barbarians". The real reasons of this historical ignorance, was, of course, not so much the "barbaric behaviour" of the Avars, — they were not "more barbaric" than the Christianized Franks — but the fact that the Avars were faithful to their ancient religion, and — just like their Hun forefathers, — did not feel to replace it with the Christian religion. (Let me note here, than two hundred years later the monastic chroniclers showed the same resistance to present true information about the coming Viking and Magyar invaders. Their attitude promptly changed when the Vikings and the Magyars became Christians. Historians know very well the effect of the Viking appearance on the ethno-linguistic and cultural map of Europe. Well, the Avars ruled over Central and East-Europe for two hundred years, having common frontiers with the Franks, Italians, Slavs, Greeks, etc. Could we believe that in this time-period, which represented about eight generations, — the Avars did not mingle with the ethnic environment?)

One of the newest historians, Victor Padányi mentioned an interesting case, which was quite unknown for the western historians, even as a hypothesis. (#145). According to Padányi's opinion, — and he is using strong evidence in his book, — the original name of Charles Martell was Karulu, and he received his other name Magnus in baptism. The background was the following:

Karulu Magnus was born as the illegitimate son of his father, Pepin II (#146). Padányi supposes, that the unknown mother was Avar by origin, because "Karulu" was a typical Turanian name, meaning "black hawk". (Kara: black, Olu: hawk). "Karulu" was later Latinized to Carolus, and, as we know, he received the title "Martell", when he, as the mayor of the palace, united all Merovingian kingdoms under his rule, and halted the Moslem invasion of Europe in the battle of Tours (or Poitiers, 732. #147). The coat-of-arms of the "Caroling" Dynasty shows a black hawk, a fact which is peculiar in itself, because this was the very first time when a Frankish nobleman used anything else in his family-emblem other than a cow, bull, or wolf. (#148).

(This hypothesis needs more historical investigation in the future, but, as additional facts, we may mention that this great hero of Christianity was the very first "Carolus" in European history, that he was called "martell", because he used his (also typically Turanian) mace in his battles, and he was a peculiarly short, black-haired, slightly Mongoloid-faced man among his red-haired, tall Franks. His grandson, the great Charlemagne (#149) was red-haired again, but his descendants, were all short, dark-brown types, far from the nordic look.)

Of course, the Carolingians did not respect this (supposed) relationship with the Avars. In 795-796 defeated them, and when the Frankish army appeared even at the Tisza, the power of the Avar Empire was over.

#145: V. Padányi: **"Dentumagyaria."** Cr. 2: "Le maricle grec' and the' konsolidierte Barbarei' " pp. 50.51.

#146: Pepin II of Heristal, Mayor of Austrasia and Neustria, d. 714.

#147: (714-741: Mayor of Austrasia and Neustria). Martel, or martell: hammer.

#148: The black-hawk coat-of-arms of the Karolings was imitated later by the Hohen-zollern, Habsburg and Romanow dynasties, — as two-headed eagles. (Special note: hawk was also "olu" in ancient Hungarian, and still "ölyv" in modern Hungarian of today.)

#149: (771-814).

The fall of the Avar Empire gave an opportunity to the Bulgars to take over the political and military power in the Carpathian Basin, especially in Transylvania. In 805

"... Khan Krum, after contributing in cooperation with the Franks to the fall of the Avars, created a strong Bulgarian Empire on both sides of the Danube." (#150).

Krum himself (#151) was perhaps the greatest Bulgarian ruler. He was born in the Carpathian Basin himself (in Pannonia, or in Transylvania), and rose to power as a result of his victories over the Avars. He never sympathized with the Turanian Avars, and he was the first Bulgarian ruler, who encouraged the Slav elements a the expense of the Hun-oriented Bulgar aristocracy. Under his successors the Bulgars were almost completely Slavized. (#152).

After the death of Charlemagne, the Carolingian Empire gradually disintegrated. Beginnig with the ninth century, the ethno-linguistic picture of the Danubian Basin drastically changed again. The Avars returned to Cetral Asia. In the German part of the disintegrated Frank Empire an ambitious king, Arnulf (#153) attempted to rebuild the imperial glory, — with the aid of Asiatic newcommers. (#154). In the western part of the Basin Sviatopluk, a Moravian prince tried to maintain his position against the Germans. (#155). In Transylvania, — especially in the Theiss-Mures-Transylvanian Alps triangle, — the Bulgars were the dominative ethnic elements. In 865, Boris I (#156) converted his people to Christianity. In 889, he voluntarily retired to a monastery. His son Vladimir (#157) belonged to the "Hun-Party" of the aristocrats. In 893 Boris re-emerged from retirement, put down the anti-Christian revolt, deposed and blinded his son and completed the organization of the Church, making the Slavonic liturgy general in its application. (#158). Boris' younger son, Symeon was the first Bulgarian ruler to assume the title of the "Tsar". (#159).

In 890 the Russian Chronicle reported the Magyars passing by Kiev, evidently on a national migration: „The Ugri crossed the chain of mountains which today are still called the mountains of the Ugri." (#160). In 892, and 894 many chronicles reported Magyar appearance in Transylvania and the other parts of the Danubian Basin. They were tribes in outpost-duty, partly in alliance with Arnulf's Germans, partly collecting experiences, and returning with reports to Arpád (#161) about the situation in the "Inheritance of Attila." (See MAP V. p. 34).

Árpád insured the success of the Hungarian Conquest with international alliances. One of these was alliance with the German Arnulf, the other one was alliance with Byzantium (#162) against Tsar Symeon.

In 896 the "Hetumoger" crossed the Transylvanian mountains, and occupied the Scythian-Hun-Avar inheritance. Transylvania became part of Hungary of more than one thousand years. (#163).

#150: O. Haleczky: **"Borderlands of Western Civilization."** Ronald Press Co. New York, 1952. p. 23.

#151: (808-14).

#152: The Bulgarian language and writing is absolutely Slav today.

#153: (887-899; from 896 not only King of Germany but Emperor.)

#154: He found good connections with the coming Magyars against the Slavs.

#155: (870-894); He united the Moravians, Bohemians and Slovaks.

#156: (852-889).

#157: (889-893).

#158: Preslav was the capital at this time. Boris returned to monastery. (D: 907).

#159: (893-927).

#160: The Magyars were called "Ugri" (Ugor) by the Kievans.

#161: Son of Almus, ruler of the Magyars from c. 886 to 907.

#162: With Leo VI (the "Wise"; 886-912). Tsar Symeon attempted to conquer Byzantium. Alliance with the Magyars saved Constantinople.

#163: "Hetumoger" ("Hét Magyar"): the "seven tribes" in ancient Hungarian.

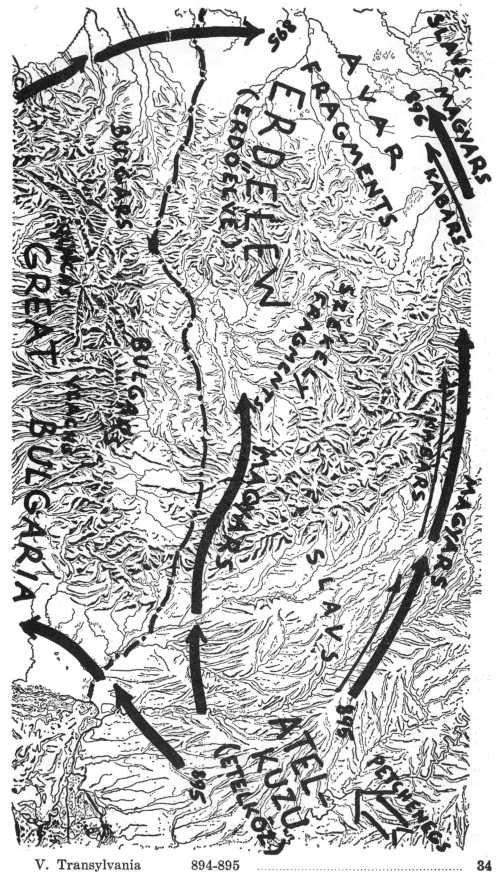

SLAVS.
MAGYARS
895
KABARS
AVAR FRAGMENTS
895
BULGARS
ERDÉLEW
(ERDŐ-ELVE)
BULGARS
BULGARS
MAGYARS (VLACHS)
SZÉKEL FRAGMENT
GREAT BULGARIA
MAGYARS
MAGYARS
MAGYARS
SLAVS.
PETCHENEGS
895
ATEL-KUZU.
(ETELKÖZ)
895

VI.

THE PROBLEM OF WALLACHIAN ORIGIN AND EARLY MIGRATION

We learned from the previous chapters that (a) the Roman legions did not have any associations with the local population; it was against military regulations, especially in the frontier-provinces. (b) The Daks (who were probably a mixture of dominating Scythian elements and subjected Thracian elements) hated the Romans so much, that they rather commited suicide, instead of attempting any type of communication with the conquerors. (c) The Romans were forced to withdraw in 271. (d) The (almost completely unpopulated) Transylvanian Basin was overrun by Visigoths and by Ostrogoths in the 4th century, and by Huns in the 5th century. (e) The Lombards and the Gepids strengthened the Germanic character of Transylvania so much, that it was called "Gothia" throughout many generations by contemporaries. (f) This Germanic character disappeared, when the Turanian Avars re-conquered the "Inheritance of Attila", and Transylvania became part of a new Scythian Empire again for more than two hundred years. (g) The gradual disintegration of the Avar Empire represented advantage for another Ural-Altaic tribe-organization, the Bulgars, who also claimed themselves the descendants of Attila. The Bulgarian domination replaced the Avar domination in Transylvania, especially in the southern part of the Basin. (h) The northern part was probably populated by the Székelys (Hun or Avar descendants), who were awaiting the reappearance of a new Turanian wave of their ethno-linguistic relatives, for the repeated conquest of Attila's Empire. (i) The expected "reconquest" came at the end of the 9th century, when the Magyars (dominated by chieftains, who were proud of their Hun origin) crossed the Carpathians, united themselves with the Székelys and occupied the Danubian Basin (including Transylvania). (j) The Hungarians are inhabiting the Danubian Basin as the dominative ethno-linguistic (Ural-Altaic) population. Hungary is their fatherland for almost one thousand and one hundred years. Transylvania (after about 1020 years) was cut down from the body of the Hungarian Kingdom by the Treaty of Trianon of 1920 and presented to Rumania. (k) One of the most important "scientific" bases of the Rumanian claim was the so-called "Dako Roman continuity", that is: the Rumanians in Transylvania are the actual descendants of the "Dako-Romans", a population, which was born — as a new ethno-linguistic unit — through the intermarriages of Roman soldiers with the subjected Daks.

Rumanian historians — employed and paid by the postwar "Greater Rumania", — attempted to convince the historians of the world, that the basic thesis of the Rumanian delegation in Paris was right, because (1) the Visigoths, Ostrogoths, Huns, Lombards, Gepids, Avars, Bulgars did not leave any ethno-linguistic traces in Transylvania, (2) the fact that Transylvania was for more than one thousand years the integral part of the Hungarian Kingdom, (or it was a Hungarian-speaking Principality) represents nothing else, but an illusion. and finally (3), only one thing is absolutely true: the Rumanians of Transylvania are actually Dako-Romans, descendants of Romans and Daks, populating Transylvania since the time of Emperor Trajanus.

Did the representatives of the Great Powers believe the Rumanian delegation's story?

They probably did not. However, for a person like Clemenceau, historical science did not play any role. The foundation of a strong Little Entente on the eastern side of Germany was the main idea. At the time of the Treaty of Trianon, the delegates were nervous and tired, because of the previously discussed Treaty of Versailles. Wilson was very close to a final nervous breakdown. Lloyd George was, as usual, cynical and ignorant. Clemenceau was a "practical man". He was not too sensitive dealing with historical evidence. The loser did not have an opportunity to produce any evidence, and Hungary was a loser. Consequently, Clemenceau was happy to receive any "evidence" from the Rumanian delegates. He was tired too. He wished to finish this unpleasant business. He, the only person among the Big Four, who was educated to deal with ethno-linguistic problems of East-Central Europe, accepted every "document", any proposals from the delegates of the newly created artificial states, — because it was dictated by the very interest of France. The national interest of his fatherland was more important for "the Tiger", than the ethno-linguistic problems of an Eastern-European province. At the end of 1920, he, Clemenceau represented the only real political power in Paris. All the others were actually puppet-assistants already. He signed his name, and Transylvania, for the first time in her entire history, — became part of the Rumanian Kingdom. The new "Dako-Romans" in Bucharest received one of the wealthiest areas of Europe.

After this it became the duty of the Rumanian historians to justify the incorporation of Transylvania into Rumania.

It was an ungrateful task. From the previously mentioned and quoted details, we must realize, that Iorga, Ghyka and others could only present "assumptions", they could suppose hypotheses, but they could not base their story about the Dako-Roman continuity in Transylvania on any document, or on any archeological source.

Most of the historians of the world did not follow the philosophy of Clemenceau. After all, they did not feel right to put their "national interest" before historical objectivity. (#164). They did not believe that the Wallachians, instead of moving west and north into Transylvania from the other side of the Carpathians, moved in the opposite directions; leaving Transylvania, populating gradually the Moldavian and Wallachian principalities.

Denying the "Dako-Roman continuity" in Transylvania, it will be our duty in this chapter to investigate the real origin of the Wallachians.

The first question, that we have to ask is this: should we investigate the origin of he Wallachians as a "race", or as an "ethno-linguistic" group?

"The origins of the Rumanians point to many different components. — feels Louis Elekes, one of the experts of the Wallachian problem. (#165) "This is not astonishing if we consider that all European nations have experienced a considerable mixture of blood, so that in most cases the racial basis is no longer recognizable. This is naturally the case with the Rumanians, who lived at one of the most troubled points of the continent and thus were exposed to many and varied foreign influences."

If we are not looking for a race, we have to concentrate on the birth of a special ethno-linguistic mixture, amalgamation of certain Romanized elements on the Balkan peninsula.

#164: One famous exeption was the older Seton-Watson, who fully adopted the Rumanian stories and (under the name of "Scotus Viator") enthusiastically fought in his books, trying to create historical bases for the "rightful" existence of the Little Entente states.

#165: L. Elekes: **"The Development of the Rumanian People."** (**Hungarian Review,** 1941, p. 678).

Did the Rumanian language originate from the Latin?
The answer should be unquestionably: yes it did.
"Rumanian is derived directly from the low Latin spoken in the
Imperial era. In syntax and grammar it reproduces Latin forms
of striking purity. Words dealing with agricultural pursuits,
however, are generally of Slavic origin." (#166).
Some of the Rumanian linguists were "careless' enough to announce
frankly the actual content of the Rumanian language. For example
"... according to Cihac, Wallachian linguist, the Rumanian
language could be divided into the following vocabularly-groups,
— as far as the origin of the words is concerned:

Slavic origin	45.7%
Latin origin	31.5%
Turkish origin	8.4%
Greek origin	7.%
Magyar origin	6.0%
Albanian origin	0.6%
Total	100.0% (#167)

The Rumanian national customs are distinctly reminiscent of Latin Italy.
"It is still customary in many Rumanian villages to attach a small
coin to the finger of the dead after an ancient Roman custom of
providing the soul with its fare across the Styx ... Rumania's
national dance, the Calausaré, commemorates the rape of the
Sabines to this day." (#168).
Professzor Giurescu, Rumania's most distinguished historian since the
death of Professor Iorga, says in his "Rumanian History", that historians
should not be employed by extreme nationalistic forces.
"On the same page on which Professor Giurescu ostracizes exag-
gerated patriotism, he says that the history of the Rumanians is
based on four positive and unissailable facts: (1) that the Rumanians are one of the oldest peoples in Europe, (2) that the Dacians
were an elite people of the ancient world; (3) that the Rumanians
are the oldest Christian peoples of south-eastern Europe; and
(4) that they are the only people in these regions who can boast
of an uninterrupted political continuity." (#169).
After a careful sutdy of our previous chapters, hopefully there is no
need to repeat the available counterevidences against these, quoted, more
than absurd statements about "the oldest people", about the Dacians as
"elite people" of the Classical World, about those "oldest Christians", and
about their "uninterrupted political continuity" in the storm of the great
Gothic, Hun, Lombard, Gepida, Avar, etc. migration. Probably the fact
that Transylvania was a Hungarian territory for more than one thousand
years, represented only an unsignificant episode in this "uninterrupted
political continuity. — for Professor Giurescu, who declared so many
times that a historian should avoid any false brand of patriotism "which
exalts everything connected with one's own nation and underrates all
things foreign." (#170).

#166: Leon Dominian: "The Frontiers of Language and Nationality in Europe". Am.
Geogr. Society of N.Y., Henry Holt and Co. 1917, p. 166.
#167: I. Szakonyi: "The First Historical Notes about the Wallachians and the Hist.
Bases of the Dako-Roman Theory." (Kanadai Magyarság, 1966. IX. 24.)
#168: L. Dominian: "The Frontiers of Language and Nationality, et." p. 161.
#169: Zs. Szász: "Rumanian History." (The Hung. Quarterly 1941. pp. 198-99.)
#170: Ibid. p. 198.

Who were the ancestors of the Rumanians?

The ancestors of the Rumanian people were a neo-Latin tribe, which, according to the conclusions of recent historical research, developed in the course of the second to seventh centuries A.D. on the Balkan Peninsula, in the immediate neighbourhood of the Albanian territory, by the "Latinization" of the former Illyrian-Thracian population. The early Wallachians were a people of nomadic mountain herdsmen and lived an uneventful life in primitive little communities; that is why historical evidence is so scanty.

The mixing of races began already in the 1st and 2nd century when wealthy Roman landowners settled Italian mountain-herdsmen in large numbers on their estates in Epirus.

> "This shepherd-society, in an area which is Northern Greece of today, in the excellent hiding-places among the mountains of Epirus, survived all the storms of the medieval migration, increased in size and mixing its original vulgar language with Slavic and Greek elements, began its movement in about the 10th century into the lower Danube area." (#171). (See MAP IV. p. 29).

Byzantine sources have mentioned three main junctions of the Wallachians. Beginning with the 9th and 10th centuries a large group populated the Pindos mountains, in Thessalia. The second significant group, the so-called "Arumuny"-Vlachs, populated the Balkan Mountains and the area north of these mountains, up to the lower Danube. (This territory belongs to Bulgaria today.) The third, and probably the largest group populated the area at the Adriatic Coast, including North Albania, Western-Macedonia, South Dalmatia. This area was more-less identical with the old Roman-Illyria. This group mixed itself with Slavic, Thracian, Albanian, Illyr and Romanised Dalmatian elements.

After the 9th and 10th centuries, sources were mentioning not three, but four fragments of the Wallachians. The shepherds in the Pindos mountains (the "Megleno-Rumuns") remained still in Northern Greece, the "Arumuns" of the Balkan Mountains slowly moved into the direction of Macedonia and Albania, the third group, the Illyrian "Istro-Rumuns" wandered as far as Istria, where a few thousand of them have survived.

In connection with our main topic, we have to concentrate on the fourth fragment. This branch (probably from "Aurumuns") did not follow the movement (toward west) of their fellow-herdsmen.

> "The fourth branch turned north-east and crossed the lower Danube in the course of the tenth and eleventh centuries. In the tirteenth century we find them mentioned in the Banat and in southern Transylvania as subjects of the King of Hungary." (#172)

The Slavization of the Balkans was significant especially in the ninth and tenth centuries. This was the age, when the Ural-Altaic identity of the Bulgarians also disappeared.

> "The immigration of the Slavs did not fail to influence the ancient Rumanians. That is clearly proved by many Slav features in Rumanian ethnical development and by the richness of the Rumanian language in Slav elements, which goes so far that on this basis several earlier scholars numbered the Rumanians among the Slav peoples." (#173).

> "...The mountains saved the Latin character of Rumanian speech." — felt L. Dominian, one of the most significant expert

#171: Tamás Karsa: "Remarks to the Authorization of the Dako-Roman Theory." ("Hungarian Life", Toronto, May, 1964.)

#172: Zsombor Szász: "Rumanian History." (The Hun. Quarterly", Autumn, 1941, p. 199.

#173: Louis Elekes: "The Development of the Rumanian People." ("The Hungarian Quarterly." Winter, 1941, p. 680.)

of the European ethno-linguistic problems. (#714), and discussing the still existing remnant of the Wallachian groups on the Balkans, he added: "The nomadic character of these isolated adherents of a Latin language is shown is many of their villages, which are occupied during part of the year only... A territory of Romance languages extending continuously from the Atlantic to the Black Sea probably existed prior to the immigration of Slavs into south-eastern Europe. The areas of Romansh, Friulian, Ladin (#175), Albanian and Rumanian are remnants of this ancient language zone."

Interestingly enough, the Rumanian historians did not even mention the other Wallachian groups, which were so clearly introduced and described by historians and geographers. They knew, that mentioning the main Wallachian settlements, would lead the readers to the logical consequence; that is: the Wallachian migration originated on the Balkans and moved gradually northwards, first into the lower Danube-valley and later, in the thirteenth century, into Transylvania. The "official" interest desired to prove that the actual migration began in Dacia, and gradually moved southward. Ghyka is very happy to find a term "Roumania' as opposed to the barbarian territories north of the Danube" in an "inscription from Sirmium of about 580" (#176), but he does not say anything more about the mentioned, but not introduced mysterious document. (#177). Also Ghyka mentions a case, when "... The Avars themselves in the seventh century (618) established in Pannonia a Romanized population that had been taken from the Balkans", (#178), without realizing, that with this "careless" sentence, he actually said something which did not seem to aid the idea of the "Dako-Roman continuity", but the Balkanic origin of the Wallachians. (#179). He calls the Wallachians, appearing in Northern Bulgaria in 860, simply "the descendants of the Dacians" again (#180), and he feels that mentioning Nestor's Chronicle in connection with the Wallachian (Volochii) appearance south of the Transylvanian Alps, he proved something. Actually he did not prove anything, because the Kievan chronicler simply noted here that "... the Wallachs attacked the Slavs of the Danube and settled among them." (#181). These Slavs came with the Bulgars from north-east, and of course clashed with the migratory Wallachians, who moved into the opposite direction, from south to north. The too much [and well paid] enthusiasm of the Rumanian "historians" sometimes resulted in a "blind alley". Fortunately for Bucharest, its historians did not take too big risk turning history upside-down. "Might was right", anyways.)

Unquestionably some of the migratory Wallachian herdsmen crossed the Transylvanian Alps and entered into the Basin itself in the ninth century. The Rumanian historians are pointing out very happily, that even the Hungarian Chroniclers were mentioning the "Pastores Romanorum" at the time of the Conquest. This was true. Southern Transylvania, — as we mentioned in our previous chapter, — was part of the Bulgarian "Tsardom" before the Hungarian Conquest. Tsar Simeon tolerated the migration of the Wallachian shepherds from the lower Danube north, to the other side of the Transylvanian Alps. (See MAP V. p. 34.)

#174: L. Dominian: **"The Frontiers of Language and Nationality in Europe."** pp. 162-165.

#175: They are in Switzerland.

#176: M. Ghyka: **"A Documented Chronology of Roumanian History."** p. 23.

#177: The mentioned date associates with Princus' victory over the Avars. The Byzantines were still called "Romani" in the early Medieval Ages.

#178: M. Ghyka: **"A Documented Chronology... etc."** p. 21.

#179: They recrossed the Danube and settled in Salonica in 678.

#180: M. Ghyka: **"A Documented Chronology..."** p. 26.

#181: **Ibid.** p. 22.

VII.

THE EFFECTS OF THE HUNGARIAN CONQUEST ON THE ETHNIC TRANSFORMATION OF TRANSYLVANIA

At the time of the Hungarian Conquest, Transylvania was sparsely populated by various peoples, mostly of Slav origin. The most dominative element of them was the Bulgarian. As we mentioned before, the triangle formed by the Maros (Mures), and by the Eastern and Southern Carpathians, was actually one of the provinces of the Bulgarian Tsardom. Symeon (893-927), the second son of Boris I, ruled over the territories, from the Maros River, south to the political frontiers of the Byzantine Empire. His reign was filled with wars against Byzantium, and the Magyar appearance in the door of Europe was associated with the fact, that the Byzantine emperors encouraged the westward-migration of the Magyar tribal-organization, and used them as allies against the ambitions Symeon.

The Tsar of the Bulgars concentrated against Constantinople, but his administration was good enough to keep even southern Transylvania under control. The population in Bulgarian-dominated Transylvania was not all Slavic. The Bulgarian aristocracy could still preserve its Turanian character, (although their language was almost completely Slavicized already), and (as we already mentioned in the previous chapter), the Bulgarian administration permitted various, mostly Wallachian, elements to leave the lower Danube district, and to enter the Transylvanian Basin. (See MAP V. p. 34, again).

In the meanwhile the Magyars, driven westward by the Patzinaks (or Pechenegs), advanced into Transylvania in 895-896. (#182).

> "... Tradition, corroborated by modern historians, has it that these Hungarians found in the eastern mountains a people akin to themselves in race and language, the Székelys, who were the descendants of Attila's Huns and who, joining forces with them, helped them to defend the eastern borders. (#183). (#184).

In connection with the Hungarian Conquest, one problem appears, and this problem divided the historians. The question was: Did the Conquest actually begin with the occupation of Transylvania, or the Conquest took place in the central river valleys, and the occupation of Transylvania represented only a second step in the coming decades?

Macartney supposes, that "at the end of the ninth century the Magyars entered Hungary, and a century or so later achieved the conquest (or occupation) of Transylvania. They pressed up the valleys of the large rivers, notably the Somes (#185), and established themselves in the more fertile portions of the western half of the 'land beyond the forest'." (#186). Many other historians did not agree with this view. According to them, the Magyars penetrated into the Basin crossing the North-eastern, Eastern and Southern Transylvanian mountains. The occupation of Transylvania was the first step of the Conquest, which was followed by the occupation of the whole Danubian Basin.

#182: The Patzinaks (Pechenegs, or in Hung. the "Besenyős") represented a much stronger military power at this time. They were also Turanians.

#183: Zs. Szász: "Hungarians — Rumanians." (Hung. Quarterly, 1941. Winter. p. 589.)

#184: We mentioned already the uncertainty of the Székely origin. (Hun, or Avar).

#185: "Somes" is the Rumanian version. The Magyar term is: "Szamos".

#186: C. Macartney: "Hungary and Her Successors." Oxford University Press, London, Royal Institute of International Affairs. 1937. p. 254.

The truth was probably somewhere in the middle. The Magyar tribes crossed the Carpathians at many crossing points in the autumn of 895. Levente, Árpád's oldest son entered the Carpathian Basin from the south, using the Danube valley as a natural gateway into the Basin. (#187). Another tribe-concentration under the leadership of Gyula (#188) crossed the mountains at the Eastern Carpathians, and penetrated into Transylvania. Árpád himself led he majority of the Magyars, and entered the Basin on the North-Eastern Carpathians, at Vereczke. His main troops met with the Székelys, and this, major, tribal concentration managed the conquest of the Central Plain. In the next year (and we mus keep in mind, that the next year was actually 896, which is the traditional date of Conquest!), the chiefs, following Árpád's order entered the Maros and Szamos valleys from the west, attempting and finding connections with the other two tribal systems. Macartney was right mentioning that the actual, and detailed occupation of Transylvania only followed the conquest of the Great Plain, but he forgot the simultaneous activities of the two minor tribal systems. It is understandable that it was much more difficult to conquer and keep under control a mountaneous area, than a plain. However, Macartney goes too far supposing that the full conquest of Transylvania took place only "a century or so later." (#189). Transylvania was not absolutely unknown to the Magyars. Beginning with 893, they executed many attacks against the Slavs of Sviatopluk the Great from their previous home, Atelkuzu. (#190). They crossed the Carpathians at the same points, which served finally as main roads to the Conquest. They crossed Transvlvania many times. Having troubles with the Patzinaks and Symeon's Bulgars at the same time, they were sensible enough to dominate Transylvania as soon as it was possible. The Transvlvanian mountains served, since the Conquest, as the natural frontier against both the Patzinaks (from the East) and the Bulgarians (South-east). (#191.) The Székelys received again their original frontier post.

Medieval Hungarian Chroniclers agree that on the western part of Transylvania the Kende (Kond) and the Ond tribes settled down, the eastern side was occupied by the (mentioned) Gyula (Gylas) tribe. (#192). In some of the Chronicles, this Gyula, or Gylas appeared as "Gelou, dux Blacorum". (#193). Rumanian historians, of course, used this opportunity with great enthusiasm. (#194). Actually, those "Blachii" (Wallachians were nothing else but the "Pascua Romanorum" (Pastores Romanorum), who were the subjected herdsmen of the Bulgarians before the Conquest (#195), and who were dominated by the tribe of Gyula from then on.

#187: Levente himself died in the battle against the Bulgarians. Árpád did not see his son again after 895.

#188: The term "gyula" (with small "g") meant "judge". Later it became a male given name. Gyula was the head of one of the most powerful tribes. The fact that the most westerly Patzinak tribe was called also "Gyula" caused considerable confusion among historians. (Inf.: Henrik Marczali: "Magyarország Története." Athenaeum, Budapest, 1912. pp. 68-69.)

#189: St. Stephen (997-1038) was the king one century later. In his time every part of Transylvania was systematically divided and administered.

#190: "Atel-kuzu" ("Between waters"). It was the area between the Dnieper and Sereth Rivers. (In modern Hungarian: "Etelköz.")

#191: According to the medieval chroniclers, Zalán was the name of the Bulgarian governor, who, in the name of Symeon, attempted resistance.

#192: Inf.: C. A. Macartney: "The Magyars in the Ninth Century". Cambridge, Univ. Press, 1930. p. 118.

#193: Ibid.

#194: M. Ghyka: "A Documented Chronology of R. History." pp. 33 and 36.

#195: Inf. Macartney: "Studies on the Early Hung. Hist. Sources." p. 111.

In connection with the conquest of Transylvania, we have to mention a historical problem, which did not have any relation to the ethno-linguistic transformation of Transylvania by the Conquest. However any discussion about Transylvania would be imperfect without mentioning it.

Simon Kézai, one of the most important chroniclers of Medieval Hungary, did not use the term Transylvania very often. Instead of it, he used the words "septem castra" which mean Transylvania. (#196).

Macartney had extensive speculation about the real meaning and origin of this sort of nomination. (#197). He was unable to find a convincing solution to the problem. Two possibilities were available. Let us introduce both of them.

In the time of Kézai, Transylvania became the home of a considerable number of Saxons (#198). As we know, the Transylvanian Saxons, (and even the Central European Germans), called Transylvania "Siebenburgen". Consequently the name "Septem Castra" was a translation from German into Latin.

Macartney, — and other historians before and after him, — were not satisfied completely with this explanation. They took into consideration that not only Kézai, but other chroniclers had mentioned the "Septem Castra" term and among these there were some, who wrote their chronicles before the Saxon settlement, or who were not aware of the term "Siebenbürgen". (#199). Thus, Macartney, and others still left open the second possibility, according to which the words "Septem Castra" represent a reference to the Seven chieftains ("Hetumoger"), who probably established temporary camps in the first part of the Conquest on Transylvania.

We may add to this speculation something, which makes the terms "Septem Castra" (Seven camps, seven forts) even more general; seven was the "lucky number" (probably from ancient mythical reasons) of almost all the Turanian tribes at this time. Most of the Ural-Altaic tribe-organizations represented seven (and not six or eight) tribes. (#200).

If this is true, that "Septem Castra" did not refer to "Siebenbürgen", but to the seven camps of the "Hetumoger", then we have actually another evidence, that the conquest of Transylvania was not only an integral part of the Conquest, but it was the first step! (This conclusion, of course, could sill compromise with Macartney's who was probably right believing, that the extensive, detailed occupation of Transylvania could some only much after the formal, political conquest.

What was the probable ethno-linguistic situation of Transylvania in the years following 896? (See MAP VI. p. 43).

The Magyars did not populate the Transylvanian Basin as heavily as they did the Great Plain. However, the mentioned Ond and Kond (Kende) tribes ruled the permanent settlement is Western Transvlvania, at the sources of he three Körös Rivers. The Székelys guarded Hungary at the Eastern Carpathians. South of there the people of the powerful Gyula-tribe settled down. The majority of the defeated Bulgarians left the Basin southward, toward the lower Danube-valley, but probablv some of them remained. The forests and caves were hiding some of the Vlach shepherds, who were ambitious enough to live on the land of warlike horsemen, far away from the Wallachian relatives at the lower Danube.

#196: Simon Kézai wrote his Gesta around 1285. (Ladislas IV' rule).

#197: In his **"Studies on the Early Hungarian Historical Sources."** pp. 39-41.

#198: We are going to discuss the story of the Saxon settlement in Chapter IX.

#199: For example the "Chronicon Budensis" (1332), which was actually the rewriting of much earlier (unknown) chronicles.

#200: The tribe of the Kabars (a Khazarian tribe, which adopted Judaism) joined the "Hetumoger". They were forced to fuse with one of the tribes. The Magyars did not wish to change the number of their tribes.

VIII

TRNSYLVANIA AS AN INTEGRAL PART OF THE
MEDIEVAL HUNGARIAN KINGDOM
(PART I: THE ÁRPÁD-DYNASTY AND "ERDÖELVE")

Before dealing with the role and problems of Transylvania (or as it was called by the early Magyars: "Erdöelve") under the rule of the Árpád dynasty (#201), we have to discuss two main questions. These questions are not connected with any particular rulers of the mentioned ruling dynasty. They are general questions, and connected usually with every territory, occupied by a newly arrived conquering nation.

(a) How did the Conqueror deal with the conquered (ethno-liguistically non-related), and subjected peoples?

(b) What was the internal and external (#202) role of a certain province (in our case: Transylvania) in the newly created political and military construction?

Answering question "a", it will be quite understandable, that the sentence "dealing with the subjected peoples" does not refer to the Conquest itself, but rather to the relatively peaceful times following the actual Conquest. The Conquest itself could be interpreted as the series of bloody battles, and the Hungarian Conquest represented a hard task for the "Hetumoger" facing and defeating the resisting troops of the Pannonian Slavs (#203), and of the South-Transylvanian Bulgarians. (204). We can not expect "humanitarian" behaviour from the Conqueror against the "minorities" on the battlefield. We may expect moderate, or despotic attitude from the Conqueror in the years following the actual Conquest, against the defeated and subjected minorities.

In answering question "a", we have to examine the Turanian tradition as to dealing with subjected non-Turanian peoples. This tradition appeared quite clearly in the Empire of Attila, and in the Empire of Baján, in the Avarian Khaganate.

Attila, the Hun, subjected the Ostrogoths, Visigoths, Gepids, Rugians, Scirians, Heruls, Thuringians, Alans, Burgundians, and Ripuarian Franks with his iron hand. These peoples were not ethno-liguistically related to the Huns; they were almost all Germanic tribes. Attila used their military service. Attila probably did not feel that their chiefs were equal with the Hun "aristocracy", but the King of the Huns did not humiliate them, did not interfere with their internal problems, and he did not force them to give up their ancient traditions, or to abandon their ancient language. After the disintegration of the Hun Empire, the Germanic tribes kept and exercised their preserved traditions. The Hun domination was quite moderate (#205). The German ethno-linguistic continuity was undisturbed.

The Avars inherited this Turanian tradition. They were also savage in attack, and they proudly believed in some sort of Turanian "superiority" above the peoples of their European environment. However, they were also quite moderate to the subjected ethnic groups. The Transylvanian Valley remained "Gothia" and the Germanic fragments there were not forced

---

#201: The successors of Árpád ruled Medieval Hungary until A.D. 1301.

#202: Of course, we do not use the terms "internal" and "external" in their modern meaning.

#203: Successors of Sviatopluk the Great.

#203: Zalán, appointed governor by Tsar Symeon of Bulgaria, and his hard resistance was well described in old chronicles. Later it was romanticized in a famous Hungarian epic poem. (Vörösmarty: **"The Flight of Zalán"**. (1823).)

#205: Even the horrified monks did not condemn Attila in this respect.

to leave their ethno-linguistic traditions, by becoming Avar instead. The Avars probably despised the Pannonian Slavs, because the ancient traditions of Asia, and even Europe, taught them this attitude. It was not "ethnic discrimination" at all. It was simply the attitude of the military-minded horsemen against the humble farm labourers. The words "to look down" could be interpreted in their original meaning in the age of the Great Migration. The horsemen actually "looked down" both on the foot soldiers, and on the horseless peasants. The Avars, just as all the coming tribal-systems, were excellent horsemen. Children (both boys and girls) learned horseback riding not much after their first walking experiences. The subjected ethnic fragments grazed cattle and goats, but they seldom used horses. The "superiority" of the Turanian tribes above the subjected peoples was not a conscious ethnic superiority. It was simply the physical and psychological superiority of the armed horsemen above the humble peasantry. Of course, this fact often coincided with the actual ethno-linguistic differences between them. (Later, in the course of political and social evolution, the "horseman" became a "knight", and the subjected or enslaved peasants became "serfs". The social difference between thm oftn coincided again with ethno-linguistic difference, but the "discrimination" of the serfs was simply part of the contemporary feudal system, and it was not deliberate ethnic discrimination. Eastern Europe has had much more complex ethno-linguistic regionalism than Western Europe already in the early Medieval Ages. Feudalism has had its special ethno-linguistic complexity.)

Reading the books of some (over ambitioned) "historians", who were trying to introduce Medieval Ages as the scene of "ethnic discriminations", let us keep in mind: we could not expect "democratic methods" from a feudal system, and secondly, in the natural athmosphere of ethnic regionalism, minority groups appeared much more often in the role of vassals or serfs, than in the role of dominating lords. If a "historian" condems the lord, because he expresses superiority above his (let us say) ethnic-originated vassals or serfs, and if this "historian" tries to fabricate a case of "ethnic discrimination" from this, he simply does not understand the Medieval Ages and the feudal system. (Dealing with Medieval Hungary in this and the coming chapters, I would appreciate, if the reader could keep this aspect in mind.)

Did the migratory Magyars adopted the relatively moderate, Turanian method, as far as dealing with subjected minorities is concerned? Yes, we have every reason to suppose it.

The Magyars were a member of the great Ural-Altaic (Turanian) language-family. They preserved the traditions of Finno-Ugric and Turco-Tatar-Mongol cultural inheritance. In the time of the Conquest, they were not absolutely homogeneous themselves. The leading families were proud of their Hun origin, the simple horseman was probably rather Turkish in appearance and attitude (#206), the lowest classes were supposedly partly Finno-ugric herdsmen, partly enslaved Caucasians, Bulgars and Slavs. One fragment of one of their tribes was the Judaist Khabars (Kabars), who joined them since the Khazarian Khaganate. (See #200 on p. 42 again.).

In the long course of their wanderings, the Magyars were subjected by the Great Bulgarian Kingdom at the Volga, and later by the Khazars. They enjoyed the relative freedom of a subjected people under a more powerful Turanian overlordship. They knew, that they could earn respect,

---

#206: The Byzantine sources called the coming and conquering Magyars as "Türks" The crown which was sent by Michael Dukas VII (Parapinakes) — 1071-1078) Byzantine Emperor to Géza I (1074-1077) in 1074, has an inscription, which indicates that it is presented to the King of "Türkia."

even a privileged position, if they served the ruling dynasty well. (#207). In their migration from the Northern Caspian to the Carpathians, the Magyars experienced this themselves. Following the Turanian tradition, they subjected less powerful tribes, but they did not force their amalgamation into the main ethno-linguistic body. (#208). The subjected tribal-fragments had contact only with the leading chiefs. In other aspects they were quite separated, and nobody disturbed their life, nobody interfered into their traditions. They paid tribute, or their military service was needed. However, "linguicide" did not take place; they remained Kabars, Bulgars, or Slavs untouched. Being the subject of one of the Magyar chieftains, the subjects received protection.

I feel I gave an answer to Question "a" already. The Conqueror transferred its ancient tradition into the Carpathian Basin too. The resisting Slavs, Bulgars were defeated, and partly even annihilated with the usual rigour of the Turanian attack, but tribes, who paid homage received a sort of Asiatic gallantry as an answer. They were subjected, but not necessarily enslaved. They received the opportunity to continue their ancient traditions quite freely. Nobody attempted to "Magyarize" them, as some of the "historians" supposed. Following the early medieval (both Asiatic and European) traditions, the subjected peoples were forced to pay tribute. The fact that the Slavs remained Slavs, the Wallachians remained Wallachians, represents the evidence in itself that one thousand years of Hungarian domination did not force the ethnic minorities to leave their ancient ethno-linguistic traditions and to become Magyars.

In Transylvania, the Székelys did not feel themselves an ethno-linguistic minority. They spoke the same language as the Magyars, probably with a slightly different dialect. Regarding themselves Huns, realizing that only the most noble leading families were Huns among the Magyars, the Székelys adopted the attitude that they were some sort of "aristocratic" tribe and they proved their faithfulness through good service in guarding the Eastern Carpathians against the storming Patzinaks (Pechenegs), and later the Cumans (#209), and the Tatars. (#210). Most of the Balgarians crossed the Transylvanian Alps after the defeat of Zalán, returning to Moeasian Bulgaria. Supposedly, they took with them subjected Slavs, Germans, most of the Wallachians. Some of the Bulgarians probably voluntarily remained. The remnants were Bulgarians who still preserved their ancient Turanian ethno-linguistic traditions and who did not wish to join the Slavicized life of the Balkanic-Bulgars. They probably welcomed the Magyars as relatives. The "Blachii" (Wallachians) represented a very small, unsignificant minority. They did not exist together, as one homogeneous group. They were scattered on the high mountains, grazing their sheep, or hiding themselves in the depth of dark caves. They knew the well concealed roads on the Transylvanian Alps very well. They could return to the valley of the Lower Danube, to their relatives at any time. They had good reason for not going. The Bulgarian Tsardom did not treat the Vlachs very well. They were in an enslaved, humiliated position. In Transylvania nobody bothered them. They were free, their messages of invitation encouraged the Balkanic Wallachians to migrate to Transylvania. They began to multiply. (See MAP VII. p. 47).

Now, let me answer Question "b": What was the external and internal role of Transylvania in the newly created political and military construction?

#207: Álmos (father of Árpád) collected tribute from Kievan State to the Khazarian Khanganate. Another Magyar, Lebed, became a sort of "Prince" in Khazaria.

#208: Main ethnic body (as we mentioned) did not really exist.

#209: "Polovtski" in Slavic languages, "Kun" in original Hungarian.

#210: They were the "Mongol Proper" in most of the western history books. They invaded Hungary in 1241.

Let us take a look first at the external role, examining the political frontiers at north-east, eash, and south of Transylvania.

The north-eastern frontier touched Kievan Russia. The Kievans have had close cooperation with Byzantium, but since the Cumans occupied the large area north of the Black Sea, the Kievans couldn't keep up this connection. (#211). Good relationship with Transylvania, especially with the ruling Gyula-family could secure a relatively safe route to Byzantium for Kiev in the time of Vladimir the Saint (#212) and his successors. (#213). (See MAP VII. on p. 47. again).

The Székelys, combined with other Magyar elements (ruled over by Gyula and his successors,) defended Eastern Hungary. The Patzinak power disintegrated under the pressure of the Cumans, an even more powerful Ural-Altaic combination. The Cumans were not able to penetrate into Transylvania (#214), but they occupied Wallachia, south of the Transylvanian Alps, as far as the lower Danube, pushing back the weakened Bulgars into the area which is identical to Bulgaria of today. (#215). (The Bulgars have had common frontiers with Hungary only from Nándorfehérvár (#216) to the Iron Gate, where the Danube leaves traditional Hungary.)

Transylvania represented the diplomatic connections between the Hungarian Kingdom and Byzantium to a large extent. The Greek-Orthodox religious influence touched Transylvania the most. Many of the Magyar chieftains (later noblemen) converted not to Roman, but to Byzantine Christianity, volunteered to represent Hungary in Constantinople. The external role of Transylvania under the Árpád dynasty was identical to its role during the one thousand years of Hungarian domination; it was a final eastern frontier-land of Europe, facing the Russian steppes (#217), and it was a natural, transitional bridge to the culturally and economically different Orient.

The external role of Transylvania created a special internal role for Transylvania in the Carpathian Basin. Transylvania was much closer to the political, cultural and economic athmosphere of the main Danubian Basin, than to Kievan Russia, or to the Balkans, but certain foreign influences, which were natural consequences of its external role, somehow effected the birth of a special Transylvanian identity. The high Transylvanian mountains have had a role here too. The highlander is different from the man of the Plain. The high mountains could offer natural fortifications for political oppositions in the frame of a medieval kingdom. It was partly effected by foreign influences, but partly connected with geopolitical factors, that Transylvania became the citadel of ancient, pagan traditions against the forceful Christianization of the Hungarian kings (#218); it became a citadel of Byzantine Christianity against the same, central effort, and in the time of Reformation, it became the citadel of Protestantism against the violent Counterreformation of the Habsburg Emperors.

#211: Sviatoslav (964-972) was killed by the Patzinaks on his way back to Kiev. His successors were often blocked from Byzantius by the Cumans.

#212: (978-1015). He converted the Russians to Christianity in the eastern Byzantine form.

#213: The greatest of them was Iaroslav (1019-1054) "the Wise."

#214: Only a small fragment of them requested asylum in Hungary before the Mongol invasion. They took flight from Khan Batu.

#215: Additionally to their external troubles, the Bulgars were weakened simultaneously by the appearence of the Bogomil Heresy.

#216: This old Danubian town is called Belgrade today.

#217: Russia was not considered as part of Europe in the Medieval Ages.

#218: Beginning with St. Stephen (997-1038), the first king of Hungary.

Answering these main questions, let us take a look at the role of Transylvania, as part of Hungary, during the rule of the Árpád Dynasty, — in a chronological sense.

Christianization, of course, was not so simple and smooth, as some of the medieval monks described. The pagan Magyars in the tenth century represented the same threat to Western Christianity, as did the appearance of their earlier relatives the Huns and the Avars. The horrified West believed that the Huns and Avars came back. (Nineteenth century historians denied these beliefs, but today, — as we mentioned, — we have more and more evidence, which seem to aid the medieval assumptions.) The Christian World declared the lightning-fast attacks of the Magyars as the "end of the world", and the Pope, himself, saw in them the executors of the "last judgment." (#219).

The Hungarians undertook several ravaging incursions into the West, "crossing the Alps seven times on horseback, and twice reaching clear to the shores of the Atlantic." (#220). (#221). The invaded Germans, Italians, etc. believed that they were facing the whole Magyar army. Today, we know, that only the western tribes were involved in these adventures. The Magyars, settled in Transylvania, did not feel any interest to participate, and their relative independence from the ruling dynasty gave them special opportunities to deal with their own problems. On the other hand: the threat of Patzinak or Cuman attack bound them to their position too.

King S. Stephen (#222) centralized royal power and introduced Latin Christianity, suppressing eastern (Byzantine) Christianity by force. He also crusaded against paganism. As I mentioned before, both the Byzantine, and the pagan opposition found their strongholds in Transylvania.

Which was the "real Hungarian" from these, the "mission" of the first Hungarian king, or the counter-attacks of the "pagans" or even the "Byzantine Hungarians"?

Hungarian historical traditions were often associating the role of St. Stephen with the "only right" Hungarian role. After all, he was the first king of Hungary, he was the founder of the hingdom, he was the great Christianizer of the country, and he was the builder of the "Land of the Holy Crown" (#223). I tend to disagree with the Hungarian historical traditions. St. Stephen was unquestionably a great medieval ruler, but forcing the Magyars to become part of Western Christendom was not an activity, which could be described as "national". He was a faithful Roman Catholic first of all, and only secondly was he a good Hungarian. To be part of Christendom was the "internationalism" of the Age. Trying to connect Hungary to the interest of Byzantium seemed to be "more patriotic", because it represented a resistance against the forced Roman Christianization, which (with its German, Latin and Slav missionaries) threatened the Magyars with the grateful disappearance of the original Turanian identity.

#219: Berengar I (888-924).

#220: Zathureczky: **"Transylvania, Citadel of the West."** p. 12.

#221: They were actually stopped only when Otto the Great (936-973) decisively defeated them in the Battle of Augsburg. (955). From this time the Magyars began to settle down.

#222: See also #218. His father, Géza, Duke of the Magyars, did not wish to become a Christian. "I am wealthy enough to serve two gods" — he said.

#223: The upper part of this crown was sent to Stephen from Pope Sylvester (Gerbert of Aurillac; 999-1003). (The crown was not only a means of coronation but the symbol of the Hungarian Constitution, including the participation and protection of the subjected — partly ethnic — provinces!)

Continuing this speculation, I would like to express my opinion, — which, as I mentioned before, more, or less, opposes the Hungarian historical traditions. If we accept the "Byzantine line" in Transylvania as partly the representative of the Byzantine "interest", but partly as the Hugarian "national" resistance against the Roman "internationalization", we have even more reason to respect the "pagan uprisings" against the Hungarian kings, as the appearances of the national cosciousness in the age of a possible "linguicide". The priests and monks, invited into Hungary were Germans and Slavs. The language of the Church (and the schools around it) was, of course, Latin.

The citadel of both the "pagan" resistance (#224), and of the Byzantine resistance (#225) was Transylvania. Thus, opposing the traditions, let me say at this point, that Transylvania represented much more the original Magyar identity, and the desire for ethno-linguistic preservation, than the Hungarian mainland itself, with its legendary ruling dynasty.

The "pagans" resisted not only Christianization, but also the new political structure, founded by St. Stephen. They wished to preserve the ancient tribal political structure in Transylvania. The final destruction of the tribal system (#226) was important for the royal dynasty not only for political reasons. Transylvania — just like in Roman times, — was the main source of salt in Eastern Europe. In the time of Béla I (#227) the salt-mining and distribution was well organized in Transylvania. (#228).

According to most of the sources, Transylvania was quite heavily populated in the time of Géza I (#229), and the large majority of the population were Magyars (including the Székelvs). (The great Wallachian migration did not begin before the thirteenth century.) According to some of the sources, even Patzinaks (as refugees) appeared among the frontiersmen, in the defence of the eastern border. They were Turanian relatives of the Magyars, consequently, they assimilated into the body of the Magyars, very fast. (See MAP VII. on p. 47 again).

If Transylvania represented an important part of Hungarian history, because, (in the tenth and eleventh centuries) it was the main citadel of Byzantine and pagan resistance, its significance became even greater in the twelfth century,wh en Byzantium was able to establish a temporary suzerainty in Hungary. (#230). Consequently, Transylvania, the land which proved to be the most faithful to the eastern Christian traditions, received a special privilege from both the Greek Orthodox kings and from Byzantium itself.

#224: Stephen defeated an anti-Christian insurrection in Transylvania in 1002. (The term "anti-Christian" is somewhat much better, than the term "pagan". The early Magyars were condemned as "pagans", because to a Roman Christian monk, (the chroniclers), every one, who did not wish to convert himself to Roman Christianity, was a "pagan". Actually the ancient Magyar religion was a version of the dualistic Zoroastrianism, which influenced Western Christianity by St. Augustine in the beginning of the fifth century.

#225: Gyula and his family were converted to the Eastern Christianity. The mother of St. Stephen, wife of Géza, was the daughter of Gyula. She, (Sarolta) was a Byzantine Christian, educated in Constantinople.

#226: Peter Urgeolo, son of St. Stephen's sister, and the doge of Venice (King of Hungary· 1038-46) defeated the last serious revolt of Vatha, leader of the anti-Christian insurrection.

#227: Andrew I (1047-61) restored the royal power. His younger brother was F la I (1061-63). He was succeeded by Solomon (1063-1074).

#228: Inf. Marczali: "Magyarország Története." p. 91.

$229: (1074-77). He was mentioned already in connection with the crown sent by Michael Dukas, Byzantine Emperor. (See #206).

#230: Following Géza I, St. Ladislas (1077-95), Coloman (1095-1114), Stephen II (1114-31), Béla II (1131-41), Géza II (1141-62) became the king.

50

1156 A.D. was probably the year, which represented the highest point of Byzantine influence in Central Europe. Géza II was forced to recognize Byzantine suzerainty in this year. Following the rule of Géza II, the emperors of Constantinople realized that Hungary (and of course Transylvania with her) belonged more and more to the Western Christendom. (#231). Settlements of Saxons in the southern Transylvania regions represented a defense line against possible Greek invasion from the South. (#232). Béla III (#233) was the last hope for Byzantium. He had been educated at Constantinople. To the deep disappointment of Manuel Comnenus (#234), this great, ambitious emperor, after returning to Hungary, Béla III married the sister of Philip Augustus of France (#235), and established not only a close dynastic connection, but also a close cultural-religious connection with (Roman-Christian) France.

Beginning with this, the kings of Hungary were closely allied with Rome again. (#236). Byzantium witnessed the appearance of Magyar Crusaders, representing Western Christianity, in the coming years. (#237). When the Mongol Invasion penetrated into Hungary (#238), Béla IV (#239) felt that the Hungarian resistance represented not only the self-defence of the Magyars, but the defence of Western Christianity facing the menace of Asiatic barbarism.

Leaving the Hungarian Kingdom for a while, let us take a look at the Wallachians again. Following their activities mostly from the writings of Rumanian historians, the first logical question should be this: could the Rumanian historians associate Wallachian history with Transylvania between the ninth and thirteenth centuries?

The answer is, — to the bitter unsatisfaction of Bucharest, — no, they could not. Iorga did not even mention Wallachians in Transylvania until the late Middle Ages. (#240). Ghyka was forced (by the available documented facts) to concentrate on the Balkans, where the warlike Vlachs were incorporated into the Bulgarian kingdom. The first mention of Vlachs in a Byzantine source is about the year 976, when Cedrenus relates the murder of the Bulgarian Tsar Samuel's brother by Vlach wayfarers. (#241), (#242). Ghyka indicates, that in the time of St. Stephen, southern Transylvania was still populated by "ducem Bulgarorum and Slavorum" and he supposes again, that some Vlachs were among them. (#243). It is from Anna Comnena (#244), in the second half of the 11th century, that we first hear of a Vlach settlement from Thessaly (N. Greece), which was called Great Wallachia. Interestingly, Ghyka put the same Wallachs in the lower Danube (!) in the service of the coming Cumans. (#245).

#231: Géza II was succeeded by Stephen III (1162-1172).

#232: The Saxons were settled down by Géza II. We will return to the Saxon problem in Chapter IX in details.

#233: (1172-1196).

#234: (1143-1180). Succeeded by Manuel Alexius II (1180-1183).

#235: Philip II Augustus (1180-1223). (He was one of the leaders of the Third Crusade (1191) with King Richard and Frederick Barbarossa, but quarreling with Richard, returned to France.)

#236: Béla III was succeeded by Emeric I (1196-1204), and by Ladislas III (1204-1205).

#237: Under Andrew II (1205-1235) in 1217.

#238: 1241. The invaders were led by Khan Batu, (the right hand of Djengiz).

#239: (1235-1270).

#240: In his "A History of Roumania."

#241: Samuel (976-1014) ruled W. Bulgaria, which was not touched by the Kievan invasion of Sviatoslav. (Cedrenus was one of the Byzantine chroniclers.)

#242: Ghyka: "A Docum. Chronology of R. History." p. 45.

#243: Ibid. p. 36.

#244: Daughter of Alexius Comnenius (1081-1118).

#245: Ghyka: "A Documented Chronology, etc." pp 46-47

Ghyka was slightly confused here, or — and this could be another possibility, — he was not confused himself, but rather he tried to confuse the western reader, giving the impression, that actually the whole Balkans was dominated by Wallachian ethno-linguistic groups. As we described before, it was not the case. The Vlach nomadic herdsmen represented a very unsignificant "ethnicum", and in the twelfth century they were clearly separated into small groups, dominated by Greeks, Albanians, Slavs, or Bulgarians. The Thessalian Vlachs were far away from their relatives on the lower Danube. The Thessalians gradually assimilated into their ethnic environment. The Lower Danubians became much stronger. They amalgamated with the Turki-Cumans. They were

> ". . . enriched by a new ruling class. That is why, in medieval Rumanian documents, most of the nobles have Turki names; . . . they prove that a considerable part of the Rumanian leaders in the Middle Ages was a Turki origin, and for a long time remained faithful to Turki customs." (#246), (#247).

When Ghyka mentions a sentence, like ". . . the Wallach' state' endowed with a certain degree of organization" (#248), he forgets to mention "only" the main thing; the Wallachians were organized by these warlike Turanian nomads, — and not by themselves. (The courageous Ghyka became so enthusiastic about his glorious findings about "organization" and "state", that he goes so far, that in his following sentences he did not mind to put a "Rumanian-Cuman duchy in Transylvania" in the twelfth century! (#249), (#250)). I have to confess, that sometimes Ghyka serves us with useful documents. After 1156, when Byzantine suzerainty gradually declined in Hungary (see on the top of p. 45), Constantinople attempted to use force!

> "In 1166, Manuel Comnenus assembled a large number of Wallachs for his army in the regions bordering on the Black Sea in order to attack the Hungarians." (#251).

Byzantium was defeated. Hungary became part of Western Civilization under the rule of the Árpád Dynasty. It was only a small consolation for Byzantium, that the Vlachs were converted to Greek Orthodoxy. In the beginning of the 13th century they began their gradual migration into Transylvania, attempting to escape from the Cuman and Bulgarian domination. Their "upper classes" were assimilated into Cumania and Bulgaria; only the lower class-elements, the still nomadic herdmen decided to cross the Transylvanian Alps. Hungarian documents were mentioning some infiltration in 1206 (#252). This infiltration continued,

---

#246: L. Elekes: "The Development of the Rumanian People." p. 681.

#247: The looks of most of the Rumanians are still Turkish. The ethnic customs are almost identical with the customs of Turkey Proper. This was not because of the long Moslem domination. Their racial identity was Turko-Slav mixture already in the 11th, and 12th centuries. The ancient Latin element was hidden in the language of the lower classes.

#248: "A Documented Chronology of Roumanian History." p. 38.

#249: Ibid. (See MAP VII. on p. 47).

#250: It was true that some Vlach herdsmen migrated north as far as the Polish populated southern Galicia. (1164). Even a passage of the "Niebelungenlied" mentioned the Vlachs (under their leader Ramunc) in association with the Poles (around 1200). (Inf. Enc. Britanica. "Vlachs" p. 229). These Wallachians migrated to Galicia from their Cuman overlords, east from the E. Carpathian Mountains crossing Moldavia, but not Transylvania.

#251: Ghyka: "A Documented Chronology of Roumanian History." p. 46. (Note: many of the Vlachs did not wish to participate in this Byzantine invasion, and their resistance led to the revolt of their chiefs, Peter and Assan against the Byzantine domination in 1189.

#252: Into the Transylvanian district of Fogaras.

and only few years later the Vlach populated not only tre Fogaras-district, but the Transylvanian side of the Southern Carpathians.

The "Golden Bull" of Andrew II (See #237 again), forced upon the king by the lesser nobility (#253), became the carter of feudal privilege in Hungary. (#254). The constitutional dialectic called the various Hungarian provinces as "the countries of the Holy Crown" (See #223 again). In case the king disregarded or violated the Constitution, the people had the right to resist with the use of weapons. (#255). Of course, this feudal privilege represented — in a way — provincial privilege too, because the feudal constitution (following the great patterns of Charlemagne's Frank Empire) presented a much higher legal respect to large provinces, like Transylvania, usually ruled by one member of the royal family. (#256).

Transylvania definitely did not have "self-government" at this time, but its autonomy was quite close to it. The central government of the king permitted almost free hand to the royal "Prince" of Transylvania. His relative autonomy based not only on the personal respect of the Prince, but on the fact, that the important provinces somehow inherited the un-written "legal system" of the ancient tribal life, where the chieftains of the various tribes administered their internal problems quite independently from the "Megyeri" ("Magyar") tribe, which was the tribe of Almus and his son Árpád, the Conqueror.

> "This principle of self-government and tolerance toward foreign groups, together with the respect for the liberty of others, pre-vailed in the same way within the Christian Hungarian Kingdom. It became expressed in the autonom district-system, in the self-government of the 'free royal cities', and later in the territorial, political and cultural autonomy given to those ethnic groups which came to find refuge under the Holy Crown. The constitu-tional relationship between the 'countries of the Holy Crown" were similar to the structure of the British Commonwealth." (#257). (#258).

One of those ethnic groups, which found protection, and even privilege under the Holy Crown, was the group of the Saxons. We will discuss their case in the next Chapter, but — dealing here with the Wallachian infiltra-tion into Transylvania, — let us mention an interesting note of Ghyka:

> "An edict of King Andrew II of Hungary in 1222 for the estab-lishment of the Teutonic Knights in Burzenland speaks of the land of the Brodnicii, east of the territory granted to the Teutonic Order. And a Papal Bull of the same year, repeating this passage of the royal edict, replaces 'ad terminos Brodnicorum' by 'ad ter-minos Blacorum' as if these two terms were interchangeable." (#259).

#253: The lesser nobility called "gentry" demanded privileges (led by the king's own son Béla). (Later Béla IV; 1235-1270).

#254: It exempted the gentry and the clergy from taxation, granted them freedom to dispose of their domains as they saw fit, guaranteed them against arbitrary inprisonment, etc. The "Golden Bull" followed the English "Magna Charta" seven years later, but it was "more democratic" in a sense: the English pattern strengthened the high nobility at the expense of the King; the Magyar pattern represented an alliance between the King and the middle nobility at the expense of the high nobility.

#255: "Jus armis resistendi."'

#256: In many cases, Transylvania was ruled by the heir to the throne.

#257: Zathureczky: "Transylvania." p. 15.

#258: This was the main reason why the Magyar State-concept suited to fulfil the role of the bridge between East and West in the Danubian Basin.

#259: M. Ghyka: "A Documented Chronology of Roumanian History." p. 40.

These "Brodnici", mentioned by Ghyka, populated the area between the Sereth and the Dniester. They appeared to be a mixture of Slavs and Wallachians, speaking a very vulgarized Latin dialect. Many families of this group migrated into Transylvania in the 13th century, crossing the Eastern Carpathians, and also many of them migrated into Polish Galicia. (See #250 again). The remnants became the Moldavian Rumanians. (#260).

The Wallachian infiltration probably caused some sort of anxiety in Hungarian royal circles. Encouraged by informations about ethnic freedom in Transylvania, the Balkan-Wallachians continued their migration from the Lower Danube and from Bulgaria. The waves of newcomers settled not only in South Transylvania, but almost everywhere. Máramaros, Déva, Hunyad, Lugos and the Bánát became Wallachian districts, and these areas were called — just as Fogaras in the beginning of the 13th century — "Silva Vlachorum" (#261).

The anxiety was connected not only because the Wallachian infiltration, which resulted an ethno-linguistic transformation in many parts of Transylvania. Béla IV (See #253 again) received the terrible news about the coming invasion of the Mongols. (#262). Remembering that the narrow flatland between the lower Danube and the Southern Carpathians served as the highway of Eastern aggressions against the Carpathian Basin (#263), the King organized in 1235 a large Hungarian settlement in southwest Transylvania. This autonom settlement was called the "Bánság of Szörény." This settlement became the frontier-guard of this strategically important region, attempting to defend the Danubian Basin against any attack coming from the south, crossing the so-called "Foscani Gate." (#264). (As a consequence of the Balkanic-Wallachian infiltration, even this pure Magyar settlement was populated by more and more newcomers in the middle of the 13th century.)

Our topic (and especially this chapter) familiarizes us with the history of the entire Danubian Basin, but no reason to detail events, which were not in direct connection with Transylvania. Thus, we will not analyze the Great Mongol Invasion in Hungary in detail, we will only mention the effect of this invasion on Transylvania.

The Mongol chief Temujin (#265), who was proclaimed supreme ruler as Chinjiz Khán (Mighty King) of all the Mongols, conquered northern China and Azerbaijan, later Georgia and northern Persia. After capturing Bokhara, Samarcand and Khorasan (1219-20), the Mongols faced a united Russian-Cuman army at the Kalka River. The Mongols defeated this united force (#266), but after their victory, they returned to Asia.

After 1237, Ogotai, successor of the Great Chinjiz Khan decided to conquer the whole Eurasian Continent. Mongol armies under Batu (#267) overrun and conquered southern and central Russia. After invading Poland (#268), they penetrated into Hungary, crossing the north-eastern, eastern Carpathians and the Transylvanian Alps. Béla's army was overwhlemingly defeated at Muhi at the Tisza River. Even the king was

---

#260: Pope Gregory IX (1227-1241) wrote a letter in 1234 to Prince Béla, informing him about the Wallachs under the rule of the Cumans. (Inf. Ghyka: **"A Documented Chronology of Roumanian History."** p. 55.

#261: "The Forest of the Wallachians."

#262: First from Julianus, a Dominican monk, returning from Asia, secondly from the Cuman refugees. (They were settled down by the Danube & Tisza.)

#263: Huns, Avars, Bulgarians, even one branch of the Magyars, later Turks, and finally the Red Army in 1944 used this gateway to enter into the Basin.

#264: Even today, more than 200 town-names remind us of Bánság's Magyar origin.

#265: (1162-1227).

#266: Battle of the Kalka River (1223).

#267: Actually commanded by Khán Sabutai.

#268: In the time of Boleslav V (1227-1279). The Mongols invaded in 1241.

obliged to flee to the Adriatic. The Mongols followed him, but suddenly gave up their conquests when news arrived of the death of the Great Khan. They returned to Asia. (#269).

The Mongol invasion left the Danubian Basin devastated. (#270). The mountainous Transylvanian regions offered better opportunities for hiding, than the Great Magyar Plain, but even the Transylvanian Magyar population suffered significant manpower losses.

In time of great danger, all of the Magyars (knights and peasants alike) became automatically, and voluntarily soldiers, appearing as defenders of the nation, and even more, appearing as defenders of Christianity (#271) against the aggressive forces of Asia. Consequently, the manpower losses were associated, almost exclusively, with the Magyars, and Székelys in Transylvania too. The Wallachian immigrants did not really consider Transylvania as their homeland yet. They did themselves in the forests, and caves of the mountains, or — even worse — they appeared often in the service of the Mongol chiefs as guides.

When the last Mongol hordes (#272) disappeared from Transylvania, the Wallachians reappeared from the forests and caves. (#273). The successors of Béla IV (#274), attempting to populate the devastated areas and ignoring the danger of ethno-linguistic transformation of Transylvania, donated further estates to Wallachian newcomers, who crossed the Transylvanian Alps after 1241. Most of them settled in Bihar (Rum: Bihor, Máramaros (Rum: Maramures), Hunyad (Rum: Hunedora) and Fogaras (Rum: Fagaras). On 11th of March 1291, the Assembly of Gyulafehérvár (#275) recognized the Transylvanian Wallachians as a "nation" with rights equal to other member nations under the Holy Crown. (#276). (Few decades later the Hungarian Kingdom established two other "voievodines", called "Havasalföld" (#277), and Moldova.)

Andrew the Third was the last king of the native Dynasty. Mentioning him, let us take a look at the ethno-linguistic situation in Transylvania at the end of the 13th century.

Even without evidence of any census, we may suppose, that the number of the infiltrating Wallachians had grown considerably in this decisive century. The Magyars and Székelys did not reproduce themselves so extensively as the Wallachian shepherds. The Magyars died on the battlefields, or were exterminated during the Mongol Conquest. The Wallachians hid themselves very well; reappeared after the danger, and invited new groups of their nationality from Wallachia and Moldavia. We do not have statistical records about the Magyar-Wallachian setlments in Transylvania at the end of the 13th century, but we do not have any reason to believe that the Wallachians represented more than about 30% of the Transylvanian population. (#278).

#269: According to historical traditions, Batu Khan returned, because he desired to succeed the Great Khan. Zathureczky ("Transylvania" feels, that Batu returned, learning that W. Europe was fortified. The Mongols ruled over Russia for many more centuries. This rule characterized the Russian look, attitude and political philosophy.

#270: After their disappearance, the Magyar nobility was allowed to build castles and these soon became bases for feudal warfare.

#271: It is clear in Béla IV' letter to Pope Innocent IV (1243-54) in XI. 11, 1252.

#272: They were called "Tatars" in Hungary, because of their Turkish appearance.

#273: Rogerius' "Carmen Miserabile" (after 1241) mentioned "Transylvanian knezates, characteristic of Rum. communities." (Ghyka: "Docum. Chron." p. 57.)

#274: Stephen V (1270-72), Ladislas IX (1272-90) and Andrew III (1290-1301).

#275: Rum.: Alba Iulia. (The Rumanians identified "Gyula" with the Lat. "Julius").

#276: "Cum universis nobilibus, Saxonibus, Syculis et Olachis". Ghyka: Doc. p. 54.

#277: Snowy Plain.

#278: The Census of Várad (1256) did not mention any Wallachian names.

The slight ethno-linguistic difference gradually disappeared between the Magyars any Székelys in the 12th and 13th centuries. Where did they settle down?

"At all events, — answered C. A. Macartney (#279), — we find them, occupying in compact masses the head waters of the Maros (Mures), the Aluta, and the Nagy Küküllö (Tarnava Mare), in the extreme east of Transylvania; and there we find their descendants to-day. They retain, indeed, a strong local and 'tribal' patriotism. They differ, in their own eyes, from the other Magyars only in being more Magyar than they."

The Székelys enjoyed the privileges of the "frontier peoples". (#280). They were all "free men" and elected thir own Count, who held office direct from the King.

"Their social organization long preserved many traces of the early 'tribal' system followed by the Magyars themselves before their settlement and political reorganization. Thus all their land was held in common, private property vested chiefly in cattle." (#281).

The Wallachians, — as we mentioned in our previous pages already, — populated Bihor, Maramures, Fogaras, and other mountainous areas.

"If you look at the country today where Magyars and Roumanians live together, you will still find the mountain portions, and especially the tops, settled by Roumanians, and the lowlands settled by Magyars, who also enter the mouths of the valleys; because the one has always been fond of the mountains and the other has always been fond of the plain. (#282).

The Magyars, the Székelys and the Saxons (#283) had thus occupied at the end of the 13th century practically all the agricultural, and, by their standards, habitable area of Transylvania. "The question so ferociously disputed to-day is — where were the Roumanians at that time?" — asked Macartney (#284).

The answer is simple. Existing still in caves, or living in small villages on the tops of high mountains, the Wallachian shepherds were still quite isolated from the political history of Transylvania. Their life was quiet. They did not know the World around them. In every family there were great many children. Crossing the Transylvanian Alps, more and more relatives joined them from Balkanic Wallachia.

#279: In his "Hungary and Her Successors". ("The Treaty of Trianon and its Consequences." Oxford University Press, London, Royal Institute of International Affairs, 1937.) p. 255.
#280: Somewhat similar to those of the Saxons (discussed in the next Cr.)
#281: C. A. Macartney: "Hungary and Her Successors." p. 255.
#282: Count Paul Teleki: "The Evolution of Hungary and Its Place in European History. "The Macmillan Co., New York, 1923. "Making the State." p. 39.
#283: Settled by the Árpád Dynasty since the beginning of the 12th century.
#284: "Hungary and Her Successors." p. 255.

IX

TRANSYLVANIA AS AN INTEGRAL PART OF THE MEDIEVAL HUNGARIAN KINGDOM
(PART II: THE TRANSYLVANIAN SAXONS)

The beginning of the Saxon settlement in Transylvania was associated with the Patzinak and Cuman invasions against the Danubian Basin in the first decades of the 12th century.

"As the Hungarian settlers were unable to provide adequate protection against the growing number of Pecheneg and Cumane invaders from the south and the east, Hungarian kings invited German (Saxon) settlers to migrate to the southern districts between 1160 and 1220." (#285).

Stephen II, and Béla II (See #230 on p. 50) were quite weak rulers. Their reigns were still associated with internal dynastic truggles. They did not have time to concentrate on Transylvania, and on the dangers facing the Danubian Basin on the eastern frontiers. Géza II (See #231 on p. 51) was the first, who — even at the time, when he struggled with the growing Byzantine efforts, — realized the necessity of new Transylvanian settlements.

The first Saxons, who were Germans from the Moselle region, were settled in 1150 in the southern Transylvanian region. Géza II felt that the Saxons would represent considerable aid in the defence of Transylvania, not only against the eastern (Patzinak, Cuman, etc.) invaders, but they could fight (together with the Székely frontiersmen) against the Greeks, if Byzantium tried to enforce its influence with a possible military adventure. (#286).

The Saxons did not arrive in one group. The first group came from the Moselle, the second from the Lower Rhine area. The Hungarian kings granted them uninhabited but fertile lands. The new settlers were quite content in their new environment, and invited their relatives from the Moselle or Lower Rhine area. The Saxon settlements were well populated and well administered already in the time of Stephen III and Béla III. (See p. 51, and #231, 232 and 233).

"They were honest, hard working farmers and artisans who founded towns and villages and come to constitute the body of the burgher class." (#287).

Additionally to the Magyars and Székelys (who were the warrior nobles), the Saxon burghers were the third "free nation" in Transylvania, forming the political body, the "populus" of the country. (#288). In the time of Emeric I and Ladislas III (see p. 51, #236) they received a growing respect from the other two bodies of the "populus".

Unquestionably, this growing respect was connected not only with their hard work, well known administrative, organisational sense, but occasionally apparent military discipline. The Magyars did not like the Germans very much, but is was also true, that the Royal Family often employed German knights in the Court. The Hungarian feudal nobility learned many useful military, legal, technical, etc. customs from the Germans. The German language was accepted as the second foreign language after Latin.

#285: Osterhaven: **"Transylvania."** The Reformed Review, Michigan.

#286: See p. 51 again.

#287: Zsombor Szász: **"Hungarian-Rumanians."** p. 589.

#288: The recognition of the Wallachians as a "nation" did not come before **1291.** (See p. 55, #257 and 276).

When the merchants of Lübeck and Bremen founded the Order of the Teutonic Knights, and when the name of this Order became associated with the crusaders, the respect of the German knights rose even higher in Hungary, especially in the circles of the high nobility in Pannonia.

The middle nobility and the peasantry did not like them so much. The Germans were too proud, and they used every opportunity to express their (believed) social and military superiority. When a large group of the Teutonic knights arrived in Transylvania under Hermann von Salza, who was the first "great grand master" of the order, they were not welcomed by the natives. Andrew II attempted to negotiate with the Teutonic Knights between 1221 and 1224. He planned to create a strong bulwark against the Cumans. Von Salza had too many and too difficult conditions for his Order. The Hungarian king felt, that giving too many privileges to the Teutons would provide a certain danger for the Royal House from the side of the Magyar gentry. 1222 was a very significant year in Hungarian history. It was the year of the foundation of the first documented Hungarian Constitution, the "Golden Bull." (See p. 53 and # 254). Andrew II refused to grant the required special privileges to the Teutonic Knights.

"After the failure of their negotiations with King Andrew II of Hungary, who hesitated to accept their conditions for a settlement at the border of Transylvania, they seized the opportunity of creating a German state at the Polish border." (#289 and #290).

After the departure of the Teutonic Knights, the Transylvanian German settlement lost something from its significance, but the Magyars, especially the Transylvanian Magyars got rid of quite an unpleasant element. (#291). Other Germans, (the original Saxon settlers) were granted far-reaching outonomy, as registered in King Andrew II' Charter of 1224.

"The king's favour was connected with the fact, that the Saxons ...did not join the Teutonic Knights; they remained faithful... The king alowed, that the Saxons could elect their own judicial authority, their own priests, etc." (#292). (#293).

The royal authority assigned to the Saxons

"... a good portion of the land: the whole cultivable area lying within the southern mountains and bordered roughly by the Mures, (Maros) and the Tárnava mica (Kis Küküllö) on the north and west of the Aluta on the south-east. Other Saxon settlements centred round Brasov (Brasso, Kronstadt) in the far southeast and Bistrita (Bistritz, Beszterce) in the north-east." (#294).

#289: Oscar Haleczki: "Borderlands of Western Civilization." The Ronald Press Co., New York, 1952. p. 71.

#290: Hermann, who was the intimate friend of Emperor Frederick ("Stupor Mundi" 1211-1250), received the call to Prussia in 1229, from Conrad of Masovia, Duke of Poland, to aid him in the Christianization of the pagans on the Baltic.

291: The Teutonic Knights built stone forts (without the permission of the king), issued their own coins, and attempted to create an independent state in the southeast corner of Hungary. (Finally, a Hungarian army forced them to leave Hungary in 1226.)

#292: Inf.: Henrik Marczali: "Magyarország Története." Athenaeum, Budapest, 1912 p. 148.

#293: Their privileges regarding administration, military service, courts, and taxation remained in effect almost unchanged until 1867.

#294: C. A. Macartney: "Hungary and Her Successors." p. 254.

There was also an outlying settlement around Szászrégen (Rum: Reghinul Sásesc, Ger: Sächsisch Reen), south of Beszterce, which although not forming part of the Saxon organization proper, has preserved much of its national character, while

"... even in the west, the towns such as Kolozsvár (Rum: Cluj, Ger: Klausenburg) were originally German, although they became Magyarized after a few centuries." (#295).

The question is this: why did the king give such a remarkable Charter to the Saxons? Why were they granted with so exceptionally good terms? (#296).

We may answer this way: (1) The importance of the Saxons was far greater than in the modern ages in Transylvania; they were relatively more numerous in the Middle Ages than they are today. (2) They were assigned the dangerous position of frontier guards, thus, the king felt, he had to give them special privileges which should hearten them in their task and ensure their loyalty. (3) This loyalty became very clear, when the Saxons did not join the Teutonic Knights in their effort for complete independence, and King Andrew II was grateful for this loyalty in a stormy age, which endangered the king's authority by the feudal high-nobility anyway. (4) The Magyars were not too enthusiastic over town life. The first towns in Transylvania were founded by those Saxons settlers. The King realized the significance of towns and valued the coming of the burghers (middle class) in the age of feudal anarchy very highly.

On the other hand, the departure of the Teutonic Knights represented true luck for Hungary, especially for Transylvania. When they left Hungary in 1226, "even the Pope declared that they were snakes, kept warm in the king's heart." (#297). (#298). They represented a permanent danger to Poland not much after their invitation by Conrad of Masovia. After their unification with the Livonian Knights (#299), they virtually exterminated the native population in Prussia, they erected a most formidable barrier to Polish access to the sea, and in the coming centuries their dangerous activity was responsible in a large part, that the unfortunate Poland became the victim of expansionistic effort from both (German and Russian) sides. (#300).

The Transylvanian Saxon settlement represented a positive factor in the history of Hungary. The expulsion of the Teutonic Knights was justified not only by the contemporary Hungarian public opinion, not only by the pope, but, — knowing their activities in and around Prussia, — by History itself.

#295: C. A. Macartney: **"Hungary and Her Successors."** p. 254.

#296: They were accepted as a single "nation" under their own elected Count, who held office directly under the king. In internal affairs they were allowed to have almost completely independent self-government. Additionally to this, their territory, the so called "Sachsenboden" became a strict national reserve, on which no other nationality was alowed to encroach!

#297: Quotation from: H. Marczali: **"Magyarország Története."** p. 149.

#298: Honorius III (1216-1227).

#299: 1237.

#300: They invaded Poland first in 1326, and they emerged triumphant in 1333. The Poles were able to defeat them only in 1410 (in the Battle of Tannenberg). Prussia was secularized only in 1525 by Albert Hohenzollern of Brandenburg, but the Teutonic Order itself survived until 1809 and was later revived in 1840, under the Habsburgs (with its original functions, e.g. ambulance service in war.).

X.
TRANSYLVANIA AS AN INTEGRAL PART OF THE MEDIEVAL HUNGARIAN KINGDOM
(PART III: THE ZENITH OF THE HUNGARIAN POWER)

After the Hungarian Royal House of Arpád died out in 1301, on the constitutional right of free election, the nation chose kings from the female lines. The extinction of the ruling dynasty led to a period of conflict, during which Czech, German, and Italian parties each attempted to put their candidates on the throne. Wenceslas, son of the king of Bohemia (#301), only thirteen years old, was first elevated, but could not maintain himself. The same fate befell Otto of Bavaria. (#302). Hungary itself, was already an essentially feudal country. Some of the great magnates and bishops owned large territories. Their wealth was associated with political and social power. Many of them enjoyed relative independency, especially in times, when the king was weak, or the king was too young and inexperienced. They were called "little kings". The lower nobility (the gentry) gradually became the most patriotic element of the country. They organized the provincial governments; they had, to a large degree, control of the administration. Also the nobility (high and middle) free from taxation, was responsible for defense, but here again, only the gentry represented a positive factor; the "little kings" were often too selfish, too individualistic, and they usually did not associate national interest with their own interests. One of these powerful lords was Mathias Csák, who ruled over large areas in Northern Hungray (which is Slovakia of today), the other one was Ladislas of Transylvania.

It seemed, in 1308, that the dynastic struggle was over, and with the victory of the Anjou-line Hungary found a good solution. Charles I (Charles Robert of Anjou), who was the grandson of Mary, the daughter of Stephen V. (#303), was elected. He established his capital at Visegrád and introduced Italian chivalry and western influences to Hungary.

Without detailing the significance of his rule, let us turn to the effect of the new king on Transylvania.

First of all, it is important to mention, that, after 15 years of effort, finally Charles Robert was successful in subduing the "little kings". The defeat of Ladislas of Transylvania was very important. The powerful lord dominated over Magyars, Székelys, Saxons, and Wallachians in a real dictatorial way. After his fall, all the ethnic groups were grateful to the king. Encouraging mining in Transylvania, Charles Robert simultaneously tried to please the various groups in this multinatioal land. The domestic peace he brought to this country enabled the people to resume their fairs. At these, various nationalities appeared in their respective national costumes.

> "Magyar, Saxon, Slovak, Roumanian, Serb, all met on the friendliest terms and learned to respect, and understand one another." (#304).

#301: Wenceslas ruled Hungary from 1301 to 1304 .He was the son of Wenceslas II (1278-1305) of Bohemia, one of the last kings of the Premyslid dynasty. The young Wenceslas was the great-great-grandson of Béla IV. (See #239).

#302: Otto von Wittelsbach (ruled Hungary from 1305 to 1308) was actually the grandson of Béla IV. (His mother, Elizabeth was Béla's daughter.)

#303: Stephen V's daughter, Mary, married Charles II, King of Naples. Their grandson was Carobert, or Charles Robert.

#304: A. B. Yolland: "A History of Hungary." Turul, Budapest, 1928. p. 50.

Studying Charles Robert's attitude towards ethnic minorities, especially to Wallachians, it is interesting to note, that the king distinguished them if they were living in Transylvania, or if they were outside of it. For example, he encouraged Wallachian setllements on the North-East Carpathians, guaranteeing their freedom, but, on the other hand, turned against the newly founded "Voivody" of Wallachia, when the head of the new, small state, Bassarab disputed Szörény with him. (#305, #306). He was succeeded by his son.

> "The first act of the new King, Louis the Great (1342-82), who ascended the throne at the age of seventeen, was a visit to the tomb of St. Ladislas at Nagyvárad. The young monarch desired thereby to symbolise his intention of imitating the example of his sainted predecessor and of devoting his life and energy to the consolidation of the the the powers of Hungary." (#307).

Why did I quote this sentence? For many reasons. First of all; Nagyvárad was one of the ancient Magyar cities in Transylvania. (Its name is "Oradea" today). Secondly: by visiting a Transylvanian city at the very beginning of his rule, the great Anjou king wished to demonstrate, that he realized the traditional role of Transylvania, as not only integral, but actually the most Hungarian part of the Kingdom. Thirdly: Nagyvárad was the city of St. Ladislas the Saint (#308), and the new king wished also to demonstrate that the Anjous were willing to follow the Dynasty of Árpád in the just, wise government of the country.

The national minorities received protection in Transylvania, and in every other part of Hungary. (At this point it will be necessary to mention, that Louis was tolerant in ethno-linguistic matters, but not in religious matters. He wished to be a "second Ladislas the Saint," regarding himself the "apostolic" King of Hungary, the protector of Roman Christianity. Consequently, he was not too friendly to the Wallachians, because of their Greek-Orthdox religion. (#309).

Louis followed in his father's footsteps. He endeavoured to establish his suzerainty over all the neighbouring petty kingdoms. Alexander, the wayvode of Wallachia, at once took the oath of allegiance. Uros, prince of Serbia, accepted his overlordship. The Wallachians and Cumanians of Moldavia yielded to his persuasions and adopted the Catholic faith in large numbers.

Dealing with Moldavia and Wallachia, it is understandable, that Transylvania received an extraordinary strategic importance in the age of Louis the Great. The Székely frontiersmen took extraordinary part in these foreign affairs, when the Tatars were driven out of Moldavia. The Székelys were directed by Andrew Laczfi. (Moldavia, after this, became one of the provinces of the powerful Anjou kingdom.)

#305: The new Wallachian settlements were in Máramaros (Maramures), and in the ccunties Ung, Bereg and Ugocsa.

#306: Ivan Bassarab was the Cuman military leader of the Wallachians at this time. Charles Robert actually desired to occupy Wallachia, but the local forces resisted successfully. (Inf. H. Marczali: "Magyarország Története." p. 204, and M. Ghyka: "A Documented Chronology of Roumanian History." p. 57.

#307: A. B. Yolland: "The History of Hungary." (In the "View of Trianon's Hungary." Gabriel Bethlen Press, Turul Association, Budapest, 1928. Ch. VIII. "The Angevin Kings of Hungary." p. 50.

#308: (See p. 44, #230). St. Ladislas (cannonized 1192) was the first great king after St. Stephen. He supported the pope in his conflicts with the Holy Roman Emperor. Pope Urban II (1088-1099) appointed him as the leader of the First Crusade, but Ladislas died in 1095, in the year of preparations. (First Crusade: 1096-99).

#309: Many of the Wallachians refused to be converted to Catholicism and left for Moldavia, uniting themselves with Cumans and with Slavo-Roumanians. (Brodnici). (1352). The name of their leader was Bogdan.

Under Louis of Anjou, Hungary became one of the Great Powers of Europe. After having balanced for centuries between the German and Byzantine Empires Hungary passed into the sphere of French influence and of French-Italian culture. The great king's court became a meeting place for the scholars and artists. After 1370 (when Louis was crowned King of Poland too, #310), his power reached its zenith. His dominions stretched from the Baltic Sea to the Black Sea and the Adriatic; practically the whole Balkans acknowledged his suzerainty. (See MAP VIII, p. 63).

"During this century Transylvania served as a pivot of expanding Hungarian influence. The princes of Moldavia and even some Wallachian princes became tributaries of the Hungarian kings, and Hungarian influence prevailed there until, 1460." (#311).

Transylvania was unquestionably one of the most favoured provinces of the Holy Crown at this time. Her economic and cultural standard was one of the highest in Europe. All the ethno-linguistic groups enjoyed the good circumstances equally, although it is mentionable that only Magyar and Saxon students studied at the University of Pécs #312. The Wallachians did not use their opportunities. They remained on the high mountains. They were quite satisfied with life, but they did not have the desire for education. Most of them were absolutely illiterate. Universities, colleges, parochial schools required the knowledge of Latin. The Transylvanian Wallachians were much more "cultured" than their Moldavian, or Wallachian relatives, but the large majority of them did not read and write even in their own native language.

The Transylvanian Vlach peasant and shepherd did not wish to imitate his Magyar or Saxon neighbours although the Anjou kings offered them opportunities for this. Nevertheless, in the light of the brilliant Kingdom, they gradually transformed themselves. Their life-standard, their homes, Greek-Orthodox churches, their personal looks became bette, more cultured. Transylvania was one of the diamonds of Europe in this era. Simultaneously Moldavia and Wallachia were very backward countries.

"Conditions in both Wallachia and Moldavia remained extremely primitive for a long period after their foundation. There were no real towns. Both countries were completely isolated. Education was almost unknown. Even the Church was backward and unorganized, served mainly by Slav priests." (#313).

We may add to this quotation, that the situation did not change in Moldavia and Wallachia later, when these provinces did not belong to Hungary anymore. "With us" said Bratianu, one of the Prime Ministers of Rumania (#314), in the course of a public lecture, "the Middle Ages began when they ended in other countries . . . We were outside the civilization of Europe." (#315).

#310: He became King of Poland in 1370, after the death of Casimir the Great (1333-1370). By an agreement already with Charles Robert (1339) Casimir, who had no direct heir, promised the Polish crown to Louis.

#311: M. E. Osterhaven: "Transylvania. The Pathos of a Reformation Tradition." p. 16.

#312: Founded by Louis the Great in 1367. According to many historians it was actually the second Hungarian university. The first one (founded in the 11th century) did not receive the university-status from the pope. The University of Pécs was one of the first Central European universities.

#313: R. W. Seton-Watson: "History of the Roumanians." Archon Books. Hamden and Contennicut. 1963. p. 29.

#314: He was premier many times between 1909 and 1927.

#315: Inf. from Zsombor Szász: "Rumanian History." (The Hungarian Quarterly, Autumn, 1941. Vol. VII. p. 205.

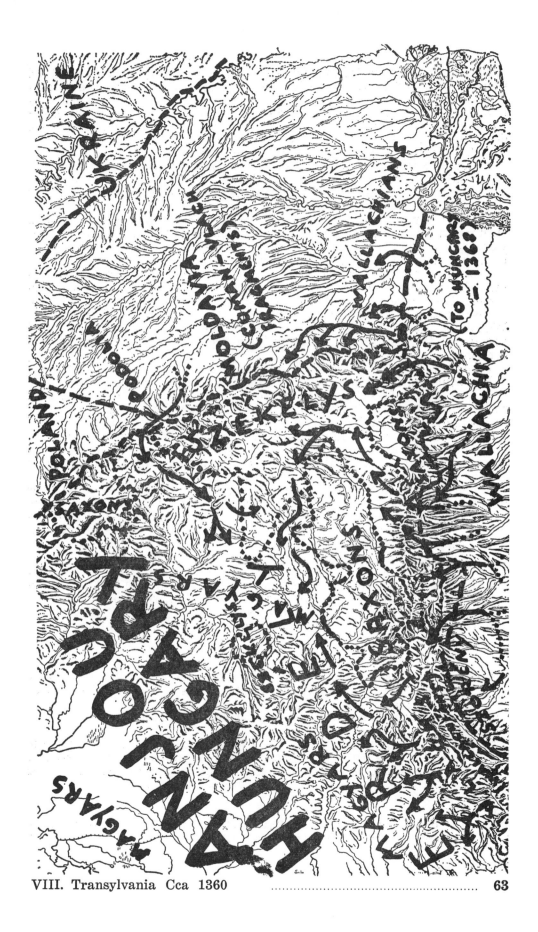

The Roumanian historians of the twentieth century concentrated all their efforts to "create" historical evidence for their dream, the "Dako-Roman continuity in Transylvania". They could not find any. Then they tried to find documents, which seemed to prove that the Wallachians were actually not Wallachians, but "Roumanians". They found some documents, although not too many; for example

> ". . . in 1345 a letter written by Pope Clement V (#316) to King Louis of Hungary . . . the Sovereign Pontiff states that several 'Olahi Romani' were living in Hungary." (#317).

"This is the first time that Wallachians are called Romans!"—rejoiced Ghyka (#318).

Thus, we may read hundreds of pages from ambitious Rumanian authors, in which they were investigating their Roman origin, in which they were, almost childishly happy at finding very modest traces. It is really too bad, that they did not spend at least some of their energies, to investigate the social, or psychological reasons, which prevented the Wallachian herdsmen from producing their own intellectuals throughout so many centuries. They were certainly not oppressed in the Anjou-age in Transylvania; nobody controlled their ethno-linguistic "culture" in Moldavia and Wallachia. However, the opportunities of the Anjou Renaissance could not decoy these illiterate "Romans" out from their forests, caves and cottages.

(Could we call Louis' steps onthe Balkans, as "imperialistic expansion"? Knowing the internation circumstances, we could not do so.

It was during Louis' reign that the first signs of the Turkish menace to European Christianity began to appear. (#319). The King of Hungary was chiefly concerned in preventing the Turks from extending their power over Wallachia and Bulgaria, whose rulers were endeavouring to throw off their allegiance to Hungary by joining hands with the new-comers. Hungary's external steps were aimed at saving the Carpathian Basin and defending European civilization.)

When Louis died in 1382, Hungary, and especially Transylvania, was an interesting example of the early European artistic Renaissance. Sculpture flourished as an art side by side with fresco-painting. The most celebrated Transylvanian sculptors of the age, Martin and George Kolozsvári, were responsible for the statue of St. Ladislas at Nagyvárad, and also, probably, for the statues in the cathedral at Kassa. (#320).

In 1382, Mary of Anjou (daughter of Louis) became the ruling Queen. (#321). She was married to Sigismund of Luxemburg, who became guardian of the Kingdom. (#322). In 1387, Sigismund, (who became German Emperor in 1410 and King of Behémia in 1436), took authority over the country. His reign marked a great decline in the royal power, due in large

---

#316: M. Ghyka, the author of this quotation mentions Pope Clement V. It is a mistake again. He couldn't write a letter in 1345, because he died in 1314. Ghyka means probably Pope Clement VI (1342-1352).

#317: M. Ghyka: "A Documented Chronology of Roumanian History." p. 60.

#318: Ibid.

#319: The Turks had taken Adrianople, and were threatening Constantinople itself. Emperor John V (Palaelogus) (1341-1376) came to the Court of Louis, at Buda. Asking aid, he offered his return to the Western Church. (He offered the same thing to Pope Urban V, 1362-1370, in 1369 (Avignon).

#320: Kassa is Kosice today. (Slovakia).

#321: (1382-1385).

#322: His position was challenged by Charles of Durazzo, who was able to secure the throne for himself for a brief period (1385-1386).

measure to Sigismund's constant absence from the country and his practice of selling royal domains in order to get money for his far-reaching schemes elsewhere.

In general Sigismund relied on the towns and lesser nobility against the great magnates. (#323). Occasionaly visiting Transylvania, (#324) he communicated mostly with the local administrators of the cities instead of the Transylvanian high nobility.

Transylvania's significant strategic position received once again special importance during Sigismund's reign. The Turkish menace came nearer. After 1369 Murad I (#325) conquered Bulgaria. (#326). In 1371 the Serbs were defeated. (327). In 1389, the Turks defeated a coalition of Serbs, Bulgars, Bosnians, Wallachians and Albanians. (#328).

Bayazid I, the succeeding Sultan (#329) began the siege of Constantinople in 1391. The siege was still on, when Sigismund led his famous "Crusade of Nicopolis" (1396) to aid Byzantium against the Moslems. He was supported by Balkan rulers and by French, German, and English knights. (#330). The Crusade was not successful. After an initial success Sigismund's army was completely overwhelmed. (As a result of this defeat, Sigismund evacuated Dalmatia (#331), the Turks dominated the Balkans, and the southern frontier of Transylvania suffered repeated Moslem raids.)

Let us leave the Turks for a while, and let us return to Transylvania. It will be important, because at this point I arrived to a Transylvanian character, to the only one, who was quite well known by the students of the North-American Continent, — by students who like to watch horror-movies. In connection with Sigismund's rule and especially with Transylvania, we have to mention "Count Dracula, the Vampire" too.

This Dracula-business began in the year of 1408, when the King founded an order of knights called the Order of the Dragon.

> "One of the first things to be done, in those days when people wore fancy dress as an everyday matter, was to design a good rousing uniform for the Knights of the Order, and they were accordingly done up regardless in a scarlet tunic and a short green cloak, while their insignia consisted of a double gold chain with a curled-up dragon." (#332).

This Order — for Dracula is merely one of the corruptions of the word dragon — was the source and origin of the Dracula legend. In 1431, a young Wallachian, the son of the Voivode of Wallachia, came to the court of Sigismund. In the same year, as the symbol of the feudal relationship, Vlad (this was his name) also received the membership of this Order. When he returned to his rather backward part of the world, his people, who had very little idea of the world of chivalry, failed to understand what the dragon meant. In fact, they were so misguided as to think that it was the mark of the evil. When the Knight of the Dragon, ("miles draconis"),

---

#323: Who inprisoned him for four months in 1401!

#324: It was the best royal baer- and stag-hunting area for centuries.

#325: (1359-1389).

#326: Shisman, ruler of Bulgaria, became vassal of the Turks.

#327: The battle took place at Cernomen on the Maritza River. In 1386 the Turks captured Nish and Lazar of Serbia also became a Turkish vassal.

#328: This famous battle took place at Kossovo. (June 20; traditional date: June 15). Lazar of Serbia was killed in this battle. Murad, the Sultan was also assassinated just after it, by a Serbian. He was succeeded by Bayazid I (1389-1402).

#329: One of the greatest ruler of the Moslems.

#330: Both the Roman and Avignonese popes sent their blessings to Sigismund.

#331: The Venetians took over the domination of Dalmatia.

#332: Stephen Csabai: **"The Real Dracula."** (**The Hungarian Quarterly**, Autumn, 1941. Vol. VII. No. 2. pp. 327-28.

began his rule in Wallachia, his people, who were apt to confuse religion with superstition and fear of magic, simply took the dragon to be a sign of a fir munderstanding with the power of darkness, and called the Voivode "dracul", the dragon or the devil.

This name was transferred to his son, whose name was also Vlad, and who became famous for his cruelty. This Dracula was a capable soldier, but he was also a well known sadist. We know, that he left the Greek Orthodox Church and became a Catholic. He engaged in the defence of Christianity. All these things did not prevent him from having a very scandalous private life. We do not have historical evidence about his sex-cruelties. According to historical information, his cruelties were carried out, regarless of sex. Was he a vampire, or not, — we do not know, perhaps he was not. (After all, he was only an East-European, who did not have the bizare and sick fantasy of the average North-American film-spectator.) He was "only" a quite "moderate" sadist, who actually would not "satisfy" the American and Canadian public. Consequently the show-producers transformed the real Dracula into a real, western-type monster. (Such mild errors in the Dracula films, as calling the Rumanians Slovaks, making the Wallachian Count a Székely, confusing topographical and other details will not surprise the European immigrant anymore, if he spent time enough to get acquainted with the level of the public education, (especially educational level in history and geography) in the high schools of the "brave, new world". The Dracula-films actually made an important service. Without them, the average North-American would know about Transylvania even less. (If the unlucky immigrant came to Canada or to the United States, and he was incidentally from Transylvania, people will tell him: "Ah yes, you are from the country, where those awful vampire Counts come from." As a matter of fact, this modest knowledge about East-Europe is better than nothing!)

Leaving Dracula, looking for more serious Transylvanian topics during Sigismund's reign, we have to mention the peasant rebellion of Transylvania in 1437-38. According to Macartney

"... the unrest was fanned by the spread from Bohemia of Hussite doctrines, which took hold especially in north Hungary, and was embittered by the cruelty with which the heretics were persecuted. (#333). The ... peasant revolt broke out in the very last months of Sigismund's reign, as the result of the action of a bishop in Transylvania in claiming the title in money. It spread over much of Transylvania, and gained considerable temporary successes before it was put down." (#334).

A consequence of this revolt was the birth of an institution, the "Union of the Three Nations" under which the Hungarian nobility, the Székelys and the Saxons formed a league for the mutual defence of their interests. (#335).

Some of the modern Rumanian historians would have us believe, that the rebellion of 1437 was actually the revolution of the "subjected Rumanians" against their Hungarian lords. This is a misinterpretation. The causes of this revolt were both political and religious. The peasants (Magyars and Wallachians alike) rose to vindicate their right to migrate at will and to ensure liberty of conscience. The Union (mentioned above) was a typically feudal cooperation of the feudal class against the peasantry. The fact, that the Wallachians were all peasants will not make

---

#333: John Ziska, a brilliant soldier led the Hussites to many victories. After Ziska's death (1424) Procop the Great continued the Hussita effort. Sigismund became king of Bohemia (1436) and he defeated the Hussites, but their movement spread to Slovakia and to North Transylvania.

#334: C. A. Macartney: "Hungary." Edinburgh, University Press, 1962. p. 50.

#335: The "Union of Kápolna." ("Unio Trium Nationum Transylvaniae.")

a "Rumanian revolution" from the peasant rebellion of 1437, in which much more Magyar peasants were involved than Wallachian, and which was led by the Hungarian Antal (Anthony) Budai Nagy. (#336). Did the peasantry revolt against discrimination? Yes, they certainly did, but it was the discrimination by the feudal nobility, and not ethno-linguistic discrimination. As a reaction against extreme feudal-lordship, the peasants revolted against the feudal-system in almost all of the European countries in the 14th and 15th centuries. The special multinational environment of Transylvania gave an unusual complexity to the peasant revolt of 1437, — and presented a special opportunity to Bucharest to „rewrite" history, introducing the peasant rebellion as some sort of Rumanian "national" uprising against Hungary. It is a fact, that the Wallachian shepherds, and peasants joined their Magyar neighbours from the same social class, but this fact did not make a national revolution from this peasant rebellion.

After the death of Sigismund, Albert, his son in law succeded him to the throne. (#337). In the very same year Europe learned a name, which was associated with heroism and with the defence of the civilization of Christian Europe for many years.

"The Ottoman hosts were besieging the fortress of Szendrö (Semendria); they were driven back by the heroic courage of a band of Transylvanian horsemen, led by a knight. This knight was John Hunyady." (#338).

This victory marked the beginning of the golden age of the famous Hunyady family.

"Through the Hunyady family from southwestern Transylvania, the province played a major role in Hungarian and European history between 1440 and 1490." (#339).

According to Wallachian legends, the real name of John (János) Hunyady was actually Jan Szibinyani, and he was of Vlach origin. (#340). We do not have evidence about the origin of the Hunyady family. It a fact that the Hunyadys belonged to the class of the Magyar gentry already. John Hunyady was a very able military leader, and the reign of King Vladislav I (#341) was distinguished chiefly by the continued victories of this talented Transylvanian, who became the Vajda (vaivode) of Transylvania in 1441. He defeated the Turks in 1442, when they invaded Hungary, and he led the Crusade in 1443 against the Turks. (#342). When the Crusaders took Nish and advanced to Sofia Sultan Murad (#343) made the ten year Truce of Szeged. Serbia was freed and Moldavia and Wallachia returned to the Hungarian protectorate. „Hungary was indeed fighting the battles of Christendom; and the sympathy and admiration of the Christian world was lavished on her soldiers." (#344).

It was not Hunyady's, but King Vladislav's fault, that Hungary, encouraged by the Pope, broke the truce, and renewed the Crusade again.

#336: He belonged to the Magyar middle nobility (gentry). For some reason he associated himself with the interests of his peasants.

#337: Albert of Habsburg (1437-39). He was the husband of Sigismund's and Mary (of Anjou)'s daughter, Elizabeth.

#338: A. B. Yolland: **"The History of Hungary."** Ch. IX. "The Reign of Sigismund." p. 60.

#339: M. E. Osterhaven: **"Transylvania."** pp. 16-17.

#340: After 1918, the Rumanians destroyed all the Hungarian historical monuments in Transylvania, but they did not touch the monuments of Hunyady.

#341: (1440-1444). He was also the king of Poland as Vladislav VI. (of Jagello.)

#342: It was preached by Papacy, and composed from Magyar, Polish, Bosnian, Wallachian and Serbian troops.

#343: Murad II (1421-1451).

#344: A. B. Yolland: **"The History of Hungary."** Ch. X. Hunyady and the Turks." p. 64.

"Drakul (#345), the vaivode of Wallachia, also came with an army of 10,000; and he (already, no doubt, planning treachery) endeavoured to persuade Vladislav to turn back." (#346). The Hungarians were left in a hostile country. The two Emperors forgot their promises. (#347). The ill-prepared Hungarian effort ended with the disaster at Varna in Nov. 10, 1444. King Vladislav was killed in this battle.

Hunyady escaped from the rout;

". . . but as he was returning home in disguise, Drakul, the treacherous waywode of Wallachia, took him prisoner and offered to sell him to the Sultan, who refused the offer." (#348), (#349).

1445 also represents an important date in the history of Transylvania. The Parliament held on May 7, 1445, decided to divide Hungary into seven districts, each to be under the control of a Captain. (#350). The position of Hunyady, as the "vajda" of Transylvania was renewed, but he became also the Captain of Transylvania and the trans-Tisza districts. Hunyady used his new power to ensure the security of Transylvania before the possible, new confrontation with the Moslems. He employed mercenaries. This addition made the Transylvanian forces more powerful. Drakul was driven out from Wallachia. Then Hunyady attempted to liberate the Balkans from the Turks. He was supported by the pope. (#351), who sent John Capistrano to the aid of the Magyars. (#352).

"In 1456, János Hunyady won a world-renowned battle over the Turks at Belgrade, remembrance of which is still being expressed in the Christian world by ringing the church bells at noontime." (#353).

Belgrade (Nándorfehérvár), — and temporarily East-Central Europe, was saved by the heroic Transylvanian. The European courts hastened to express their admiration and their gratitude. And it is true, that the ringing churchbells of the five Continents every noontime still represent the memory of the great Hunyady. Pope Calixtus III (#354) ordered the bells to be rung every noon in all churches, and this regulation is still in effect in our days.

The price what Hungary had to pay for the victory was a heavy one. Hunyady was infected with the plague. He was taken to Zimony (this ancient Magyar town is called "Zemun" today), where, on August 17, he died. His remains were burried in the church he himself had founded at Gyulafehérvár. (#Rum: Alba Julia).

We have many reasons to believe, that the world knew much more about Transylvania in those days. All Europe mourned Hunyady's death. Hungary mourned the great military leader and governor of the Kingdom. (#355). Transylvania mourned its heroic Captain. The Vlachs mourned "Jan Szibinyani". Even the Sultan exclaimed: "He was my

---

#345: Identical with Dracula (mentioned before).

#346: A. B. Yolland: "The History of Hungary." pp. 65-66.

#347: Frederick III (1440-1493) the last Holy Roman Emperor (from the House of Habsburg) ignored the promises of his predecessors. John VIII (of Palaeologi) (1425-1448) was involved with internal troubles, and surrounded by Turks even at Constantinople.

#348: Yolland: "The History of Hungary." p. 66.

#349: According to Csabai ("The Real Dracula"), the Wallachian voivode was involved in the defence of Christianity. Yolland introduces him as a traitor.

#350: The temporary militarization could be justified by the Turkish danger.

#351: Nicholas V (1447-1455).

#352: John Capistran, Saint (1385-1456) Italian, Franciscan preacher.

#353: Zathureczky: "Transylvania." p. 17.

#354: Calixtus III. (1455-1468).

#355: He was appointed governor beside the young Ladislas V (1444-57), the son of Albert of Habsburg, from 1444.

foe, but I grieve for his death! The world has lost its greatest man."
(#356).

The turks were kept away for several decades, while Hunyady's son, the Transylvanian-born king, Mathias Corvinus (#357), built an empire of strength and culture in the Danubian Basin. When he died at 47, he left Hungary a dominant state in central Europe and a decisive factor in European diplomacy.

Mathias did not govern the Kingdom from the castle of his family in the Transylvanian Vajdahunyad. He governed from Buda (#358) and later from Vienna (#359). Both of his courts represented great wealth and luxury, centres of Renaissance learning. (#360).

After Mathias' death, Ladislas II, King of Bohemia, was elected King of Hungary by the nobles. He was a weak and ineffectual ruler (#361), who allowed the work of Mathias Corvinus to be undone within a few years. He gave up Mathias' conquests (#362), and arranged dynastic marriages with the Habsburgs. (#363).

This policy led to a formation of a national party among the Hungarian nobility. Transylvania became the citadel of the Magyar resistance again, — not for the first time, and also not for the last time in her history. The national resistance against the activity of the king was led by Stephen Zápolya (or Szapolyai), the Vaivode of Transylvania.

Simultaneously, the Transylvanian (and Pannonian) peasantry attempted again the revolt against the ruthless exploitation of the aristocrats. The revolt of 1514 was organized and directed by George Dozsa, a former soldier of the Hunyadys. The rebellion was supressed in a sea of blood by John Zápolya, leader of the nobility. (#364).

Louis II. the son of Ladislas, succeeded his father at the age of ten. His reign was marked chiefly by the spread of the Protestant Reformation, This movement first took root in the German (in Transylvania: the Saxon) areas and in the towns, and was vigorously opposed by the nobles. (#365). In these years of internal troubles, the Turks took Belgrade, beginning their victorious advance into Hungary. (#366). In 1526, the Turkish army (#367), broke into Hungary and defeated King Louis (Lajos, #368) in a famous battle of Mohács, in which the young king himself fell on the battlefield. This battle has always been considered as perhaps the greatest national catastrophe in Hungarian history. It must be considered as a major landmark, which marks the beginning of the Habsburg reign over Hungary, a reign that lasted for almost 400 years. The 150 years of Turkish conquest was nothing else but a long illness, after which Hungary was able to recover. The Habsburg domination represented a much more terrible catastrophe, which was closely associated with Hungary's (and Transylvania's) problems even in the twentieth century.

#356: Inf. from Yolland's **"The History of Hungary."** p. 70.

#357: Mathias Corvinus, the "Just" (1458-1490). (The younger son of J. Hunyady)

#358: Where he founded the third university of Hungary in 1470.

#359: He counquered from Frederick III in 1485.

#360: One of his courtiers, the Italian Bonfini heard the gossip about the Roumanian (Roman) origin of the king. Following the feudal custom, he worked out the origin of Mathias back to the "divine Aeneas."

#361: (1490-1516). He belonged to the Jagello dynasty.

#362: In order to secure recognition from the Habsburgs.

#363: Both his son and his daughter were married into the Habsburg family.

#364: The supressed rebellion was followed by the "Tripartitum" of Verböczy, a constitution, which established the equality of all nobles and fixed the system of serfdom on the peasantry.

#365: In 1523 it was declared punishable by death, but despite of it, the ideas of Protestantism spread in Hungary, especially in Transylvania.

#366: In 1521.

#367: More than 100,000 against 20,000 Hungarians.

#368: Louis II (1516-26) was only 20 years old, when he died.

XI

THE INDEPENDENT PRINCIPALITY OF TRANSYLVANIA

Louis' death was followed by a hot contest over the succession. The West-Hungarian nobility hoped for German aid against the Moslems, thus they elected Ferdinand of Habsburg, brother of Emperor Charles V. (#369). The national party concentrated in Transylvania again, — as so many times before and after 1526 in Hungarian history, — and they elected John Zápolya as king. (#370). The civil war between the two kings lasted for two years. Zápolya was defeated. Then, he appealed to the Turks who supported him vigorously, (#371). By the Peace of Nagyvárad (#372) the two kings recognized each other, each ruling part of the Danubian Basin. Zápolya became vassal of the Turks. Ferdinand continued the war against them.

In 1540 John Zápolya died. The Turks recognized his infant son, John II (Sigismund) Zápolya. (#373). The civil war was on again. Ferdinand began the invasion of Transylvania. The Turks used the opportunity of the civil war. Penetrating deeply into Great Hungarian Plain, they invaded and took Buda. (#374).

Transylvania, under John Sigismund Zápolya was still a vassal state of the Turks, but was left almost entirely free. The Habsburgs held only a narrow strip of western and northern Hungary, and even for this they long paid tribute to the Turk. (375). (See MAP IX. pp. 71).

The Transylvanian constitutional system grew out of the previous political structure of this land. The indirect government of Transylvania (before 1526) did not suggest any ways of separation, because the king could have taken into his own hand at any time the administration of the land. Transylvania was an integral part of the Kingdom. However, the fact, that Transylvania had her own administration by the Vajda (Voivode) and this structure built on the cooperation of the three "nations" (#376), made the transformation into an independent Principality relatively easy.

> „When, as a result of the Turkish occupation, the Kingdom itself fell apart, and in accordance with the Speyer treaty in August 1570, the independent Transylvanian Principality was established, even the people of Transylvania regarded the situation as interim and born of necessity." (#377).

What does this quotation really mean?

Not less than the fact, that the Transylvanians did not desire permanent independence. Following the Hungarian tradition, they felt themselves as the true and volunteer subjects of the Holy Crown, thus in the Speyer Treaty (mentioned in the quotation) the young Transylvanian king was ready to abdicate voluntarily from the Hungarian throne for the benefit of the Emperor Maximillian (#378), and recognizing the sovereignty of the Hungarian Crown over Transylvania, took the title of "Serenissimus Princeps Transylvaniae" ("Duke of Transylvania") only.

#369: Charles V (1519-1556) was the older brother of Ferdinand. (1526-1564; King of Hungary and Bohemia; being the husband of Anna, sister of Louis II). Beginning with 1556, Ferdinand became the Emperor of Germany.

#370: (See p. 69 again.) John Zápolya as king ruled from 1526 to 1540.

#371: Suleiman (the Magnificent; 1520-66) was the Sultan this time.

#372: The city is called "Oradea" today. The Treaty was arranged in 1538.

#373: (1540-71). He was born from Zápolya's marriage with Isabel of Poland.

#374: 1541.

#375: Some of the historical maps show Transylvania as part of the Moslem Empire after 1526. These maps are fals. Transylvania was under Turkish protection against the Habsburgs, but in internal affairs it was independent, paying only tribute to the Turks — just like the Germans did.

#367: See pp. 66-67 and #335.

#377: Zathureczky: **"Transylvania."** pp. 19-20.

#378: Maximilian II, son of Ferdinand (1564-1576).

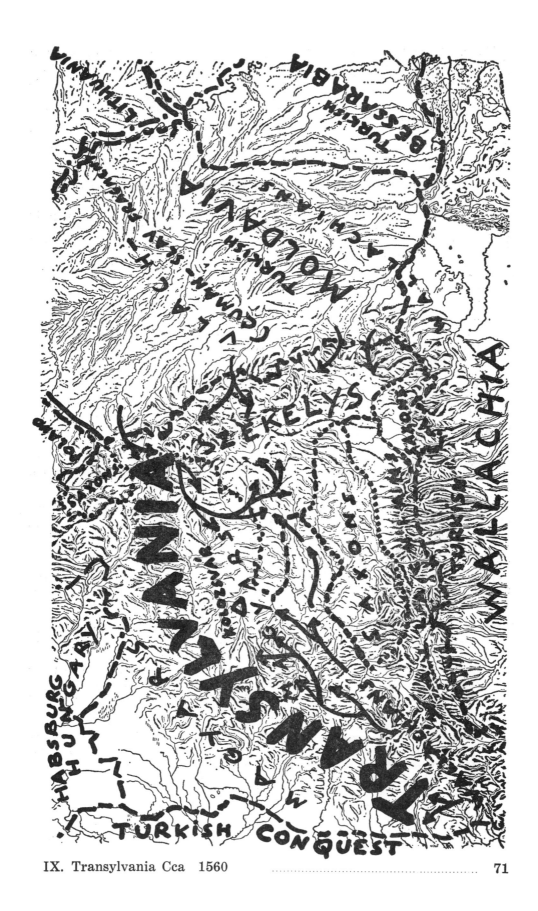

IX. Transylvania Cca 1560 71

Thus, Transylvania was independent from the rest of Hungary, but this independency did not mean the desire to separate its political future from the "Holy Crown". The Transylvanians did not call their leaders "vajda" (Voivode) anymore. Changing this term to the term of Prince (Duke), they wished to express that (1) Transylvania appeared on a much higher status since 1526, and (2) the Transylvanians will always be faithful to the Holy Crown, so even the Transylvanian Prince is (and will be) subject of the King of Hungary, — if the King (crowned with St, Stephen's crown) rules according to the interest of Hungary. Consequently (3, — and this was clear in the mentioned Speyer Treaty of 1570) the Transylvanian political ruler should abdicate from the title of King and should be satisfied with the title of Prince.

If the title (and position) of the Prince of Transylvania was a quite changeable part of the new Transylvanian constitution, the other part, — which was associated with the "Three Nations" tradition (#379) proved to be a stable one.

Under Cardinal Martinuzzi, Transylvania was organized as a State in 1542.

> "In 1542, at Torda, the three nations of Transylvania, i. e. the Hungarians, the Székelys and Saxons, renewed their former alliance. The Prince (Hung: Fejedelem) elected by them was to rule jointly with the Transylvanian Estates, according to their constitution. The Prince resided at Gyulafehérvár, and was assisted by a council composed of twenty-two members, seven for each of the three nations and one representing the Prince himself." (#380).

Ghyka, the Rumanian historian has an interesting remark, according to which "Mohács (1526) . . . caused a break of 340 years in the Hungarian domination of Transylvania." (#381).

Does this sentence represent the truth?

No, it does not. Ghyka tries to confuse his readers, by attempting to introduce the centuries of independent Transylvania, as an age, in which this land "was not Hungarian" at all, because "it was not attached to the Imperial Crown of the Habsburgs."

He could not mislead the experienced reader, who knows history. The student of history knows that (1) Habsburg domination was not necessarily identical with "Hungarian domination," (2) Hungarian domination could be associated with the "Holy Crown", but not with the Imperial Crown of the Habsburg emperors, and (3) the Princes of Transylvania were Hungarians themselves, finally (4) two "nations" of the three, — the Magyars and the Székelys, — regarded themselves Hungarians.

#379: It will be probably peculiar for the reader, that the Wallachians did not appear among the founding "nations" in the constitution. The answer is this: (1) the Transylvanian Wallachians were recognized as one of the "nations" already in 1291 (See p. 55, and # 176), but the "Three Nations" constitution was based only on the "Union of Kápolna" (1438; — See p. 66, #335 again) (2) In the 15-16th Century only the nolibily was indentical with the "nation"; we could not find too many nobleman among the Wallachians. (3) The "Magyar nation" of Transylvania meant: the Hungarian noblemen and probably some of the Wallachians, who deserved the title of noblemen in the Turkish wars. (4) The Wallachians represented still a little minority and their representation in the Constitution seemed to be justified this way — by the feudal-minded majority. (5) Realizing that "Magyar nation" meant actually the nobility, (with non-Magyar elements among them), it will be quite clear also, that the term "nation" did not mean necessarily an ethno-linguistic, but rather an abstract political idea in the 16th century.

#380: D. Sinor: **"History of Hungary"**. G. Allen & Unwin, London, 1959. p. 164.

#381: M. Ghyka: **"A Documented Chronology of Roumanian History."** p. 73.

Ghyka, and other Rumanian historians like to mention the independent Transylvanian Principality, because they feel, that referring to these 340 years during which Transylvania did not belong to Buda, represents an argument against Hungarian historians, who are talking about the "One thousand years of Hungarian domination in Transylvania, since the Conquest to Trianon."

Macartney's opinion on this is the following:

"At the same time, when Hungary was partitioned between the Turks, the Habsburgs, and the Princes of Transylvania respectively, there was no genuine separation between Transylvania and that true Hungary which was at the time more of an ideal than a reality. The Princes of Transylvania were themselves Magyars, and the preponderance of the Magyar element among their subjects was accentuated by two important facts: one, that Székelys of this period lost most of their ancient privileges und became entirely assimilated with the Magyars . . ; the other, that the Transylvanian Princes held during long periods large tracts of predominantly Magyar territory outside the western frontiers of Transylvania proper. They regarded themselves, indeed, and were regarded, as the bulwark of Hungarian national liberties." (#382).

Some of the Rumanian historians did not try to convince their readers with the "independent, non-Hungarian Transylvania" idea, (like Ghyka did) because (as above) it was easy to disprove. Iorga, and his group (#383) gave up this attempt and they tried to introduce the Transylvanian Principality as some sort of Moslem subject, merely a Turkish province during many centuries. (#384). Of course, it was only another way of falsification.

"Transylvania became, after 1526, a separate principality, under a national prince. This land became practically independent, and it maintained its independence in the sixteenth and seventeenth centuries, though paying formal tribute to the Sultan. This tribute was merely formal, and the Sultan was quite content to have a formal acknowledgment of his supremacy, and his troops never garrisoned the country. The clever diplomacy of able Magyar princes ruling Transylvania prevented the German and Turkish Emperors, who ruled large parts of the world, from subjugating this little state in Europe." (#385).

Of course, the Rumanian historians attempted the underestimation of the significance of the independent Transylvanian principality, because they felt it very insulting that the Wallachian minority did not have a possibility to become the fourth "nation" in the Constitution of 1542. (See p. 72, #379 again). At this point they tend to confuse feudal discrimination with ethno-linguistic discrimination again. The Wallachian nobility (and — as we mentioned — only the nobility was identical with the "political nation" this time,) — was represented in the Magyar County Nobility, which "was only by title 'Magyar' though it was not purely so by race; others being made nobles exactly like the Magyars." (#386).

#382: C. A. Macartney: **"Hungary and Her Successors."** p. 259.

#383: Seton Watson had a tendency to be a follower of Iorga in his **"History of the Roumanians.",** using only Rumanian sources for his books, ignoring to take the ideas of feudalism into consideration, and being partly under the effect of his father, (the notorious "Scotus Viator"), who used historical writings as one of the means "to justify" the Paris Treaties of 1919-20).

#384: Under their effect, on some of the western historical maps, Transylvania appears as part of the Moslem Empire!

#385: Teleki: **"The Evolution of Hungary."** p. 61.

#386: **Ibid.** p. 64.

Rumanian historians, speculating about the history of the Rumanians, and trying to deal with Transylvania, as part of Rumanian history, were usually very quiet about the three centuries-long Transylvanian Principality. Reading the previous pages, we could understand why this happened. It was very hard, if not impossible, to prove that (1) the Transylvanian Principality was not a Hungarian domination, and — if it was ruled by the Magyars, — (2) it was not independent at all; it was only a subjected province of the Turkish Empire.

Reading Iorga, Ghyka and others, we will find out, that the Rumanian historians devote only a few pages to these important years of Transylvania, because its development did not seem to fit into the theory of the "Dako-Roman continuity." Let me add a very important reason to all this; the Transylvanians did not use their independency to convert themselves to Greek Orthodoxy (to the religion of the Wallachians) or to Mohamedanism (which was the religion of the Turks). The Transylvanians (nobility and peasantry alike) used the independency from the Habsburgs to accept Protestantism, so that during the late 16th century the larger part of Transylvania became either Calvinist (the Magyars and Székelys), or Lutheran (the Transylvanian Saxons).

> "The Diet held at Torda in 1557 asserted the freedom of religious practices and the scale was slowly tipping in favour of Protestantism: first Lutheranism, then Calvinism. From 1571 onwtrds Unitarianism was also recognized, and the Transylvanian constitution was based on the axiomatic equality of the three nations (Hungarian, Székely, Saxon) and of the four religions (Roman Catholic, Lutheran, Calvinist, Unitarian). This was a remarkably liberal attitude for the epoch, and it seems to be unparalleled in other parts of Europe . . . Religious freedom became an idea accepted by all in Transylvania, and this caused that country to become its champion during the Counter-Reformation." (#387).

> "The basic principle of this statehood was the 'una eademque libertas', the same and equal liberty for all'. This liberty-ideal was not only expressed by the continuous liberty wars against the Habsburgs, but most of all in the very statehood of Transylvania itself, in its political system and mental attitude . . . The Law of Transylvania (#388) clearly stated that 'there shall be no differences between Hungarian members and the Roumanian members of the nobility' ('Valachus ipse nobilis cum Hungaris nobilibus et verificationem et juramenti depositionem in Judiciis facere peregareque tenentur')" (#389).

Thus, during the 16th and 17th centuries Transylvania became the citadel of Hungarian Protestantism. However, Protestantism was not associated with the fanatism of the Reformation, (as it was in many other parts of Europe at this time), because "the surprising fact is that between 1544 and 1574 some twenty-two laws granting freedom for the practice of new theological opinions were enacted by the Diet of Transylvania. No other parliament anywhere passed so much legislation concerning religious freedom in so short time. And it was in the 16th century!" (#390).

#387: Denis Sinor: **"History of Hungary"**. Ch. 18: "Reformation, Literature." pp. 185-186.

#388: Act VI. of the Law of 1540.

#389: Zathureczky: **"Transylvania."** Ch. V: "Transylvania in Light of History." p. 21.

#390: M. Eugene Osterhaven: **"Transylvania. The Pathos of a Reformation Tradition."** "Freedom of Religion and Conscience in Transylvania." p. 22.

Of course, the Princes of Transylvania tried to spread Protestantism in Moldavia and Wallachia. They were not successful. The great result, however, of their cultural influence was the creation of the Rumanian ecclesiastical language and ecclesiastical literature. "Rumanian books were printed at the time at the expense of Hungarian nobles, and Prince George Rákoczy I (#391) gave orders to found a Rumanian ecclesiastical school and a Rumanian printing press." (#392).

This whole movement was of course a part of the struggle af Transylvania for freedom of creed against Catholicism. When fighting for it themselves, they had to give it to other people.

As the heir of the humanistic-renaissance kingdom of Mathias Corvinus (See previous chapter), the Transylvanian Principality took over the legacy of the Hungarian European culture.

"The first book printed in Hungarian appeared in Transylvania in 1527. Toward the end of the same century, some 18 printing establishments were at work within the land. Together they published 380 books, 180 in Latin, 139 in Hungarian, 15 in German, 10 in Roumanian, 9 in old Slavic and 7 in Greek language." (393).

In the 17th century, there were already 44 printing establishments at work. Besides original works, they published a large number of translations from French, English, Italian. Dutch and German writers, mostly from philosophers and clergymen.

Beginning with 1555 appeared a specifically Transylvanian lyric of the age. They are still respected as the first diamonds of the Hungarian national literature. (#394).

"The centers of public education were "Collegiums", where side by side with young noblemen, a large number of lower class children became educated." (#395).

The students were instructed partly by Hungarian professors (who received their degrees at foreign universities) (#396), partly by foreign professors of great international prestige. (#397). Young Transylvanians visited foreign universities in increasing numbers, financed by the dukes of Transylvania, who did not question the racial, linguistic, or religious belongings of the students. (#398).

The Transylvanian Princes and noblemen gave powerful aid to the unfoldment of the Rumanian culture. In addition to the mentioned case of Prince Rákoczy I, let me mention the names of a German and of a Magyar publisher. In the year 1564 Mr. Mayor and Mr. Miklos Forro jointly published the Evangelium in Rumanian language. Prince Kristof Báthory established a Rumanian printing shop in Gyulafehérvár, where the very first Rumanian book appeared printed in Latin letters in 1570.

At this point appears the question: in what percentage did the Rumanians appear in the Transylvanian population in the 16th and 17th centuries?

#391: We will mention him later in this chapter.

#392: Teleki:"**The Evolution of Hungary.**" p. 65.

#393: Zathureczky: "**Transylvania.**" p. 24.

#394: In 1555, Sebestyén (Sebastian) Tinody-Lantos published in Kolozsvár (Rum.: Cluj) his famous "Verses Krónika...... (Eng.: Chronicles in Verses), and in 1569, appeared the most typical literary work of that era, printed in Abrudbánya, the "Comedy about the Treason of Balassi Menyhért."

#395: Zathureczky: "**Transylvania.**" p. 24.

#396: The Universities of Pécs and Buda discontinued instruction during the time of Turkish occupation.

#397: Martin Opitz, John Alsted, Henry Bisterfeld and Isac Basire.

#398: For example, in Wittenberg, between 1586 and 1640, more than 300 Transylvanian students received diplomas. In Lynden, between 1620 and 1650, there were 231 Transylvanians enrolled. (Inf. Zathureczky: "**Transylvania.**")

Interestingly enough, the Rumanian authors did not mention numeric evidence, altough some statistics were available from original documents. Instead of using them as references, the historians of Bucharest were satisfied with general ,and simplified remarks. For example Iorga in his work says: "The Rumanians of Transylvania are more numerous there than the Serbians are in Hungary." (#399). And later in the same book: "The Roumanians were the great majority of the inhabitants of the country." (#400).

Let me quote other (non-Rumanian) sources now:

"At the end of the sixteenth century the Rumanians formed about one-quarter of the population of Transylvania, about 100,000." (#401).

"At the beginning of the sixteenth century, the entire population of Transylvania numbered 425,000 souls, of whom about 100,000 were Rumanians." (#402).

"Lupu Vazul, Voevod of Moldova, reported in a letter to Istanbul in 1643, that 1/3 of the population of Transylvania was Roumanian." (#403).

"According to the census made by the Jesuits between 1658 and 1662, Transylvania had a total population of a half million people, of which about 240,000 was Roumanian." (#404).

"In 1700 the Rumanians were not more than a quarter of a million in Transylvania." (#405).

"At the beginning of the eighteenth century their numbers had risen to about 250,000, approximately half of the entire population." (#406).

Thus, in the time, when Transylvania fought her Protestant freedom-fight against the Habsburgs, and struggled for her national existence against a surrounding Moslem world, in the time when so many Magyar soldiers died on the various battlefields, — the Wallachian infiltration continued into Transylvania, and the natural reproduction of the Transylvanian Wallachians was also much higher than of the Hungarians. Using the quotations above, it was quite clear, that the Magyar poulation (including the Saxon minority) grew from 200,000 to 250,000 only, between the 16th and 18th centuries. The Rumanian population grew from 100,000 to 250,000. (At the end of the 18th century, the Rumanians were already in majority, but Iorga was wrong stating this already for the 17th century.)

Returning to historical chronology, let me mention, that shortly after John Sigismund died (1571), the Estates of Transylvania elected Stephen Báthory to succeed him. (#407). Transylvania had great respect in Europe at this time. This respect appeared, when the people of Poland offered to the Prince of Transylvania the Polish crown. Báthory accepted the offer, and he became one of the greatest kings in Polish history. He (#408), appointed his brother, Christopher Báthory, as Prince of Transylvania. (#409).

#399: Iorga: "A History of Roumania." ("Roumania in the late Middle Ages") p. 100.
#400: Ibid: (Sixteenth and Seventeenth Centuries.) p. 153.
#401: Teleki: "Evolution of Hungary." p. 83.
#402: Zsombor Szász: "Hungarians — Rumanians." p. 590.
#403: Zathureczky: "Transylvania." p. 40.
#404: Ibid. p. 40.
#405: Teleki: "Evolution of Hungary." p. 83.
#406: Zsombor Szász: "Hungarians — Rumanians." p. 590.
#407: (1571-76). Selim II (1566-74) was the protector of the Báthorys.
#408: (1575-1586). He defeated Ivan the Terrible (1533-84) in 1581.
#409: (1576-81).

After the short rule of Christopher, his son Sigismund Báthory became the ruler of Transylvania. (#410).

"Educated by Jesuits, he offered to make an alliance with Rudolph for the purpose of driving the Turks out of Europe. He declared himself ready to acknowledge the suzerainty of Rudolph and to secure him the succession if he died without heir." (#411 and #412).

The Estates of Transylvania had no faith in the genuineness of the Habsburg intentions and feared the vengeance of the Porte. They refused to endorse the policy of the Prince. Báthory's policy encouraged Rudolph's ambitions, but did not promise to benefit Transylvania, or the general Hungarian aim for independency.

The Habsburgs began the so-called Long War against the Turks. (#413). This war resulted in a very confused social-class-, and ethnic situation in Transylvania. The Estates (the Magyar, Székely and Saxon groups alike) formed a conspiracy against Sigismund Báthory, but he overruled the internal alliance, executed the leaders of the planned coup and confirmed his alliance with the King by wedding the Archduchess Maria Christina.

The Transylvanians were forced to participate in the war against the Turks. They were not too happy to do so, because the Moslems were tolerant about the Transylvanian independency and religious freedom, and it was possible that in the case of Christian victory, Transylvania would become only one of the Habsburg provinces and the Transylvanian Protestantism would face danger by the political, cultural and spiritual forces of the rising Counterreformation. (#414).

In 1599 Andrew Báthory, a Cardinal succeeded his cousin as Prince of Transylvania. The Habsburgs wished to secure the Austrian overlordship, the Magyars and Székelys were confused: they did not really know which neighbour was worse: the Moslems or the Habsburgs. Unquestionably these Protestant groups formed the backbone of the Hungarian nationalism, and Transylvania again, even more, than ever before, became the citadel of Hungarian identity and independency.

It was in the course of these campaigns against the Turks, that Michael "the Brave", voivode of Wallachia, intervened, and for a year (1600) actually united Moldavia and Wallachia with Transylvania as a single state. He had his secret agreement with the Habsburgs and he was also "careful" in over seeing the murder of Prince Andrew Báthory. He began to rule Transylvania with the sword.

". . . But he allowed his self-confidence and arrogant conceit to carry him too far. He insulted Rudolph and provoked the self-respect of the Transylvanian nobility. Basta, Rudolph's general sent by the King to bring Michael to his senses, was welcomed by the Estates as a veritable saviour. The cruel tyrant was routed and fled to his own country." (#415).

Interesting to note here, that this one-year incident of uninvited intervention appears in "history-books" written by Rumanian historians as an early appearance of Rumanian "nationalism". The interventionist Michael appears as a national hero, who attempts to "reconquer" Roman-Dacia. Iorga calls the Magyars and Székelys as "dirty and ferocious bar-

---

#410: (1581-98).

#411: Yolland: **"The History of Hungary."** p. 100.

#412: Rudolf II. (1576-1612) son of Emp. Maximilian II.

#413: From 1591 to 1606.

#414: Nevertheless Gen. Stephen Bocskay defeated the Turks several times and liberating Wallachia and Moldavia, forced them to recognize the Transylvanian overlordship.

#415: Yolland: **"The History of Hungary."** p. 102.

barians" because they were impertinent enough to oppose the rule of a foreign tyrant. The Wallachian shepherds, of course, welcomed Michael. Consequently Iorga mentioned them — in connection with the Michael-affair, — as reperesentatives of "a population with traditions of a very ancient civilisation." Iorga does not understand, why the Transylvanians "regarded Michael as a terribly inconvenient leader," and, continuing his "very special" approach, the Rumanian historian notes, that "Michael also wanted the ports of Maramuras, the Banat, and the whole country as far as the Theiss"(!). Of course the Magyars refused to present their country to this megalomaniac adventurer. Iorga is most unsatisfied about this "arrogancy", and calls the resisting nation "Imperialists", which expression makes us thing about the unusual semanticism of this term in the mind of some historians. (#416).

Basta, the general of the Habsburgs, attempted to rule Transylvania alone. The Transylvanian Magyars recalled Sigismund Bathory and did not wish to obey the German agent. Surprisingly, Basta united his army with the returning Michael's forces.

"The two foreigners attempted to rule jointly; but they could
not agree, and Basta had Michael assassinated." (#417).

Then, Basta revived the methods of ancient and medieval tyrants. He exacted taxes daily from the impoverished nobles; he had some of those who resisted his despotic measures buried alive: his German and Walloon mercenaries robbed and tortured the poor. The continual fighting, the ravages of the plague, and the failure of crops, had reduced the Principality to a state of misery and distress.

"Hunger-maddened parents, we are told, killed their own children and ate their bodies; and human flesh was sold in the mar-
kets." (#418).

The year of 1604 was the beginning of Counter-Reformation under Habsburg auspices, in Transylvania. The military terrorism of Basta was accompanied by the violent persecution of Protestantism. However, the misery of the country inspired the patriotism of Stephen Bocskay (#419), who in 1604 raised the standard of revolt in defence of political and religious liberty.

Bocskay defeated the Habsburgs! He became Prince of Transylvania (#420), and negotiating with Rudolf, he secured the Treaty of Vienna, by which Protestantism fas given equal status with Catholicism. (#421).

The Transylvanian attitude was classically expressed in the "Last Will and Testament" of Bocskay. "As long as the Hungarian Crown shall be in the possession of the Germans, a nation more powerful than we are, the presence of a Duke in Transylvania will always be practical and needed in support of Hungary. But when God shall be willing to return the Hungarian Kingdom, we urge the people of Transylvania not to secede from or turn against tha Kingdom, but to aid it with all their power and in complete agreement, and render themselves under the Crown according to old customs." (#422).

#416: Quotations from Iorga's **"A History of Roumania."** pp. 155-156.

#417: Yolland: **"A History of Hungary."** p. 102.

#418: **Ibid.**

#419: See #414 again on p. 77.

#420: 1604-1606.

#421: Nevertheless, the Counter-Reformation made great strides, especially among the nobility in Habsburg-ruled Hungary, due to the efforts of Cardinal Pázmány and the Jesuits. The Transylvanian nobility and peasantry resisted. Transylvania was unquestionably the citadel of both Hungarian nationalism and Protestantism, which forces were associated with the idea of Hungarian liberty.

#422: Quotation from Zathureczky's **"Transylvania."** p. 20.

The rule of Stephen Bocskay, as Prince of Transylvania, marks the beginning of a period which was called by many authors (historians and fiction-writers alike) as the "Golden Age of Transylvania." (#423). Bocskay and his successors made Transylvania a vital factor of European politics, and one of the significant cultural centres of the Continent.

At this point, it will be important to return to the Transylvanian Constitution again. We mentioned the origin of this constitution, when we discussed the peasant-rebellion of 1437, and its consequence: the formation of the "Union of the Three Nations" (pp. 65, 66). We touched on the development of this constitution, mentioning the Union of Torda, when the "Three Nations" of Transylvania, the Magyars, the Székelys and the Saxons were united again, to be the legal base of the independent Transylvanian Principality. (1542; p. 72). This constitutional system, which based itself on the close cooperation of these main political grops, crystallized itself in the "Golden Age". (We may criticize this Constitution, that the Wallachian group was not recognized as the fourth basis, but in connection with this, it will be also important to mention, that the Wallachians did not have any "middle nobility", did not have any middle class, did not have too much ambition to participate in the political life, and the very few of them, who were willing to be active, appeared as members of the Magyar nobility. Consequently the word "Nation" received some sort of political sense, and it was not identical with the ethno-linguistic group itself. Unquestionably, the Hungarians made a serious mistake by ignoring the realization of the growing Wallachian infiltration into Transylvania. They also made a mistake in neglecting cooperation with the Greek Orthodox Clergy. The Transylvanian Protestants were too busy concentrating on the dangers of Catholic Counterreformation and on the danger of the Turks. Consequently, the Transylvanian Wallach peasantry, gradually searching for protection, for religious, social and political centralization, found the solution, found the protection and center in Wallachia, where the Greek Orthodox metropolitan, or the Vaivode was always willing to advise them, hoping to use these connections in a "more tactical way" sometime in the future.)

We may criticize the Transylvanian Constitution that underestimated the significance of the growing Wallachian population, but it was also true, that this Constitution was one of the best, the "most democratic" constitutions of early Modern Europe.

> "The country was governed by an elected duke, whose legal authority was determined by the Congress, which Congress also possessed the power to remove him from office. Each nation elected 'Counselors' in equal number, to serve beside the Duke. In order to bring a Congressional Resolution, the consent of all three nations was necessary. The nations voted collectively in Congress, as a block. Later, repealing the original vote-right, the Constitution ordered that in case of grievances, the nation concerned had to turn to the other two for support, who, in their turn, had to present the case to the Duke through due process of Congress or in case of lesser grievances, to the Counselors." (#424).

The Congress consisted of one house only. The individual representatives had only discussion-rights. The vote went by nations in block. Consequently, the majority was not necessarily identical with the numerical majority of the Congress, with all its members, but of the votes of the three nations as groups.

#423: The best known of these historical fictions were: Maurus Jókai: **"The Golden Age of Transylvania."** and Sigismund Moritz: **"Transylvania."**
#424: Zathureczky: **"Transylvania."** p. 22.

The Transylvanian Saxons enjoyed complete territorial, political and cultural autonomy in this constitutional frame. In spite of the fact, that through all the centuries they stayed loyal to their German origin, they created a special branch of the universal German culture. With their scientists, writers and creative artists, they contributed a very particular color to the development of the Transylvanian regionalism and mentality.

The Wallachians did not populate any specific part of Transylvania, like the Saxons did. In other words: it was not county, or district of Transylvania, which was populated by only Wallachians, and nobody else. They were almost everywhere, exercising their traditional occupation, grazing their animals on the mountains. The valleys, cities, towns of the same district were populated by Magyars, or Székelys, so the complex ethno-linguistic situation simply did not give opportunity for the creation of an autonom Wallachian district, although the Princes of the Transylvanian Principality were willing to do so. It will be also interesting to mention that the Transylvanian Wallachians became somehow different from their Balcanic relatives. They remained Greek-Orthodox they had a growing sympathy toward their original mother-country, South Danubian Wallachia (Regatul), but

", . . . The Hungarian and German Protestantism on Transylvania exercised a decisive influence upon the cultural and political development of the Roumanians. These cultural influences, coming from the Hungarians, developed in a relatively short time the cultural and political nationalism of the Roumanians." (#425).

We may note, as an additional comment to this quotation, this: if we realize, that modern nationalism was actually a complex product of ancient patriotism, the Renaissance and the Reformation; if we realize that the French Revolution and the Napoleonic athmosphere only completed the formation of this movement; than we will also realize, that the Wallachians, — whose actual tradition did not content any trace of ancient patriotism (#426), — whose history was not touched by the Renaissance and Reformation (#427), — actually received, imported these main sources of modern nationalism from their Hungarian neighbours. They learned nationalism from the Hungarians, and — as it usually happened in history, — they used the learned movement, as a weapon against their "teachers".

Thus, the Wallachians gradually developed their own national emotions, but they did not from an organized population-majority in any part, or any district of Transylvania.

"Due to this reason, during the era of the Independent Transylvanian Principality, (1542—1690), the Roumanians were not able to become a Transylvanian nation, invested with large scale selfgovernmental rights and privileges." (#428).

The only notable cultural institution of the Wallachians was the Greek Orthodox Church. This Church was centralized outside of Transylvania, in the "Regat" (Southern Danube valley). It was under complete Balcanic-Slavic influence and its official language was not even Rumanian, but Slavic.

#425: Zathureczky: "Transylvania." (The author quotes here from Prof. Torjai-Szabó: "Ceturies of Transylvania." München, 1956). p. 25.

#426: The Wallachian population of Transylvania did not have any idea that many centuries later certain ambitious historians of Bucharest will identify them with the ancient Daks and Romans.

#427: The Balkans (where the Wallachians came from) — was occupied with Bysantinism, later by the Moslems. The Renaissance and Reformation could not extend to this peninsula.

#428: Zathureczky ("Transylvania" p. 22) quotes here from Goldis: "About the Nationality Problem", Arad, 1912,., pl. 17.

"The era of the Roumanian national consciousness began only about 1700, when half of the Transylvanian Roumanians converted to the Greek-Catholic religion, and our priests were able to study history in Rome and Vienna." — wrote Jean Slavici, Rumanian historian, in 1893. (#429). (#430).

At this point, let us return to the chronological approach of the Princes of Transylvania. (We left it, mentioning Stephen Bocskay, on p79, as one of the great Princes, whose reign marks the beginning of the Transylvanian "Golden Age.")

Bocskay died in the year of his great triumph, on December 29, 1606. (#431). His death was attributed to poison. (#432). He was succeeded by Sigismund Rákoczi (#433), soon followed by Gabriel Báthory (#434), who was one of the most tyrannical rulers, Transylvania ever had. As long as he listened to the counsels of Gabriel Bethlen, this young prince was able to rule in peace, but before long his ambition was aroused, by the unscrupulous flattery of his courtiers. He attempted to annex Wallachia and Moldavia, because he felt, that, as a ruler of these unified territories, he would be able to apply to the Polish throne too. (435). He was badly defeated by the Wallachian vajvode. Then, he came into conflict with the Saxons, whose privileges he presumed to assail.

Vienna was delighted to witness the Transylvanian troubles, and the Habsburgs attempted to turn the situation to their own adventage. Báthory was a Protestant (#436), and Vienna desired to place a Catholic prince on the throne. Bethlen, (the chief counselor) turned to the Turks for aid and the Habsburg attempt was stopped already in Northern Hungary. (#437).

Disappointed by the senseless rule of Gabriel Báthory, the Estates elected Gabriel Bethlen as Prince of Transylvania in his stead. (#438). He was one of the outstanding figures of his day, a great general and a determined and honest statesman.

"As a diplomat, he was an opportunist, adapting his plans to the needs of the moment; but he never lost his main objective. the maintenance of the constitutional and religious liberties of Hungary. He was a pupil of Martinuzzi (#439); Transylvania was to be raised to a height of power, political and military, which should enable her to act as a permanent obstacle to the growth of Turkish influence and the aggrandisement of German imperialism." (#440).

#429: Quotation from Zathureczky's "Transylvania." (p. 22). (Zathureczky noted, that he used the quotation from Jean Slavici's "Ardealul, Studiu Istoric.", 1893, Bucharest, pp. 95-96).

#430: These historians returned as Rumanian nationalists into Transylvania, but they did not use the "Daco-Roman Theory" as a tool of their nationalism. This theory was a later invention.

#431: He died a few months after the Treaty of Vienna (June 23), which declared that Hungary and her provinces should be governed by Hungarians, and which acknowledged the independence of Transylvania.

#432: The person suspected of the deed, Michael Kátai, his Chancellor, was cut to pieces in Kassa (Czeh: "Kosice") by the Prince's faithful "hajdus".

#433: 1607.

#434: 1608-1613.

#435: Sigismund III (of Vasa) ruled Poland this time (1587-1632), who succeeded Stephen Báthory (See p. 76, #408), uncle of Gabriel Báthory.

#436: The Báthorys had a Catholic and a Protestant branch too.

#437: Stephen Khlesl, German General couldn't go farther than Kassa (Kosice).

#438: 1613-1629.

#439: Organizer of Transylvania in 1540. (See p. 72).

#440: A. B. Yolland: "The History of Hungary." p. 109.

Gabriel Bethlen was the greatest Prince of Transylvania, and probably one of the greatest leaders in all of Hungarian history.

"Bethlen's rule in Transylvania marks the apogee in the principality's history. He showed that the Hungarian genius, which had animated St. Stephen, Béla IV, Charles Robert and Hunyadi, was still very much alive and needed no Habsburg nursing ta fulfil its historic function." (#441).

But Bethlen was not to the taste of Vienna; he was a Calvinist. Even worse: at the outbreak of the Thirty Years' War (#442), he openly sided with the enemies of the Habsburgs (#443), and made Transylvania a vital factor in European politics. (#444).

"Transylvania served as an important factor in the European balance of power promoted by Cardinal Richelieu (#445) and prevented excesses of Counter-Reformation activity in royal Hungary." (#446).

The British Ambassador at Constantinople early in the seventeenth century said:

"Had Prince Gabriel Bethlen of Transylvania received the same assistance which the European Powers gave to Gustavus Adolphus, he would have accomplished more for Protestantism than Gustavus Adolphus did." (#447).

Gabriel Bethlen was succeeded by his widow, Catherine (#448), his brother Stephen acting as Governor and Regent. When Catherine embraced the Catholic faith and intrigued to place Transylvania under the suzeraity of the Habsburgs (#449), the Estates compelled her to abdicate. The Regent, Stephen Bethlen proved to be a weak ruler, thus the Estates elected the vealthy magnate, George Rákoczi I to the Transylvanian throne. (#450). He was a devout Calvinist. He continued the policy of Gabriel Bethlen, but in a much more careful, and compromising manner. He managed to guide Transylvania through the storms of the European crisis. At the same time he took full advantage of the growing weakness of the Turks (#451). His rule was also a true representative of the "Golden Age of Transylvania." He was a liberal-minded ruler, and he was willing to protect especially the Wallachian minority.

The true state of this nomadic herdsman-people can be best evaluated from the Prince's decree, sent to the Rumanian Bishop of Bihar, ordering him "to preach to those poor Wallachians in their own tongue, so they may be edified by it in the knowladge of God, and led out from the shadows of superstitious errings into the clear sunshine. (This quotation

---

#441: Denis Sinor: "History of Hungary." "The Golden Age of Transylvania." pp. 191-192.

#442: 1618-1648. It ended the Treaty of Wephalia, with a French victory.

#443: He was allied with Count Matthias of Thurn (in 1619), with Christian IV, King of Denmark (1588-1648), with Gustavus Adolphus II (1594-1632), King of Sweden, but his most important ally was Frederick V (the "Winter King" (1619), the head of the Union of the German Calvinists.

#444: In the first year of the War still Matthias (1612-19) was the Emperor. He was succeeded by Ferdinand II (1619-1637), and Ferdinand III (1637-1657).

#445: (1585-1642) French prelate and statesman, founder of French absolutism, who participated on the Protestant side in the War (from 1635).

#446: M. Eugene Osterhaven: "Transylvania." p. 17.

#447: Count Paul Teleki: "The Evolution of Hungary." p. 63.

#448: He married her already in 1626. She was the daughter of George William, Elector of Brandenburg. (Through this Bethlen became the brother in Law of Gustavus Adolphus, who married Mary of Brandenburg.)

#449: She "ruled" from 1629 to 1630.

#450: (1630-1648). He was the powerful squire of Sárospatak.

#451: Under Murad IV (1623-40) the Turks were weakened by Venice and Persia.

represents evidence again of the fact that Rumanian culture and civilization (both in Transylvania and Wallachia) had its origins in the Principality itself, and started with the help, understanding, — often by the financial aid, — of Transylvanian Dukes and noblemen. (#452).

Prince Rákoczi I was followed by his son George Rákoczi II. (#453). The young Prince could not continue the successful policy of his father. He was not satisfied to be only the ruler of one of the most brilliant courts of Europe. He was too ambitious. He led a campaign to acquire the Polish crown (#454). The Turks intervened fearing the growth of his power. The Transylvanian Prince was defeated in an unlucky campaign against Poland (#455). Meantime the Eastates, acting on the instructions of the Porte, had elected Prancis Rhédey to be their prince instead Rákoczi II. (#456). In 1658 Rhédey resingned, but the return of Rákoczi to power was the signal for a renewed effort on the part of the Turks. Wild hordes of Turks and Tatars were set loose on Transylvania. Over 100,000 Transylvanians went into Turkish slavery. The "Golden Age" — and the history of the independent Transylvanian Principality with it, — was over. Ákos Barcsay unwillingly accepted the throne offered to him by Köprili (#457), his only motive was to save the country from futher ravage. The people were reduced to the verge of beggary. The Grand Vizier raised the annual tribute and demanded an enormous war indemnity .George Rákoczy II appealed to the Habsburg Emperor for help (#458), but the help did not came. On June 7,1660, he was mortally wounded fighting against the Turks. Barcsay, again elected Prince, proved incapable of action. In 1661, the Estates elected John Kemény, who choose the German alliance again in order too meet the certain danger threatening Transylvania from Constantinople (#459). Again Vienna did not send help. Once more Transylvania was given over to the ravages of Turks and Tatars; another 100,000 Transylvanians were taken prisoners and conveyed to Constantinople; mostly Székelys and Magyars of course, because the Transylvanian Wallachians were very willing to serve the Moslem conquerors. In these stormy years, due to the very high death-rate of the Magyars, and due to their forced deportation into slavery, — the Wallachians became the majority of the Transylvanian population!

Ali Pasha (#460) compelled the Eastates to elect Michael Apafi (#461). Kemény continued the struggle against the Turks, but he was killed in battle. Apafi "ruled" as a vassal of the Sultan.

The "liberation" of Hungary by the Habsburgs was a result of a prolonged war against the Turks. (#462). In 1683, Kara Mustafa was defeated, when he attempted to besiege Vienna. The Habsburgs received relief from Charles Lorraine of Germany and John Sobieski of Poland. (#463).

#452: Quotation from Zathureczky's **"Transylvania."** p. 22.

#453: 1648-1660.

#454: In alliance with Charles X of Sweden (1654-60) in 1657 invaded Poland. (Ruled by John II Casimir, 1648-1668, at this time.)

#455: His Cossack allies betrayed him to the Tatars and Poles.

#456: November 1657 to January 1658.

#457: Barcsay (September 1658-September 1659). Mohammed Köprili was the "Grand Vizier" of Mohammed IV (1648-1687).

#458: Ferdinand II (1619-1637) was succeeded by his son, Ferdinand III (1637-1657). In the time of our story, the Empire was ruled by the son of Ferdinand III: Leopold I (1658-1705).

#459: Köprili, the Grand Vizier was famous for his unlimited ruthlessness.

#460: Ahmed Köprili (son of Mohammed) was the Grand Vizier at this time. Ali Pasha was the Turkish governor of Transylvania, delegated by the Grand Vizier.

#461: 1661-1690.

#462: 1682-1699.

#463: John III Sobieski (1674-1696), one of the greatest Polish rulers.

In 1684 Venice joined Austria and Poland in a "Holy League", sponsored by the pope. (#464). The imperial generals, Charles of Lorraine and Louis of Baden, advanced into Hungary. They took Buda in 1686.

István Szakonyi mentioned an interesting example from this war. Both sides, — the Habsburgs and the Turks, — attempted to use every opportunity, every possible means, to defeat the enemy. Both the Imperial and Ottoman generals knew very well the Wallachian attitude. They knew that the Wallachians did not belong emotionally to any side, and they were always ready to betray any side for the opportunity for gifts or other benefits. The Moslems were able to subject Transylvania using the help of the Transylvanian Vlachs. The Imperial generals remembered similar "traditions", when — in the second half of the 16th century, — it was possible to manage the temporary conquest of Transylvania, "co-operating" with the Wallachians. Szakonyi notes (#465), that, when the Turks surrounded Vienna (1683), one of the Imperial officiers. Sigismund Csáky, offered some money and "special benefits" to the Wallachian voivode, who supported the Turks at this time. The voivode followed the instruction, and when Sobiesky's troops arrived, the Wallachians surprisingly attacked their allies, the Turks. It was in a critical moment of the battle. The shocked, confused Turks could not stop the stormy attacks of the Poles anymore. (#466).

The reconquest of Buda from the Turks, was followed by a German victory at Mohács (#467) and with a great victory of Eugene of Savoy at Zenta (#468). By the Treaty of Carlowitz (#469) the Habsburgs secured all Hungary excepting the Bánát of Temesvár. (Rum; Timisoara). The Hungarian Diet had fixed the succession to the throne in the male line of the Habsburgs, already in 1687. The ancient constitution of Hungary subsisted, but it fell more and more into neglect. The higher aristocracy tended to devote itself to the peasures of the Vienna court, and the opposition of the Magyar gentry (concentrated in the local assemblies or comitats) was not sufficient to stem the tide of absolutism.

Michael Apafi, the "Prince" of Transylvania, died in 1690, being succeeded by his son, Apafi II. On Dec. 4, 1691, the Emperor Leopold, after long negotiations, issued the diploma which regulated relations between him and his subjects. (#470). In 1691, the Emperor terminated the Transylvanian Principality and incorporated it into the Empire. While he abolished the Transylvanian Constitution, it still retaned almost the same principles of "Systema unionis trium nationem." (#471).

#464: Innocent XI (Benedetto Odeschalchi; 1676-1689).

#465: István Szakonyi: "The First Historical Notes about the Wallachians." (Kanadai Magyarság, Nov. 12, 1966).

#466: This incident was only one in the series of very similar cases. Studying the history of the modern Rumanian Kingdom, we will find many ocasions, when the Wallachian attitude appeared, betraying the allies in the most critical moment, and surprisingly turning to the other side for special benefits. (See also World War I and II).

#467: 1687. After this, the Turks were driven beyond the Danube.

#468: 1697. This victory brought the war to a close.

#469: January 26, 1699.

#470: Transylvania was occupied by the Imperial army under the leadership of Charles Lorraine. In the "Diploma Leopoldinum", Leopold promised religious tolerance in Transylvania and promised, that the ancient Székely and Saxon privileges will be respected in the future.

#471: The system of the Three United Nations.

XII.
TRANSYLVANIA AS A PROVINCE OF THE HABSBURG EMPIRE. (PART I.)

The year of 1690, — which was the year when Transylvania, the independent Principality became only one of the provinces of the Habsburg Empire, — was a very stormy one. The united German, Polish, Hungarian forces pushed the Turks out from the Carpathian Basin, down to the Balkans, and at the same time, Magyar patriots, realizing that their "liberation" was actually nothing else, but becoming subjects of Habsburg absolutism, attempted to use the opportunities of the chaos, fighting for Hungarian national independence.

The insurrection of Imre Thököly followed the traditions of Bocskay (#472) and Gabriel Bethlen (#473). Unifortunately, he could not find any real foreign support. (#474). The fact, that Protestant Transylvania was the real citadel of Hungarian patriotism, was again evident when the Estates, ignoring the Apafi family, elected Imre (Emericus) Thököly as Prince of Transylvania.

The Thököly-Revolution came somehow too late, and it was too isolated. In the hours of the Habsburg-Catholic triumph over the Moslems, Christian Europe did not pay too much attention to a Protestant-minded Hungarian national rebellion, which — worse yet — was manipulated through the use of a possible Moslem support. After the Peace of Karlovitz (1699), Thököly, who had fled to Wallachia, was exiled by the Sultan to Ismid (#475),, where he died in 1705.

We closed the previous chapter, mentioning the "Diploma Leopoldinum" (p. 84, #470). Let us mention it, again, because the history of Transylvania, as a Habsburg province, begins with this famous document.

Charles the Lorraine, the representative of the Emperor appeared with his German-Hungarian forces already in 1687 in Transylvania. and compelled Apafi (#476) to sign the very unfavourable Treaty of Balásfalva. This document was enforced by the appearence on the scene of Govn. Carafa accompanied by a "cartload of instruments of torture." Apafy retired to the county of Fogaras (Rum: Fagaras). The "Diploma Leopoldium" itself (1691) promised to respect the Transylvanian Constitution. based ont the "Systema unionis trium nationem", but — with special attention to Thököly's simultaneous activity, — marked the end of Transylvanian independence. Apafi II. (son of Apafi I) formaly renounced his authority as Prince of Transylvania in 1710 and George Bánffy, who was the actual, appointed Governor since 1690, "devoted his energies to compelling the "Three Nations" to reconcile themselves to the new state of things and pay their taxes regularly. For the time, the moral ruin of Transylvania was complete." (#477).

#472: See pp. 78-79.

#473: See pp. 81-82.

#474: Thököly was born in 1657 and was related to the most powerful and most patriotic Hungarian nobel families. (Zrinyis etc.) In the beginning of his revolt, he had French promises, but Louis XIV (1643-1715) did not give any aid in the critical period. He persuaded Sultan Mohammed IV (1683-1687) to undertake siege of Vienna (1683).

#475: Suleiman III (1687-91) and Mustapha II (1695-1703) did not like Thököly, because his anti-Habsburg, Protestant-Magyar nationalism seemed to be in the way of German-Turkish negotiations. Ismid is a small town in Nicodemia (Asia Minor).

#476: Apafi endeaovured to secure both French and Turkish aid without success for the mentioned reasons.

#477: Quotation from Yolland: **"The History of Hungary".** p. 124 Antony Caraffa was an imperial general of Neapolitan origin, whose system of "reign" was associated with murder, torture and terror.

The Magyar middle nobility, (which proved to be much more faithful to Protestantism and to the original Magyar patriotism, than the, mostly Catholicized, high aristocracy), and the Székelys realized, that the Emperor's promises, confirming the privileges and liberties of the „Three Nations", did not have any real political value, and his other promises, guaranteeing annual Diet for Transylvania, represented more formal than liberal values. Leopold I imposed a tribute on Transylvania, stationed a powerful imperial garrison in it, and put it under a "Gubernium" (a separate court chancellary, directed after 1694 from the "Sibenbérgische Hofkanzlei" in Vienna. During the succeeding century the pressure of Catholic and bureaucratic rule gradually broke down the old individuality of Transylvania. The privileges of the Székelys had almost vanished, and many of them had sunk into serfdom. Even the Transylvanian Saxons suffered under the terror of their (racially related) Emperor. (#478).

I mentioned in the previous chapter already, that most of the victims of the anti-Habsburg, and anti-Turkish Wars were Magyars and Székelys (See p. 83 again). The Wallachians of Transylvania did not participate in these wars, because they did not have any reason to fight against the Counterreformation, and, on the other hand, their real political and cultural center, Wallachia, was the vassalage of the Sultans, with quite good cooperation with the "overlord" in most cases. The Magyars, and Székelys died on the battlefields; the Wallachians became the real majority in Transylvania, by natural reproduction and by the increasing infiltration. (#479). In 1698 the Orthodox metropolitan and his clergy, harrassed by poverty and by Calvinist pressure, yielded to Jesuit offers and signed an act of submission to Rome, while retaining their own rites and customs. With this agreement, the so-called "Uniate Church" was born in Transylvania. By the imperial diploma of 1699 the Uniates were to have the same privileges as the members of the Latin rite, though they never in fact enjoyed the full status of the Latin Catholics. None the less the removal of some of their disabilities allowed educational and social advance to the ultimate benefit of all Rumanians. (The Orthodox who refused to join the union were deprived of all contact with their co-religionists over the border and had no proper organisation until 1759, when they were placed under the archbishop of Pest.)

The relationship between the Magyars and Wallachians was not too good in the time of the Independent Transylvanian Principality, because the Magyars were accepted as one of the "Nations", the Wallachians were not, and because the Magyars represented the ruling force of Calvinism, the Wallachians did not. This, already poisoned, relationship turned into hostility, when the Magyars and Székelys realized, that their Vlach neighbours were ready to serve any of the enemies of Transylvania, sometimes the Germans, in other times the Turks. Now, the Catholic-Greek Catholic relationship gave more purpose to the Protestant-Hungarian versus Wallachian situation.

"About the end of the seventeenth century the Roumanians of Transylvania, on which the burden of the tyranny of Magyar princes and their Calvinist aristocracy was heviest, from the religious point of view as well as the political and social, witnessed the arrival of the Austrians, proclaiming themselves the founders of a new state of things." — notes Iorga. (#480).

#478: They were saved by their great minister, Samuel Srukenthal.

#479: The influx of the Wallachians into Transylvania in the 18th cenruty was associated with the fact, that Moldavia and Wallachia was ruled by the Greek Phanariotes. The newcomers were political refugees.

#480: Iorga: **"A History of Roumania."** Ch. X. "Decadence in Eighteenth Century." p. 199.

Thus, the eminent Rumanian historian feels, that Hungarian Calvinism represented some sort of distatorship on the Wallachians. Was the occupation of Transylvania by the forces of Habsburg-Counterreformation good for the Wallachians? Not really, — feels Iorga, because the Catholics were ready to cooperate only with those, who were ready to abandon the original Greek Orthodoxy. Participation in the "Uniate Church" represented cooperation with Vienna. Interestingly enough, even the Greek Catholic Wallachians could not receive the title of the "Fourth Nation" (additionally to the traditional Three Nations) from the Emperor. (See pp. 93,96).

The foundation of the "Uniate Church" had another significance. The Wallachians did not assimilate with the Magyar-Székely population, because (1) the Wallachian language was very different from the Magyar; (2) the Wallachian way of life (shepherds on the high mountains) was very different from the life of the agricultural population of the valleys; and (3) the Orthodox faith was very different from the Protestant preaching and puritan philosophy. The appearance of the "Uniate Church" which was actually a handshake between Catholicism and Byzantinism at the expense of Protestantism, represented also an alliance between the Imperial conquerors and the Wallachian subjects against the common enemy: the Protestant Magyars. The "Divide et Impera" policy, which became an very typical Habsburg tactic in the nineteenth century, appeared already in the eighteenth century in Transylvania, with this classical example.

The Greek Uniate Church was not only a religious, but a political institution too. Vienna attempted to create a good ally in Transylvania by this Church: the Wallachians. "However, two thirds of the Transylvanian Rumanians resumed Orthodoxy by the mid-eighteenth century in spite of Habsburg attempts to keep them in the Roman fold." (#481).

During this time the seminaries of the Uniate Church produced the first educated elite of the Transylvanian Rumanians. This elite was also the first Rumanian gorup, which really felt Transylvania as their home. The uneducated (even illiterate) Wallachian mass — as Macartney expressed, — "lived with one foot in Hungary. Many of them were shepherds, whose periodical migrations took them regularly across the frontiers." (#482). Most of the Transylvanian Wallachians saw Wallachia (as Moldavia) as their real home, and "... even the agriculturalists decamped readily across the Carpathians if times were hard — just as they immigranted, as casually, when conditions were unusually severe in Wallachia or Moldavia." (#483).

Was the Habsburg attempt successful with the "Uniate Church"? Yes, it was, but only partly. The Uniate Church was an anti-Hungarian organisation, so the Habsburgs were able to create a cultural-political center against those "dangerous and rebellious Magyars." On the other hand, the Rumanians (even in the Uniate Church) represented a Rumanian national movement, working in harmony with their Orthodox fellow-Wallachians. It was quite disappointing for Vienna. Supporting the Transylvanian Vlachs, they created a force against the Magyars, but they created one more nationalistic element too. (One example was the Horia-rebellion. See p. 94—96).

We mentioned already, that, due to the heavy Magyar and Székely losses in the time of wars, due to the enormous Wallachian reproduction and

---

#481: M. Eugene Osterhaven: "Transylvania." p. 18.
#482: C. A. Macartney: "Hungary and Her Successors." p. 261. Note: In the last decades of the 18th century, two Uniate theologians, Gregory Sinkai and Peter Maior, studying at the Roman college, found food for thought in the similarity of the Latin and Rumanian languages. On their return to Hungary, they worked out a history of the Rumanian people on these new bases. (Inf.: Zsombor Szász: "Hungarians — Rumanians." p. 593.)
#483: C. A. Macartney: "Hungary and Her Successors." p. 261.

infiltration, the Transylvanian Rumanians represented already a majority. Comparing the census of 1794 to the previous statistical dates and assumptions, we have the following ethno-linguistic transformation in Transylvania:

	TOTAL POPULATION	WALLACHIANS	%
Beginning of the 16th century:	425,00	100,000	23.5
Beginning of the 18th century	500,000	250,000	50
Census of 1794	1.300,000	800,000	61.5 (#484)

During the 18-th century, which was that of the Phanariote rule in the Wallachian and Moldavian principalities, the Wallachians in Transylvania increased at an enormous rate. In 1794, from the 1,300,000 total Transylvanian population there were 350,000 Magyars and Székelys, 150,000 Saxons and 800,000 Rumanians, thus within a century their numbers increased at the enormous rate of 220 per cent!

Returning to chronology, it will be important to mention that the Habsburgs learned already in the beginning of the eighteenth century, that even the defeated, heart-broken, weakened Magyars were able to begin a great attempt for national independence, a revolt, which adopted the best patriotic traditions of the Bocskay, Bethlen and Thököly revolutions and freedomfights. The head of the movement was Francis Rákoczi, a descendant from the Transylvanian Rákoczy dynasty; thus Transylvania was once more the main focus of Hungarian emotionalism.

The revolt of Francis II Rákoczi (#485) was the result of widespread discontent with the policy of the Vienna goverment. Ultimately the movement became a real social upheaval. Rákoczi soon controlled most of Hungary and even began to threaten Vienna. His flag declared the main philosophy of his freedomfight: "Pro Patria et Libertate"! (#486), and the "Kurucz" spirit was alive again. (#487). Rákoczi was Catholic himself, but he was followed by hundreds of thousands of all religions, thus this new anti-Habsburg revolution could not be associated with the struggle of Reformation against Counterreformation. It was a pure Magyar war for independence against Austrian imperialism.

In 1707, the Hungarian Congress of Onod declared officially the dethronement of the House of Habsburg, giving the power of "regent" to the Duke, Ferenc Rákoczi, unitil free elections could be held. "Thus the decree of Onod restored in principle the National Kingdom and the territorial unity of the country. Due to the fact that the elected Duke of Transylvania and the Regent in whom the Hungarian Congress invested the Royal Powers was the same person, in idea and in practice, the re-unification of Hungary and Transylvania became materialized." (#488).

However, the Rákoczi Liberty War ended in defeat. Rákoczi's followers accepted the Peace of Szatmár (May, 1, 1711; #489), by which the Emperor (#490) promised respect for the Hungarian constitution and redress of grievances, Rákoczi himself refused these terms and took refuge in Turkey. (#491.

#484: (See also p. 76). Inf. from Zsombor Szász: **"Hungarians — Rumanians"** pp. 590-1. ("The Hungarian Quarterly 1941.)

#485: He was the stepson of Imre Thököly. (His mother was Ilona Zrinyi).

#486: "For Fatherland and Liberty!"

#487: The "Kuruczs" were the soldiers of Thököly against the pro-Austrian, pro-Catholica "Labanczs".

#488: Zathureczky: **"Transylvania."** p. 26.

#489: Rákóczy's ally, Louis XIV did not send any aid again. The "Sun King" was busy with his war against Britain.

#490: Leopold I died in 1705 and was succeeded by Joseph I, his son (1705-11).

#491: He died in Rodosto (Turkey) in 1735.

Apart from the fact that it put an end to hostilities, the Peace Treaty of Szatmár (Rum: Satu Mare) contained little to make the Hungarians rejoice. Te conditions in it were more severe, than those refused by Rákoczi in 1706, and concessions were made on four points: "(1) A general amnesty to everyone (#492), (2) Religious freedom, (3) Respect for the Constitution as formulated at the Diet of 1687—8, and (4) Convocation of a Diet to discuss matters further." (#493).

The two main points, which in the past were so strongly made by Rákoczi, i.e. the independence of Transylvania, and foreign guarantees that the treaty would be adhered to, were not mentioned!

Joseph I (See #490 again) was succeeded by his brother Charles VI in 1711. (#494). When Michael Apafi II (#495) died in 1713, Charles simply took the title of Prince of Transylvania too. When the last corner of Hungary was recovered from the Turks in 1718, the area was not added to Transylvania, although it was part of it before. "The area, baptised the 'Bánát of Temesvár' (Rum: Timisoara) was kept as a separate crownland, administered, like the Military Frontier, from Vienna." (#496 & #497).

The system of government, in all of the Habsburg provinces, was autocratic. "The Transylvanian Diet was, indeed, convoked regularly, but it was so packed with ex-officio members as to forfeit any claim to represent the people. The military administration in the Bánát and the Military Frontier was purely authoritarian." (#498) The democatic evolution of the Transylvanian Principality could not continue under Habsburg domination. This evolution, which could solve even the minority problems, (probably similarly to th esolution in Switzerland, if not promptly, but sooner or later,) was paralysed by the force of Habsburg absolutism. This system was bad enough in Hungary Proper, but in the complex ethnic circumstances of Transylvania, it was even worse. In purely Magyar-populated areas the Habsburg power was usually represented by an Austrian authority. This situation provoked anti-German emotions in this area. Vienna was "careful enough" (keeping the "Divide et Impera" idea in mind) to appoint a quite rectionary, usually Catholic, aristocrat, as government official, to the Wallachian populated districts. Consequently, the hostility appeared as an ethno-linguistic, minority bitterness; it did not turn against Vienna (most of the poor, illiterate Wallachians, did not even know about the existence of a city under this name), but against the "cruel Magyar "domnu" (#499), who seemed to be the main end original source of their discrimination. The Wallachians did not realize, that Magyar, or Székely peasants were under the same, absolutistic authority; they did not know, that the large majority of the Magyar middle nobility (the "gentry") was attempting to fight for a free Transylvania, They did not know, and they did not care. The ruling aristocrat was a Magyar. It was enough.

In these stormy years, when in Hungary, in this basically peasant country, where the patriotic middle nobility followed the examples of western

---

#492: Including Rákóczi, if he took the oath of allegiance.

#493: Inf. from Denis Sinor: **"History of Hungary."** "The Rákóczi Rebellion." p. 227.

#494: (1711-1740).

#495: See p. 84.

#496: It was only in 1779 that it was liquidated, its southern fringe being attached to the frontier, while the remainder was organized in counties. (See **MAP X.** on p. 90).

#497: Quotation from C. A. Macartney: **"Hungary."** "The Eighteenth Century." p. 103.

#498: **Ibid.**

#499: "Domnu" is lord in the Rumanian language. (A vulgarised version of the Latin "Dominus")

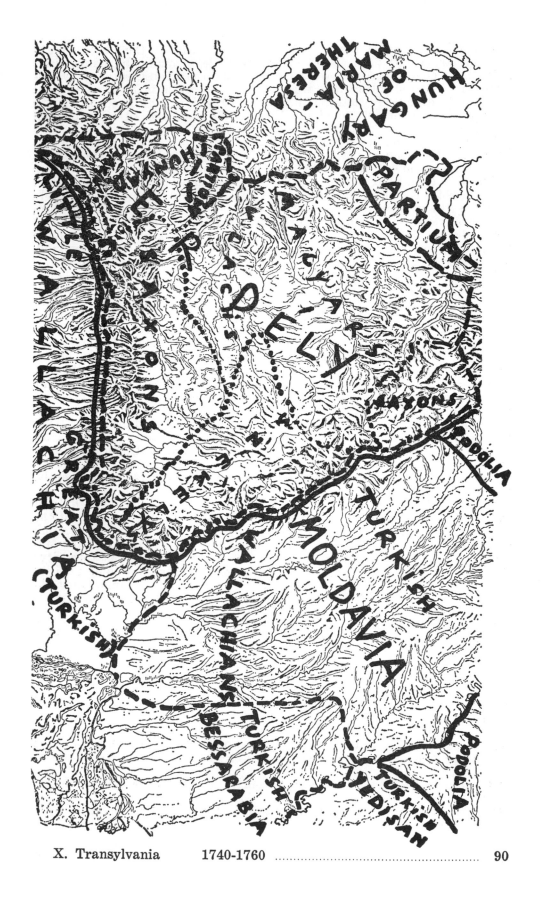

European countries, and turned gradually to be a Middle Class (only dangerously too late,) — there, the problems of feudalism, and their association with Habsburg absolutism, provoked minority bitterness against the "ruling" Magyars. Were the Magyars actually in ruling position? No, as a nation, they were not. Was the Magyar nobility in ruling position? The answer is again: no, it was not. Only part of the Catholic high aristocracy was in a ruling position, but this part of the Magyar high nobility was partly Germanized already, did not speak the language of the forefathers, or, if did, than in a broken form. They were not Magyars "emotionally" anymore; they became courtiers around the Habsburgs, and — as feudal lords, — they opressed, and exploited their serfs, Magyars and non-Magyars alike.

The Protestant high nobility and the gentry (from both religions) did not respect these opportunist characters, as Magyars anymore. They were actually "traitors" from the points of view of the patriotic Hungarians. However, even if they did not serve the Magyar national interest anymore, even if they were not Hungarians in their conscientiousness anymore, they certainly had Hungarian names, and many of them had non-Hungarian serfs on their giant lands. The hostile relationship between Germanized aristocrats, and Magyar peasantry was actually a poisoned feudal relationship, and it turned to be a Magyar bitterness against Vienna. The feudal relationship between the very same Germanized Hungarian aristocrat and his Wallachian serfs turned to be an "ethno-linguistic problem'.' The fate of Hungary was, that the problems of feudalism were accompanied with the problems of Austrian authoritarianism in the complex athmosphere of multinationalism. (#500).

Charles VI was without male offspring. His principal endeavor throughout his whole reign was to secure the various lands which were united under the scepter of Austria against division after his death. Hence he established an order of succession under the name of "Pragmatica Sanctio" which decreed that: (1) the lands belonging to the Austrian Empire should be indivisible and (2) that in case male heirs should fail, they should devolve upon Charles' daughters, the eldest of whom was Maria Theresa, and their heirs according to the law of primogeniture. (#501).

Vienna enforced the acceptance of the "Pragmatica Sanctio" first in Transylvania (1722) and only after it, in Hungary (1723).

The Wallachian infiltration continued in the eighteenth century into Transylvania in increasing rythm. (#502). Life was definitely better in Transylvania — even in feudal circumstances — than in the Phanariote and Moslem dominated Moldavia and Wallachia. Ghyka informs us that the Wallachians migrated westward from Transylvania up to the River Tisza, and other waves of Macedonian Wallachians came to Transylvania and the Banat. (#503). In these circumstances, the ambitious "Innocentius Micu-Klein, who in 1729 became the Uniate bishop, sent petition after petition to Vienna demanding at first only religious but later also national and political rights for his people." He was the first, who mentioned the Dako-Roman theory, and demanded equal rights with the other Transylvanian nationalities. (#504). Vienna was too powerful to compromise.

#500: Of course, before and after World War I, it was "fashionable" to speak about Magyar "dictatorship" over "those poor ethnic minorities." The diplomats of the "Little Entente" were "practical" enough to "associate" feudal problems with the Magyars as a nation.

#501: In case of the extinction of his line, the daughters of Joseph I and their descendants were to inherit.

#502: See statistics on p. 88.

#503: Inf. from Ghyka: "A Documented Chronology of Roumanian History." p. 89.

#504: Quot. from Zs. Szász: "Hungarians — Rumanians." p. 592. Note: Micu-Kein followed the trend of theologians, mentioned in Note: #482, p. 87.

and refused to discuss the matter, but the Viennese officials were "clever" enough — as usual — to mention, that they were forced to reject the Wallachian request "because of the sensitivity of those Hungarian lords." The Habsburgs hoped that inciting the nationalities on one to another, and especially inciting the smaller minorities against "the most dangerous" nationality, the Hungarians; Vienna will be able to rule over the Carpathian Basin. The Magyar nobility usually received certain gossips from "reliable sources" in Vienna, about the "possible dangers" of Slav and Wallachian movements, — and interestingly enough, the leaders of the very same movements — from other channels of the Imperial Court — received signs of "sympathy", or even "kind encouragements." (The historians of the Little Entente, who attempted to introduce the internal problems of the Austrian Empire, as Austro-Hungarian authoritarianism" on the"on the neck of those poor, exploited nationalities," did actually more than oversimplified history; they actually falsified it. It was quite unfortunate, that many of the western historians simply adopted those falsifications, without any individual, objective approach, careful investigation in depth, and without conscientious, and objective criticism.)

Transylvania remained one of the most important provinces of the Habsburg Empire, throughout the eighteenth century. It was important, as a factor of internal policy and also as a significant area, as far as external policy was concerned. The Turks realized, that in Transylvania Protestantism was still the main cultural and political factor, and Protestantism was facing Vienna with hostility. When the Turks supported Joseph Rákoczi (son of Francis Rákoczi II) against Austria, Constantinople was diplomatic enough to "appoint" him as "Prince of Transylvania" and offered him the land of his forefathers as reward for his possible victory. The Moslems were in the way of gradual decline (#505), and they could not find their previous fortune again; Joseph Rákoczi died in Viddin. (#506). (See situation bw 1740—1760: MAP X., p. 90).

Charles VI died in 1740, and with his death, the male line of the Habsburgs was extinct. According to the "Pragmatica Sanctio", his daughter, Maria Theresa became the Empress. (#507).

Maria Theresa inherited the best political advisers from his father. Following their advices, she left Transylvania in its original status. It was a separated province from Hungary Proper. This solution was good for the Transylvanian Protestant nobility, (which worried about the possible domination from Hungarian Catholic aristocrats), but it was good for Vienna too, (because the Habsburgs did not wish to face the power of one united Hungary). In the mean time, the Habsburgs realized, that, as "chief patrons" of Catholicism, they have extraordinary opportunities to weaken Transylvanian Protestantism, and the power of Magyar resistance with it. In the cases of mixed marriages, the Empress often interfered, and especially in Transylvania, she took the child from the Protestant mother, not so much for the benefit of the Catholic father, but for the benefit of the Counterreformation. (#508). Cimultaneously, the Habsburgs were always very generous in formalities. Such a generosity was a separate court chancellary, "Gubernium" and Thesauriat".) (#509).

#505: After the Treaty of Karlowitz (Jan. 26, 1699), the Turks were forced to sign the Treaty of Passarowitz (July, 21, 1718). (They lost the Banat of Temesvár, N. Serbia and Little Wallachia.) See also p. 89, #497.

#506: He died in 1738. (Inf. from Asztalos-Pethö: **"A Magyar Nemzet Története."** Lantos Publ., Budapest, 1933. p. 339.)

#507: She became Queen of Hungary and Bohemia, Archduchess of Austria. Marrying Francis Stephen of Lorraine, they became founder of the Habsburg-Lorraine Dynasty.

#508: Inf. from Asztalos-Pethö: **"A Magyar Nemzet Története."** p. 328.

#509: Political-military, and administrative offices. (See p. 86 again.)

The policy of Vienna gradually effected the previcusly respected, now humiliated Protestant high-, and middle-nobility. They were not in the focus of political and social events anymore. The Transylvanian Saxons were quite happy, that they had a German-speaking domination over the province. (#510). The Wallachians also received some sort of patronage from Vienna, not so much on political, rather on social and educational levels. Some Rumanians emerged from serfdom, when Maria Theresa in 1766 extended the system of the Military frontier to three Wallachian districts in Transylvania. Peter Aron, bishop of the Uniate Church — with the permission of of Vienna, -opened the first, Wallachian speaking, high school and Greek Orthodox Seminary, opening a special source of Wallachian culture and progress in Transylvania. It will be important to mention, that, in case of "special patronage of ethnic groups", Vienna was "careful" enough to hint, that these charitable activities were against the resisting and jealous Magyars. The Saxons and Wallachians acknowledged this "discreet information", forgetting that their fathers, and grandfathers received the same, or even more generous patronage from the Princes of the independent Transylvanian Principality. (For example, see pp. 82, 83 again.)

But the Habsburg Empire had many other means. "It is no wonder, that in Transylvania the equality of religions came to naught. The Diet had the right to nominate as candidates for each office three members each of the Lutheran, Calvinist, Unitarian and Catholic confessions. The King always chose a Catholic, even if he received the least votes. So the Goverment became Catholic." (#511). Catholic government, of course, represcented a security for Vienna against any possible Magyar resitance.

The situation became even worse in Transylvania, when Maria-Theresa gave more and more power into her son's hand. Joseph II became emperor already in 1765, (but took over the power completely only after the death of his mother. (#512). He was not authoritarian in the old feudal sense anymore, because he did not adopt the "divine right" of the ruler, but he was authoritarian enough in the sense of "enlightened absolutism", because his imperial and cosmopolitan mind could not understand that the free exercise of the language of the ethno-linguistic minorities was much more than simply means of communication, but a sensitive, emotional factor, and the only means to resist assimilation, to prevent their final disappearance in the ocean of millions. The young Emperor belived, that he would be able to create a strong, centralized, national State from his multinational Empire, simply by centralized administration and through strict Germanization. He realized that Transylvania represented some sort of citadel of Protestantism, and also citadel of Hungarian resistance. Visiting Transylvania in 1773 and in 1783, he gave rise to rumours that the serfs were to be liberated and armed against their masters, knowing well, that a rumour, like this could excite the Saxons and Wallachians, and it could simultaneously harm the Protestant Magyar nobility. It was not enough. He actually abolished the Transylvanian constitution in 1784, dissolving the three "Nations."

> "Joseph's brother and successor, the shrewd and circumspect Leopold handled this situation. He rejected, however, a 'Supplex Libellus Vallachorum' in which the Roumanians of Transylvania had asked for recognition as a 'nation' " (#513).

#510: H. Marczali notes in his **"Hungary in the Eighteenth Century"** (Cambridge, Univ. Press, 1910, p. 161) that "the Saxons in Transylvania did all in their power to put themselves under Austrian supremacy" already in the 17th century. (A letter from 1614 to Emperor Matthias).

#511: **Ibid.** p. 263.

#512: In 1765, he became co-regent for the Austrian lands, with his mother, without much influence.

#513: C. A. Macartney: **"Hungary"** "Renaissance and Reform." p. 125.

From these "contraversal" activities of Joseph and Leopold could be quite easily realized that the Habsburgs attempted to use the smaller minorities only as instruments against the Hungarians, but they did not have any plan to reward those nationalities with political rights. The policy of "Divide et Imera" was actually very similar to the international "Balance of Power" system. According to the plan of Vienna, the balance with the Magyars on one side, and with the other nationalities on the other side, will secure the "unity" of the Empire. As long as the Habsburgs were able to play the role of the "balancer", they certainly could preserve their power. It was a dangerous game, but the Habsbugs were excellent gamblers; they could play this game for many centuries.

An interesting example of the Habsburg tactic in Transylvania was the activity of Austrian forces in 1784.

Joseph II declared his "Edict of Tolerance" already. (#514). Within eight years from now, 700 monasteries were closed and 36,00 members of orders were released in the Empire. (#515). The connection of the ecclesiatical order with Rome was weakened. (#516). The feudal burdens were reduced to fixed norms, and attempts were made to abolish completely personal servitude among the peasants.

The political advisers warned the Emperor, that the Church was the most faithful, and most useful ally of the Empire, dealing with non-Catholic provinces, like Transylvania. Joseph II stopped the movement of "literalization." As we mentioned before, he did not belive the "divine origin of Monarchy", but — realizing that the Hungarian Holy Crown was much more, than simply a means for coronation, but somehow the representation of the ancient Magyar constitution, — he was cautious enough to transport the Holy Crown from Pozsony (Slovak: Bratislava, Germ: Pressburg) to Vienna, pretending, that his activity was associated with the original Constitution. He sent more troops to Transylvania, and his agents attempted to have "better cooperations" with Saxons and Wallachians.

We will remember from previous information (#517) that the Wallachian Uniate Church received a special task in Austro-Wallachian cooperation.

> "The inadequacy of the concession, either to improve the conditions of the Roumanians or to conciliate them, was shown by Horia's savage rebellion of 1784, which was still more savagely repressed." — wrote Macartney. (#518).

The excellent British historian, who proved to be one of the best in Danubian history, oversimplifies at this time. A closer, a deeper look at this Wallachian rebellion, will give us an opportunity to realize: (a) the methods of Rumanian historians, and (b) the methods of the contemporary Habsburg policy.

The Wallachian revolt was organized and led by three peasants, Horia, Closca and Crisan. Horia was a well to do peasant, who knew Joseph personally. He complained to the Emperor about the feudal injustices in Transylvania. Joseph II listened to him with sympathy. (They met in Vienna).

#514: Oct. 13, 1781.

#515: There still remained, however, 1324 monasteries, with 27,000 monks and nuns.

#516: Pope Pius VI (1775-1799) tried to deter Joseph II from his anti-clerical policy. He ran to Vienna himself (1782) to talk with the Emperor. Not much later (1789) the Pope could not care about Austria anymore. He was confronted with the radical anticlericalism of the French Revolution.

#517: p. 87.

#518: C. A. Macartney: "Hungary and Her Successors." p. 262.

On his return, Horia told the peasants that the emperor supported them, and had "ordered him" to lead them in resistance to the nobles. The rebellon spread all over the central mountain district, and even extended into the Maros (Mures) valley. It was soon defeated by the united forces of the nobles. Joseph II disclaimed any sympathy for the rebels. Horia was executed on the wheel at Gyulafehérvár. (Alba Juria..)

"Roumanian historians are inclined to treat this as a nationalist rising. The nobles against whom Horia fought were Hungarians, and it is possible that the national motive played a part. But the movement was essentially a social revolt of the peasant masses against the nobility." — wrote Hugh SetonWatson about the rebellion of Horia. (#519).

We may understand, that the "historians" of postwar Bucharest had a hard task to present a satisfactory interpretation o fthe Horia rebellion. They certainly could not mention that the Wallachian minority had good relationship with the Habsburgs. (The postwar Rumanian government attempted to be even more anti-Habsburg in the 1920-es than its Little Entente partners.) Thus, they could not write about the possible, secret Habsburg support of Horia. But the leader of the Wallachians clearly told, that he had the sympathy, even the permission of the Emperor for the uprising! Was the "national hero" of the Wallachians an ordinary liar? The Rumanian historians could not suggest this version either. They could not propose any alternative, which would please Bucharest. What to do then? They chose a simple, but not too historical way. They mentioned that the "revolution of Horia" was a real, glorious, national uprising "against those cruel Hungarians." (#520). Xenopol, Rumanian historian goes so far, that he characterizes the rebellion in this way:

"The Wallachians remained very foderate. They did not rape the Hungarian nobel ladies, but they re-baptised them by force, and they forced them to marry with one of the Wallachian peasants, -usually with the murderer of their parents or husbands. It was true that the Wallachians executed every nobleman, who came in their way, but they did not manage these executions themselves. They asked the gypsies to do this. Thus the Rumanians, even in their great excitements, still maintained their original greatness of mind." (#521).

Tasting the real Rumanian "greatness of mind", realizing another example of the historical methodology of the postwar Rumanian historians, let us take a look at the Habsburg attitude in connection with this rebellion.

We really do not have any evidence about Joseph's promises to Horia. Using the careful language of Vienese diplomacy, the Emperor probably did not send Horia clearly to kill the Transylvanian Protestant nobility. He, or his advisers probably encouraged Horia, impressings on him, that the Protestant Magyars were the common enemies for both Catholic Austrians and Greek-Orthodox Wallachians. The encouraged Horia simplified the received encouragement to his fellow peasants. Members of both the Uniate, and the Orthodox Churches came to join the rebels. The rebellion

#519: Hugh Seton-Watson: **"Eastern Europe"**. Archon Books, 1962. pp. 59-60. (The author was usually under the influence of Little-Entente historians, but often he realized the right conclusions and did not follow his "masters" in their falsifications.

#520: Rumanian historians like to "generalize." Discussing the peasant uprisings, looking for "scapegoats", they blamed the Magyar peasantry too, together with their landlords.

#521: Quotation from: Jeromos Szalay: **"Románok Erdélyben"** ("Rumanians in Transylvania." (Hungarian Life, Toronto, 1964.)

was associated with unpercedented horror. Groups of (usually drunk) Wallachian shepherds and peasants ruthlessly murdered thousands of innocent men, women and even aged and children. Encouraged by the (real, or supposed) support of the Emperor, the Wallachians robbed not only the castles, but the humble houses of Hungarian peasants. If an unfortunate woman was in their way, she was raped by many of them, finally murdered. If she was incidentally a Hungarian, nobel lady, wife of a mechant, or even a peasant girl, then she was tortured after her rape and before her murder.

Curiously enough, the large army of Austria was stationed in the very close neighbourhood of the horror. We have to suppose, that probably Horia did not lie; or he said the truth perhaps sometimes. The Imperial army "did not interfere." The horrible slaughter happened before their eyes. The Habsburg forces began their movement only, when the united troops of the Transylvanian Hungarians crushed the criminal bands. Then the Imperial army moved very fast, and the first thing that the Austrian generalt did, was the disarmament of both the Hungarian and Wallachian sides. Vienna had good reason for this. The Protestant Magyar gentry heard about Joseph II's previous agreement with Horia. The Wallachians witnessed the cruel execution of Horia, "friend" of the Emperor. The Horia-rebellion is a very important lesson. It gives a good picture about the Habsburg policy in Transylvania; it introduces the national attitude of those Wallachians, who preserved their "original greatness of mind", and finally: the falsification of this event represents a good example about the methods of postwar Rumanian historians too. (#522).

Joseph was succeeded by his younger brother, Leopold II in 1790. (—1792). The new emperor's short rule was associated with many excitements in Vienna; the echoes of the French Revolution were being heard all over Europe. Transylvania received the great news too. "The principles of 'Egalité, Fraternité, Liberte', the desire of the peoples for a liberal parlamentarian form of government and constitutional rule, aided by the increase of national feelings, stirred new unrests." (#523). (#524).

Francis I inherited from his father the throne at very dangerous time, the time of the Napoleonic wars. (#525). The Emperor received the unpleasant news about the execution of his aunt Marie Antoinette (#526), and he gave his answer executing the "Hungarian Jacobins" led by Abbot Ignatius Martinovics. (#527).

Transylvania witnessed the Napoleonic wars with a sort of divided interest. Even the Hungarian interest was divided. The high aristocracy (Catholic and Protestant alike)) sympathised with the efforts of the European Coalition to overthrow the Republic of France. (The Protestant nobility was monarchist too; they believed in a national monarchy, by the election of a king of Magyar origin.) The emerging Hungarian middle class sympathised with the French Republic and hoped that the Napoleonic victory would liberate Hungary from the Habsburg yoke. One of the tragedies of Hungarian history, that, when Napoleon issued his famous Manifesto to the Hungarian nation, (on May 15, 1809,) calling on them to throw off the Habsburg yoke, to assemble on the Field of Rákos and elect a king of their own, — the Catholic high aristocracy was able to force the Hungarian loyalty to side with the Habsburgs! (#528).

#522: Some of them felt that the Horia rebellion was identical in greatness to the French Revolution!

#523: Zathureczky: "Transylvania." p. 27.

#524: The Wallachian nationalists were disappointed when the Habsburgs rejected the "Suppliex Libellus Vallachorum" in 1791. (See p. 93. #513.)

#525: (1792-1835).

#526: The unfortunate Queen, wife of Louis XVI (1774-1792) was the youngest sister of Leopold II, and daughter of Maria Theresa.

#527: He was a republican, but his attempt for a free Hungary, followed the great traditions of Bocskay, Bethlen, Thököly and Francis Rákóczi.

#528: This decision was probably fateful for Napoleon too.

Public opinion was always a very flexible, uncertain, and hardly measurable thing, but it was usually even more complex in a multinational country like Transylvania, where a large part of the population (the Wallachians) was not really informed about the current events or was informed too late), because of their illiteracy. Reading the various sources, we could find very wide variations of effects, emotions, opinions about Napoleon's activity. His surprising marriage with Arhduchess Marie Louise (#529) resulted in a sort of disappointment among the nobility and the gentry. The conservative Protestants were disappointed, because Napoleon, (— who was still the individualized Hope itself for many Transvlvanians, —) did not mind marrying a Catholic Habsburg princess. The Gentry, (many of them effected by the French Revolution) were disappointed, because Bonaparte, who once proudly said, that he was the "Son of the Revolution" betrayed the original revolutionary spirit, marrying "another Marie Antoinette." It was clear now, that the incorporation of the Papal States with France was not "real" Anti-Catolicism, — (as it was hoped by the Protestants,) only "simply" French imperialism. Napoleon's East-European policy caused confusion too. The foundation of the Grand Duchy of Warsaw (#530) could be considered as liberation, and most of the Transylvanians sympathized with the idea, that the Grand Armv appeared protecting" the country of Stephen Báthory" against the Russians. The French invasion of Russia was regarded as an unnecessary campaign, which would not result in anything good. The French retreat effected nothing else in Transylvania but a sort of malice. Székelys, Magyars, Saxons. even the Wallachians realized that Napoleon did not represent the Great Revolution anymore. He was only one of the megalomaniac, and imperialistic emperors.

When Austria turned against France and participated in the Wars of Liberation (#531) there were many Transvlvanians in the united Austrian armv. The Hungarian regiments distinguished themselves, particularly at the battle of Leipzig (#532). In 1814. the Hungarian Hussars, under Colonel Joseph Simonvi, were with the Allies at Paris, and many Transylvanian Magvars, Székelys, and Saxons were in his troops. (533).

Were these Hungarian and Transylvanian officers simply military adventurers? Did they participate in the struggle simply because they became pro-Habsburgians? No, they did not. They only hoped, that performing loyality and military courage, they could request just administration, and, at least. semi-independence for Hungary and Transvlvania from the Emperor. They were "loyal" for a hoped imperial gratitude.

They did not know the Habsburgs very well. The Metternich System (#534) appeared, with the power of the victorious Austria in all the provinces. After 1815, rigid censorship, elaborate espionage, supervision of all political, social institutions, characterized life in Transylvania. Vienna was especially suspicious for any supposed appearance of nationalism, Hungarian, or Wallachian. Metternich received wide powers from the Emperor, but Francis himself acted as a minister of "internal affairs," (meaning "internal" by the business of any province, German or non-German-speaking, in the Austrian Empire). In Transylvania, the police had su-

---

#529: Apr. 1810. (Napoleon divorced Josephine, marrying the daughter of Francis)
#520: Founded in 1307 already by Napoleon, by the Treaty of Tilsit. Russia recognized its formation from Polish territory. It was ruled by the Kings of Saxony.
#531: Austria declared war on France in Aug. 12. 1813.
#532: Oct. 16-19, 1813. It was often called the "Battle of Nations."
#533: March 31, 1814.
#534: Clemens, Fürst van Matternich (1773-1859) became the leading spirit of this international system, which as "Holy Alliance" secured the status quo with reactionary conservatism. repressing liberal-nationalistic uprising with espionage, censorship, and often with arms.

preme authority, spies were everywhere, letters were opend. Both in Hungary, and Transylvania Francis I attempted to rule, without summoning the Diet.

Napoleon was defeated, but the spirit of the French Revolution spread everywhere, and it arrived to certain parts of Eastern Europe, actually only after 1815. The Metternich system did not face the French giant anymore, but it faced the reappearance of new ideas, new movements, enthusiastic daughters of the Great Revolution: Nationalism and Liberalism. These movements acted as twins, because freedom for the individual, freedom for society meant freedom for the national minority too. This new, political renaissance put the "ethno-linguistic nation" into the place of the "political nation". "National selfdetermination", which was one of the great realizations of the French Revolution became great idea, and desire, espacially in East-Central Europe, where nationalities traditionally played significant historical roles, — together, or against each other.

The Magyars and Wallachians arrived at the self-realization again, that they are nations, and in this revolutionary artmosphere of liberalnationalistic emotions, every nation felt the right to demand independence, and selfdetermination for their political, social, economic future. The Saxons became nervous too, but, of course, their reason for excitement was the suspicion, that nationalist uprisings will threaten their comfortable status quo. In Hungary Proper the enforced Diet of 1825 represented exclusively the still semi-feudal nobility. Here the lower house (Table of Deputies) were the real reformers; the upper house (Table of Magnates) did not wish to go to far, because their members, the Germanized, Catholic high aristocracy had almost identical interests with Vienna. (#535). "The magnates rejected the porposal for a resititution of complete religious liberty" — wrote Professor Yolland, — "they rejected the civil code, the bill for the establishment of a system of credit and a national bank, the resolution relating to the use of Hungarian instead of the Latin language; and the proposal for the support of the Polish revolution. (#536). They rejected the resolution relating to the union with Transylvania!" (#537). (Thus, the Germanized, Catholic, ruling aristocracy actually became the traitor of the Hungarian national interest. They were the instrument of the reactionary Habsburg policy, and nothing else. What a paradox of history, that the Slav and Wallachian minorities, appressed by these Magnates, identified them with the Hungarian nation herself!)

The gentry, (significant factor in the formulation of the appearing Magyar middle class) realized that unification with Transylvania fits the theory of national selfdetermination, it reperesented the return to the ancient idea of the "Holy Crown", and it could also result in a Danubian stronghold against the Habsburg power. "In Hungary, every Diet from 1715 to 1832, discussed the possible reunification with Transylvania" (#538).

Simultaneously, the Rumanians demonstarated for their own national recognition. "George Barit, Cipariu, and others were responsible for the great national demonstration . . . They cheered for the new nation as 'an integral an autonomous part of Transylvania on a basis of equal liberty'." (#539). Thus, they did not advocate unification with Wallachia Proper!

#535: The moderate wing of the Reformers, inspired by Count Stephen Széchenyi (1791-1860), aimed primarily at cultural and economic progress. The radicals, led by Louis Kossuth (1802-94) sought independence from Austria, and parliamentary govt. for Hungary. Francis Deák (1803-76) urged a middle course, with Magyar autonomy and with parliamentary regime.

$536: (1830-31). Brutally crushed by the Russians at Ostrolenka. (May, 26).

#537: Yolland: "A History of Hungary." p. 156.

#538: Inf. from Ferenc Kölcsey: "Historiai Vázolatok a Két Magyar Haza Egyesülése és Magyarországnak a Részekhez való Joga Felett." (K.F. Összes Művei, Szépirodalmi Könyvkiadó, Budapest, 1960. p. 1230.).

#539: N. Iorga: "A History of Roumania." "The Roumanian Renaissance". pp. 227-8.

In 1836, the Diet in Hungary Proper won its first victory, when Magyar was substituted for Latin as the official language in Hungary. (#540). Agitation for reform gathered vigor in the coming years. (#541). Simultaneously nationalistic feelings grew among the Transylvanian Wallachians too.

"Aa the Diet of May 1834, the two Roumanian bishops of Transylvania renewed their memorial of 1791 (#542), asking to be alowed, as in the past, to enjoy the status of the fourth nation. The request was rejected as not justified. A new memorial was presented to the Diet (of Transylvania) by bishop Vasile Moga. The Diet of 1842—43 passed the Joseph Teleki bill suppressing the Roumanian language in all branches of public life, even in schools and churches." (#543).

What happened? Nothing else, but this: the national feeling among Transylvanian Magiyars and Székelys became so enthusiastic, that it appeared not only as a resistance aganist Austrian Germanism, but as an oppressive force aganist national minorities. Being informed about the Reform Age in Hungary Proper, being informed about the desire for the unification with Transylvania, the Transylvanian Hungarians adopted the union with Hungary and

". . . pending its achievement, demanded a more dominating position for the Magyar element in Transylvania. The Diet had been convoked again regularly sice 1837, and in 1841—2 its Magyar members put forward a motion to make Magyar the exclusive language of the Diet, the "Gubernium" and the other central offices, and of higher education." (#544).

(Thus, Ghyka has here a point, but — as usual, — he goes a little bit too far with his interpretation, and even with his presentation of facts. (a:) Joseph Teleki was not a typical representative of Magyar chauvinism, — as Ghyka tries to introduce him, — because he was one of the Germanized aristocrats, who attempted to serve the Matternich system, with his provocative bill. The System was ready — in the times of crisis — to give up Germanization temporarily, using the "Divide et Impera" tactic instead of it. The introduction of the Teleki-bill, — and its enforced acception by the Diet, — proved to be an excellent insrument to divide the nationalistic forces in Transylvania. (b:) The bill did not "Magyarize" the elementary education and did not touch the Orthodox churches. Thus, Ghyka here goes too far with his "documents". (c:) Teleki is certainly a traditional Hungarian name, so Ghyka identifies him with the Magyars. As an example, let me mention here the name of Baron Samuel Josika also, the appointed Governor of Transylvania, by Metternich. He had an ancient Hungarian name too, but he was the narrowminded servant of the Metternich svsthem, a Germanized, feudal lord. Could we identify him with the Reform Age of the Magyars?)

The Reform Age (essentially expressing the growing emotions of liberalism and nationalism in Hungary) reached a revolutionary-minded hight in the elections of 1847. The Liberals returned in a large majority to the Table of Deputies. (#545). Deák now united the various Liberal groups on a compromise program of reform, the so called "Ten Points". (#546).

#540: Ferdinand I (1835-48), the weak-minded and incapable son of Francis I, was the emperor at this time. The real ruler was — of course — still Prince Clemens Metternich.

#541: As editor of a newly founded (1841) organ of the radicals, the "Pesti Hirlap" (Pest Journal), Kossuth attacked Austria violently.

#542: See p. 93 (and #513), and p. 96 (and #524) again.

#543: Quotation from M. Ghyka: "A Documented Chronology of Roumanian History." (p. 92).

#544: C. A. Macartney: "Hungary." pp. 150-151.

#545: (Where the patriotic gentry-middle class was the leading spirit.)

#546: Afterward known as the "March Laws."

Among the various liberal-nationalistic demands (#547), we could find the demand for the incorporation of Transylvania, as one of the most important ones. Deák's program was accepted by the Table of Deputies, but was combated by the conservative Table of Magnates (#548), The Deputies began negotiotion with the Imperial Goverment itself, and had reached a deadlock, when news of the February Revulution in Paris (#549) reached Hungary and precipitated the revolutionary movement.

The Reform Age was also the golden age of Hungarian national literature, associated with the literary and artistic movement of Romanticism of contemporary Europe.

"This great age extended from 1820 to 1867. It saw the national element becoming the essential basis of poetry. It saw a language, made supple by the labors of the preceding generation, molded into the utmost perfection of form. The richest harvest was in the fields of the epic and of the lyric." (#550).

Unquestionably, the Hungarian (and Transylvanian) literature (previously effected by the European waves of enlightenment and by the spirit of the French Revolution) came under the influence of the Reform Age, which was actually the age of Liberalism and Nationalism. " The rising political enthusiasm of emergent independence was carrying Hungarian poetry forward into a Romantic movement of intense feeling and brilliant achievement, where the form and pressure of high thoughts were made manifest with finality of power and beauty." (#551). Fierce indignation against Austrian oppression and intense pride in the national past animated Hungarian poetry, prose and art in the liberal-nationalistic-minded Reform Age. Many of th Hungarian literary classics were born in Transylvania. (#552). This land also gave birth to many well known Hungarian scientists of the early 19th century.

"Among the best known scientists of the day were Farkas and John Bolyai, father and son, the latter being the founder of non-Euclidean geometry; and the explorer, Alexadner Csoma de Körös whose grave is located in Darjeeling, India." (#553 and #554).

The liberal and nationalistic demands of the Hungarian Reform Age was confronted with the Metternich system in Transylvania too. This confrontation could not lead to compromise with the way of peaceful negotiation. The initiative, which was given by poets and writers, and was taken over by politicians, could not find solutions in reform meetings. The political clash between imperial absolutism and liberal-nationalism could continue only — just like in Paris, Berlin, Milan and Vienna — in one way. Transylvania was on the road of revolution.

#547: Responsible government, popular representation, larger liberty for the press, right of public assembly, religious liberty, universal equality before the law, universal taxation, abolition of serfdom with compensation to the landlords, abolition of the "aviticitas", the rigid system of entail dating from 1351.

#548: At this point, let me remind the reader again, that the Wallachians (and their postwar historians) identified these reactionary, pro-Austrian aristocrats with the Hungarian nation.

#549: Febr. 22, 1848. Workers, students demonstrated in Paris against Louis Philippe (1830-1848) and against parliamentary corruption.

#550: Watson Kirkconnell (Univ. of Nova Scotia): "The Magyar Muse." (Kanadai Magyar Ujság Press, Winnipeg, 1933. p. 20.

#551: Ibid.

#552: For example Ferenc Kazinczy (1759-1831), Ferenc Kölcsey (1790-1838), Mihály (Michael) Tompa (1817-1868), etc.

#553: Quotation from M. E. Osterhaven: "Transylvania." p. 18.

#554: Csoma de Körös was one of the greatest explorers of Asia. The young Transylvanian wrote the first English-Tibetian dictionary in 1834.

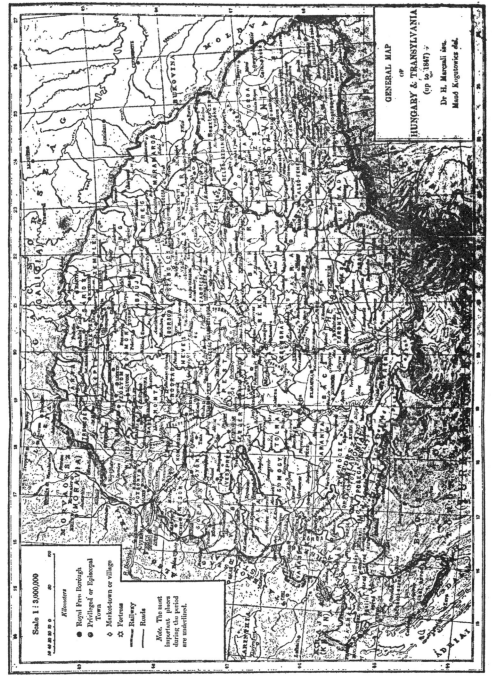

For Explanation of Map see pp. xv—xvi.

Cambridge University Press.

XIII.
TRANSYLVANIA AS THE PROVINCE OF THE HABSBURG EMPIRE.
(PART II: REVOLUTION — REACTION — COMPROMISE.)

The news of the February Revolution in Paris aroused much excitement in Vienna and in Pest. In a daring speech Lajos (Louis) Kossuth denounced the Metternich System and demanded responsible goverment for Hungary, mentioning many times, that Transylvania, this ancient citadel of Hungarian patriotism must return to its mother-country.

The restlessness began in Pest on March 3, 1848. Stimulated by the boldness of the Hungarians, the Vienese middle class began to demonsrate too against their own imperial authorities. In their petitions to Emperor Ferdinand I, they expressed not only their sympathy to the Magyar Liberal-nationalists, but they indicated that Hungary should not be divided into two separeted parts and Transylvania should be united with Hungary proper, because, after all, these two parts represent one, and only one country, the ancient patria of the Magyars since 896. Mostly the liberal-minded Vienese students demonstarated very enthusiastically beside the Magyars and, through mismangement, the popular commotion led (on March 13) to clashes between the demonstrators and the troops. On the same day, Metternich resigned and left the country.

What could the Emperor do in these circumstances, when not only the oppressed provinces, but his own Austrians turned against Habsburg authority? On March 15, in his Manifesto, he abolished the censorship, and promised the convocation of a constitutional assembly. Simultaneously, in Buda and in Pest, the happy and enthusiastic Magyars began some sort of over-emotional celebration of the coming freedom. (#555). The Hungarian Table of Deputies adopted the entire Ten Points of Deák, which thus became the March Laws (See #546, p. 99), equivalent to a constitution. Transylvania received the great news, that "the land of the Székelys" became a province of Hungary again! (#556).

The Table of Magnates (trying to be "loyal" to Ferdinand) opposed the "March Laws" vigorously, but to the great surprise of the aristocrats, (who did not realize the poor position of the Emperor in Vienna itself), Ferdinand accepted the Hungarian demands. (March 31.) But it was not enough. The „glorious five days of Milan" (#557) gave evene more opportunities for the Magyar liberals. Ferdinand agreed on the independency of Hungary, joined to the rest of the Habsburg possessions only through a personal union. (#558).

> "On Apr. 11, Ferdinand gave his royal sanction to the laws discussed and passed, without opposition, by the diet of Pozsony. (Slov: Bratislava, Germ: Pressburg) These included . . . the union of Transylvania with Hungary." (#559). (#560). (#561).

#555: Alexander Petöfi (1823-1849) one of the greatest Hungarian poets, and his friends became the leaders of the civil demonstration.

#556: Of course, the Saxons and Wallachians did not receive this news with happiness.

#557: March 18-22, 1849. The Milanese Italians hated the Austrian yoke, and the news from Vienna and Pest encouraged them for their own revolution. On March 22, Piedmont declared war on Austria.

#558: On March 31, the Croats, on Apr. 8 the Czechs demanded semi-independency, and constituent assembly.

#559: Quot. from A. B. Yolland: **"The History of Hungary."**

#560: Other laws were: resp. Cabinet, extension of franchise, popular suffrage, equality of citizens before the law, abolition of feudalism, etc.

#561: On May 30, the Transylvanian Diet voted for the Union with Hungary.

On April 25, the Emperor promulgated a constitution for Austria. The constitution set up a constitutional regime with a responsible ministry. This decision was very satisfactory for the Austrian liberal middle class, pacifying for the Magyar liberals both in Hungary Proper and in Transylvania, but it was bad news again for the Transylvanian Saxons, and for the Wallachians, Trying to explain this, we have to remember, that these two nationalities were "minorities" in a province, which was a minority in itself. They had the position of the "double minority", consequently, only good relationship with Austrian authoritarianism could represent them security against the Hungarians. Transylvania's reunion with Hungary, and Hungary's independence from Austria had a bitter meaning for the Transylvanian Saxons: they were not members of the "ruling race" anymore; they became ethno-linguistic minorities again. The Wallachians still blessed the memories of the Habsburg "Divide et Impera" system, which represented sometimes surprising opportunities for them at the expense of the Magyars.

"The Roumanians met, on May 15th, on the Field of Liberty at Blaj; Auguste Treboniu Laurian formulated their claims in sixteen points. The Diet of Cluj (Hung: Kolozsvár), on 21st June, voted in favour of equality of rights for the Romanians of Transylvania; those of the Banate and of Hungary asked for an analogous privilege." (#562).

Losing Habsburg authoritarianism, which, strangely enough, became a natural ally of the Wallachians in Transylvania (especially in the times of Joseph II, #563), the Rumanians looked southward to Rumania Proper, for solidarity, and, if necessary, for aid. Let us follow their attention, and let us take a look at the history of Rumania at this point.

In 1774, Rumania was still a province of the Moslem Empire, but in this year by the Treaty of Kuchuk Kainarji (#564) Russia was given certain rights of intervention in behalf of the Danubian principalities, Moldavia and Wallachia, which were still ruled by "hospodars" (#565) appointed by the sultan. (#566). In 1802, Russia (#567) forced the sultan to promise to appoint the "hospodars" for seven years only, and not to remove them without Russion consent. Russia gradually became some sort of "protector" of the Wallachians against the Moslems.

By the Treaty of Bucharest of 1812 (#568) Bessarabia was detached from Moldavia and ceded to Russia, and by the Treaty of Adrianople (1829) Russia strenghtened her protectorate and secured for the principalities complete autonomy. (#569).

#562: M. Ghyka: "A Documented Chronology of Roumanian History." "Roumanians of Transylvania and Banate." p. 92.

#563: See the story of the Storia rebellion again. Pp. 94-96.

#564: July 21, 1774. The Ottoman Empire was defeated by the Russians (1762-72) of Catherine II (1762-1769). Moldavia and Wallachia remained Turkish, but Russia reserved the right to intervene" on their behalf."

#565: Usually Phanariot Greeks.

#566: Selim III (1789-1807).

#567: Ruled by Alexander I (1801-1825).

#568: May 28, 1812. Mahmud II (1808-1839) was in real trouble since 1806. The Russians invaded the Empire again and he faced a revolution even in Constantinople by the restless Janissaries. He was glad to accept this Treaty, by which he gave up Bessarabia to the Russians.

#569: Invaded by the Russians of Nicholas I (1825-55), the Turks actually lost authority over the Wallachians. Russian troops were everywhere; the Moslems gradually evacuated these provinces and the Russians appointed the „hospodars" now — for life time!

Between 1829 and 1834, the Russians continued their occupation. The Moldavians and Wallachians were grateful to Count Kisselev, the Russian governor, who made them realize that their new conqueror had the same Greek-Orthodox religion. Count Kisselev proved to be a good protector of the Wallachians. He took precautions against the plague, organized a Wallachian militia, reformed the finances and abolished trade restricitions. In 1832 a group of Wallachian boyars (landed gentry) worked out an "Organic Statue" under Russian auspices. According to this, an assembly of boyars was to elect the prince from among their own numbers. He was to be elected for life and irremovable without Russia's concent. ,#570).

After 1832, Moldavia and Wallachia witnessed a great economic expansion, because Western Europe became a good customer for Rumanian grain. The Lower Danube became an important water-way for steamboat transportation. Commercial connections with France was accompanied with French literary influence. Many Rumanian students went to Paris, learned ancient Roman and French history. They returned with the experiences of real French revolution-mindness and they brought with them the feling that they were not only the relatives of the great French nation, but they were both — Frenchmen and Rumanians — late children of the great Roman Empire!

The Rumanian students in Paris met not only the "sons of the Great Revolution", but they met with Polish immigrants too. These immigrants were the refugees of the Polish War of Independence against the Russians. (#571). The Rumanians did not care that these Poles were actually defeated by their Russian "protectors". The main point was, that they could learn the emotional memories of an enthusiastic freedomfight against an authoritarian despot. The students, not much after their return, became leading middle-class elements of a coming revolution.

The revolution of June 1848 demanded a liberal regime from the Russians (#572). The Russians made a surprising step. They agreed with Turkey at this time, invaded the two Rumanian principalities and put down the revolution. (#573).

The Transylvanian Wallachians witnessed these exciting happenings with growing enthusiasm. They felt that they actually belang to Wallachia. Receiving the utopian assumption, that the Wallachians were "Romans", accepting the gossips, that Transylvania itself was a province of the Roman Empire sixteen hundred years ago, they fabricated a philosophy, according which the Transylvanian Wallachians should be united with Moldavia and Wallachia Proper, without returning to their brothers on the Balkans. They began to witness the Hungarian Revolution against Austria with growing interest too, waiting for further opportunities. It was unquestionable, that they would not support the Magyars and the Székelys, but they would take the first chance for their own interest.

On May 17, Ferdinand and his family fled from radical Vienna to Inns bruck. From June. 1848, it was cleir, that Austria faced the revolt of Bohemia too (#574) and had heavy losses in Lombardy. (#575).

Beginning with September, the famous "Divide et Impera" policy resulted in positive effects for the Habsburgs. Vienna was able to instigate the Croatians against the Magyars, and in Sept.17, Baron Jellasich, Ban of Croatia, began an invasion of Hungary!

#570: The result was an olligarchic system, which continued until 1856.

#571: Paskievich, the Russian general crushed the Poles at Ostrolenka (May 26, 1831.) Many of the refugees found temporary home in Paris.

#572: The leaders were Constantine Rosetti, Ion and Dmitri Bratianu. The hospodar accepted a liberal constitution and fled.

#573: September 1848. According to the Convention of Balta Liman (May 1, 1849), the Russians and the Turks occupied the Wallachians jointly.

#574: June: Pan-Slav Congress in Prague; June 17. Prince Windischgraetz crushed the revolutionary movement.

#575: General Radeczky defeated the Piedmontese army at Custozza (July 24).

The Babsburg administration was in a much stronger position at the end of this stormy summer of 1848, than in the beginning of the year. Vienna discarded the constitution previously promulgated by the government and drew up a new document, which was only pronouncedly democratic. (#576). Its only act of lasting importance was the emancipation of the peasants from feudal burdens. (#577).

In October, it became clear, that the Habsburg government attempted to use the extreme nationalisms of the various ethnic minorities against the "most dangerous" minority; the rebelling Magyars. Jellachich, Bán of Croatia was made "Commander-in-chief" of the forces operating against Hungary. (#578). Simultaneously, in October, began the attack of the Wallachians, (with continuous murders, and arsons) against the peaceful Hungarian towns and villages. These horrible attacks represented the „popular" continuation of the loud, but actually unsuccessful meetings of Blaj (Hung: Balázsfalva,) and Cluj (Hung: Kolozsvár). (See p. 103, and #562 again). The Wallachian leaders, (esp. one of them, named Ságuna) turned from the political steps to the means of revolution. This revolution, using the "vendetta-system" of the Balkans, turned against the Hungarian population itself.

"Both Saxons and Roumanians took the Austrian side against the Magyars, the Roumanians being encouraged by promises of selfgovernment." — noted Macartney. (#579).

"The murders and arsons began with the spiritual leadership of the Saxons, and with the presence of the Austrian troops." — wrote Marczali (#580). — "Saveru Axente, Avrám Jancu, and Francu Mikas were the Wallachian leaders (#581). The Wallachian peasants received "passure"-s (#582) from the Austrian officiers for their activity, and these Wallachians commited such dreadful crimes against the elderly, women and children, that even the Austrians were ashamed at what was going on under their authority. The password was: the total extermination of the Magyars!"

The peasant rebellion was authorized and supported by Vienna, was advised by the Saxons, was organized by the "Dako-Roman" agents of Wallachia Proper, and was actually led by the Greek Orthodox "popes" (#583).

"The Walachian peasants totally exterminated the Magyar population of Nagyenyed, Abrudbánya and Zalatna. They annihilated one half of the Hungarian population in the county Hunyad. The hordes of Avram Jancu and Saveru Axentie secured the Wallachian majority in Transylvania." (#584).

Interestingly enough, most of the Rumanian historians "did not know" anything about the slaughters of October, 1848. M. Ghyka only mentions, that "... The Roumanians declared themselves for the Emperor and fought the Hungarians." (#585). He does not mention that their peasant hordes

---

#576: The "Reichstag" made its declaration in July 22, 1848.
#577: Which became law on Sept. 7, 1848.
#578: He was driven back by the Magyar troops.
#579: C. A. Macartney: **"Hungary and Her Successors."** p. 262.
#580: Henrik Marczali: **"Magyarország Története."** (Eng.: The History of Hungary.) Athenaeum, Budapest, 1912. "The Freedomfight". pp. 667-668.
#581: The Wallachians called them "tribunus", adopting the Roman titles.
#582: Permit.
#583: The popes: Greek-Orthodox priests.
#584: Tamás Karsa: **"Remarks to the Authorization of the Dako-Roman Theory."** "Hungarian Liberty", Toronto, 1964. p. 4.
#585: Ghyka Matila: **"A Documented Chronology of Roumanian History."** "Roumanians in Transylvania and Banate." p. 92.

did not fight against regular (or even irregular) Hungarian trops, but invaded, ignited and, in many cases plundered, murdered and raped the peaceful Transylvanian population.

The Wallachian leaders were probably quite satisfied with the result. An important consequence of the slaughters was that the Wallachians represented an even greater majority in Transylvania, than before the bloody October of 1848. Following this

"... Through their bishop Saguna (#586), they presented a memorial to the Emperor on 25th February 1849. This memorial once more stressed the antiquity of the Roumanians in the Transylvanian regions, and the fact that they constituted the majority of the population. It asked among other things for the Union of all Roumanians in the Monarchy into one single autonomous nation under the crown of Austria, and that the Emperor should assume the title of Grand-Duke of the Roumanians." (#587).

Vienna was probably also satisfied with the result of the bloodshed in Transylvania. The Emperor's answer arrived in which „The Emperor promised to satisfy their demands 'with the shortest possible delay and to general satisfaction." (#588).

In the mean time, the Liberal revolution of Vienna was crushed. The revolutionary mob murdered Count Latour, the minister of war (Oct. 6), but at the end of this month (Oct. 31) Windischgraetz, aided by Jellasich bombarded Vienna, and ruthlessly executed the revolutionary leaders. (#589). On Dec. 2, Emperor Ferdinand abdicated. It was engeneered by Prince Felix Schwarzenberg (#590). He induced the heir to the throne, Archuduke Francis Charles, to forego his rights in favor of his eigteen-year-old son. Francis Joseph I ascended the throne. (#591) According to Prince Schwarzenberg, the young Emperor was not bound by any of the promises of his predecessor to the Hungarians. The efforts of the government were now concentrated on the campaign against Hungary. On Jan, 5., Windischgraetz occupied Buda and Pest, and at the end of April, General Görgei, Commander of Chief of the Hungarian army was forced to evecuate nearly all of Hungary In the same month, the Hungarian Diet, meeting temporarily at Debrecen, proclaimed the Hungarian Republic and elected Lajos Kossuth as "responsible governor-president."

The Austrian army did not prove itself strong enough against the revolutionary troops, which reoccupied Buda in May 21, 1949. In June, Vienna accepted the offer of Tsar Nicholas of Russia to aid in the suppression of the Hungarian revolution. Few weeks later Gen. Paskievich (#592) invaded Hungary from the north while the Austrian general Haynau led the invasion from the west. The Hungarian army defended only Transylvania, but not for long. The defence was almost impossible. The invaders represented an overwhelming military majority, and the Wallachian hordes used every chance again for murders and plundering. Görgei put up a vigorous resistance, but on Aug. 9, he was decisively defeated in the battle of Temesvár. (Rum: Timisoara). Two days later, Kossuth abandoned his position in favor of Görgei and fled, with many other leaders, to Turkey. (#593). On Aug. 13, Görgey sur-

#586: See p. 105. He received the title of "Baron" earlier from Vienna. He was a member of a Macedonian Vlach family, which settled in Transylvania in the 18th century.

#587: M. Ghyka: "A Documented Chronology of Roumanian History." pp. 92-93.

#588: Ibid. p. 93.

#589: Including Robert Blum, delegate from the Frankfurt Parliament!

#590: (1800-1852). Dipl. adjunct of Radeczky, iron-willed adherent of the restoration and even extension of the imperial power.

#591: (1848-1916). He was Francis Joseph II for the Hungarians.

#592: He was the ruthless suppressor of the Polish Revolution of 1830-31. (p. 98, #536). (See the main directions of invasion on MAP XII, p. 107).

#593: Later, he attempted to convince Millard Fillmore (13th President of the USA) to interfere against Austrian despotism. (1851-1852).

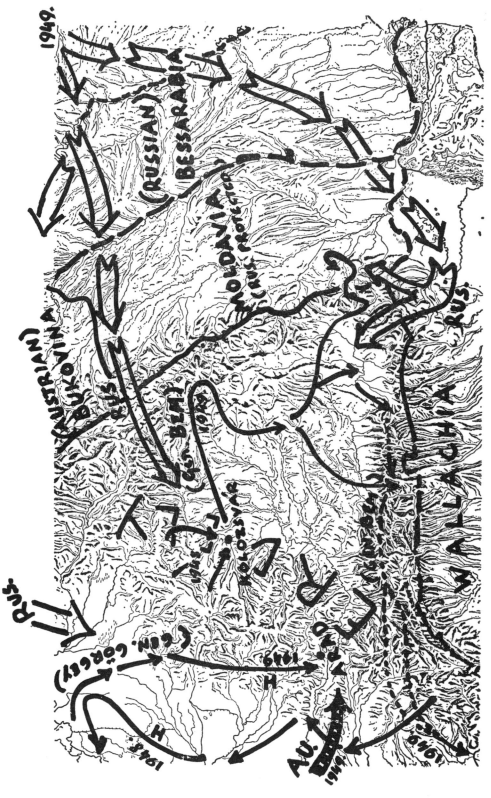

rendered to the Russian commander at Világos. Despite promises of ce-
lemency, General Haynau visited sanguine vengeance of the Hungarians
at the bloody assizes of Arad. Nine generals were hung and four shot. It
was not enough. On the very same day (Oct. 6, 1849) Lajos Batthyany,
prime minister of Hungary was executed at Pest, and in the following
months, thousands of officers, and civilians (many women among them)
were tortured, imprisoned, executed (Petőfi, the great poet was killed by
the Russians already in the battle of Segesvár).

Between 1849 and 1860, the so-called "Bach-system" represented despotic authoritarianism and the revenge of the Habsburg Dynasty in the
reoccupied lands. The same years represented some sort of hopeful age
for the Transylvanian Wallachians and Saxons. The Constitution of March,
1849 already indicated a better position for the Rumanians in the centralized Austrian system. "On 10th January 1850, the Roumanians of Transylvania, the Banate and Hungary repeated their demands of February
25th, 1849; the bishop of Oradea (Hung: Negyvárad), Vasile Erdeli, sent
a similar petition, and on 10th April, the Synod, meeting at Sibiu (Hung:
Nagyszeben) did likewise." (#594).

Simultaneously, Moldavia and Wallachia Proper were not inactive. Can-
tacuzenu, minister of Duke Cuca of Moldavia already made a plan, which
was identical to Great Rumanian attempts of 1918. (#595).

Vienna suspended the constitution of 1849 in 1851, and ruled the Empire by bureaucratic methods, simultaneously undermining the life of the
various nationalities by a policy of vigorous Germanization. This policy
was associated especially with the name of Alexander Bach, minister of
the interior. Hungary lost its historic identity, and Transylvania (#596)
became a separate province again.

Not much after 1850, it became clear, that the "hopeful age" of Wallachians and Transylvanian Saxons did not turn into a "golden age." The
"loyal" Rumanians and Germans suffered the same fate as the "rebel"
Hungarians. The new Constitution (1851) abolished the Saxon privileges,
and the Wallachian peasants learned again, that betrayal of their Magyar
neighbours, loyalty to the Emperor, did not pay a high profit. They became oppressed people again, and Vienna was careful again to rule over
them with Germanized, Catholic aristocrats, with original Magyar names.
(The Austrian diplomacy experienced, that this system worked very well
before, consequently it could work well sometime later.)

Restauration and reaction was associated with Catholicism once more.
A Concordat with the Catholic Church (1855) gave the Church extensive
power, especially in matters of education.

At the end of the 1850—s Austria was weakened again by the results of
the Crimean War (#597), and by the War with France and Piedmont.
(#598). The "Bach regime" ended with the "October Diploma" (1860) issued by the Emperor; it set up a federal constitution which recognized
wide autonomy for the various provinces. The Hungarians, led by Deák
(#599) opposed this settlement, and demanded the restoration of their
own liberal constitution.

#594: M. Ghyka: "A Documented Chronology... p. 93.

#595: Cuca was a very ambitious man. On January 24th, he became the Prince of
the united Moldavian and Wallachian principalities. Unfortunately for him, the
Austrians did not respect his position. He was replaced in 1866 by Prince Carol
of Hohenzollern, as Prince of Roumania.

#596: With Croatia and Southern Hungary.

#597: (1856-59). This war undermined Austria's international position, and ruined
the finances through prolonged mobilization.

#598: (1859). The Austrian forces could not fight with full heart, because there was
an always returning gossip about a coming Hungarian revolution.

#599: Ferenc (Francis) Deák was already mentioned on p. 98 (#535), and p. 99
(#546).

Three months later, the "February Patent" of the Emperor interpreted the "October Diploma." (#600). According to this interpretation, the planned, new constitution will set up a bicameral parliament, but the described electoral system would give an autocratic, even despotic ruling apporutnity to the German elements in the Empire. The negotiations with Francis Deák and his fellow Hungarians failed; Hungary and Transylvania was ruled administratively and autocratically again.

Vienna tried to display strength again, but the bluff did not work. Everybody knew that Austria was not able to preserve its original imperial power. The advisers of the Dynasty began negotiations with the „most dangerous" national minority, the Magyars, again. The negotiations opened in 1865, and, when the Austrian army suffered one of its most humiliating defeats from Bismarck's Germany in the Seven Years War, at Königraetz (Sadowa; July 3, 1866), it was sure, that the Austro-Hungarian negotiations were very favourable for the Hungarians, probably at the expence of the other natinalities. (#601).

What type of policy was adopted by the minorities of Transylvania during these new circumstances?

The Transylvanian Saxons took the Austrian side against the Magyars in the freedomfight of 1848/49. They hoped for privileged positions from Austria. When the struggle ended, the Saxons did not receive any imperial gratitude: disappointingly they were overruled by absolutistic measures too. "In the brief semi-constitutional era of the sixties, however, during which the Magyars abstained from co-operating, the Saxons and Roumanians left alone together, established the Roumanian 'nation' and its two churches on a footing of equality with the other 'received' nations and churches, and proclaimed the equality of the Magyar, German, and Roumanian languages in official business." (#602).

The Saxons seemed to be quite satisfied with this solution, the Wallachians were not. They looked ot the growing areas of the Moldavia and Wallachia Proper with real nationalistic pride, and their dreem was not acknowledged equality anymore, but to force the union of Transylvania with the other two (Wallachian populated) provinces. At this point, let us take another look at the history of Moldavia and Wallachia Proper again. (We discontinued the discussion of their history in 1849, with the Convention of Balta Liman; p. 104, #573).

In 1853, Russia occupied both Moldavia and Wallachia again, following a dispute with Turkey. This led to the Crimean War. (#603). On Aug. 8, 1854, the Russians evacuated these provinces, which were occupied by Austrian troops (#604) in agreement with Turkey.

The Austrians still controlled Moldavia and Wallachia, when, in 1856, in the Congress of Paris, Napoleon III (#605) appeared as patron of these principalities. (#606). Turkey and Austria opposed the idea, but England and Russia sided with France. It was finally decided that the sultan (#607) shoul summon popularly elected divans to ascertain the wishes of the population. At the same time an international commission was to investigate and suggest an organization.

#600: February, 1861.
#601: The Hungarians loyally participated at the Austrian side in this war against the Germans.
#602: C. A. Macartney: **"Hungary and Her Successors."** p. 262.
#603: The European powers protested against the occupation.
#604: Until March, 1857.
#605: Napoleon III: emperor from 1852 to 1870.
#606: Under the influence of Mme Cornu and Ion Bratianu, Wallachian diplomats.
#607: Abdul Mejid (1839-1861)

In March 1857, Austria evacuated Moldavia and Wallachia Proper. In the elections every kind of pressure and corruption was employed to debar the unionists, who were consequently defeated. After an international storm, in which almost oll the European powers participated, new sections were held, which resulted in great victory for the unionists. In the next year, in a conference at Paris, the powers decided to establish the "United Principalities of Moldavia and Wallachia", with separate but identical administrations. In January, 1959, Col. Alexander Cuza (Cuca), a relatively unknown officer, became the elected prince of Moldavia. (I mentioned this ambitious Wallachian nationalist on p. 108, #595, already). Very soon, he secured his election by Wallachia too, and his position was really strengthened, when Napoleon III recognized him. This imperial recognition was followed by other powers too.

On February 5, 1862, the sultan (#608) allowed the fusion of the two legislatures. The union of the two principalities was recognized, and known by the new name of "Rumania."

Cuza had probably very good connections with the leaders of the Transylvanian Wallachians. The union of Moldavia and Wallachia was quite easy with the support of Napoleon III. The opportunity for continuation was open. The Austrians were weak already, the Hungarians were still weak.

> „The Wallachians are ready for any treason", —wrote General
> Klapka, one of the heroic leaders of the Hungarian freedomfight,
> — they are trembling from the Russians, they are frightened of
> the Austrians, and they hate us. Even the most moderate of them
> desires the annexation of Transylvania to Wallachia. They hope,
> that both Austria and Hungary will collapse in blood, and Tran-
> sylvania will fall to their feet as a ripe fruit." (#609).

Cuza could not grasp Transylvania, and he could not keep his rule even in Rumania. In 1866, he was kidnapped by his opposition and was forced to abdicate by a conspiracy of Conservatives and Liberals, who desired rather a foreign prince. The Assembly at once offered the position to the Count of Flanders, (#610), who declined. Then, few months later, the provisional government (with the secret approval of Napoleon III and Bismarck) proclaimed Prince Charles of Hohenzollern-Sigmaringen. A plebiscrite approved of the action and Charles arrived at Bucharest on May 22. (#611).

The Transylvanian Wallachians proved in these stormy years that their main political interest was closely connected with Rumania Proper. In 1861 already, they met at Nagyszeben (Sibiu) and declared their sympathy, to Col. Cuza's united Principalities. When, on February 11. 1861, the Transylvanian Diet voted for the union of Transylvania with Hungary, the Wallachians protested. The Diet repeated this motion in 1865, and the Wallachians protested again. (#612).

> "The Compromise of 1867, however, re-united Transvlvania with
> Hungary and, while retaining the autonomy of the received
> Churches (among which the Roumanian Orthodox Church now
> at last found a place), abolished all special national privileges and
> proclaimed the equality of all Hungarian citizens, irrespective
> of their race or language." (#613).

#608: Abdul Aziz (1861-1876).

#609: Asztalos-Pethö: **"A Magyar Nemzet Története."** (Engl. The History of the Hungarian Nation." "The abszolutizmus", p. 416.)

#610: The Count was the son of Leopold II of Belgium. (1865-1909).

#611: Charles (Rum: Carol) ruled Rumania from 1866 to 1914.

#612: Inf. from M. Ghyka: **"A Documented Chronology of Roumanian History."** p. 94. (Note: In 1861, the Rumanian Cultural Society, the ASTRA (created in Transylvania) became the strongest tool of the Rumanian political movement. In 1881, it co-operated with the "Liga Culturala" in Bucharest working for the unification of all Wallachians in "Great Rumania".)

#613: C. A. Macartney: "Hungary and Her Successors." p. 262.

Unquestionably the Compromise (or, in its original name, the "Ausgleich") represented very important changes. These changes appeared not only as the agreement between the two strongest national elements in the Austrian Empire. These changes appeared also as victory of liberalism over reactionary conservativism.

The "Ausgleich" was largely the work of Francis Deák, seconded by Julius Andrássy. According to the new political organization. Hungary received again the ancient lands of the crown of St. Stephen, and the Magyars were permitted to dominate the minorities through the constitutional system of 1848. Did the Constitution of 1848 advocate the authoritarian rights of the feudal aristocracy? No, it did not. The Constitution of 1848 was a typical liberal-national-constitution, (See the 10 Points, or March Laws again, p. 100, #547), which included responsible government, popular representation, freedom of the press and freedom of religion, equality before the law, abolition of serfdom, etc. When the Ausgleich of 1867 returned to the ideas of 1848, it represented the return of liberalism in its original revolutionary ideals, and it also represented the defeat of absolutistic conservativism. In spite of this fact, it is interesting to mention that Rumanian historians tended to mention the "Ausgleich", as some kind of reactionary agreement at the expence of the subjected social classes and nationalities, as the intrigue of aristocrats against the ethnic groups.).

The two States were joined in personal union through the monarch. The comon ministries were: foreign affairs, war and finance. In annual delegations, composed of sixty members of each of the two parliaments, they were empowered to decide matters of common interest.

The age of the Austrian Empiere was over. The birth of the Austro-Hungarian Monarchy represented no final solution yet in this great trend of liberal-democratic evolution, but Francis Deák and Gyula Andrássy did not feel that the "Ausgleich" was some sort of final result. They felt, it was a good beginning for the creation of a Danubian liberal-democratic Confederation. If it did not happen according to their ideas, it was not their fault.)

Transylvania was returned to Hungary Proper again, and it became an integral part of the Hungarian Kingdom. The new era of constitutional government was welcomed by all parties. All Churches and languages received egual freedom. All special national privileges were proclaimed as equal. Any citizen of Transylvania could fel himself as equal, regardless of his racial, religious, or linguistic origin.

The autocracy of the Habsburgs was replaced by a constitutional system, no liberal enough yet, but with open oportunities for more liberalization. Did the new regime bring satisfactory solutions to the minority problems?

Unfortunately, it did not. "Open violence and undisguised absolutism were to be replaced by a policy of obstruction and intrigue. The 'nationalist question' of Hungary was about to enter a new phase." (#614).

#614: A. B. Yolland: "The History of Hungary." pp. 173-174.

XIV.
THE DUAL MONARCHY AND TRANSYLVANIA. PART I:
"MAGYARIZATION."

The main essence of the "Ausgleich" was, that Hungary was formually recognized in her historical boundaries, as an independent kingdom, with its own constitution, parlament and government. The first prime minister was Count Julius (Gyula) Andrássy, prominent in the long negotiotions before the signing of the Compromise. "In addition to the person of the common ruler who was to be crowned as king of Hungary, the ties with Austria, where that same ruler would continue to be an emperor, were reduced to the creation of the three 'joint ministries'." (#615 and #616).

"The act of Coronation had served as the outward symbol of the reconciliation of Dynasty and Nation." (#617).

The Austro-Hungarian Monarchy, a liberal-constitutional state formation, created in the Danubian Basin a tremendous economic upswing and prosperity. "Together with the industrial and commercial urban development, the entire social structure of the country began to change. Sadly enough, the political changes did not keep in step with the social changes." (#618). Deák's and Andrássy's plan was, that the "Ausgleich" would be the great beginning of a social-national-liberal evolution, which would transform the Austrian Empire into a constitutional Danubian Confederation, where every individual, every social class, and every national minority would find its satisfaction, even happiness. Unfortunately, the expected evolution did not follow the "Ausgleich" — especially as far as the gradual solution of the ethnic problems were concerned.

Unquestionably, every citizen of the Monarchy enjoyed the same rights provided by the law. The change from a feudalistic system to a liberal-constitutional state filled the middle class with enthusiasm. and turned their attention to legal problems. All the political activities of this era were concentrated on the discussions of constitutional questions. The mistake of the leading politicians was that, dreaming about a great and prosperous future. discussing rather abstract political problems, they did not pay enough attention to the fact, that presenting eguality to the (ethnic) citizen still did not solve the problem of he ethno-linguistic minority, as a group; and political democratization in itself was not a magic formula, which would cease the hostilities of certain ethnic groups from one day to the next.

The booming economy created a prosperous middle class and a tremendously large class of urban bourgeoisie. But,again these members of the new, and powerful middle class, were Hungarians! For example, in Transylvania, the Walachian shepherds and peasants were not touched by this booming industrial and commercial revolution. If they hated the Magyar feudal landlord, if they associated the problems of feudalism with their (supposed) ethnic discrimination before; now they turned emotionally against the urban bourgoisie, because he was living in a clean home, and not in a dirty cottage; because he was educated and not illiterate, because he tended to imitate the Western European, and not the backward Balkanic customs; because — he happened to be a Magyar, and not a Wallachian.

#615: See theprevious page.
#616: Quotation from Oscar Halecki: **"Borderlands of Western Civilization."** The Ronald Press Co. New York, 1952, pp. 330-331.
#617: A. B. Yolland: **"The History of Hungary."** Ch. XXI. "Modern Hungary." p. 174.
#618: Zathureczky: **"Transylvania."** p. 29.

The large masses of landholding peasantry also benefited from the richness of the Monarchy, except the landless farm laborers. The landless rural population was still backward. Many of them, — if they were Magyars, — migrated to America for higher wages. Many of them,— if they were Wallachians, — looked (their real cradles: Moldavia and Wallachia,) to united Rumania for salvation.

One of the experts of the Rumanian problem, Louis Elekes raised the question: did the Transylvanian Wallachians really feel Transylvania to be their homeland? If they did, then why did it happen, that they betrayed this unfortunate land so often, sometimes for the benefit of Austria, in other cases for the benefit of the Turks? If, they did then why did they continue their nomadic life, wandering to various parts of this land, returning to Wallachia Proper, and reappearing again, crossing the Transylvanian Alps so many times? If they felt themselves Transylvanian, then why did they use every historical opportunity to attack the innocent and defenseless houses of their Magyar neighbours, why did they murder and rape them so many times, why did they burn the houses of their "fellow" Transylvanians? If the landlord happened to be a Hungarian, and they were serfs, did this fact justify this type of activity? If they represented a backward illiterate ethnic minority, did this fact give an excuse for these horrors? Could the Transylvanian Wallachians ever be faithful Transylvanians, if their hearts, if their political emotions were always connected with their ancient Balkanic homeland, Wallachia?

"At the beginning of the modern era, the Rumanian people stabilized and thereby laid the foundation of a subesequent national development." — wrote Louis Elekes (#619). — "But there is a difference between a people and a nation. The essence of this difference was the subject of many discussions; and we do not yet recognize clearly which is the most important of its numerous ethnical, cultural, political and other factors. But one thing is certain: a nation in the European sense of the word can only be formed by a people which is closely attached to the land it occupies, which feels its dewelling-place to be a home and is living a well-organized life on it. All this, as we have seen, happened comparatively late with the Rumanian people . . . National life in Rumania was not so deeply rooted in social life as in the western conutries of Europe."

Commenting on this quotation, we may say, that (a) for a long time, the Rumanian people had no considerable say in the government of their country on the Balkans. Their masters were usually foreigners, but even their ruling classes did not take a great part in the affairs of the state. There existed no organic connection between state power and society in Rumania. (b). The Transylvania Wallachian was emotionally always part of his Moldavian, or Wallachian stock: he settled or wandered in Transylvania as an alien. He also felt everything alien around him, but he was waiting for political or economic opportunities, using those opportunities sometimes in very drastic ways.

The focal point of the Rumanian nation was unquestionably in Wallachia Proper. The Transylvanian Vlach did not feel Transylvania as his homeland, even if he was bron there and hins family lived there for many generations. The Transylvanian-Rumanian political leaders usually came from Wallachia Proper, and they settled in Transylvania only to "organize". When their patron, the Austrian autocracy seemed to fall, the Wallachians realized, that perhaps Transylvania could be theirs, by taking it

#619: Louis Elekes: "The Development of the Rumanian People." pp. 686-687.

from the Magyars. What a marvelous opportunity! Then — to the terrible disappointment of Rumania, — the Magyars compromised with the Austrians, Transylvania became on integral part of the Hungarian Kingdom, the Magyar minority became the majority again, and they could not do anything else, but a wait the next opportunity presented by history. But how long?

The Constitution of Dec. 21, 1867 was the masterpiece of liberal ideologists. It contained the complete catalogue of the basic human rights, limited the power of the government, introduced the responsibility of the cabinet, and contained directives concerning the equality of all nationalities.

". . . . But exactly this point shows, that the doctrinemakers of the liberal state were unable to give life to the they had created. The spirit of the constitution would have requested that a nationality-law be drawn up which could have secured national autonomies from the town councils up to the ethnic universities. But the Parliament, in spite of its own Constitution, never settled this problem." (#620).

This Constitution was a work of idealists, who did not have too much practical sence. All nationality groups were equally entitled to the exercise of free elections, to representation in the Parliament, to their free press and to any other kind of cultural, economic and religious establishments. These establishments were not only allowed but were generously supported by the Hungarian Government. The law (Sect. 44 — 1868) clearly stated that "all the citizens of Hungary form one political nation, therefore every citizen of the conutry, no matter to which ethnic group he belongs, is an equal member of the nation." (#621). This law meant that in Hungary, not only the majority group belonged to the ruling nation, but even the smallest ethnic group was a member of it.

The "Nationality Act" failed to satisfy the ambitions of the Rumanian extremists. It was based on the respect for the freedom of the individual. It was not enough: Transylvanian Rumanians resented their lack of territorial autonomy! "In 1868, the Francis Deák Bill was pessed" — cries out M. Ghyka (#622). "It was robbing the Roumanians from all the rights granted them by the Diet of 1863."

Of course, the Rumanian historian goes too far again with his conclusions. In the Diet of 1863, the Transylvanan Wallachians obtained equality of rights. In 1863, it meant equality with the other Transylvanian "Nations", the Magyars, Székelys and Saxons. Now, in 1867, the liberal Constitution and Nationality Law did not "rob" these rights.

"The separate Transylvanian Constitution and the system of the three "nations" were abolished and in their place the Hungarian Parliament passed its famous 'Nationality Law', the first of its kind in Europe, which, while maintaining the Hungarian charcter of the State, granted general and complete equality to the various nationalities." (#623).

The Wallachians demanded territorial autonomy now! Ethnic equality did not give an opportunity to join Wallachia Proper! Territorial autonomy seemed to be the way, which could represent a political "right" to dispose with Transylvania, and " perhaps" to join the Moldavian-Wallachian union. Not receiving the demanded autonomy, the Wallachians took up an attitude of passive resistance.

#620: Zathureczky: "Transylvania." p. 35.
#621: Ibid. p. 31.
#622: M. Ghyka: "A Documented Chronology of Roumanian History." p. 95.
#623: Zsombor Szász: "Hungarians — Rumanians." p. 595.

Even if the Rumanians were disappointed at losing the opportunity of territorial autonomy, they were certanly satisfied with the possibilities of cultural development.

"Onisifor Ghibu, professor of the Kolozsvár (Cluj) Rumanian) University, tells us in his books written in 1915 (#624): ". . . As an autonomous body the Rumanian Greek Oriental Church at Hungary and Transylvania, by virtue of the rights ensured in 1868, independently administers, directs and manages — subject to the full maintenance of the sovereign's supreme control — its own ecclesiastical and educational affairs and trust funds in every important respect." "School-inspectors have no immediate authority over our schools." "Parents are free to send their children to school they choose." "The language of tuition and the curriculum are determined by the bodies maintaining the schools." "In all Rumanian denominational schools (in Transylvania) the language of instruction is Rumanian." etc. (#625).

The Hungarian Parliament felt that the management of the minority problem was not only liberal and democratic, but it was one of the best solutions comparing similar situations in contemporary Europe. The main concern was, how to cooperate with Austria. On May 4, 1868, in face of opposition from the Independence Party, Andrássy's government agreed to the establishment of a common army for the Dual Monrchy, with German the language of command.

Following the "Ausgleich", let me mention two legal changes, which irritated the Transylvanian Wallachians. One of them was, that the Concordat with the Papacy was suspended.

The question could be raised: why would a change, like this, irritate the Wallachians? After all, they were not Catholics. Were they not happy with this liberal change?

As we remember, the Concordat with the Catholic Church gave the Church extensive power. (See p. 108). We will also remember, that the Wallachians were not hostile towards the Church and against the Habsburgs, because Church authoritarianism, and Habsburg despotism could secure their position against Transylvanian Protestant Hungarians. The emperors often exercised the tactic of "Divide et Impera", and both Austria and the Wallachians received benefit from this tactic. The Wallachian "Uniate Church" also represented the alliance of Catholic Austria and Orthodox Rumania. Now, in 1870, the suspension of the Concordat with the Papacy, (which was actually a reply to the promulgation of the dogma of papal infallibility, #626) reminded the Transylvanian Vlachs, that the "good old days" were over, and they could not hope anymore for the patronages of Habsburg autocracy, or Catholic clericalism.

The other irritating legal change was, that the Jews Act (in 1867) already abolished the political disabilities of the Jews. The Wallachians (both in Transylvania and in Wallachia Proper) were quite extreme antisemites. The Hungarian Jews were grateful for the liberalization; they became important factors in social and economic life, they assimilated with the Hungarians to a large extent. They did not feel themselves "Jews" (in the racial sence of this term) anymore, as in Russia, Poland and Rumania. They became Magyars (keeping their Israelite religions) in language, culture and spirit. Hungary gained exellent, faithful citizens with them. This was enough for the Wallachians to become more anti-Hungarian and more antisemitc at the same time.

#624: Onisifor Ghibu: "Viata si organizatia biserceasca si scolari in Transilvania si Ungaria and Scola romaneasca din Transilvania si Ungaria.

#625: Quot. from: Andrew Fall: "Hungarian Culture — Rumanian Culture. (Danubian Review. 1940. Vol. VIII. No. 6. November, pp. 9-10.)

#626: Dogma of Pius IX (1846-78) proclaimed on July 18, 1870.

In 1875, Kálmán (Coloman) Tisza formed his Liberal Party. (#627). The elections gave the new party a great majority. which proved that public opinion was enthusiastic about liberalization, and losing feudalistic tendencies. Kálmán Tisza became Prime Minister in Oct. 1875, and he was able to keep this position until March 1890. Accepting the Compromise, he devoted his energies to strengthening the Magyar position in Hungary. One main charcteristic of his system was centralization.

"Hungary, where the regional autonomies had long been repealed by the Habsburgs, yielded to centralistic tendencies of the Monarchy, and so the districts, losing their intended political roles, became solely administrative units. The effectes of this change were felt the most in Transylvania, where the Constitution had secured for centuries complete self-government for different nationalities." (#628).

During the time of Habsburg absolutism, until the "Ausgleich", the Transylvanian districts were administered by German speaking Austrian officials. This system was not unpleasant for the Transylvanian Saxons at all, because they could consider themselves some kind of "ruling" nationality. We saw, from the previous chapters, that system often represented a sort of benefit for the Walachians, because they realized, that friendliness with the Austrians at the expense of the Hungarians, could offer opportunities. Then did not have their own middle class-inteligentsia, they could not administer themselves, their cultural focal point was in Wallachia, outside the Transylvanian Basin, — thus the presence of Austrian officials was quite a satisfactory solution for them. One important effect of the "Ausgleich" was, of course, that, after 1868, the administrators were mostly local dignitaries usually of Magyar origin, nominate dby the Emperor, who was also the King of Hungary. This was a very unhappy change for Saxons and for Wallachians. The Saxons, in view of their numerical inferiority confined themselves to building up a close organization for the defense of their social and religious individuality. Their economic, social position was satisfactory, they were hard workers, living in beatiful, clean towns and villages. Their ancient national satus was abolished in 1876, so they were not a "nation" anymore in its original political sence, but, of course, they were recocnized as a nationality, and they could enjoy their ethnic rights — supported by the 'Law of Nationalities", just like any other ethno-lingustic group.

The situation became more and more extreme in Wallachian circles. They were a majority of the Transylvanian population itself, although they remained a very little minority, if we calculate only the middle class and, of course, they were a small minority of the whole population of the Hungarian Kingdom. The growing Rumania across the frontier represented an important factor in the ambitions of some local Wallachian dignitaries. ("Many Roumanian politicians, who later played great roles in the post World War Roumania, began their political careers as renresentives of those districts, where the Roumanian population was in the majority." (#629).

The economic development of Hungary gave free opportunities to everyone to became a member of the political-minded middle class, with absolute disregard to his nationality. But because the middle, and upper clas-

---

#627: Kálmán Tisza (1830-1902). The new party was composed from the Independence Party (which made the Compromise), and from the Deák Party, (which was a party under the personal leadership of Francis Deák.)
#628: Zathureczky: "Transylvania." p. 29.
#629: Ibid. pp. 29.30.

ses were almost exclusively Hungarian in language after the "Ausglaich" those members of the other nationalities, who came up into these classes through their own efforts became rapidy assimilated into these classes, and most of them lost their original national identities.

"Rumanian politicians called this natural assimilation of the individuals, as 'Hungarization', or Magyarization'. The fact was, that 'Hungarization', or 'Magyarization', as a planned program, never existed. It would have been against the Hungarian Constitution. Nonetheless, there was a definite assimilative effect at work within the bourgoisie and the middle class toward the newcomers into these classes. It was simply the law of assimilation exercised by a higher culture on an inferior one." (#630).

Postwar Rumanian history books and newspapers tried to introduce this natural assimilation, as a well-planned ,and aggressively directed linguicide, which attempted to force the disappearance of ethno?linguistic minorities. Here, at this point, it will be important to mention, that many western newspapers after he first Wourld War, still overexcited by victory, and extreme nationalism, and — as usual — hungry for sensations, were happy to report the "horrors" of "Magyarization." It was also true, that many of the western historians (in countries, where natural assimilation simply meant the adoptation of the English, or French languages by any newcomer), used the materials of these newspapers and well paid Little Entente-"historians", as their only sources. Consequently, assimilation into the English or French society was still regarded as a natural, and even enefiting process, but the same thing, when an individual, or a group gradually assimilated in Hungary, was called "Magyarization", with the accent, which was tended to impress the reader, that here some sort of organized crime was commited.

Of course, the Rumanian historians were working hard to investigate and to produce extreme cases. These extreme cases (and they were always possible to find in a complex society) were introduced as typical cases. M. Ghyka quoted one sentence. that he found in a Hungarian newspaper (the "Kolozsvár", 3rd August, 1891). According the sentence: "Only brutal force can impress the uncivilized masses." (631). (Did this shameful sentence really appear in this paper? Regretfully, yes, it did, but Ghyka could not find any other similar sentence anywhere, so he was happy, and proud to produce this one, as his great evidence, ignoring the well known fact, that using "brutal force" by political administration could be the illegal activity of an overambitious official in Hungary, but "brutal force" was a general standard in the Balkans, where the people of Mr. Ghyka came from.)

He refered to the fact that many names were "Magyarized" in Transylvania at the end of the 19th century, as some kind of crime. "As a result," — he said — "whereas from 1840 to 1910, Hungarians in Transylvania showed an increase of 48.7 per cent, the Roumanian population, (which was the more prolific of the two) showed only an increase of 19.1 per cent." (#632). Additionally, he was writing about "suppression of Roumanian schools", about the "unjust" foundation of a Greek Catholic (Uniate) bishopric in Hungarian language, as examples of "brutal oppression." (#633).

#630: Zathureczky: "Transylvania." p. 30.
#631: M. Ghyka: "A Documented Chronology of Roumanian History." p. 98.
#632: Ibid.
#633: Ibid. pp. 98-99.

Could we say, that "Magyarization" was nothing else, but a natural integration? Could we say, that "Magyarization" meant only the voluntary assimilation of individuals into a higher culture, or for a better political, social, economic opportunity? We still feel, that in most of the cases it was natural, it was voluntary. Rumanian, Slav, and -- under their influence, — some Western historians did not pay attention to the fact, that the large majority of the "Magyarized' individuals originated from intermarriages. Their fathers, or their mothers were Hungarians. In circumstances, like these, their "Magyarization" did not need too much "enforcement"; these cases represented nothing else, but the pracitical care of the parents to choose the way of life for their son, which seemed to offer more opportunities.

Nevertheless, the Ministry of Kálmán Tisza, especially after 1880, devoted its energies by strengtening the Magyar position in Hungary, notably by various school and language regulations designed to Magyarize the new generation among the subject nationalities. Was the Government more nationalistic with this activity than other European governments in this time? No, it was not. We are in the nineteenth century, which was the "golden age" of nationalism. Hungarian nationalism was extreme enough (under the effect of the spirit of this age, and as a reaction after the absolutistic Habsburg regime), but definitely not more extreme, than French Chauvinism, English Jingoism, and Italian Irredentism. Was "Magyarization" sometimes so extreme, as to discriminate against other ethno-linguistic feelings and minority rights? Yes, it was somtimes (altough, let us repeat, only in a minor extent), but it was never so extreme, never so authoritarian, as Austrian Germanization in the age of Habsburg absolutism, or Russification in the time of the Romanovs, or in the time of the "Red Tsars", or Slavization of other linguistic groups in the countries of the Western and Southern Slavs. „Anglicization" on the British colonies seemed very natural by Englishmen, because those territories were recognized as natural extensions of the British crown. The Hungarians had somehow a more justified reason to "Magyarize", after all their political and social organizations were on an area, which was Hungary for one thousand years. They were not colonies, where the various native peoples naturally resisted against the activities of the imperialist conqueror. They were areas, which belonged to the Hungarian crown since the ninth century, and where not the dominating nationality (like in the cases of England and France), but the ethnic minorities were the newcomers, (which was, of course not the case in Slovakia and Coratia, but it was definitely the case in Transylvania).

Anglicization, Germanization, Russification, Slavization, Magyarization, — these are often antidemocratic approaches. Thus, I am not defending any one of them I am only calling attention to the fact, that we should not justify any activity of the Past, doing nothing else, but using the "democratic" morality of the present. "The Nation-Concept of the 19th century became interwoven with the ethnical and the language concepts. Because, during the feudalistic era and even after 1868, the political nation was the Hungarian, the desire became more prevalent that the member nations should speak the Hungarian language. This brought forth the false notion that those who could not speak the language could not be good Hungarians nor good patriots." — wrote Zathureczky (#634). „This cretated a big propaganda movement on behalf of the Hungarian language, called 'Magyarization', which had more noise than affects and the logic of which was in direct oppostion to the facts." (#635).

#634: Zathureczky: **"Transylvania."** p. 32.

#635: Quotation from Ottlik:**"Pax Hungarica."**, quoted from Zathureczky's **"Transylvania."** p. 32. ("Magyarisation" was less inhuman than the nationalist persecution devised after 1918. It only harmed Hungary. It won the hatred of the masses of non-Magyar nationalities, and strengthened the hands of various nationalist leaders." Seton-Watson: **Eastern Europe between the Wars**, 1962. p. 43.

The leaders of the Transylvanian Rumanians, of course, realized the fact, that their people were mostly peasants and herdsmen. They also realized, that without a certian degree of assimilation they were unable to rise into the commercial or administrative middle-class, since they had no such classes within their own ethnic group. These leaders, mostly the Greek Orthodox priests, felt, that they were loosing their people. They protested with every possible means against the assimilation of the Wallachians. They realized that the real source of this assimilation was not so much the activity of the government, or the propaganda of some extreme newspapers, but rather the fact, that the (Hungarian) father, or mother of the child decided this assimilation voluntarily, for his (or her) benefit. The Wallachian leaders felt, that the Hungarian father (or mother) was an "alien", or "traitor" in these Wallachian families, and voduntary assimilation was — from the point of view of the Rumanian Orthodox Church — a manifestation of hostility against the Rumanian interests.

"They saw the solution of their problems in the creation of ethnic autonomies and in the federation in these autonomies. In spite of the fact that in the concept of the Habsburg Empire there was no place for such autonomies, while on the contrary, the original idea of the Hungarian State-Concept was based on regional autonomies until the Habsburgs abolished them, the leaders of the ethnic groups showed loyalty only to the Vienna court and not to the Hungarian homeland." (#636).

From the point of view of the Hungarian officials, this attitude seemed to be a hostile behaviour. The Hungarian government often justly regarded the ethnic problem as part of the oppressive Habsburg policy against the territorial integrity and unity of Hungary. After 1867, the "Divide et Impera" system actually did not exist in Vienna anymore, but mutual suspicions among ethnic groups indicated that the dark shadow of the "Divide et Impera" was still present in its effects, and consequences. "In 1878" — complains Ghyka, — "an electoral law reduced the Roumanian representation in the Diet to a negligible minority." "In 1879, a school law was passed which the Hungarian rulers intended to be a crushing blow: it introduced the obligatory teaching of Hungarian in all elementary schools, both religious and muncipal." (#637).

Two Roumanian metropolitans (#638) went to see the Emperor in order to protest, and in the next year, the Wallachians produced in their conference at Nagyszeben (Rum; Sibiu) a nine point programme, demanding "equality of rights." The School Law of 1879 was extended, in 1882, to secondary religious schools. The Rumanians protested again, "which this time found an echo in the Kingdom of Roumania," (Titu Maiorescu, D. Sturdza, P. Carp, and others). (#639).

It was true, that the government of Prince Carlo (#640) paid more and more attention to Transylvania. On Apr. 24, 1877, Rumania was invaded by the Russians during the war with Turkey, but Rumania entered the war in May, on the Russian side and proclaimed independence. The Treaty of Berlin (1878) recognized the full independence of Rumania. (#641). On May 23, 1881, Prince Carol was proclaimed king of Rumania. Two

---

#636: Zathureczky: "Transylvania." pp. 32-33.

#637: Quotations from Matila Ghyka: "A Documented Chronology..." p. 95.

#638: Miron Romanul and John Vancea.

#639: M. Ghyka: "A Documented Chronology... etc." p. 95.

#640: (1866-1914).

#641: The Rumanians were obliged to cede Bessarabia to Russia in return for the mush less desirable Dobrudja. The Rumanian government was obliged to promise protection to the Jews of Moldavia. Actually, nothing was done, and anti-Semitism became the main policy both in Rumania and by the Wallachian leaders in Transylvania. (See explanation on p. 115 again).

years later Rumania managed an alliance with the Monarchy. Bucharest regarded this alliance, as alliance with Vienna only, and not as an alliance with the Austro-Hungarian combination, (#642), attempting to create a situation in Transylvania, which was hoped to be silmilar to the Habsburg-Wallachian connection in the time of Joseph II and Horia (#643) against the Magyars. Bucharest was encouraged by the fact that Francis Deák died in 1876, and they felt, that his disappearance from the political scene, could lead to the happy co-evistence of Austrian absolutism, and Wallachian nationalism. In these cricumstances it was quite understandable, that the Wallachian metropolitans took their complaints to Vienna, and not to Buda, and Francis Joseph was "the Emperor" to them, and not the "King of Hungary."

"A law passed in 1891 to Magyarize kindergartens" — wrote Ghyka (#644), — „the national conference of Sibiu decided to present without delay a new memorial to the Emperor." (#645). "In 1891" — wrote N. Iorga, (#646) — "legal action was taken against the Roumanian leaders, whose great crime was that they wanted to submit to the Emperor at Vienna, in the form of memorandum, the grievances of four million loyal subjects. The paper was returned to them by the Hungarian Chancellory unopened." (#647). On year later, Tural Popovici (encouraged by both the Rumanian National Party, and by Bucharest) appeared with a petition of Rumanian students of Transylvania with various protests. (#648). It was followed by other protests, and when Hungary began preparation for the celebration of the Milennium (#649) the political situation was very stormy in Transylvania. The Magyar and Székely population shared the patriotic enthusiasm of the Hungarians in Hungary Proper. The Saxons were guite ignorant, but they were willing to participate in the exhibitions and parades. The Wallachians proved to be extremely hostile, and showed once again, that they regard Rumania and not Hungary as their homeland. In an article G. Clemenceau (#650) aided the anti-Hungarian feeling in Transylvania to a large extent. The article appeared in the "La Justice" (#651), and "it caused great repercussions abroad and roused Roumanian opinion in Transylvania." Thus, Wallachian nationalism was supported by French chauvinism long before the War. As a reaction to this, the Hungarians, preparing for the Millenium Celebrations, suppressed the Rumanian National Party. (#652).

The Magyars looked forward to the Celebrations in the athmosphere of tension and mutual distrust.

#642: The Alliance (Oct. 30, 1883) was part of the Triple Alliance System (1882). One factor was the Rumanian fear of Russia. Did the Rumanians "shelve their irredentist aspirations in Transylvania" with this alliance? Some western historians believe so. We feel, that Bucharest tended to aid this irredentism, attempting to co-exist with the Emperor only.

#643: (See Chapter XII. p. 94. again.)

#644: M. Ghyka: "A Documented Chronology ..." p. 95.

#645: Ghyka and other Rumanian historians usually did not mention at all, that the children in kindergartens and schools had the opportunity to be instructed in their own native languages too, (besides Hungarian language).

#646: N. Iorga: "A History of Roumania." p. 249.

#647: He was also mentioning "monstrous trials" "throwing innocent men into prisons" without documentary evidence. He describes Wallachians as "loyal subjects." Did the following years really justify this term?

#648: He was sentenced to five years inprisonment, but not only because of his protests, but as a spy and agitator against national interest.

#649: 896-1896: one thousand years of Hungary in the Carpathian Basin.

#650: (1841-1929). The "Tiger of Versailles" was only a young liberal-nationalist at this time. In his articles, already advocated for a French-Slav-Rumanian coexistence against German-Austrian "authoritarianism." He was not anti-Hungarian, but "pro-Rumanian" against the Dual-Monarchy.

#651: May, 12, 1894.

#652: This Party (hand in hand with the "Liga Culturala" in Bucharest) openly advocated for the creation of "Greater Roumania" (inc. Transylvania). (See also p. 110, #612).

XV.
THE DUAL MONARCHY AND TRANSYLVANIA.
(PART II: FROM THE MILLENNIUM TO TRIANON.)

The year of the Milliennium found the Magyars one of the proudest and most ambitious peoples of Europe.

"The Magyars were bursting with new energies. The Union had deprived them of the special position which they had held in Transylvania, where they had wielded a power out of all proportion to their numbers . . . It was therefore with great courage that they attacked the gigantic task of moulding Transylvania in the Magyar image." (#654).

We may understand this pride and ambition, if we remember, that the Magyars were ready to celebrate that their forefathers conquered the Carpathian Basin one thousand years ago, but, on the other hand, this ambition seemed to be too extreme, if we keep in mind, that, for example in Transylvania, the Magyars felt themselves highly superior above the Wallachians. Unquestionably, the educated middle class always adopted some sort of feeling of superiority above rural, and above illiterate population, — and in this situation the Magyars happened to be the middle class intelligentsia, and the Wallachians were the herdsmen, and peasantry. Even understandig this, it will be still uneasy, if not impossible to justify the fact, that "an ingeniously devised franchise practically excluded the Roumanians from parliamentary representation, while all the forces of the courts and the police were mobilized to repress any local political activity." (#654).

Here, again, we may find some explanation for the rigid administration in Transylvania. The Hungarian officials knew very well, that the local "activists" were not working for ethnic equality, but to force the union of Transylvania with Rumania itself. No State of the World would witness this type of activity without radical interference. But on the other hand again, with the possible extension of political rights, with granting a sort of limited autonomy, could not the Hungarian administration appease the ethnic groups in Transylvania? Could not a diplomatic appeasement separate the Transylvanian Vlachs from the provocative, chauvinistic forces of Rumania?

The joy caused by the coming Millennium Celebration was foreshadowed by a national mourning. On March 20, 1894, Louis Kossuth died at Turin. (#655). Transylvania participated in the national mourning, which unfortunatelly increased the hostility on both Magyar and Wallachian sides. Remembering Kossuth, the Magyars became more nationalists the Wallachians became even more hostile against the Hungarians.

"The year 1896 was a landmark in the history of Hungary. The Millenium Exhibition displayed the progress which Hungary made in her efforts to further the cause of universal culture." (#656). The Székelys and

---

#653: C. A. Macartney: **"Hungary and Her Successors."** p. 263.

#654: **Ibid.**

#655: In the previous decade there had been a marked revival of the Independence Party, the leadership of which was assumed by Kossuth's son, Francis. This Party fought for further independence for Hungary.

#656: A. B. Yolland: **"The History of Hungary."** p. 179.

the Transylvanian Magyars participated in the Celegrations in colourful national dresses, and their appearance was welcomed with great enthusiasm in Budapest. (#657). The Saxons were welcomed too, and they felt themselves once again rather on the Magyar side. When they heard the speech of the Emperor-King, (appearing in Hungarian national dress), which expressed harmony between the Dynasty and the conutry, they felt, that their presence was justified. Mentioning other nationalities from Transylvania, let us say, that Ruthenians, Bulgarian market-gardeners, and Gypsies were there too, all in their colorful national costumes. The Transylvanian Slovaks and Serbians joined the groups of their fellow nationalities from Slovakia and the Banate. The Transylvanian Jews did not appear as a separate national group. In Hungary and in Transylvania only the Polish-originated, so-called Orthodox Jews regarded themselves as a separated etthno-linguistic group. (#658). The "neolog" Israelites were proud and happy to feel themselves members of the Magyar middle class. (#659). (#660).

The Celebration introduced Hungary's industrial progress too. At this point, it will be quite significant to mention, that the industrial development of of Transylvania was still far behind that of Northern and Western Hungary, thus this province appeared rather as the "land of Hungarian patriotism," and a "land of a golden economic future."

The Wallachians, of course, ignored the celebrations. Ghyka informs that a Wallachian group managed a counter-meeting" on 9th June 1896, in the Swoboda Hall, in Vienna. (#661).

Before returning to the Wallachian problem, which was of course, the main ethnic problem in Transylvania, let us take another look at the Saxons, at the end of the nineteenth century.

> "The Saxons had laid the foundations of their communal life too truly for the edifice to crumble easily. The autonomy of their church round which their life centred henceforward, was buttressed by a solid income derived from foundations and from selfimposed taxation, and, with the help of this, they were able to keep up a remarkably high cultural standard . . . But they had become purely self- regarding, save that they watched, as in mirror, the progress of events in the far-off German conutries of which they always felt themselves the outpost." (#662).

Beginning with the "Compromise", the Transylvanian Saxons were quite loyal to Hungary, they did not cooperate with the Wallachians anymore, because they realized, that they had much more in common with the Magyars, and they certainly did not sympathise with the idea of Rumanian unification. Remaining in Hungarian Transylvania represented remaining in Europe. Being part of a Rumanian Trasylvania seemed to be a disgusting possibility for the Saxons, because it could mean being part of the Balkans which seemed to be inferior.

In 1903, began the Austro-Hungarian dispute over the army. An increase in the number of recruits was vigorously opposed by the Independence Party, which insisted on the use of Magyar insignia and the substitution of Magyar for German as the language of command. The other

---

#657: Buda and Pest was united in 1873.

#658: Most of them came in the late 19th century from Galicia and Moldavia.

#659: (See p. 115).

#660: At this point, let us mention, that Transylvania was populated with some very limited number of Karaites and Armenians too. (Inf. C. A. Macartney: **"Hungary and Her Successors."** p. 269.)

#661: M. Ghyka: **"A Documented Chronology..."** pp. 96-97.

#662: C. A. Macartney: "Hungary and Her Successors." p. 263.

contemporary problem was, that more and more landless peasants emigrated from various parts of Hungary and Transylvania to the United States and to Canada. (Their emigration had basically economic reason. They left for a larger piece of bread, — but they left their hearts in Hungary. Many letters from the other side of the Atlantic seemed to prove, that the famous epigram has some right: "Extra Hungariam non est vita, sic est vita, non est ita. #663).

1904 was the benning of the very extensive nationalistic activity from the Wallachian side again. In this year, the Orthodox bishopry in Transylvania composed a declaration on the subject of the modification of the school laws:

"Our Church and our People will faithfully carry out their duty towards the Fatherland, but they will not give up their language, for it has been written about this people that it prefers its language to its life." (#664).

This declaration was followed by others, and in more and more extreme sentences. "Magyars and Roumanians nibbled away the fringes of their old national preserve, and even invaded its cities." (#665). The Wallachians were fighting for more and more rights, and the Magyars stubbornly did not give them anything, that they demanded. We mentioned already, that the Hungarians realized that the Wallachian demand for autonomy was actually only the first step for the planned unification with Rumania, thus the Hungarian officials did not wish to grant this autonomy. However, the reason of mutual hostility was connected not only with the present problem, but with the past too. "A Magyar writer, Dr. A. Balogh, who investigated demographic questions for the Hungarian Government at the beginning of the nineteenth century, concluded that, of all the nationalities of Hungary, the Roumanians were the largest gainers on balance, and were responsible for more of the Hungarian losses than any other race." (#666). Budapest faced here, not only the Wallachian minority, but Bucharest too. "Public opinion in Roumania . . . became increasingly conscious of the national unity of all Roumanians and increasingly desirous of translating this into political union . . . The great majority of Roumanian opinion in both countries was at heart in favour of such a readjustment." (#667).

After the Ministry of Count Stephen Tisza (#668), the Géza Fejérváry Cabinet introduced the Universal Suffrage Bill (#669). (It could be step toward liberal-democratization.) This, and the Bosnian annexation crisis of 1908, (#670), led the Transylvanian minority problem away from the focus of public interest, but only temporarily.

In 1910, the Wallachian Orthodox bishopry began its struggle again. It complained that Hungarian officials falsified the Constitution and the "Law of Nationalities" of 1868. ("In al denominational schools, wheather they enjoy State grants or not, all subjects are to be taught only in Rumanian", comes with the counterevidence Andrew Fall, quoting from the "Lex Aponyi", mentioning other evidence, which seemed to prove that "the Rumanians were free to establish schools", and "the bishops of the denominational Churches were members of the Hungarian Upper House." (#671).

#663: "Outside of Hungary there is no life, and if there is life, it is not the same." (The epigram was created by the Italian Coelius Rhodinginus in the 15th century.)

#664: Ghyka: "A Documented Chronology . . ." p. 97.

#665: C. A. Macartney: "Hungary and Her Successors." p. 262.

#666: Ibid. p. 266.

#667: Ibid. p. 268.

#668: Son of Kálmán Tisza. Hist 1st Ministry was from Oct. 1904 to Feb. 1905.

#669: July, 1906. (Unfortunately it remained only a proposal).

#670: Oct. 6, 1908.

#671: Andrew Fall: "Hungarian Culture — Rumanian Cutlure." pp. 11-12.

The Rumanian leaders of Transylvania found themselves often in a quite strange, and almost unsolvable situtation. On one hand, they were fighting against Hungarian officials "for more rights" in schooling, but on the other hand, they had always a hard time to convince their own fellow Wallachians, that schooling, education is a good thing. The average Wallachian in Transylvania (with the exception of the very small middle class group,) did not like to send his children to school.

"As late as 1910, 72 per cent, of their population was illiterate, and the vast majority (1,246,639 persons out of 1,472,021 whose profession was recorded) were still peasants or herdsmen." (#672).

The Wallachians of Transylvaniia had high-schools of their own. These high-schools were patronized by the Hungarian Government financially, but no Hungarian official interfered in the system, or in the curriculum. It was up to the Wallachian population, it was up to the actual need among the population, to establish more high-schools, but this need just did not appear. The Wallachians, of course, were not excluded from the Magyar speaking establishments, and if any of the young Wallachians appeared in a Hungarian school, it was natural, that he had to expect, that he will study his subjects in the Hungarian language, or — using the term of the postwar Little Entente historians, — he will be "Magyarized". Interestingly enough, in certain Transylvanian, Wallachian-populated districts, where the need really existed for building more Rumanian high schools, the Rumanian religious and political leaders refused to do so, and instead if it, they advised the parents to send their children to Bucharest, where the teaching (especially the teaching of history) was extremely anti-Hungarian. For the Wallachian leaders of Transylvania it was much more important to build up an anti-Hungarian, relatively small, but chauvinistic middle class, than to build more schools in Transylvania itself and to give general help to educate their illiterate population.

Of course, many of the newly trained and prepared Rumanian intellectuals remained in Rumania Proper. They represented an important alliance for the Rumanian intellectuals to "liberate" the Wallachian relatives of Transylvania. On the other hand, the Transylvanian, Rumanian speaking, middle class remeined very small. (#673).

	Magyar	German	Rumanian	Total
Primary schools	1,265	254	1,145	2,664
Apprentice schools	61	13	1	75
Burger schools	55	7	3	65
Training colleges	8	3	3	14
Secondary schools	30	9	5	44
Special schools	23	3	1	27
High schools	7	-	3	10 (#674).

#672: C. A. Macartney: "Hungary and Her Successors." p. 266.
   (Note: The Baron Béza Fejérváry Cabinet was succeeded by the Cabinet of Dr. Alexander Wekerle, who governed with the support of the coalition parties. (1906-10). In 1910, this Cabinet was succeeded by the Ministry of Count Khuen-Héderváry, in which Stephen Tisza was the dominating figure.)

#673: In 1910, we could find about 15,000 Magyar intellectuals, and only 6,093 Rumanian intellectuals in Transylvania. (Inf. Macartney: "Hungary and Her Successors." p. 266.)

#674: Statistics from Ibid. 264. (Note: The Rumanian High Schools were all theological academies. All the Rumanian schools were denomanational. When a State school was founded in a minority district, it was always purely Magyar.)

Taking only the main nationalities of Transylvania, comparing the changes from the Census, from 1846 to 1910, the Magyar, German and Rumanian population developed as follows:

	1846		1857		1880	
	Number	%	Number	%	Number	%
Magyars	368,540	24.35	569,742	26.21	630,477	30.25
Germans	222,159	14.68	202,114	9.30	211,748	10.16
Rumanians	916,015	60.53	1,287,712	59.24	1,184,883	56.86
Others	6,601	0.44	114,096	5.25	56,940	2.73
	1,513,315	100.00	2,173,704	100,00	2,084,048	100.00

	1890		1900		1910	
	Number	%	Number	%	Number	%
Magyars	697,945	31.00	814,994	32.90	918,217	34.28
Germans	217,670	9.67	233,019	9.40	234,085	8.80
Rumanians	1,276,890	56.72	1,397,282	56.40	1,472,021	54.92
Others	58,711	2.61	30,703	1.30	54,044	2.00
	2,257,216	100.00	2,476,998	100.00	2,678,367	100.00

(#675).

These figures show a small, but steady increase in the percentage of Magyars. The statistics do not seem to prove any aggressive "Magyarization". Supposedly, any Englisch, French, German, or Russian territory, where the official language was English, French, German, or Russian, minority ethno-linguistic groups could not develop in the measure showed above. The increase of the Magyars was rather at the expence of the Germans and the minor nationalities than of the Rumanians. Unquestionably, however, "Magyarization" would have a larger effect on the Rumanians, if they had any willingness to go school. As we mentioned before, most of them did not appear in any school, and if they did so, they went rather to Bucharest to take high school education, than to a denominational Transylvanian sccool.

"Magyarization" was almost exlusively registered in the towns. The following figures will prove this:

	1880		1910	
	Total Pop.	Magyars	Total Pop.	Magyars
Kolozsvár (Rum: Cluj)	30,363	24,199	60,808	50,704
Brasso (Brasov)	29,584	9,827	41,056	17,831
Beszterce (Bistrita)	8,063	574	13,236	2,824
Fogaras (Fagaras)	5,307	1,734	6,579	3,357 (#676).

"The total urban population rose from 217,926 in 1880 to 350,268 in 1910. The Magyar element rose from 105,824 (48.6 per cent.) to 205,728 (58.7 per cent.) The Germans sank from 23.8 per cent. to 16.1 per cent; the Rumanians from 24.0 per cent. to 23.4 per cent." (#677). These figures were proving quite clearly, that the Wallachian leaders in Transylvania, and the extreme nationalists in Bucharest did not have too much reason to complain about "aggressive" Magyarization. The Transylvanian Saxons had much more reason to do so. If they did not, it could be answered with the fact, that these Saxons settled in Transylvania since the 13th century, and many Saxon families had intermarried with Hungarian families. They could send their children to German-speaking schools in Transylvania, in Hungary Proper, or to Austria or Germany, if they wished. If they sent their children to Hungarian schools, probably they did not mind "Magyarization" at all.

#675: C. A. Macartney: "Hungary and Her Successors." pp. 264-265.
#676: Ibid. p. 265.
#677: Ibid.

Now, let us take a look at the population of the Transylvanian towns, according to the census of 1910, in a more detailed way:

Town	Number of inhabitants	Magyars	Germans	Rumanians.
Kolozsvár (Cluj)	60,808	50,704	1,676	7,562
Brasso (Brasov)	41,056	17,821	10,841	11,786
Nagyszeben (Sibiu)	33,489	7,852	16,832	8,824
Marosvásárhely (Targu Mures)	25,517	22,790	606	1,717
Resica (Resita)	17,384	2,713	9,435	3,796
Beszterce (Bistrita)	13,236	2,824	5,835	4,470
Gyulafehérvár (Alba Julia)	11,616	5,226	792	5,170
Segesvár (Suceava)	11,587	2,687	5,486	3,031
Székelyudvarhely (Odorhei)	10,244	9,888	212	115
Nagyenyed (Aiud)	8,663	6,497	163	1,940

These figures (678) show that the Rumanians were a village-dwelling and not a town-dwelling people. (We may have another, very important conclusion: any ethno-linguistic map, which attempted to introduce ethno-graphic situation in a given time, when one of the ethnic groups was basically town-dwelling, and the other ethnic group was basically village dwelling, must be false in itself! The ethnographic map is able to give impression about "populated territory" only. A city, or a town represents only a small point on the map. In a city, or in a town, population is usually much bigger, than in the area around the town, or in the mountains. In 1910, for example, the Rumanians represented 54.92% of the total population. The ethnographic maps were giving the impression, that the Rumanian population must be more than 70%. In 1920, Bucharest produced for the Treaty of Trianon falsified etnographic maps, which coloured the absolutely unpopulated areas as Rumanian-populated territories. This "diplomatic" step gave the impression to Clemenceau, Lloyd George and to President Wilson, that actually almost all Transylvania was a Rumanian populated province. Consequently it should belong to Rumania.)

Now, let us take a brief look at the main religions:

Greek Orthodox	794,864
Greek Catholic	749,404
Roman Catholic	375,325
Calvinist	399,312
Unitarian	67,749
Lutheran	229,028
Jewisch	64,074
	2,679,756

This statistic is from Osterhaven (#679), using the census of 1910. (If we compare these religious groups with the population-statistics on p. 125, it will be quite easy to realise, that the Greek Orthodox plus Greek Catholic (1,544,268) population is more or less similar to the Rumanian population; the Calvinists, Roman Catholics, Unitarians (842,386) were more-less Hungarians, the Lutherans were the Saxons. Part of the Jewish population (the Orthodox appeared in the "Others" column, the other part (the Neolog) among the Magyars.)

In 1913, Stephen Tisza became the Prime Minister (#680), exercising far-reaching authority not only in Hungary, but in the councils of the Dual Monarchy. In Transylvania the Rumanian irredentist agitation deve-

---

#678: Sigismund Bátky: "Ehe Ethnography of Hungary." (In "View of Trianon's Hungary." Gabriel Bethlen Press, Budapest, 1912. p. 278).

#679: M. Eugene Osterhaven: "Transylvania." p. 13.

#680: His second primeministership was from June 15, 1913 to May 23, 1917.

loped rapidly. The government suppressed it to the best of its ability, but thereby created much ill-feelling in Rumania Proper. Tisza was eager for an understanding especially with the Rumanians, but like all Magyar statesmen, he rejected the idea of universal suffrage, which would have given the subject nationalities a voice in political affairs, (#681), and would at the same time have enabled the lower classes (both agrarian and industrial proletarians) to challenge the domination of the upper classes.

Rumania became gradually more powerful, and exercised more and more influence both in France and the Balkans, Of course, Bucharest, complaining about Magyar authoritarianism in Transylvania in Paris, and actually everywhere in international diplomacy, was much more extreme in nationalism, in suppression of ethno-linguistic minorities, and in class-autocracy, than the Hungarians themselves. In 1900, Bucharest was in serious tension with Sofia (Bulgaria), because of their conflicting aspirations in Macedonia. In 1905, Rumania was very hostile towards Greece, (and this hostility extended until 1911), because Athens treated the Kutzo-Vlachs in Macedonia in an oppressive way. Large numbers of Greeks were expelled from Rumania in these years. In 1907, the Moldavian peasants rebelled against the cruel treatment of Rumanian officials. This insurrection was put down by military force and martial law proclaimed throughout the country. In 1913, Bucharest agreed with Bulgaria by which the latter was to cede Silistria as compensation for gains made in the First Balkan War. (#682). The Rumanians demanded more, and on July 10, 1913, declared war on Bulgaria, joining with Serbia and Greece in the Second Balkan War. (#683). Bulgaria was rapidly defeated, and in the Treaty of Bucharest (#684) the Rumanians received Northern Dobrudja.

On June 14, 1914 Tsar Nicholas of Russia and his minister, Sazonov appeared at Constantza and Bucharest. The Russians and Rumanians agreed to co-operate in the event of the closure of the Straits in a Turkish-Greek war. The Russians attempted to suggest, that Rumania should join the Entente Powers, but the Rumanians (#685) refused to commit themselves to intervene in the event of an Austrian attack upon Serbia. (#686) On Aug. 4, 1914. Rumania proclaimed neutrality in the World War. (#687).

"In 1914, when the Great War broke out, Rumania was a member of the Triple Alliance. But that Alliance was very unpopular in Rumania and had become more so during the Balkan Wars, so that it was never submitted to Parliament for ratification, or made public in the country . . . When the Entente threatened to break off negotiations and leave Rumania to her own devices, Bratianu (the Premier) yielded, and on 17th August 1916 concluded a treaty with the Western Powers." (#688).

Ten days later, Rumania declared war on the Austro-Hungarian Monarchy! According to the promise of the Entente, "she was to receive the southern part of Bukovina, . . . Transylvania, Hungarian territories almost up to the Tisza (Theiss) river, and the whole of the Banate." (#689).

#681: The Univ. Suffrage Bill (July, 1906) did not became a law. Note: the subject nationalities represented 52% of the total population.

#682: Its outbrake was on Oct. 18, 1912, between Bulgaria, Serbia and Greece on the one hand and Turkey on the other. Turkey was defeated. (May 1913.)

#683: June 29—July 30, 1913.

#684: August 10, 1913.

#685: They were actually members of the Triple Alliance since 1883.

#686: Nicholas II (1894-1917) knew two weeks before Saraievo, that Austria was going to invade Serbia in the near future. (His visit to Bucharest helps the assumption, that Russia was ready for war, and the Black Hand provocation was supported not only by Belgrade, but by Russia herself.)

#687: August 4, 1914.

#688: Zsombor Szász: "Rumania at the Paris Peace Conference." (Danubian Review. October 1940, Vol. VIII. No. 5. p. 12, and p. 14.)

#689: Ibid. p. 14.

Since the spring of 1916, the Russian government had been redoubling its efforts to bring Rumania into the war. Many members of the Rumanian government hesitated, some of them even worried about the growing Russian influence, suspecting that Rumania could be a victim of Russian imperialism towards the Balkans. Others, again, were rather pro-Austrian, or pro-German. Pro-Germanism appeared around the King, who was of German origin(#690), but some others felt, that co-existence with the Habsburgs could save Rumania only from Russification, or Balkanization. (#691). However, the majority of the Rumanian politicians were opportunists, remembering that the growth of Rumania was, step after step, the result of some coinciding historical opportunity, which opportunity, expected, or anexpected, gave a chance, and then another chance again, to make the, originally little and weak. Wallachian province, into, what was Rumania in 1916. The success of the Brusilov offensive (#692), and the readiness of the Russian government and its allies to recognize the Rumanian claims to the Bukovina and Banate as well as to Transylvania, resulted in the conclusion of a political and military agreement.

August, 1916 was a very disappointing month for the Central powers, because Rumania declared war on Austria-Hungary on August 27, and when Germany gave her answer the next day, declaring war on Rumania, on the very same day, the former member of the Triple Alliance. Italy, also declared war — on Germany! (#693). Rumania received the war-declarations of Bulgaria and Turkey (#694), but it was quite clear now, that the Central powers were facing too strong forces on the other side, and — Rumania put herself on the "right" side of the balance again!

However, it seemed, that the timeing was wrongly chosen, in entering she war. The Rumanians should probably have entered the war in June, when the Russian offensive began, but they had wanted to wait for the harvest, and were, in fact, very poorly prepared even in August. They began the invasion of Transylvania on August 28, and took Brasso (Rum: Brasov, Germ: Kronstadt), and Nagyszeben (Rum: Sibiu, Germ: Hermannstadt). Their successes were due to the fact, that Hungary did not expect any attack from a member of the Central Powers, and did not concentrate forces in Southern Transylvania. From the points of view of Vienna and Budapest, the Rumanian invasion of Transylvania was a tracherous step. After the initial surprise, the Austro-Hungarian and German forces, hastily assembled in Transylvania and commanded by the former chier of staff, General von Falkenhayn (#695) counter-attacked the Rumanians on Sept. 27—29. They surrounded the Rumanian forces at Nagyszeben (Sibiu). Simultaneously, a Bulgarian-German force, under General von Mackensen invaded the Dobrudja, took Silistria, Constantza, and Cernavoda. (#696). On Oct. 7—9, Brasso (Brasov) was reconquered, and the Rumanian invaders were pushed back into Rumania Proper.

Gen. Falkenhayn did not stop, and began to penetrate into Wallachia on Nov. 10-14. The Rumanians were between two fires: Falkenhayn and Mackensen. The Rumanian government moved to Jassy. Bucharest fell into the hands of the Central Powers. (Dec. 6.).

#690: Charles (Carol) of Hohenzollern-Sigmaringen died on X. 10. 1914. His illness was very much connected with the fact, that the govt. discontinued the treaty of alliance with Austria. He died of heart attack.

#691: Dr. Vajda-Voevod, Rum. pol. leader, who later became prime min. of Great-Rumania, wrote in 1913 in the "Osterreichische Rundschau". "Without the presence of a strong Austria-Hungary, Roumania would be easy prey for Russian imperialism." (Inf. Zathureczky: Transylvania." p. 41-42.)

#692: Beginning with June 1916, until Sept. 1916.

#693: The Italians denounced the Triple Alliance on May, 3, 1915, and declared war on Austria already in May, but only on August 28, 1916 on Germany.

#694: August 30, September 1 respectively.

#695: Replaced by Hindenburg on August 29, as chief of staff.

#696: From September 10 to October 25.

How did the population receive the the Rumanian invasion and the news about the final collapse of the Rumanian army?

Of course, we can not speak here about any common "public opinion." From the two invaded cities, Nagyszeben (Sibiu) was mostly Saxon-populated, and the Saxons, very understandaby, did not desire any "Rumanian unification". In Brasso (Brasov) the situation was similar in a sense, that here the Hungarian population represented the large majority, and they were very happy to hear about the defeat of the Rumanian forces. Generally speaking, the tension in Transylvania was more extreme, than ever before, and, especially in areas, where the Wallachians represented the majority, the situation was quite close to civil war.

In the spring of 1917 revulution broke out in Russia, the Russian army collapsed, the Russian soldiers abandoned the Rumanian front, leaving the Rumanian army in the lurch. Towards the end of the year the Rumanian government concluded an armistice, which was followed at the beginning of 1918 by a preliminary treaty (March 5, 1918), and on May 7, in the definitive Treaty of Bucharest, Rumania was obliged to cede Dobrudja to Bulgaria and to turn over the Transylvanian passes to Hungary.

Six months after the Peace of Bucharest, in the autumn of 1918, the Central Powers collapsed. They had lost the war.

> "The irredentist Rumanians, first of Bessarabia, then of Bukovina and later of Transylvania, signified their desire for union with the Rumanian Kingdom. In November the Rumanian Government again declared war on the Central Powers, Mackensen withdrew his troops, and for the second time the Rumanian army invaded the now absolutely defenceless Transylvania." (#697).

Hungary was not in the position for selfdefence at this time. On Oct. 17, 1918, the Hungarian parliament, in reply to Emperor Charles (#698) declaration of "reorganization" of the Monarchy, declared complete independence from Austria, except for the personal union. At the end of the same month Count Michael Károlvi, an extremely liberal and republican, provoked, and led a revolution. Consequently the National Council proclaimed Hungary a republic. The affairs of Transylvania were not in the focus of the revulutionary government, and Count Károlyi (without military forces) could not defend Transylvania anyway.

"On December 1, 1918, the Transylvanian Wallachians and (surprisingly) the Saxons, the latter induced by large scale concessions, declared the union of Transylvania with Rumania without the assent of the Hungarians and Székelys." (#699). "The resolutions passed by the Rumanian National Council in Gyulafehérvár (Alba Julia), were accepted as the voice of the people, in spite of the fact that neither one of the two other Transylvanian national groups were represented at that convention. The first point of that resolution declared, 'the unification of all Roumanians and the territories inhabited by them with the Kingdom of Roumania." (#700).

Count Károlvi was not in the position to send any aid (political or military) to the Transylvanian Magyars and Székelys. On Jan. 11, 1919, he became appointed president of the republic (#701), but on March 21, he resigned in protest to the Allied decision to assign Transylvania to Rumania. The Communists (most of them sent by Lenin) took the opportu-

---

#697: Zsombor Szász: "Rumania at the Paris Peace Conference." p. 15.

#698: On Nov. 21, 1916, the old Emperor, Francis Joseph died, and was succeeded by his grandnephew, Charles. (Son of Otto, younger brother of the assassinated Francis Ferdinand).

#699: M. Eugene Osterhaven: "Transylvania." p. 19.

#700: Zathureczky: "Transylvania." p. 5.

#701: The government at once proceeded with the work of dividing the large estates among the peasants.

nity, and on the same day they declared the formation of a "Socialist-Communist government under Alexander Garbai (president) and Béla Kun (foreign affairs). Béla Kun soon took the next step, declaring the Sommunist Dictatorship.

Even the Communist ("international-minded") government realized, that the disarmed, defenseless Hungary could be very easily the victim of the bloodthirsty, revenging Czechs, Rumanians and Serbians, whose extreme nationalism turned into imperialism, realizing the free opportunities for conquests, which will be probably justified by the Western Allies. On March 28, Hungary declared war on (newly formulated) Czechoslovakia (#702) and proceeded with the reconquest of Slovakia. On April 10, 1919, the Rumanians (already conquering Transylvania, but looking for opportunities, which were far beyond their previous dreams) began to invade Hungary. (#703). They were on the way to Budapest, when Béla Kun, and his fellow Communists were involved mostly with internal problems. (#704). On Aug. 1, Béla Kun realized that the Rumanian forces were going to conquer the Hungarian capital, and the Hungarians would not adopt the Soviet communist system anyway. He fled to Vienna in face of the Rumanian advence. On Aug. 4, the Rumanian troops occupied Budapest, and did not evacuate until Nov. 14. They left Hungary Proper only on February 25, 1920, but reinforced Transylvania with more Rumanian troops.

The people of Hungary were happy when the last Rumanian soldier left Hungary, even if they took everyting with themselves, which was movable. The Hungarian public opinion was concentrated on the important internal changes. Already on Aug. 6.1919, Archduke Joseph took control as state governor, but was forced by Allied protests to resign. (#705). On March. 1, 1920, Admiral Nicholas (Miklos) Horthy, commander in chief of the forces, became the appointed regent and head of the state. On March 23, he proclaimed Hungary a monarchy, with the throne vacant.

Simultaneously, oppressive policies were undertaken by subsequent Rumanian officials against the Hungarians and Székelys in Transylvania. "About 150,000 civil servants and teachers were expelled from their positions . . . "Constitutional" and extra-constitutional means were used to reduce the importance of the Hungarians, and police terror was applied widely". (#706).

On June 4, 1920, the Hungarian Government signed the Treaty of Trianon, by which the thousand year old Hungary was shorn of almost three-quarters of its territory and two thirds of its inhabitants. The Czechs received Slovakia, the Serbians took Croatia and Slavonia and part of the Banat of Temesvár (Rum: Timisoara), Rumania received the rest of the Bánát, and, of course, Transylvania. The Rumanians also received part of the Hungarian Plain. Even Austria had the opportunity to keep western Hungary. (Burgerland). (#707).

#702: The Czechoslovak National Council declared its independence on Oct. 18, 1918. On Oct. 30, the Slovak National Council voted for union with the Czechs.

#703: Simultaneously, a provisional ("white") government was set up by Count Julius Károlyi (brother of Michael), Count Stephen Bethlen, Admiral Horthy, and Archduke Joseph, at Szeged under French occupation at this time. (It was called a "Counterrevolution" by the Communists).

#704: On June 24, the Communists declared the "Soviet Constitution."

#705: He was actually a Habsburg!

#706: M. Eugene Osterhaven: "Transylvania." p. 19.

#707: Hungary was also forced to pay reparations, to keep an army of only 35,000 men, to assume part of the old Austro-Hungarian debt.

Matila Ghyka commented on the Treaty of Trianon in this way:
"The Treaty of Trianon did not grant Transylvania to Roumania, but only ratified an existing state of affairs and voluntary unions based on the simple fact of the Roumanian majority in provinces of which the Hungarian masters had never attempted to gain the affection." (#708).

Thus, the Rumanian historian calls the surprising occupation of a defenceless neighbour country by a former "ally" as "existing state of affairs", he calls a meeting where the Magyars and Székelys were not even invited a "voluntary union", and he feels that Transylvania, citadel of the Hungarian Protestantism, and citadel of Hungarian patriotism troughout one thousand years, was a province, of which the Hungarian masters had "never attempted to gain the affection."

Let me introduce some general statistics about the consequences of the Treaty of Trianon; dealing only with the actual decisions, as immediate consequences:

From the 325,411 square kilometer territory of the Hungarian Kingdom, 232,448 square kilometers were divided up among artificially created, new, multinational states. From a population of 20,886,487 (of which 54.5% were Magyars), 13,271,370 were placed under foreign domination, including 3,319,579 Hungarians.

Out of these, more than three million Hungarians, 1,704, 851 became subjects of the Kingdom of Greater Rumania.

The population figures given by the Hungarian census for this area were as follows:

By Language	Total (#709)	In Transylvania only
Magyar	1,704,851	918,217
German	559,824	234,085
Slovak	30,932	2,405
Roumanian	2,800,073	1,472,021
Ruthene	16,318	1,759
Croat	2,141	944
Serb	54,874	
Other languages	96,431	48,937
Total	5,265,444	2,678,368 (#710).

The westernmost strip of the large area, presented to Rumania in Trianon, had a large Magyar population, almost without any Wallachian district. It was assigned to Rumania for "strategic reasons", but the extreme Rumanian claim for a western boundary on the Tisza (Theiss) was rejected. Bukovina too returned to Rumania after almost a century and a half under Habsburg rule. The Rumanian troops occupied Bessarabia, using the opportunity that Russia was not in the position to defend it. The division of the Banat with the Serbs was negotiated directly.

Wallachians, both in Transylvania, and Rumania, were in a happy excitement, when they received the fantastic news, that Transylvania will be part of Rumania from now on. The unfortunate country was under Rumanian military occupation for many months, but somehow, Rumanian

#708: M. Ghyka: "A Documented Chronology... p. 102.
#709: These figures include population not only of historical Transylvania, but other territories, received by the Treaty of Trianon from Hungary; areas from the Hungarian Plain, Maramaros (Maramures), and part of the Banate.
#710: From C. A. Macartney: "Hungary and Her Successors." p. 252. (Compare with our previous statistics, on p. 125). (Also, see ethnographic map on p. 133.)

officials, and the literate part of the Wallachian population knew, that Transylvania was never part of Rumania in previous history, and the Wallachian majority in Transylvania appeared only in rural areas, and was caused by a continuous infiltration from the Balkans. It took several months, until Bucharest was able to truely realize the new situation, and gradually changed the military conquest into administrative annexation.

The Saxons were not happy, but they represented a too small number, surrounded by other nationalities. They received many promises from Bucharest, and they acknowledged with satisfaction, that the king of Rumania was of German origin. They knew, that the Hungarian officials will lose their positions, they also knew that Rumania did not have enough afficials to replace them. New opportunities seemed to arrive to the hard working circles of the Transylvanian Saxons.

How about the Hungarian emotions? Until the last moment, they were hoping, that the 10th point of Wilson's famous "Fourteen Points" ("Opportunity for autonomous development for the peoples of Austria-Hungary") will be accepted by the "Big Four". Trianon was a disappointing answer; the peoples of the Dual Monarchy did not get free opportunity of autonomous development. The Czechs, Serbians and Rumanians received their rewards (the Serbians for provocation, the other two for treachery). On the ruins of the multinational Monarchy, three other artificial, multinational states were built (The irterwar years proved that Austrians, Hungarians, Slovaks, Ruthenians, Székelys, Saxons, Slovenes, Croats were innocently, and cruelly punished for war-crimes which were actually commited by Macchiavelist diplomats and generals on both sides of the pre-war Balance of Power).

Transylvania, the very heart of Hungarian patriotism, the pearl of European Calvinism, this typical Central European cultural region, (where — as result of endless Wallachian infiltration — 54% of the rural population became Wallachian); — Transylvania, which was part of Hungary for more than one thousand years, — became part of the Rumanian Kingdom, part of the Balkans.

ETHNOGRAPHICAL MAP — See opposite page

#711: This map is a reproduction of Count Paul Teleki's **"Ethnographical Map."** (Based on density of population, according to the census of 1910, noting only the main nationalities.)

#712: Count Teleki's **"Ethnographical Map"** was an additional attachment of his **"The Evolution of Hungary."** The same map appeared in C. A. Macartney's **"Hungary and Her Successors,"** and the same map again, in smaller form, in **"A View of Trianon's Hungary."**

XVI

TRANSYLVANIA AS A PROVINCE OF THE RUMANIAN KINGDOM.

The "peace" treaties, forced upon Europe after World War I, paralyzed the historic and economic functions of the Danubian Basin. They did not even serve their alleged purpose, that is, to solve the nationality problems. Only the roles changed. The new minority groups, created by the treaties, were mercilessly exposed to the most chauvinistic discriminations by new, artificial, multinational states.

The Paris treaties included carefully outlined instructions for the protection of the ethnic minorities. Nevertheless, these instductions were completely disregarded by Rumania, and by other successor states of the Dual Monarchy. Could, or did the League of Nations give aid, in case of request, to any of the ethnic minorities?

"... There was no place for the Hungarians to present their grievances. The League of Nations lent a sympathetic ear, but was anable to enforce the respect for the so-called 'minority rights'." (#713).

Rumania, which emerged from the Great War with greatly expanded frontiers, quickly learned, that satisfaction of territorial demands did not in itself bring contentment or prosperity. "Bessarabia and Transylvania suffered economically not only from the cutting of the historical ties with Russia and Hungary but also from the centralized financial and banking system by which the politicians of the Regat unified and exploited them." (#714). "In Transylvania, the large Magyar minority, well over a quarter of the total population, had lorded over the Rumanians for at least seven hundred years, and still had the feeling of belonging to a master race. In the interwar years, the Rumanians did not deprive the Magyars of their schools . . . but Bucharest did, however, require all civil servants to pass a Rumanian language examinition, and often used this to discriminate unfairly against Magyar applicants." (#715).

Professor Wolff, who wrote the sentences, quoted above, really did not belong to the group of the pro-Hungarian historians, but even he realized, that the Paris peace treaties provoked much more bitterness and dissatisfaction, than ever before. How about Hugh Seton-Watson, the other pro-Rumanian, pro-Slav historian, who inherited so much from his father, the famous R. W. Seton Watson's anti-Hungarian feelings? How did he feel, about the new position of Transylvania?

"... the Hungarians . . . became second-class citizens in Transylvania. They kept most of their schools, although the Rumanian authorities interfered with the teaching in them in a number of irksome ways . . . Roumanian officials . . of Regatean origin flooded the province. Although it was reasonable that knowledge of the Roumanian language should be expected of all State employees, the examination was often deliberately unfair, and came to be regarded simply as an excuse to kick out old, and refuse admission to young, Hungarian officials." (#716).

Already on Sept. 14, Rumania joined the League of Nations, promising "democracy", and liberalistic methods with minorities. Simultaneously "the Transylvanian Roumanian 'Directing Council', backed by the Regat troops, exercised a national dictatorship, leaving the Saxons within limits, to manage their own affairs, but keeping a tight hold over the Magyars." (#717).

#713: Zathureczky: "Transylvania." p. 43.

#714: Robert Lee Wolff: "The Balkans in our Time." p. 126.

#715: Ibid. p. 144.

#716: Hugh Seton-Watson: "Eastern Europe Between the Wars. 1918-1941." pp. 300-301.

#717: C. A. Macartney: "Hungary and Her Successors." p. 291.

Bucharest introduced the parliamentary system, with a single parliament. The Rumanian parties, of course had an overwhelming majority. The Constitition emphasized the unitary and national character of the State. The same Constitution also stated specifically that minorities, as such, were not recognized as forming corporate bodies. In the excitement of a victorious, extreme nationalism, Bucharest declared Greater Rumania as a "national state", knowing that the Wallachian population represented only 71.9% of the total population, and knowing, that in Transylvania the Wallachians represented only 46.1% of the population. (#718).

The Transylvanian Magyars, with few exceptions, refused to recognize the existence of enlarged Rumania, until after Hungary had ratified the Treaty of Trianon. Then they formed two parties which in 1922 fused into a single body, the "Magyar National Party." (This party did not really have a chance to represent the Hungarians in Rumanian political life. "At the first elections, for example, 30 of the 33 candidates which they put up were disqualified, and only one elected.") (#719). (#720).

Of course, the Wallachian emotionalism was quite understandable, looking from their points of views. In the prewar Jews they formed the national proletariat, and now, that they received the power of the State behind them, they attempted to create a national upper and middle class. This ambition could be achived only, and most easily, at the expense of the Magyars, Germans and Jews.

"The most vigorous assult of all has, indeed, been made not against the Magyars but against the Jews." (#721).

Anti-Semtism, and anti-Hungarianism in Transylvania was about the same thing for long time, because the "neolog" Jewish middle class asimilated with the Hungarian middle class, and proudly confessed themselves Hungarians. In Moldavia and the Regat the Rumanian anti-Semitism turned against Orthodox Jews, and it was hard to estimate, if it was hatred against an alien race, or social hostility of a national proletariat against bourgeosie elements. One interesting signaficance of the anti-Hungarian hostility was, that after 1920, the most extreme nationalism originated in Bucharest, and not by the Transylvanian Wallachians, and even in Bucharest, the youngest Rumanian generation proved to be the most extreme.

Studying the modern history of Transylvania, it could be clear for the student of history, that the minority problems of this land were always very compex. The "minorities" faced usually the majority of Transylvania itself, but also the oppression of some outside power, which supported this majority. In other cases, the outside power supported the minority against the Transylvanian majority. In other cases again, both majority and minority faced the oppression, or manipulation of an alien power, and it was up to the political attitude of any of these, that this alien power will co-operate with the national majority or minority. In the previous chapters we could find examples for all these possibilities. After 1920, Wallachians in Transylvania did not represent a majority (if we calculate Rumanian Banate), but they were supported by Rumania proper, with which they were an overhelming majority.

#718: In Transylvania itself, the Vlachs represented about 55%, but Rumania received areas from the Hung. plain and from the Banate, where they represented only 39.6%. Stat from: R. W. Watson: **"A History of the Roumanians."** (Archon Books, Cambridge, Univ. Press, 1963. pp. 566-567.)

#719: The Magyar claim to represent the Moldavian "Csángo Magyars" was also rejected.

#720: Quotation from C. A. Macartney: **"Hungary and Her Successors."** p. 291.

#721: **Ibid.** p. 288.

The younger Seton-Watson, — who proved to be much more objective than his father, R. W. Seton-Watson, (the ill-famed "Scotus Viator"), — was very wise to write this:

"Transylvania ... cannot be considered as a Roumanian province with a Hungarian minority or as a Hungarian provice with a Roumanian minority. It is the home of both Roumanians and Hungarians, both of whom have lived there far longer than any historical records that can be considered as reliable. Until the two nations can live together in peace and friendship it is inconceivable that the conutry can have any prosperity or security." (#722).

Unfortunately, the Dual Monarchy did not realize this before the war. Bucharest seemed to be even more extreme in narrowminded nationalism. In 1920, King Ferdinand (1914—1927) "ousted the Transylvanian Beasant Premier Vaida-Voevod, elected after the war, and installed the war hero, General Avarescu." (#723). "Under Avarescu and the Liberal Premiers who succeeded him, a policy of rigid centralization was introduced. The National Councils of Transylvania, Bessarabia, and the Bukovina were dissolved, and the whole conutry divided into Departments, under Prefects appointed directly from Bucharest ... The special wishes and susceptibilities of the Transylvanians were disregarded ... Transylvania was forced to bear the brunt of the national taxation, while financial eliques in Bucharest monopolized the pickings." (#724). (#725).

Rumania, as member of the League and being allied with Czechoslovakia and Yugoslavia, #726) felt that no power in the world could stop her from dealing with her newly occupied provinces. in any manner she wished. Hungary was certainly too weak to interfere in defence of the Transylvanian Magyars and Székelys. (#727). In 1922, the position of Hungary slightly changed. She was admitted to the League of Nations. (#728). From this time on, Hungarian revisionism, which actually began in 1920 already, could appear not only in pamphlets, in newspapers, in speeches, but on the international stage of the world.

We already mentioned the psychological importance of the Carpathian Mountains. "Magyars felt that when Rumania stepped across the Carpathians, it was as though the natural wall against Asia had crumbled" (#729). "All tourists in Budapest saw the enormous statue of Hungary mourning the lost provinces, north, east, south and west ... Between the wars the national motto became the celebrated 'Nem, nem, soha' (No, no, never)." #730).

#722: H. Seton-Watson: "Eastern Europe Between the Wars." pp. 271-272.

#723: R. L. Wolff: "The Balkans in our Time." p. 126.

#724: Bucharest was courageous to do this, ignoring that the Paris treaties alienated Hungary (because of Transylvania), Russia (because of Bessarabia), Bulgaria (because of Dobrudja) and to a small extent Yugoslavia (because of the division of the Banate).

#725: Quotation from C. A. Macartney: "Hungary and Her Successors." p. 282.

#726: Alliance with the Czechs (Apr. 23, 1921), with the Serbians (June 7, 1921). Bucharest even managed a defensive treaty with Poland and Hungary (March 3, 1921) against the Russians.

#727: The historical storm continued in Hungary even after Trianon. King Charles attempted to occupy the throne on March 27, and Oct. 21, 1921. Regent Horthy refused, because of the ill-feeling about the Habsburgs, and because of he possible threat of the Little Entente. Burgenland's dispute with Austria (Aug.-Dec. 1921).

#728: The Cabinet of Cout Sephen Bethlen (Prime Min. 1921-31, and master of consolidation) received this opportunity on Sept. 18, 1922.

#729: John Flournoy Montgomery: "Hungary, The Unwilling Satellite." (The Devin Adair Company, New York, 1947. "The Downfall of Rumania", p. 130.)

#730: R. L. Wolff: "The Balkans in Our Time." p. 143. (The term "Trianon" was also mentioned this way: "tria Non", ("three not").

Interestingly enough, when postwar Hungary was still considered by many of the poswar governments as a semi-feudal state, Rumania was able to present some impression in Geneva as a "democracy". Unquestionably, this impression was connected not only with France, (which attempted to use the League as a police-institution, guarding the defeated nations), but with the fact, that Rumania was allied with Masaryk's Czechoslovakia, and in the 1920-es, it was too early to recognize for the, usually naive, western eyes, that even this "champion of Democracy", who was able to influence President Wilson with the flood of his democratic ideals (#731), after 1920, in practice, seemed to adopt the idea af George Orwell:

> All pigs are created equal — but some pigs are created more equal than others." (#732).

Yes, history proved that political democracy in itself was unable to solve minority problems. "From the point of view of fair play, principles of democracy based on the majority rule can only be successfully applied in the governments of homogeneous societies, where the chance to become a majority is always open to the (political) minority groups. Ethnic minorities, however, do not have this opportunity", (#733) ". . . Because the majority rule is the strict consequence of democracy, democracy is always inclined to become an oppressive domination toward those elements of society which, due to some conditions originating in their very nature, are of a permanent minority status." (#734). "Instead of the establishment of crude majority rule, democracy was thus actually aiming at something different from liberty: the rule of the 'best few', winning their laurels in free competition". "No negative safeguards of democratic equality could be reckoned with to save the 'under dog' in this period of postwar-nationalism. For a rule which provides that subjects belonging to different nationalities must be treated as equals without discrimination, actually means that no one may claim preference on grounds of belonging to a nationality; or to put it more forcefully: that all subjects must be treated as if they belonged to one single nationality." Because the successors of the Monarchy were also multinational states, the "majorities" in these states" . . . always inclined to suspect members of minorities — evidently not always without good reason — of disloyal sentiments towards the State to which they are bound by no ties of sentiment or tradition." (#735).

Thus, in Eastern Europe, where the democratic revolution was not only the revolt of the poor against the rich, but the revolt of the conquered nation against the conqueror, where extreme nationalists and generals dictated "democracy", where revenge and the "security of the victors" was more important than "national self-determination"; — "democracy" — strangely enough, — became identical (and let us use the words of Orwell again) with the dictatorship of "some pigs" who were "more equal than others."

#731: "In internal affairs as in foreign, democracy must be our aim." "Genuine democracy will be economic and social as well as political." "In our Democratic Republic, freedom of conscience and toleration must not be merely condified but realized in every domain of public life. Democracy is the political form of the humane ideal." (T. G. Masaryk: **"The Making of a State".** London, 1927. pp. 390, 394, 441.)

#732: George Orwell: **"Animal Farm."** 1946.

#733: Zathureczky: **"Transylvania."** p. 5.

#734: L. Ottlik: **"The Minority Problem Yesterday and Today."** Szemle, p. 106. (Quoted by Zathureczky, in **"Transylvania".** p. 5.)

#735: László Ottlik: **"Democracy and the Multi-National State."** (**"Te Hungarian Quarterly."** Vol. IV. Winter, 1938/39, No. 4. pp. 587, 590, 591).

In a multinational state "political democracy" usually has "side effects", which seems to be "quite democratic" for the members of the "dominating" nation, but does not seem democratic at all for the members of the national minorities. "Democracy is not a way of governing, whether by majority or otherwise, but primarily a way of determining who shall govern and broadly, to what ends." (#736).

Can a multinational state, (which bases the methods of governing on nothing else, but only on "political democracy") survive? In a multinational society, (where the minorities, being differently constiutted by their traditions, cannot ascape the feeling of oppression,) the "democratic" parliamentary routine becomes sooner or later, not the means to survive but the means to disintegrate. "The society where such a situation prevails is actually in a state of latent dissolution, for it contains elements which can never be reconciled to its constitution." (#737).

Already in the 1920-s, it became clear, that even "democratic" Czechoslovakia was not able to remain truly democratic in multinational circumstances. Avarescu was much more "realistic" then Masaryk. He realized earlier, that Rumania would be able to preserve Wallachian political overlordship only through the means of national dictatorship.

> "The Roumanians have never considered that they had any serious chance of conciliating the Magyars, and . . . they have not even thought in worth while to attempt to detach from them any particular social element, such as the workers or the peasants. Their chief attacks have, of course, been directed against the politically active classes . . . Generally speaking, they have regarded the Magyar minority as an irreconcilable enemy." (#738).

The Rumanian "Land Reform" was a good example that "Parliamentary Democracy" was not democracy at all, without economic democracy.

In 1923, when both Hungary and Rumania began to deal with economic reconstruction (#739), Bucharest introduced a "Land Reform", which "took 2,718,146 acres of land from Hungarians, (mostly small landowners) and handed this over to the Roumanian population and the Roumanian churches. The owners of these properties were recompensed with valueless government bonds." (#740). This action, which was originally directed only against the Hungarians, was camouflaged as a reform aimed against the big landowners. "The truth was, that even according to Roumanian statistics, of the 5,461,200 acres of agricultural land in Transylvania, only 1,904,635 acres were owned by farmers possesing more than 100 acres . . . Almost half of the land confiscated from the Hungarians was taken from small farmers with less than 100 acres." (#741). (#742).

> "The Land Reform has a nationalist character which deserves attention. In Transylvania, Bácska and Bánát, side by side with Roumanian and Serbian peasarts, were landless Hungarian peasand labourers. These, as belonging to the 'enemy nation' received a less than equitable share of the lands of their former Hungarian masters." (#743).

The long dispute between Hungary and Rumania regarding the disappropiation of Transylvanian landsholders who had opted for Hungarian citizenship, and whose property rights were laid down in the treaties, —

#736: H. B. Mayo quotes MacIver in his **"An Introduction to Democratic Theory".** Oxford University Press, New York, 1960. p. 59.

#737: L. Ottlik: **"Democracy in a Multi-National State."** pp. 586-587.

#738: C. A. Macartney: **"Hungary and Her Successors."** p. 285.

#739: The League adopted a scheme for economic reconstruction of Hungary. This continued until June, 1926.

#740: Zathureczky: **"Transylvania."** p. 44.

#741: Zathureczky quotes (p. 44) M. Constantinescu: **"L'evolution de la reforme agraire en Roumanie."** 1925. p. 247.

#742: Macartney introduces the actual landholding situation using the statistics from N. Moricz: **"The Fate of the Transylvanian Soil."** (1934).

#743: H. Seon-Watson: **"Eastern Europe Between the Wars."** p. 79.

began in 1923, and it was still on in 1930. All efforts by the League to effect a compromise failed. (#744).

On March 27, 1923, the new constitution of Rumania (mentioned on p. 135 already) abolished the three-class system of voting and introduced the secret ballot. "Though corrupt and unpopular, the Liberals met with no united opposition, and were able to rig elections to their own advantage . The new constitution . . . made Rumania a strongly centralized state . . . The Transylvanians in particular resented the degree to which they were governed from Bucharest. The measures guaranteeing civil liberties were so worded that in practice it was easy to limit their exercise." (#745).

> "The sufferings of the minorities during the inter-war period were due fundamentally to two causes, the bad system of Government . . . and the identification of nationality with the State apparatus. It is inconceivable that national minorities can enjoy decent treatment in States organised on a basis of economic exploitation, social oppression, corruption, torture and terrorism. Not only the minorities, but all but a few members of the majority nation suffer from these things, and to talk in such conditions of human rights and protection of minorities is merely a joke in bad taste." (#746).

The discriminations appeared against the Magyars, of course, not only in their political, and social, but in their economic life. "Taxation has undoubtedly been discriminatory. Certain taxes exist which affect minorities almost exlusively." (#747). Shops, courageous enough to sell non-Rumanian books, Hungarian engineers, and other minority professionals had to pay extra taxes, for various "reasons". The minority taxpayer had to pay his taxes on time, or he was fined unmercifully. "The so-called 'Comisia Econamica Speciala', which was set up for the purpose of nationalizing Roumanian industry', concerned itself in practice with all important minority firms in Transylvania, which were obliged to take Roumanian directors on to their boards." (#748).

Parallel with the economic persecution, the Rumanian Government undertook an all out offensive against the Hungarian schools. Hungarian, as a language of instruction was abolished and its use forbidden in all the public schools. "In many cases, children were cruelly beaten for using their language among themselves during the recess." (#749). Both Protestant and Catholic parocial schools (some of them established in the 15th centuries) were closed down. (#750). The American Committee for the Rights of Religious Minorities reported: "The administrative oppression, the violent enforcing of the Roumanian language, . . . the aggressive hostility, . . . all these are aimed for the total destruction of the minority school system. The laws of 1925 serve as oppressive political and nationaylistic tools against the minorities." (#751).

In 1911, Hungary (blamed always with "Magyarization") permitted 2,813 public schools, in which Rumanian was the language of instruction. In 1926 there were no schools left at all for the use of the Magyar lan-

---

#744: The details of the land dispite were described, and documented in Francis Daák's **"The Hungarian-Rumanian Land Dispute."** (**"A Study of Hungarian Property Rights in Transylvania under the Treaty of Trianon."** Columbia Univ. Press, New York, 1928.)

#745: R. L. Wolff: **"The Balkans in Our Time."** p. 127.

#746: H. Seton-Watson: **"Eastern Europe Between the Wars."** p. 272.

#747: C. A. Macartney: **"Hungary and Her Successors."** p. 322.

#748: **Ibid.** p. 323.

#749: Zathureczky: **"Transylvania."** p. 44.

#750: While in 1918 there were 8 parochial type colleges in Transylvania, in 1927, there were none.

#751: **"The Religious Minorities in Transylvania."** Edited by the American Committee, The Bacon Press, Inc. Boston. 1925. (From Zathureczky, pp. 44-45.)

guage. Let us quote now from a newspaper, trying to illustrate the situation. The "BRASSOI LAPOK" wrote on Dec. 14, 1925: "The new teacher, Mr. Clements Tratiu, who was sent recently by the government to the village of Csikjenöfalva, in his efforts to enforce the new language regulations of the Government, handed out such beatings to his pupils, that on the first day the parents had to carry home twenty-four badly beaten children from the schoolhouse, who were unable to walk." (#752). This sort of situation was not rare at all in Transylvania in the inter-war years. Only one thing was rare here. Not too many Hungarian newspapers were courageous enough to discuss school problems under the dark shadow of the Rumanian national dictatorship.

Rumanian "science" was also involved on Rumanization. Some Rumanian scientists supposed that there must be Rumanian blood among the Székelys, who have lived for centuries so close to Wallachian settlements. In more and more "schientific approaches" the Székelys were described, as "Magyarized Rumanians." The registrars (also instructed by those "scientists" of Bucharest), registering the birth of a Hungarian child, translated the names into Rumanian. "A group of medical doctors, under the leadership of Dr. Peter Ramusatu, took blood samples of 20,092 Hungarian children. Some of these children, having their names changed by the registrations, were declared Roumanians, and because their blood types were similar to the others, the group drew the conclusion and the theory, that the Transylvanian Hungarians are in reality assimilated Roumanians. The report handed in by this group received the award of the Roumanian Academy." (#753).

On Dec. 28, 1925, Prince Charles (Carol) renounced his right of succession to the throne and preferred to live in exile with his mistress, Mme Lupescu. (#754). On March 25, 1926, a new electorial law provided that the party polling 40% of the votes schould have one-half of the seats in parliament. This move was designed to prevent due representation to the various peasant parties. which were clamoring louder and louder against the existing regime. "This electoral law was somewhat on the Fascist model." (#755). It attempted to harm the peasantry, but also to harm Transylvana first of all, because the main center of the Peasant Party (which fused with the National Party of Transylvania) was in "Ardeal" (#756), and Iuliu Maniu, the champion of human rights (#757) was the respected leader. Beginning with 1928, the peasants loudly demanded the dismissal of the cabinet, and their congress at Alba Julia (Gyulafehérvár) demanded representative government, decentralization and reform. (#758).

#52: Quoted from Zathureczky's "Transylvania." p. 45.

#753: Ibid.

#754: Bratianu and the Liberals were actively hostile to the prince.

#755: Expressions from R. L. Buell "Europe. A History of Ten Years. The Macmillan Company, New York, 1930. "The Little Entente." p. 326.

#756: As we mentioned already, the Rumanians did not have any original name for the conquered Transylvania. They simply vulgarized the Hungarian "Erdély" into "Ardeal" in every-days conversations, and only gradually adopted the title "Transylvania", also from the Hungarian official (Latin) documents.

#757: He advocated rights for the Wallachians before 1920 facing the Monarchy. Now, he championed democratic rights against Bucharest.

#758: Bucharest had busy years beginning with 1926. In this year it managed alliance with Poland and France; even with Mussolini's Italy. In the next year, King Ferdinand died, and Michael (b. in 1921), son of Prince Carol, became the king (1927-30), under the guardianship of Prince Nicholas, brother of Carol. The death of the energetic Liberal leader, Bratianu gave more opportunity for the peasants, since 1928.

When Julius Maniu became premier, it was a serious victory for the peasants. He set out to purge the administration, made easier the influx of foreign capital, and improved the lots of the peasants. It seemed that Maniu would create some sort of peasant democracy, and the focus of power would be based rather on the Transylvanian Wallachians. They were much less extreme than the Regat-politicians, thus Maniu's premiership represented some measure of hope for the Hungarian minority groups too. Maniu introduced a large measure of decentralization, remodelled Rumania into seven large Directorates, based on the historic units, each enjoying wide local autonomy. In spite of his efforts, it seemed that Rumanian economy was in fateful condition already.

"Transylvania", — said Captain Cazalet in the British House of Commons, on May 10th 1928, — "for its size, should be one of the richest countries of the world and certainly one of the greatest grain-exporting countries in Europe. What is her situation to-day? She has to import wheat, and I have seen what were the finest farms in Europe, which people came from all over the world to inspect, ruined through maladministration and idiotic laws." (#759).

Maniu could not help anymore. A corrupt administration came across the Carpathians and exercised a most detructive influence on the Transylvanian economy and community. The extreme chauvinism which was expressed by that administration filled even the Transylvania Wallachians with disgust. "No one in Transylvania has gained anything by the annexation of Roumania Everyone lost. It is much worse now, than ever before." (#760). Vaida-Voievod admitted that — "law and justice had more respect in Hungary than in Roumania." (#761).

On Dec. 12, 1929, in the elections, at last free of pressure and corruption, the Peasants' Party scored a great victory. On June 6, 1930, Prince Carol surprisingly arrived by airplane, and was accepted by Maniu. The parliament (June 8) revoked the law excluding him from the throne. Michael was put aside in favor of his father and Carol II became the king of Rumania. (#762). It became clear very soon, that his return represented the return of dictatorship too. The King brought back Mme Lupescu, and attempted to establish his personal rule. On Oct. 6, 1930, Maniu resigned, because of ill health. He was succeeded by his lieutenant, George Mironescu. (#763). On Dec. 23, Ion Duca became the leader of the Liberal Party. He was one of the extreme Rumanian nationalists; his appearance represented bad news for Transylvania. On Apr. 18, 1931, the King appointed a coalition (National Union) cabinet under Prof. Nicholas Iorga, his former tutor. This was regarded as a prelude to a royal dictatorship. (#764). A new electoral law assigned 60% of the seats in parliament to "professional groups." In the June, 1931 elections, one of the most corrupt ones in Balkanic history, the Peasants' Party was defeated.

While in the Little Entente States, the minority problems forced the governments to abandon liberal-democratic systems replacing them with authoritarian, and later with Fascist methods, in Hungary, revisionism found gradual connections with Mussolini's Italy, one of the revisionist Powers in postwar Europe. After 1930, it seemed that in Central and

---

#759: **"The Hungarian Question in the British Parliament."** (Speeches, Questions and Answers thereto in the House of Lords and the House of Commons from 1919 to 1930. Grant Richards, London, 1933.) p. 364.

#760: Stephen Pop-Csicso, **"Adeverul"**, 1928. February. Quoted from Zathureczky: **"Transylvania."** p. 42, and p. 49.

#761: **Ibid.** p. 42. (From the **"Patria"**, Oct. 26, 1928.) (Note: Vaida-Voevod became Premier in 1932.)

#762: (1930-1940).

#763: Simultaneously the "optants' dispute with Hungary settled by the Brocchi Plan. (Worked out by Italy and England). Hungary was to receive contributions from Czechoslovakia and from other countries.

#764: We introduced many quotations from him in previous chapters.

East-Central Europe, cut up by superificial and irresponsible "peace" treaties, mainly only two types of states existed: "statusquo states" and "revisionist states". It also seemed, that, — as sorrowful and bloody shadows of Versailles and Trianon, — both the "statusquo" states and "revisionists" tended to adopt fascism. The "status-quo" states could not govern their artificial, multinational countries with democratic methods, and extreme nationalism in dominative position was able to oppress existing nationalism in oppressed position only by totalitarian dictatorship. The "revisionist states" were disappointed by the "peacemaking" methods of western "democracies". The rise of Italy and Nazi Germany offered new hopes for revision.

In Hungary, all the political parties (right, center or left) desired revision. The difference between the "extreme right" (antisemite) the center (monarchists, legitimists, liberals, etc.), and the left (socialdemocrats) was, that the "extreme right" (led by Julius Gömbös) tended to connect Hungarian revisionism to Italy, and later to Germany.

As a reaction after the Béla Kun Bolshevik dictatorship, the rightist elements ruled the political arena. On Nov. 11, 1926, Hungary reestablished the "Upper House", where the landed aristocracy re-appeared, altough far behind its earlier political power, similarly to the power and position of the British House of Lords. On Apr. 5, Hungary managed the "Treaty of Friendship" with Mussolini's Italy, which began her political invasion against the Little Entente and its supporter, France. From the Hungarian side, this Treaty was associated with the growing agitation for revision, which was also ardently supported in England by the Rothermere press.

> "The hope for a peaceful revision of the intolerable Trainon Treaty definitely restored legality and a stable order in Hungary." — wrote Tibor Eckhardt, former leader of the Smallholder Agrarian Party, (who was in opposition against the fascist elements, ex-Army officers, the jobless youth, the despairing rements, ex-army officers, the jobless youth, the despairing refugees, incurably homesick, clung to this idea as the last hope for the betterment of their miserable fate. No victorious king has ever been given such spontaneous acclaim as was showered on Lord Rothermere, when he visited Hungary . . . The people of Hungary stood unanimously and firmly by their single demand: the equitable revision of the unjust Trianon settlement by peaceful means. This was not warmongering, it was the only possible peace policy." (#765).

Eckhardt, and other anti-fascist elements (they represented an overwhelming majority) wished revision, but by using the means of diplomacy. Tht "extreme right" was not so peaceful. They had their own ways (#766), and connection with Mussolini, (later with Hitler), seemed to promise two things for them: (a) revision, (b) power in internal affairs. They were the loudest agitators for revision, and the Hungarian people desired revision so much that millions were ready to have alliance even with the devil himself for the sake of revision. Revisionism was the main reason, that Archduke Otto (son of Charles IV), pretender to the throne, was able to reach his majority. Not only revisionists, but anti-fascist elements favoured him. A. Habsburg seemed to be a better solution, than fascism.

#765: Tibor Eckhardt: "Regicide at Marseille." American Hungarian Library and Historical Society, New York, 1964. "The Hungarian Movement for Revision." pp. 96-97.

#766: In Jan. 1928, and in Jan. 1933, certain shipments of arms were discovered. They were shipped from Italy. The Little Entente protested. However, it was the activity of he fascists. Official Hungary was looking for peaceful means of revising Trianon, in the early 1930-s.

On August 15, 1931, France granted a loan Hungary, evidently on condition that revisionist agitation should cease. (#767). It was too late. Count Bethlen, the master of Hungarian consolidation since the War, realized, that depression, hope for revision (by Mussolini), aids the extremists in political life. Being uable to cope with the financial and political situation, he resigned. His friend, Count Julius Károlyi, took his place, but — under the pressure of Mussolini, — on Oct. 4,1932, Julius Gömbös, extreme reactionary and anti-Semite, former leader of the "Awakening Magyars" (#768) became the Prime Minister. Horthy, the Regent did not like his political attitude, but he was a revisionist, with excellent connections with Mussolini. He opposed the restoration of the Habsburgs, and promised the realization of Hungarian territorial claims, first by close co-operation with Fascist Italy, and, beginning with 1933 (#769), by co-operation with German Nazism. The signature of the Rome Protocols, establishing close political and economic ties between Italy, Austria, and Hungary (March. 17, 1934), and forming a bloc in opposition to the Francophil Little Entente, was part of his policy. (#770).

Bucharest witnessed the changing international situation with growing attention and anxiety. The historical example of the Dual Monarchy proved, that a multinational state could not survive a great international storm. Rumania had real reason for fear, looking at her 1930 census:

Total population	17,793,252	
Rumanians	12,980,033	72.95% of the total
Magyars	1,426,178	population.
Germans	740,169	
Jews	725,318	
Ukrainians	577,693	
Russians	415,217	
Bulgarians	361,058	
Turks, and Tatars	28,793	
Gypsies	278,793	
Serbs	(80,000)	
Czechs and Slovaks	(50,000)	
Poles	(50,000)	
Armenians	(12,00)	
Greeks	(10,000)	(#771).

#767: Hungary suffered severely from the general world depression.

#768: The "Awakening Magyars" were led by Iván Héjjas (relative of Horthy) after 1920. They were fascist radicals, and anti-Semites. In the late 1920-es Julius Gömbös was the most prominent member of this group.

#769: The advent of Hitler, and the National Socialist Germany led to the rapid spread of Nazi agitation to Hungary.

#770: Gömbös' hope was that Germany and Italy could both be brought to support the Hungarian claims. He rejected the Franco-Czech plans for a Danubian Federation. (Dec. 1933).

#771: Statistical numbers (not in bracket) are from Hugh Seton Watson's "Eastern Europe Between the Wars." Appendix, p. 415. His datas were from the "Statesman's Yearbook." 1944, and they contain the official Rumanian census of December 29, 1930. The numbers in bracket were estimations from C. A. Macartney's "National States and National Minorities." Oxford University Ppress, London, 1934. (pp. 510-534). Of course, these estimations did not appear in the number of the total population as minorities. In every probability, the 1930 Rumanian census counted the smaller minorities as Rumanians. Of the Magyars, about 1,200,000 populated Transylvania, the rest was in the Regat, and in Bukovina.

"According to the census of 1930, in Transylvania proper, with a population of 2,870,751, the Rumanians numered 1,657,923; thus froming only a slight majority of 56.1 per cent. Even after the expatriation of 197,000 Hungarians from Transylvania, there still remained in 1930, 826, 796 Hungarians." (#772).

On May 31, Professor-Iorga resigned, after failure to secure a loan from France, and a new cabinet was formed by Alexander Vaida-Voevod, leader of the Peasant Party. In the same year, the Peasants won a great victory in the elections, but their position was weakened by the inability of Maniu to get along with the king and by rivalry between Maniu and Vaida-Voevod. On Oct.20, Maniu took over the premiership again. (#773).

On Jan 1933, a system of League supervision of Rumanian finances was introduced for four years. In the same year Bucharest concluded a "Pact of Non-Aggression" with Russia, which recognized now Rumanian Bessarabia. On Nov. 14, 1933, Ion Duca, and the Liberals took over the Cabinet. The Peasants Party disintegrated. "Liberal Party" did not mean "liberalism" in Rumania, thus their return represented return of dictatorship over the minorities. It was not enough. Rumania took further steps on the road of fascism. On Dec. 29,1933, Duca was assassinated by members of the "Iron Guard", a fascist, strongly anti-Semitic organization, led by Corneliu Codreanu. Martial law was proclaimed at once. The Liberals attempted to resist the Iron Guard. Its leaders were arrested. George Tartarescu took over the leadership. Nicholas Titulescu, minister of Foreign Affairs tried to form an international alliance system against the growing revisionist movements in Central Europe. The conclusion of the Balkan Pact (Febr. 8, 1934) among Rumania, Yugoslavia, Greece and Turkey aimed at stopping revisionism, which associated with fascism already. However, Rumania's attempt for status-quo led her to the practice of fascism.

On May, 1934, King Carol, (with his chief "adviser", Mme Lupescu), — after a plot against his life, — was working on the establishment of a totalitarian dictatorship already. As a reaction, the Liberals allied themselves with the Peasants' Party. (#774). It was too late. The court was overshadowed by the rapid spread of fascism and anti-Semitism. In 1936, the anti-Semitic "Christian League" (#775) was the "opposition" against the fascist, and anti-Semitic "Iron Guard". The anti-German Titulescu was forced to resign. On Dec. 21,1937, the king appointed Octavian Goga, as prime minister. The new head of the cabinet (#776) at once embarked upon an orgy of anti-Semitic legislation. It was still not enough for some bloodthirsty Wallachian groups. Traditional Rumanian Anti-Semitism was associated with anti-Hungarianism again. They wished to prove, that with the adoption of an extreme totalitarian system, Rumania will resist revisionism. If Hungary was searching for fascist aid, Rumania wished to preserve domination of Transylvania, — as a fascist State!

On Jan. 18, King Carol dissolved the Parliament. On Febr. 10, he dismissed Goga. A new cabinet was formed, containing several former premiers, under the leadership of the patriarch, Miron Christea. The constitution was suspended, and all political parties were suppressed. (#777).

#772: Tibor Eckhardt: "Regicide at Marseille." p. 86.

#773: Until January 5, 1933.

#774: Even Maniu and Vaida-Voevod reconciliated.

#775: Headed by Prof. A. C. Cuza, led by the poet Octavian Goga. A wing of the Peasants' Party participated too, led by Vaida-Voevod.

#776: Actually, he gained only 10% of the votes in the election.

#777: These moves were violently opposed both by the fascist Iron Guard and by the Peasants' Party of Maniu. Only Maniu's movement aimed to return to a somewhat more liberal regime. The Iron Guard and the Government were both fascists, only the Iron Guard was more extreme.

Rigid censorship was instituted. In Transylvania, the Hungarian spirit was still very much alive. "The Transylvanian press, suffering under heavy censorship, lost its provincial character and rose to the European level. The Transylvanian Literary Guild and the Transylvanian Helicon gathered the writers and established a Hungarian Publishing Co-operative. A new and specifically Transylvanian literature was born. Struggling with poverty and by the Roumanian authoritise, the Hungarian stage reached an unprecedented peak against all odds." (#778). Just as it was in the days of the independent Transylvanian Principality of the 16—17 centuries, the Magyar culture of Transylvania, separated from Hungary proper, unfolded into a unique phenomenon of regional and national individuality. It was not part of the Rumanian culture. It was a unique part of Western culture.

The Transylvanian Hungarians — between two awakening forces of fascism, (one of them aiming to reconquer Transylvania, the other to preserve domination,) — were forced to search for strength and resources within their own numbers in order to survive. A new naitional pride and consciousness appeared. It was not Rumanian at all, but it was not identical with the emotions of Hungary proper either. (#779). The Transylvanian Jews proved to be faithful allies again. Not only through financial help, but by their writers and artists, they became part of the Hungarian culture once again.

The Transylvanian Germans, on the other hand, did not participate in this effort. They sympathised with Rumanian fascism, which was similar to the simultaneously rising Nazism in Germany. The Saxons did not like the Transylvanian Magyar-Jew associations. They were proud to belive, that Hitler's Germany became a great Power again. When fascist Rumania tried every possible way to obtain good relations with Germany, the Transylvanian Saxons received privileges from Bucharest. Facing the opposition of the Magyars, Jews, and the Wallachian Peasants' Party members of Transylvania, the Rumanian government attempted to work together with the Transylvanian Saxons at least. The Saxons were willing to co-operate with Bucharest.

Transylvanian Magyar nationalism based itself on the old. classical, patriotic ideals, without the adoptation of the semi-feudal, semi-fascist side-effects, which appeared in Hungarian revisionism, after 1930. Let me quote here one typical example of Transylvanian poetry of the late 1930-es. In this poem, the author expressed the Magyar emotions, desiring to preserve the national language and culture.

„To the Magyars of Transylvania." (from "Végvári", transl. to Engl. by Watson Kirkconnell).

"Let the inevitable come at last,
When flagging arms in anguish'd stress no longer
Can stey the ruthless avalanche of time!
Yet be our kinship stronger!
If we no more can be a shouted word,
In secret brotherhood let Magyars grow! —
To emigrate, to hide ourselves? O never!
From hence we will not go!"

#778: Zathureczky: "Transylvania." p. 46.
#779: The foundation of this new attitude of self-reliance was the large mass of the Transylvanian peasantry. The Transylvanian Agricultural Society, created by the big landowners before the war, became the organization of the small farmers. The Transylvanian Unitarian Church preserved its good connections with England, etc.

"Out of the flame of straw-fires there in left
A handful of red embers in our hearts, —
A thousandfold more hot than burning worlds
Or aught that heat imparts.
Upon each other's heart-wall, in the night
Of this our doom, we tap our rataplan,
One signal in these catacombs of death:
We stay Hungarian!"

"Here is time's depths lurk many forms of death,
And much may come to pass; but nome so clever
Lives under Heaven as can build a coffin
To bury us forever!
On poet-lips, the tree of Magyar spech
Shall sprout anew in buds and branches vernal;
Indomitable force in floods shall sing:
'Our spirit lives eternal!' "

"Ere this we have kept vigil, feigning death!
More weight than moans the muffled voice commands,
And cryptic words are mightier far than plain,
Steel'd hearts than steel-clad hands.
The down-pent muscles of the iron spring
Do not let go, but slowly gather strenght;
Greater oppression breeds but greeter power
That will strike back at length."

"Ere this we have kept vigil, feigring death!
We have stood many a storm, nor is this new,
Torn up before, we once again took root,
Whatever ill winds blew.
I do not say that worse times will not come
When, with our lives low-trodden in the mud,
No one shall hear a word or ev'n a moan:
Only our hearts' low thud —
Beating with Magyar blood!" (#780.)

The answer of the Rumanians had a very different tone. Ignoring the sad, national spirit of the Transylvanian Magyar minority, they turned against Hungary proper, with extreme hatred:
"While the Hungarian revisionist jackale contented themselves with howling at the moon, the Rumanians were content to spit in contempt. But today this concert of mangy curs has been joined by one whom, until now, we had considered as our brother." . . . "The howling jackals of the plains who turn their muzzles towards us may know that we shall nevermore be their serfs, that we shall nevermore populate their prisons. The worms may draw marrow from their bones and the spirits may make soap from the rotten fat of these fools of the plains." "God help the Hungarians on that day when the Rumanians consent to revision; because they will kick up the frontiers with the points of their boots and will wipe from the face of the earth that dirt which a fly blew unto the map of Europe and which vitiates the air" "We shall sit down in the Royal Palace of Budapest and stay there." "Let the Hungarian packs of the plains know that the Transylvanian Rumanians will delay the crossing of the Tisza by one night, by a St. Bartholomew night, in which they will extirpate every single Hungarian. (#781).

#780: The poet's name was Alexander Reményik (1890-1940). He wrote his poems in the capital of Transylvania, Kolozsvár (Rum: Cluj) under the name of "Végvári" (Eng: "Man from the Frontier-fortress.")

#781: C. A. Macartney (in his **"Hungary and Her Successors."** p. 290) quotes from the **Danubian Review** (December, 1936).

Reading these sentences of extreme nationalism and hatred, these sentences of extreme brutalities and vulgarities (#782), we should keep in mind, that Bucharest regarded the Transylvanian minority problem, as an effort of Hungary proper to "reconquer" this land some day. The Rumanian nationalist "intelligentsia" ignored the fact, that the real base of the minority problem was, that the Transylvanian Magyars and Székelys suffered from various discrimination, consequently desired some sort of change, and obviously hoped, that this change will come from the revisionist tendencies of Central Europe. Bucharest was too excited during these years, and its excitement even increased, when it was informed, that King Alexander of Yugoslavia (#783) and M. Barthou, foreign secretary of France were assassinated at Marseilles. It turned out that the assassins had operated from Hungary. Rumanian officials viewed this case as the first aggressive step of Hungarian revisionism. Acute danger of conflict developed, but the matter was finally adjusted by the League of Nations which, in a masterpiece of diplomatic circumlocution, mildly rebuked the Hungarian government. (#784). (The final investigation, actually, discovered that the assassin was a Macedonian revulutionary, working with Croat revulutionists, having headquarters in Hungary. (#785).

In Hungary, many officials sympathised with the rise of Italian and German revisionism, because it seemed, that Italy (or Germany, or simultaneously both of them) will aid Hungarian revisionism. Mussolini was much more favoured, than Hitler. The Hungarian Government considered, that Nazi power was a new reappearence of the "Drang nach Osten", and Hitler could easily reintroduce it in a much more totalitarian way, than the Habsbugs ever did. The Hungarian economic-social system could be called "feudalcapitalism" at this time. It was a quite close association of impoverished noblemen, and wealthy members of the neolog Jewish class, assimilated to be Hungarian in the last two generation. These elements wished revision, of course, but — if possible, — not by the aid of Adolf Hitler.

The elections of 1935 (#786) proved that fascist agitators could not influence the Hungarian society. On June 1, Count Bethlen and his followers (in opposition, since Julius Gömbös was the prime minister) joined the other very important opposition group, the Agrarian Party of Tibor Eckhardt, which resented the dictatorial methods of Gömbös and suspected him of plans against the constitution.

On Oct. 6, Gömbös died and was succeeded by Koloman Darányi. The new premier represented no change in "rightist" policy, but tried to follow a somewhat more conciliatory course.

The following months did not seem to fit into the Hungarian plan for revision. Hitler did not show too much interest, (and many of the Hungarian politicians did not mind this at all, because it was suspected, that any German "aid" would put the Carpathian Basin under German „protectorate"). Mussolini was busy with the Mediterranean problems and with the

---

#782: Macatney feels that the language that Rumanians were using was "typical of the language in which many young pseudo-educated Roumanians are beginning to indulge." (C. A. Macartney: **"Hungary and Her Successors."** p. 290.)

#783: Alexander I (1921-34) was the son of King Peter Karageorgevich.

#784: December 10, 1934.

#785: The headquarters was at Jankapuszta, a concentrated camp for Croat refugees. The international and national investigation could find no evidence about any connection of the Croat conspirators with the Hungarian government. (**Inf.** T. Eckhardt: **"Regicide at Marseille".** pp. 128-9).

#786: Apr. 11. (The opposition groups polled 1,041,000 votes against 908,000 for the government, but the intricate electoral system enabled the government to retain its majority in seats in the Chamber.

Ethiopian crisis (#787). The formation of the Rome-Berlin Axis (#788) involved the sacrifice of Austria by Mussolini.

It was clear now, that Italy was weak to support Hungarian revisionism, and any coming "support" form the Axis could result in more danger for Hungary, than adventage. Under these circumstances, Darányi, during 1937, drew closer to Austria, and Hungary began to seek contact with the Little Entente. The Hungarian Nazis (led by Ferenc Szálasi) protested vigorously. (This, relatively small group was almost identical (as far as character and internal policy is concerned) with the Rumanian Iron Guard, but the fact, that the Iron Guard (#789) was fascist, and was anti-Semite, did not attract the Hungarian fascists (#790), because the Iron Guard advocated the cruel discrimination against all Rumanian national minorities, not only the Jews. The Szálasi-group was revisionist too.)

On March 5, 1957, the existence of a Nazi plot was revealed in Hungary Szálasi, and other conspirators (who hoped, and worked for Hitler's interference) were arrested, but they were treated mildly. (#791).

On Oct. 11, Eckhardt and his Agrarian Party joined with the Legitimists. They represented quite different political points of views, but facing the danger of fascism, unification seemed to be the best solution. Even the Social Democrats became friendly to the idea of Habsburg restoration as the most effective way to block the fascist elements. When the various fascist groups were united to form the Hungarian National Socialist Party (#792), efforts were made to glorify the regent, Admiral Horthy, and to further his son's candidacy for the throne. (#793). On February, 1938, Szálasi was arrested again (#794) and drastic steps were taken to stamp out the Nazi movement. It was too late.

The Anchluss brought the powerful Germany to the Hungarian broder. The large German element in Hungary (#795) became more restless, and the Nazi danger became more urgent. The government was not in the position to co-operate with the Little Entente, and of course, the idea of the Hagsburg restoration became irrealistic. The Cabinet of Béla Imrédy (#796 imitated some sort of semi fascism (#797) attempting to satisfy both Hitler and the Hungarian Nazis. The acquisition of Southern Slovakia, as a result of the dismemberment of Czechoslovákia (#798) was received by a sort of confusion by many leading Hungarian politicians.

#787: The clash between Italian and Ethiopian troops at Ualual (Dec. 5, 1934) was followed by an agreement bw. France and Italy (Jan, 1935). On Oct. 3, the Italian forces began the invasion of Ethiopia, which was annexed in May 1936.

#788: Oct. 27, 1936. It was followed by the denunciation of Versailles by Hitler.

#789: The nucleus of the Iron Guard was the "Legion of Archangel Michael", formed in the 1920-es, by C. Z. Codreanu.

#790: They called themselves "Nyilaskeresztes" ("Arrow-cross"). This symbol imitated the svastika, and also tried to symbolize both Árpád, the Conqueror (the arrow), and Christianity (the cross).

#791: The Hungarian government could not go too far in the shadow of Hitler, who appeared openly as the protector of the Hungarian Nazis.

#792: Under the leadership of Szálasi, the "Hungarian Hitler."

#793: His son was István (Stephen) Horthy. The regent in his memoirs (**"Ein Leben für Ungarn", (Eng: "A Life for Hungary"**) denied this attempt.

#794: (Febr. 1938.) with 72 associates. They were sentenced to prison.

#795: C. 500,000 Germans of Hungary became enthusiastic receiving the news about the German annexation of Austria. (March 13, 1938).

#796: Formed his Cabinet on the day of the Anschluss.

#797: With the limitation of Jewish activity in business and the various professions.

#798: The Münich Conference (Sept. 29, 1938) returned some Magyar populated areas to Hungary, and established German hegemony in Central Europe.

148

These stormy series of political events were witnessed from Rumania with growing anxiety. First let me introduce the feelings of the various minority groups in Transylvania, and after, we will take a look at the position of the Rumanian government.

We mentioned already, that the emotions of the Transylvanian Magyars were not identical with the emotions of "official" Hungary, and were not even similar to the emotions of the Hungarian Nazis. Were the Transylvanian Hungarians revisionists? Yes, they were, because revisionism was the only way to get rid of Rumanian nationalistic discrimination. They sympathise with Horthy, with the former Hungarian prime Minister, Stephen Bethlen (#799), and with Tibor Eckhardt. The Transylvanian neolog Jews (assimilated to the Hungarian middle class) had good family connection with their relatives in Hungary. The Transylvanian Magyars and Székelys realized that Julius Gömbös (and, more so, Ferenc Szálasi) were fascists, — and they knew very well the character of fascism, knowing the Rumanian Iron Guard. Connection with Austria and Mussolini represented some hope for Transylvanian Magyars, but, after the Anschluss, it was clear, that Hitler's "help" will be accompanied by German domination in East-Central Europe, probably even in Transylvania. Carol managed to arrest Codreanu (#800), but his surprising visit to Hitler made clear to the Transylvanian Magyars, that Transylvania could not hope any benefit in the focus of various fascist and semi-fascist forces.

"Carol . . . ended his tour with a surprisingly successful visit to Hitler. He promised the latter increased economic collaboration but evoked Rumania's paramount interest in Transylvania and discussed the problem of the stategic importance of the Carpatho-Ukraine as a possible direct territorial and military link with Germany." (#801.

In these circumstances, the Transylvanian Magyars were divided. "A minority, influenced by the ideas of the extreme Left, remained equally opposed to the Bucharest and Budapest regimes, but the majority allowed themselves to be convinced by the intellectuals and politicians of the old Transylvanian Hungarian ruling class, and regarded Roumanian rule as the cause of all their woes." (#802).

The writers of Transylvania "have taken to heart the teaching of history and of Nature, deriving from them a messianic spirit, at higher morality, an ideal transcending racial differences . . . This consciousness of a spiritual mission rises to philosophic heights in Alexander Reményik, Transylvania's 'poet prophet' (#803) . . . "Thrown back upon themselves, the Transylvanian Magyars had to take count of their resources and draw from their own inheritance the material with which to build up a new life." (#804). However, this hoped "new life", which was planned as a "real Transylvanian life" was confused again among the forces of German, Hungarian and Rumanian fascism, and semi-fascism. Anti-revisionism was dangerous, because it represented the extremism of Bucharest, and the danger of final ethno-linguistic annihilation. Revisionism was a sweet term in Transylvanian Magyar circles only until the "Anschluss". After that it was associated with Hitler, and with Szálasi.

#799: He belonged to the Catholic branch of the Transylvanian Bethlens.

#800: He was condemned to 10 years at hard labor for treason (May, 27, 1938), and he and 13 other Iron Guardists were shot by their guards on Nov. 30. On March 6, 1939. Armand Calinescu became premier on the death of Patriarch Christea.

#801: Ghita Ionescu: "Communism in Rumania." Oxford Univ. Press, London, 1964. "Introduction", p. 55.

#802: H. Seton-Watson: Eastern Europe Between the Wars." p. 302.

#803: See pp. 145-146, and #780 again.

#804: Caspar Ernyei: "The Spirit of ransylvania." ("The Hung. Quarterly." Vol. VI. No. 2, Summer, 1940. pp. 228-229). (The same article mentions Mária Berde, Joseph Nyirö, Aron Tamássy, etc. as leading literary personalities.)

Did the Transylvanian Magyar majority desire to choose revisionism, because they were rather pro-German, than pro-Rumanian?

No, it was not the reason at all. Since the meeting of Hitler and King Carol, Germanism and Rumanian nationalism were not opposing things anymore. The official Hungarian government arrested Szálasi, just as Carol arrested Codreanu, and the Transylvanian Magyars hoped, that Budapest would be able to succeed at satisfying Hitler, and occuping (at least part of) Transylvania. The Transylvanian Magyar minority desired change, because aggressive Rumanization led to gradual "linguicide" of Hungarian minorities. The following census statistics indicate the shift brought about by the forcible Rumanization practiced among the population of the twenty-five largest Transylvanian cities:

	Hungarian sovereignty		Rumanian sovereignty	
Census	1890	1910	1938	
Hungarians	58.8%	65.3%	46.6%	
Rumanians	15.8%	15.6%	52.0%	(#805)

The hopes of the Transylvanian Magyars became more realistic, when Premier Imrédy resigned (#806), and the great (Transylvanian originated) geographer ond historian, Count Paul Teleky (#807) became the head of the next Cabinet (He suddenly suppressed the leading fascist organization, yet ot the same time, to placate Germany, joined the anti-communist pact of Germany, Japan and Italy.). When Hungary occupied Carpatho Ukraine, securing at last, the long desired common frontier with Poland, Transylvanian public opinion was, that the re-occupation of Transylvania will be the next step in this line of partial revision. (#808).

The Transylvanian Saxons viewed Hitler's successes, as a general German glory. Previously they were allied with the Rumanian officials against the Magyars, now, they changed sides again. According to their information, Hungary will be enlarged with Transylvania, but the whole Carpathian Basin will be dominated by Germany, — consequently, Transylvania will be dominated by the Transylvanian Germans! This delight was confused with many things: the best Magyar patriots of Transylvania were associated with Jews; many Transylvanian Magyars were antifascists; and, on the other hand: the Saxons found out, that Codreanu's death did not stop German-Rumanian negotiations Bucharest itself attempted to work together with Berlin.

The Transylvanian Wallachians were even more confused. Revisionism, the occupation of Hungarian populated Slovakia and Carpatho Ukraine showed, that in Transylvania, the Magyars will become the dominating factor again. But the Transylvanian Magyars were not fascists, and Bucharest, on the other hand, became more ond more fascist! What to do now? To choose fascism, and associate both with Bucharest and with Berlin at the expense of the Transylvanian Magyars? It seemed to be a logical step. But the Transylvanian Wallachians were supporters of the suppressed Peasants' Party of Maniu, and most of them were anti-fasicists! In these stormy months, the Transylvanian Magyars and Wallachians, for the first time in their history, had a common, secret, perhaps unrealistic desire: independent Transylvania!

#805: M. Eugene Osterhaven: **"Transylvania."** "Population". p. 12.

#806: The Nazis, whom he had tried to outdo in his anti-Semitic policy, had taunted him with his own Jewish ancestry.

#807: I quoted from his book (**"Evolution of Hungary".**) many times in this work. He made the best ethnographic map of Transylvania.

#808: On Apr. 11, Hungary withdrew from the League under the pressure of Germany. The elections of May, 28, 1939, showed, that the Hungarians did not choose Nazism. The government secured 180 seats out of 260.

Bucharest, in the mean time, attempted to be a faithful German satellite. King Carol knew Rumanian history very well. He knew, that Rumania was able, not only to survive, but to grow, using and practicing an old "morality": "might is right". The Wallachians balanced wonderfully in old times between Russia, Austria and Turkey. The best result of this balancing was the birth of Greater Rumania. Now, Carol realized, that the continuation of this balancing policy was necessary to survive.

"The Rumanians have always been able in the past to be on all sides and to end up with the winner. They profited very handsomely in the first war by these tactics, and King Carol apparently decided to act accordingly . . . King Carol has been considered so much of a playboy that his abilities have been underrated. He was a typical Balkan ruler, with his passions, tenacity, ruthlessness and indifference to Western opinion." (#809).

When Carol realized, that Hitler was willing to co-operate with Rumania, the Rumanian ruler became even more ambitious. He knew that he had to fight. Transylvania was at stake!

Surprisingly, the Teleki Government did not prove to be too nationalistic. Having only quite cool connections with Hitler, they did not wish to use Nazi power for re-occupation of Transylvania. On the other hand: Teleki was an ethnographer, and a liberal-minded scientist of ethnolinguistic minority problems. His idea was identical with the Transylvanian desire: to create an independent Transylvania! His foreign minister, Csáky, represented this idea in discussions with German officials.

". . . Csáky said that his present idea was that if Roumania broke up, an independest, tri-national State should be formed in Transylvania. Hungary did not wont to annex this state since the elements in it opposed to this would be too large for her to assimilate." (#810).

However, both Hungary and Rumania could not master political changes in East-Central Europe anymore. Hitler held the power of decision. Transylvania arrived to a new stage in her unfortunate history. The minority groups found themselves in a new, unpleasant situation.

#809: John Flournoy Montgomery: **"Hungary, the Unwilling Satellite."** "The Downfall of Rumania." pp. 133-134.
#810: C. A. Macartney: **"October Fifteenth."** (**"A History of Modern Hungary"** "1929-1945") Edinburgh, at the University Press, 1957. Part I., "An Axis Policy" p. 321.

XVII.

THE DISMEMBERMENT OF TRANSYLVANIA

The year of 1939 still offered various alternatives for Rumania, and Carol did not know what to choose. Miron Christea, the patriarch and prime minister died in March, and was succeeded by Armand Calinescu, minister of the interior in the former government. One month later, Great Britain and France guaranteed Rumanian independence and integrity, following the German annihilation ofCzechoslovikia and rumors of a German ultimatum to Rumania. But Carol hoped to co-operate with Hitler, because, personally he was a beliver of German victory in a coming war and, secondly, friendship with Nazi Germany could save Transylvania for Bucharest. King Carol was well informed about the returning compunctions in Britain about the Treaty of Trianon. Hitler seemed to have a better hand than Chamberlain in this game. (#811). A trade-treaty (signed in March, 1939) put the Rumanian industry under German control already. Carol was ready to extend this agreement to the political-military ground too.

Elections were held on a corporative basis in June. (#812). The new Rumanian government seemed to be strong enough. All the leading political figures (including the old Maniu) became members. Carol tried to overrule the Iron Guard, and experienced, with shocking surprise that Hitler supported them, — behind his back! However, Carol still had a hope. Receiving the news about the Ribbentrop-Molotov Pact (#813), it still seemed, that Rumania, with her traditional luck in international affairs, will be able to preserve her frontiers.

When Germany invaded Poland (#814), both Hungary and Rumania declared neutrality for different reasons. The Hungarian Government knew, that the invasion of Poland was only the "next step", and many other steps will follow it, but the traditional friendship with Poland made a declaration of neutrality necessary. Bucharest had an other reason. The "Blitzkrieg" separated it from the Western allies. Carol could not even hope for aid from the West. Carol sympathized with Hitler, but it was too early to declare this sympathy. The obvious step was the declaration of neutrality. (#815). The collapse of France in the summer of 1940 removed the last prop of Rumanian morale. Understanding that the Nazis demanded a bigger role for the Iron Guard in Rumanian political life, the king agreed to form a totalitarian national party, which included Iron Guardists, under Horia Sima.

Rumania really could not do anything else, but to obey Hitler. Consequently, Bucharest faced a very angry Moscow, and it seemed, that the traditional Rumanian luck ran out. On June 26, 1940, the Soviet Union demanded Bessarabia and Northern Bukovina. Two days later, Rumania yielded, and evacuated these territories. Bucharest was forced now, to play with open cards. On July 1, 1940, Rumanian Premier Tatarescu renounced formally the Anglo-French guarantee to his country, and stated, that future Rumanian policy will be aligned within the "new orientation in Europe."

#811: Neville Chamberlain (pr. min. from May, 28, 1937) still believed the success of the "appeasement" at this time.

#812: Women could vote and, for the first time in Humanian history, compete as candidates, but only for the senate.

#813: August 23, 1939.

#814: September 1, 1939.

#815: Carol went so far, that, when Prem. Calinescu was assassinated by the Iron Guard (succeeded by Argeseanu, later by Argetoianu, and Tatarescu), the king did not even investigate the case.

". . . King Carol tried to ingratiate himself and save his throne. But his country had other territorial debts to pay. First, Bulgaria demanded the return of Southern Dobrudja, which Rumania had acquired in 1913 as the result of the Second Balkan War.. The province had never had a Rumanian majority respite considerable efforts at colonizing it whith Rumanians." (#816.

At the Treaty of Craiova (Aug. 23, 1940) Southern Dobrudja was ceded to Bulgaria.

Simultaneously, the Rumanians planned to build a line of fortifications against Hungary, the "Imaginescu line" as the Bucharest wits called it. The Hungarians now demanded large parts of Transylvania. The negatiations began in July under Axis auspices. Carol was willing to cede to Hungary a strip of land along the frontier, but the Hungarians wanted much more.

"In August, 1940, wishing to bring all South-Eastern Europe under their control, and finding the existence of frontier disputes and revisionist claims in that region inconvenient, the Axis Dictators themselves decided to 'solve' the Transylvanian Question by Partition. The Vienna 'Award' gave about half of Trannylvania, including Cluj (Kolozsvár) and the Szekler counties to Hungary." (#817).

Hungary received about 1,000,000 Hungarians and 1,100,000 Rumanians.

Rumanian resistance in the ordinary sence was not possible. ("King Carol could, in theory at least, have threatened, to destroy the oil refineries . . . This desperate gamble might conceivably have forced the Germans to reconsider, since the Hungarians could make no equally effective threat. But Carol did not take it, despite the overwhelming weight of public opinion, which favored resistance. The decisive factor was the threat made by the Soviet ambassador . . . It is probable that the Russians were trying in this indirect way to serve notice on their allies, the Germans, that they were still interested in the country which the Avis powers were now so busy carving up without consulting Moscow." #818).

Zathureczky reports the following statistics: according to the Rumanian census,

the Northern part had	1,007,170	Hungarians,
	1,166,434	Rumanians,
	60,046	Germans, and
	160,234	other nationalities.
The Southern part had	473,551	Hungarians,
	2,067,723	Rumanians,
	481,128	Germans, and
	133,000	other nationalities. (#819).

Neither Hungary, nor Rumania was satisfied with the Vienna Arbitration. Transylvania became again the victim of Big Power policy, just as twenty years before. (Budapest and Bucharest both expected another settlement after the war). "The new borded, cutting lengthwise across the middle of the country, with complete disregard to geographical economic and administrative endowments, caused severe complications on both sides." (#820).

#816: R. L. Wolff: "The Balkans in Our Time." p. 192.
#817: H. Seton-Watson: "Eastern Europe Between the Wars." p. 302.
#818: R. L. Wolff: "The Balkans in Our Time." p. 193.
#819: Zathureczky: "Transylvania." p. 49.
#820: Ibid. pp. 49-50.

(Note: See MAP on p. 162.)

Nevertheless, the enthusiasm of Magyars was great in both Hungary and Transylvania on the great days of the reannexation. On September 4th. 1940,

"... the Regent of Hungary, as Supreme War Lord, issued an Army Order with the words, 'Forward to the ridge of the Eastern Carpathians!', for 'the injustice done by Trianon has in part been repaired'; 'We are marching now to recover a futher part of our heritage of ten centuries' were the words in which the Regent, who personally led the Hungarian National Defence troops as they crossed that section of the Trianon frontier the roads of which converge on the heart of Transylvania and the ridge of the Eastern Carpathians, defined the object in view". (#821).

The army began its march on September 5th; and in eight days with clockwork precision took possession of the territories that had been allotted to Hungary. On the first day the town of Szatmár (Rum: Satu Mare) welcomtd enthusiastically the Regent riding at the head of his troops. On the second day the old Hungarian city. Negyvárad (Rum: Oradea) became part of Hungary again. "Everywhere the Regent was received by garlanded houses and windows, trimphal arches, thunderous applause, choral addresses and songs, heartfelt jubilation and happiness shining through tears." (#822). The most important event in this long series of joys was undoubtedly the entry into Kolozsvár (Rum: Cluj), on September 15th. "Enormous crowds of inhabitants of the liberated regions made a pilgrimage to Kolozsvár, King Matthias's town, which during centuries the cradle of Hungarian national culture." (#823). "Foreigners must have wondered — and rightly wondered — how this town and all the other towns could ever have been described as and dubbed a Rumanian town: that must have been the impression conveyed by the sight of these enormous crowds of Magyars . . ." (#824). (825).

Let me quote the most interesting sentences from the Regent's message, addressed in Kolozsvár to the enhusiastic orowd:

"I am happy to be able to welcome the re-incorporated regions of Transylvania from Kolozsvár . . . After twenty-two years of bitter ordeals, what I never for a single moment ceased to believe would come to pass, is now an accomplished fact . . . Our fate has set us here on the threshold of East and West; our country was for centuries exposed to eternal warfare waged on the highway of destructive world history; and while other and more fortunate people of Europe were able to increase and augment their forces in peaceful work, the Hungarians were bleeding and being decimated and exterminated in eternal warfare . . . In the meantime foreign nationalities filtered into the country . . . Our ancestors not only received them, but granted them every liberty, ensuring them these privileges by legislation . . . It was not arms that deprived us of our territories, but the so-called treaties of peace . . . May God's blessing guide our nation towards a happy and glorious future!" (#826).

#821: Andrew Fall: "Re-incorporated areas welcome Hungarian soldiers with indescribable enthusiasm." (In the "Danubian Review," Vol. VIII, No. 5, October, 1940.) p. 1.
#822: Ibid.
#823: Ibid. p. 2.
#825: The obvious explanation of the described enthusiasm was, that the re-incorporated cities were still mostly Hungarian populated. The "liberation" of those cities and towns represented opportunities of individual freedom for the oppressed Magyar population.
#826: A. Fall: "Re-incorporated areas welcome H. soldiers ... etc." pp. 3-5.

The partial re-incorporation of Transylvania did not satisfy the revisionists, especially those who were dreaming about the return of the "traditional" Great-Hungary; all the territories which were conquered by Árpád and which were dominated by the greatest Hungarian kings.

"We must not however forget that present-day Hungary is still 120.000 sq. kilometres smaller in area than Hungary of pre-War days, the number of her inhabitants being also 7 million below the figures recorded in the days prior to the first Great War — despite the fact that there has been a very considerable natural increase during the past twenty years." — wrote John Kassay, one of the well known historians of Hungary. (#827).

"Far from settling the problem," — wrote H. Seton-Watson, — it only exacerbated feeling on both sides. Realions between Hungary and Roumania have never been so bad as since August 1940 . . . Roumania will never be content until she has recovered all." (#828).

Some Wallachians who wished to fight for Transylvania looked for the lead in Maniu, the grand old man of Wallachian-Transylvania. He hesitated, because he never supported forces of extreme Rumanian shauvinism, he probably belived the right of the Hungarians for a partial revision, and he realized, that associating with Rumanian nationalism was identical to association with Rumanian fascism. And after all: Maniu realized that Transylvania was not so much under the domination of the enthusiastic Magyars, but rather under the shadow of the Nazi-Stalinist alliance. While he hesitated, the Iron Guard, despite their pro-Greman attitude, led the national protest and demanded the abdication of King Carol, who was made the scapegoat. The king left on Sept. 6, 1940, with Magda Lupescu. leaving his 19-year-old son, Michael on the throne as Mihai I.

Before his departure he entrusted power to a general, Ion Antonescu, who formed a government consisting largely of Iron Guardists, with Horia Sima as vice-premier. The constitution was suspended and Antonescu given full powers. Germany and Italy guaranteed Bucharest, that "Rumania populated by Wallachians" will remain Rumania. It was bad news. Rumania lost about 3,500,000 subjects to the U.S.S.R., 2,400,000 to Hungary and 360,000 (by the return of Southern Dobrudja) to Bulgaria. There were rumours that Germany intended also to separate the Banat from Rumania, but in the end that territory was merely accorded semiautonomy under the large local German minority.

Antonescu, the fascist leader of Rumania, tried to have good connection with Hitler, and to use this connection for the re-annexation of Transylvania to Rumania. When Rumania was declared a "national legionary state" on Sept. 15 and joined the "Tripartite pact" on Nov. 23, (#829) Rumanian fascist offisials, insructed from Bucharest began an unprecedented oppression against Magyar individuals in Southern Transylvania (not restored to Hungary).

The Hungarian government realized that this step represented the renewed Rumanian ambitions, which lost the spirit of Clemenceau in the interwar years, but received a new „protector" now: Adolf Hitler. The Hungarian government also realized, that the Führer did not like the Magyars too much, and probably the Rumanians were willing to be "much more faithful", if necessary, to the Germans — for Transylvania. On 9th

#827: John Kassay: "New Situation in South-Eastern Europe." ("Danubian Review", Vol. VIII. No. 5., Oct. 1940. p. 7.)
#828: H. Seton-Watson: "Eastern Europe Between the Wars." p. 303.
#829: The Anticommitern Pact.

Oct. in Parliament, Count Paul Teleki, speaking of the persecution of Magyars in Rumania, amongst other things said:

"We know why these persecutions are taking place, and why they are permitted. It is in order to obtain a revision of the Vienna Award, which the Rumanian Government asked for, accepted and signed. The aim of the Rumanians is to evade or alter the Vienna-Award. which determined the new frontier but said nothing about an exchange of the populations. Another aim is to force the Magyars to opt and to intimidate those who are too resolute in spirit to flee." (#830).

The Hungarian Prime Minister warned Bucharest, that if Rumania will continue the oppression of Magyars in Southern Transylvania, Hungary will be forced to use serious political measures. Antonescu did not care. "His first meeting with Hitler was successful. By his frankness on the Transylvanian problem, for instance, on which he warned the Führer that the Rumanians would never yield, as well as by his decisiveness, he impressed Hitler as a man to be trusted." — wrote Ionescu, one of the most prominent Rumanian historians. (#831).

The Southern part of Transylvania, filled with the overflow of the Roumanian bureaucratic apparatus which had to evacuate the North, was paralyzed by confusion, and absolutely unable to establish a normal administative, economic and social order. At the same time the Northern part was re-organized by the Hungarians in a matter of weeks. "The inspired labor and the creative power of the Transylvanian Hungarians, free again to be expressed, improved the country to European standards." (#832).

Antonescu, encouraged by the friendship of Hitler, continued the oppression of the Hungarians in Southern Transylvania. ". . . The Hungarian minority was harassed in a most brutal manner by the angered Roumanian administration. Ministers, Protestant and Catholic alike were arrested and beaten . . . Beatings of Hungarians in public places, and even in their own homes, were not only encouraged by the police, but in many cases carried out by them." (#833).

In the time, when any manifestations of the Hungarian minority in Southern Transylvania, whether agricultural commercial, or cultural, were severely repressed, even Germany knew that the Transylvanian problem was only "solved" on a temparory basis by the division, and set the date of "final" arrangements after "the victorious ending of the war". The representatives of the German Government promised the entire territory of Transylvania one day to Hungary, the next day to Rumania, "using it as a whip, to force these two conutries into giving more contributions and assistance in the war." (#834). (On June 21, 1941. Hitler's armies attacked Russia.) The Germans realized that the best trick to secure both Hungarian and Rumanian "co-operations" was: to promise Transylvania to both of them!

German troops had been pouring into Rumania since September, 1940, but as the Germans had decided to reduce Rumania to complete subservience playing off the Iron Guard against Antonescu, the Wehrmacht stood by, when the Iron Guard staged a St. Bartholomew's night on Nov. 28, 1940, in which 64 prominent members of the old regime were assassinated, including Iorga, and the peasant leader Virgil Madgearu. Antones-

---

#830: Ladislas Fritz: "Feverstricken Rumania." ("Danubian Review", Vol. VIII. No. 6, November, 1940. p. 4.)

#831: Ghita Ionescu: "Communism in Rumania. 1944-1962." p. 63.

#832: Zathureczky: "Transylvania." p. 50.

#833: Ibid.

#834: Ibid.

cu now secured German support in putting down the Guard, which staged a more serious riot at the end of January, 1941, under the leadership of Horia Sima, (Vice-premier in Antonescu's "Cabinet"), and Ion Codereanu, father of Corneliu. The revolt was finally suppressed with about 5,000 casualties; Sima escaped.

The new administration formed at the end of January was mainly military, all guardists being excluded. Some 500,000 German troops were in Rumania by February and on February Great Britain broke off diplomatic relations with Rumania.

Antonescu refused to join Adolf Hitler in smashing Rumania's ally, Yugoslavia in April 1941, but all the Wallachians were behind him in entering the war agains tthe U.S.S.R., as Germany's ally on June 22.

In this difficult situtaion, Budapest followed a different path. The Hungarian Government, knowing well that open defiance would bring German occupation and the fate of Poland, tried to get involved as little as possible in the war. The Teleki Cabinet still hoped for some sort of diplomatic solution. when on December 12, 1940, Count Csáky and Yugoslav Foreign Minister Cincar-Markovic signed at Belgrade, a pact of "lasting" peace. (#835). In the next year, Hungary, this unwilling German statellite, found herself in an insolvable problem, when Hitler without any consultation with Horthy or Teleki, invaded Yugoslavia (April, 6, 1941).

Teleki received this unpleasant news already on April 3, when he was informed, that the German army had just started its march into Hungary, and Hungary's next task will be to invade Yugoslavia in "co-operation" with the Germans.

"Count Teleki simply broke down when the disaster was revealed to him. This was no longer his world. He used a pistol, but it was the bitter realization that he had signally failed that killed him." (#836).

On April 8, 1941, the British government informed the Hungarian minister in London, that the British legation in Budapest is being withdrawn because Hungary has become a base for military operations against the Alies.

While the successors of the martyr Premier (#837) still tried to be as moderate beside Hitler as possible, the encouraged Rumanians became the most amitious ally of the Führer, Sending troops to the Russian front, on Dec. 12, Rumania also declared war on the United States. (#838). The recovery of Bessarabia in the summer of 1941 was highly popular in the Wallachian populated territories, but the opposition leaders underground, in particular Maniu, strongly disapproved of the army crossing the Dniestr into Soviet territory in 1942, and of the organization of a new Rumanian province beyond the river known as "Transnistria". However, Antonescu was optimistic. After all, Rumania was always able to gain more and more multinational territories in the last century, balancing well in international conflicts. Why not do it again? If serving the Tsars, the Sultans, the Habsburg emperors, — and also betraying them in the "right" moment, — could create a Greater Rumania; then serving — and perhaps betraying — Hitler, could create an even Greater Rumania! Antonescu felt be had the key to Rumanian future in his hand, and Bucharest began to admire and glorify Hitler in the same way, as they admired and glorified Clemenceau two decades ago. Transylvania was at stake!

#835: Nevertheless, on March 25, 1941, the Yugoslavs were forced to sign the Tripartite Pact. Simultaneously, Ribbentrop "promised" that Germany will respect the territorial integrity of Yugoslavia.

#836: J. F. Montgomery: "Hungary, The Unwilling Satellite." p. 126.

#837: Ladislas Bárdossy (Apr. 1941 to March 7, 1942) and Nicholaus Kállay (March 9, 1942 to March 19, 1944).

#838: Meanwhile, Hungary was forced to declare war on Russia (June 27, 1941) and (one day after Rumania) to declare war on the U.S.A.

Now, before continuing to describe the stormy historical events, which divided Transylvania under the "blessing" of Nazi totalitarianism, and later re-united her again, under the "blessing" of Stalinist totalitarianism, — let us take a look at the statistics of ehnography again:

The population figures for the area ceded to Hungary were:

	1910 census		1930 census		1941 census
Magyar	1,125,732		911,550		1,347,012
Rumanian	926,268		1,176,433		1,066,353
German		German	68,694	German	47,501
Yiddish	90,195	Jews	139,885	Yiddish	45,593
Ruthene	16,284			Ruthene	20,609
Slovak	12,807			Slovak	20,908
				Romany	24,729
Other	22,968	Others	99,585	Others	4,586
	2,194,254		2,395,147		2,577,291

The figures for the area left with Rumania are:

	1910 census		1930 census
Magyar	533,004		441,720
Rumanian	1,895,505		2,031,447
German		Germans	475,158
Yiddish	465,814		
Other	152,820	Others	150,934
	3,047,143		3,099,259 (#839).

At the beginning of 1942, Hitler, bent on an offensive in the summer, needed as many satellite divisions as he could muster. He made a strong appeal to both the Hungarian and Rumanian governments. This took place just when the Transylvanian problem had again interposed between the two countries.

> "Ribbentrop had assured the Hungarians on 8 January 1942 that as far as the Reich was concerned, the Vienna Diktat would stand. This provoked Antonescu to inform Hitler that 'all the Rumanian soldiers on the eastern front asked when it would be possible for them to fight finally for Transylvania.'" (#840).

When the disastrous casualty list came from Stalingrad (Nov. 1942), Bucharest began to realize, that it was not so sure anymore, that the creation of an even Greater Rumania (including Transylvania of course) could be connected with the final victory of Hitler. Antonescu, the dictator still expected a miracle, but Maniu and the "Liberals" under Dinu Bratianu formed a rallying point for popular discinent with the fruits of Antonescu's pro-Axis policy, and undertook secret negotiations with the Allies during 1943. The traditional parties were supported in the desire for an ar-

---

#839: Statistics from C. A. Macartney's **"October Fifteenth."** p. 423. (Note: The Hungarian 1910 census based on "mother tongue", the 1930 census of Rumania based on "nationality". This was the reason of the "German-Yiddish" difficulty. Many Jew confessed himself as Hungarian under Hungarian regime, but as Jew in Rumanian regime. The reason of the difference between the 1941 census above and the statistics on p. 153. is, that p. 153 introduces the Rumanian census previous to the Vienna Award, the numbers above were representing the Hung. census, after the reconquest of N. Transylvania.

#840: G. Ionescu: **Communism in Rumania.** pp. 65-66.

mistice by the pro-Soviet left wing groups, the Social Democrats under Titel Petrescu and the Communists under Lucretiu Patrascanu. The average intellectual in Bucharest, — who learned in his whole life, that morality led nowhere, but the Wallachian Machiavellism led to the creation of a large, multinational state in the past, — cynicly felt once again: "If we could not re-occupy Transylvania being 'faithful' to Hitler let us try to do it, being 'faithful' to Stalin, for a change! In the beginning of World War I, we Rumanians, and Hungary, were both the unwilling statellities of the Habsburgs. The Habsburgs Emire disintegrated, the foolish Magyars victimized themselves under the ruins, and we received Transylvania, simply, because we were 'smarter', and we always knew when the time was right to turn against our 'allies'. Well, it seems to be, that we Rumanians, are facing the same problem. If we are able to manipulate well in this international confusion it could be possible, that Stalin becames our next 'Clemenceau', the foolish Magyars will remain as 'war criminals', and we could reappear again, in the 'protecting' shadow of the Great Powers, — as victors, as rightful conquerors of Transylvania!"

The speculation of the Wallachian intellectuals was very logical. The Hungarian Government witnessed the military-political situation with growing interest. In 1943, it was quite clear, that Germany lost the War. Knowing heir Rumanian neighbour too well, it was also clear, that Bucharest was searching for "old relations" with the West, and simultaneously operated with its "Leftists" in Moscow. It was also clear, that Bucharest had better political traditions both with Paris an with Moscow, than Budapest.

The Kállay Government attempted to use any available diplomatic route to make separate peace with the West. (#841). Simultaneously, Hungary tried to find connections even with the seemingly most democratic forces of Rumania. Nicholas Bánffy, Transylvanian politician and author was the connecting link between Stephen Bethlen (Budapest) and Maniu (the great old man of Wallachian Transylvania) (Kállay, himself, did not know anything about this route, but this fact did not make any difference. Thistime many "official" and "unofficial" individuals were working for "separate peace "both in Hungary and Rumania). Bánffy had a troubled time to meet with Maniu in Bucharest, because he was watched by Antonescu's secret police. Nevertheless, he met with Maniu, and tried to convince him, that Hungary and Rumania should not play an immoral game, even if the prize was Transylvania. Rumania and Hungary should turn, against the Axis at the very same time. Rumania and Hungary should negotiate in the matter of Transylvania directly, without any interference by any of the Great Powers.

Maniu was not in the position to discuss the matter officially. After all, he was only a discriminated politician in a fascist Rumania. But he hoped, that he would regain his power soon. He knew, that he has better connections with the West than Hungary, and he also knew, that Rumania would be "liberated" one step earlier, than Hungary. It represented an important time-period to win a war again, without one victory on battlefields. Maniu refused to discuss Transylvania with Bánffy. (#842).

The Casablanca Conference (Jan 14—24, 1943) was first to mention the term: "the unconditional surrender of the Axis forces". The Teheran Conference (Nov. 28, 1943 — Jan. 12, 1944) decided to "present" East

#841: One of the most important documents, which rescribes this attempt is András Tamás: "Délkeleteurópa a Diplomáciai Törekvések Sodrában." (South-East-Europe in the stream of Diplomatic Efforts." "Északi Fény", Montreal, 1961.)
#842: Inf. Lajos Kerekes: "The Political Mission of Nicholas Bánffy to Rumania in 1943." (In the Törtnénelmi Szemle" VI/2. 1963. pp. 259-261.)

Europe, as a "special sphere of regional interest" to "Uncle Joe" (#843). Already in October, 1943, the Russian army reached the Dnieper, and on March 26, 1944, the Ukrainian army reached the former Rumanian frontier. Odessa fell to them on Apr. 10, and Tarnopol on Apr. 15.

Everything happened again, according to the plans of the Rumanian politicians. Germany learned of the Hungarian manipulations for separate peace. Hitler did not trust Horthy, or any of the Hungarian ministers, — actually he never had any reason to trust them. On March 21, 1944, German troops occupied Hungary, and a pro-German pupet government (#844) was set up. Hungary could not make any independent move anymore, she was not a military, or political ally anymore, she was an enslaved German colony.

The Rumanian government surrendered when Russian troops reached the mouth of the Danube, and captured Jassy and Kishinev. It happened on Aug. 24, 1944; but — probably an even more important change was, that — one day earlier, King Michael dismissed the Cabinet of General Ion Antonescu and accepted armistice trems from the United Nations. The Coup d'état, which overthrew Antonescu and brought Rumania into an unexpected war against Germany, was largely the work of the young King himself, supported by the National Peasants and Liberals. The capitulation of Rumania trapped major units of the Black Sea naval forces of Germany (#845), thus Bucharest in the very first day of its new „metamorphosis", actually forced the gratefulness of the Allies. (#846). Stalin knew very well what was Rumania's number one desire: Transylvania! Consequently, in all of his personal or indirect message to Bucharest, Moscow repeated Molotov's public statement (made already on April 3, 1944), "making clear Russian territorial demands. but otherwise guaranteeing Rumanian territorial integrity, the implication being that Rumania would recover northern Transylvania." (#847).

The territorial clauses of the armistice between Russia and Rumania (September 12, 1944) acknowledged the Soviet annexation of Bessarabia and Northern Bukovina, but annulled the Vienna Award of Northern Transylvania to Hungary. Moscow knew its new "partner" very well. It was absolutely sure, that Bucharest would not protest against "small shanges", if Russia opens the new hope for the reconquest of "Ardeal".

In the fall of 1944, the Russian Army moved across Transylvania. "They were followed by regular Rumanian troop units and Rumanian guerila bands, which terrorized the Hungarian population by murdering men, women and children and carrying out medieval type executions in the Hungarian villages.

And how about Hungary? Could not Hungary do anything against these new events?

No, Hungary could not do anything. On October 15, in a radio address, Regent Horthy attempted the impossible. He declared armistice. He was arrested by the Germans, who nominated Ferenc Szálasi, fascist leader, as the head of the puppet government. Szálasi "continued to fight" on the German side! But the Germans know that they actually lost the War. In November, the Russians were at the gates of Budapest, but the Germans, and smaller Hungarian units still resisted savagely in Buda, which was conquered only on February 13, 1945.

#843: President Roosevelt and his wife, usually called the Russian dictator only as "our dear Uncle Joe".

#844: Döme Sztojay became the Prime Minister, and also min. of Foreign Affairs.

#845: Although some of the smaller craft escaped up the Danube before the Russian advance closed that route of escape.

#846: Especially Russia had reason to be grateful. The Rumanian "alliance" opened the way to the Black Sea, and from there to the Mediterranean!

#847: R. L. Wolff: **"The Balkans in Our Time."** p .239.

On March 9. 1945, it was annaunced that Northern Transylvania had been restored to Rumania.

Even Hungarian politicians and military personalities, already on the Russian side (#848) could not prevent this. Moscow used every benefit from the co-operation with Hungarian Liberals, Socialists, antifascist elements, but it was decided at the Crimea Conference (Feb. 7—12, Yalta) once again, that Rumania will be handled as an "ally", and Hungary as a "former enemy". Consequently, Hungary, (which became, with Rumania, and with many other nations from unwilling satellite of Germany to unwilling satellites of Russia,) began the new chapter of her unfortunate history, with conditions, which were even more miserable than her victimized East-European neighbours' conditions.

Hungary, which represented the strongest opposition within the German satellite-system against fascism, was considered now, as "the last faithful satellite" of Hitler. Rumania, — where the Iron Guard proved to be even more fascist, than the military terrorists in Italy and Germany, where the totalitarian government of Antonescu consciously fought, side by side with Hitler, in hope of an even Greater Rumania, — was considered as a "faithful ally of West an East alike, which used the first opportunity to prove her traditional faithfulness to the right side!"

It happenend this way, because Stalin, — who (according to the dream and plan of Bucharest,) actually played the role of Cleamenceau now, — wished it to happen this way. Churchill was unquestionablv a more educated, and more capable politician than Llovd George in 1920, — did not really count anymore. (It was clear. that 1945 brought a "Pyrrhic victory" for Britain. One more victory, like this, and she lost — forever.) And how about Roosevelt?

Well, the American President fit into the Russian-Rumanian plans wonderfully. Naive, and quite inexperienced in the labirinths of international diplomacy, ignorant in East-European ethno-lingusitic problems, not only influenced, but almost dominated by "Uncle Joe", ill both in his body and in his soul, — Roosevelt became a tragic reincarnation of Woodrow Wilson.

Probably the hopeful believers of the new peace, the believers of the newly created international organization, the United Nations, did not feel this wav in 1945, but in our days, disappointed bv the Cold War, by overshadowing problems of the "Balance of Terror", we my understand the feelings of the Hungarians in 1945: Yalta was another unfortunate realization of Versailles; another appearance of Trianon.

Transylvania, which was divided by Hitler, was reunited by Stalin. The dismemeberment of Transylvania was not a real solution. Did the reunification represent a solution for the minority problems of this unfortunate land? If semi-feudal parliamentarism, followed by political democracv, followed bv semi-fascist dictatorship, followed bv military fascism, could not solve the ethnic problems of this country, could we hope that Stalinistic Communism held the secret formula, which will bring salvation to the eastern part of the Carpathian Basin?

I try to answer this question in my next chapter.

#848: On Nov. 11, 1944, Hungarian General Staff Chief Vörös joined the Russians, ordered the Hungarian troops to join the Red Army, and declared, that the Horthy regime (and not the Szálasi group), was the legal one. On Dec. 24, 1944, Russia announced that a Hungarian National Assembly had been set up in Debrecen. General Vörös appeared as minister of defense, Colonel Gen. Miklós as Premier. On January 21, 1945, Miklós signed an armistice with Russia, the U.S.A. and Great Britain.

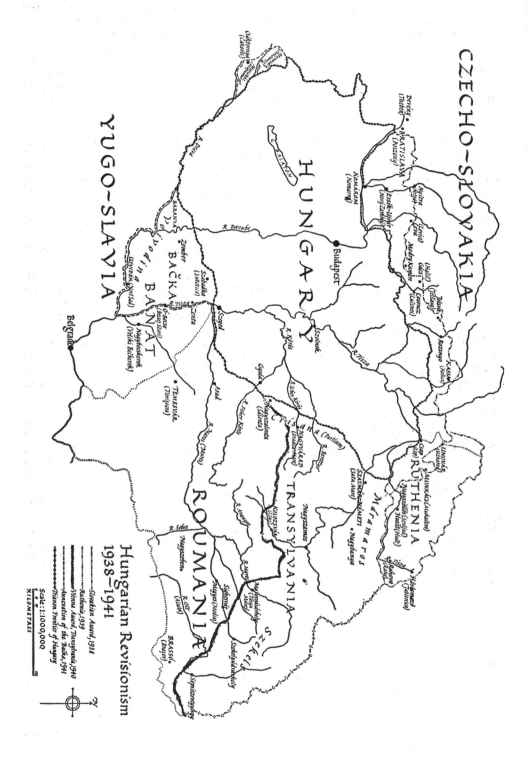

Hungarian Revisionism
1938–1941

Scale:1:1,000,000
KILOMETERS

— Slovakian Award,1938
— Ruthenia,1939
— Vienna Award, Transylvania,1940
— Annexation of the Bačka,1941
— Tianon Frontier of Hungary

XVIII.
TRANSYLVANIA IN THE SHADOW OF STALIN.

The Communists, whose organization had long been illegal in Fascist Rumania, were relatively few in number in 1944; they had no war record of partisan activity to give them prestige and few of the Communist leaders were of Wallachian origin, the majority being Russian-trained Jews, Ukrainians, or even Hungarians. How to associate the Communist movement to the traditional Rumanian Chauvinism, how to introduce these newly appeared Muscovites, as real Rumanian heroes, — it represented a real problem for Moscow. Russia actually did not need Rumania as military alliance; her strategical position represented a key for Stalin; a key which could open the doors both to Central Europe and to the Balkans; and, of course, also to the Mediterranean. The creation of a strong Communist government in Bucharest was eminently important in 1945 for the Soviet Union.

The problem appeared only in personalities in the highest Communist leadership. The Rumanians were anti-Semites and anti-Ukrainians, and they hated the Hungarians more than ever before. How to give them Jews, Ukrainians and Magyars, as — leading Rumanian Communists?

The support of the mob did not represent any problem. The Russians knew, that political morality was never the characteristic side of the Wallachians, and they will sympathise with any political force, which helped to regain Transylvania. The Communist Patry also gained reinforcement in its lower ranks from among the leaderless and disillusioned Iron Guardists, ready for violence. Moscow also hoped, that the Socialdemocrats will give support in the first years, (hoping that the Communist government is actually a "Marxist" government, consequently much better, than the disappeared Fascism.) "Later", planned Moscov, keeping the good, old Bolshevik system in mind,, "some of those Socialdemacrats will follow us, the rest of them could be easily condemned as 'Fascists', or 'Capitalists'."

Altough many of the Rumanians suspected, that Stalinism was not Socialism, and it will be hard to associate Communism with Rumanian nationalism, the newly arrived Muscovite leaders attempted to convince the people of Rumania (Wallachians and ethnic minorities alike), that actually they were Rumanians themselves, and they came to do great things: (a) they will introduce the only infallible ideology of world history, and (b) they will create (with the "great Russian Army" behind them) a more glorious, a greater Rumania, than ever before.

While the Soviet Army introduced military administration in Northern Transylvania, which was succeeded in the spring of 1945 by Rumanian administration (#849), the Communist-controlled "National Democratic Front," combined with direct Soviet pressure, finally brought results when on March 2, 1945, King Michael asked Petru Groza, leader of the Left-wing Front to from a government. (#850).

#849: With this step, Stalin gave Transylvania back to Rumania even before the peace negotiations. "On one hand, he compensated Roumania for the re-annexation of Bessarabia and Northern Bukovina, but on the other hand, there were also political reasons behind this decision. It is the usual practice of Bolshevism to prepare the introduction of communism by seemingly serving certain national interests." (Zathureczky: **"Transylvania".** p. 52.)

#850: Before Groza appeared on the scene, two minor military figures ruled the Rumanian stage: Gen. Constantin Sanatescu, and Gen. Nicolae Radescu, an open anti-Communist. They were removed at the "advice" of Soviet deputy foreign minister, Andrei Vishinsky.

The Groza Government excluded the National Peasants and Liberals, and proved highly unpopular. Hhen the Potsdam Conference (July 17 — Aug. 2, 1945) proposed the resumption of diplomatic relations with Rumania, it was "supposed" that her government was "democratic". The other condition was that Rumania should be "recognized" by the Great Powers. The U.S.S.R. immediately resumed "relations", but Great Britain and the United States refrained on the grounds of "the unrepresentative nature" of the Rumanian administration. King Michael then appealed to the three powers who, meeting in Moscov in December, 1945, "advised" that a government, broadened by the inclusion of a National Peasant and a Liberal member, should hold elections. Beginning with January 7, 1946, the representatives of the Opposition parties were included in the government. Moscow did not support this idea, — the Bolsheviks always felt, that political Opposition was such an unnecessary thing! — but in these early postwar years Stalin did not wish to provoke any hostility from the West. Thus, the seemingly "democratic" Rumanian government was formulated by British and American pressure. However, the important posts continued to be in Communists hands.

On Now. 19, 1946, the government bloc announced that it had polled 71. % of the votes in the elections. Then the Muscovites began really "to work". The elections were followed by a wave of arrests of former prominent politicians and their followers. To get rid of Antonescu was easy. After all, he was a Fascist, a war criminal. He was shot to death. That was not enough for Moscow, and the Muscovites in Bucharest. Maniu, the great old man of Transylvania was also arrested on June 15, 1947. The National Peasant party. which had the allegiance of the majority of Rumanians, was declared illegal in August 1947, and Maniu himself tried and condemned to life imprisonment on Now. 11 (He died in prison in 1952). Evidence given at the trial was used as a pretext for removing Tatarescu from the ministry of foreign affairs; Ana Pauker, a Moscow-trained Jewess, took his palce.

Meanwhile, in giving "military protection" against the Rumanian transgressions, the Soviet Union put the leftist leaders of the Rungarian minority under obligation to them.

> "Stalin gave back North Transylvania to the Roumanians under the condition that they would respect the rights of the ethnic groups. With this step, he introduced into Transylvanian the Stalinist National Policy. This policy consisted of the recognition of ethnic autonomies and it based on the federation of these autonomies. These autonomies are 'nationalistic in form socialistic in substance'. Which means that the nationality groups are Bolshevized in their own language and with respect to their national customs, but under the strict supervision of the almighty Party."
> (#851).

Thus the nationality groups are held in tight dependency on the political, economic and ideological levels. (#852).

#851: Zathureczky: **"Transylvania"**. p. 52.

#852: Note: Zathureczky (**"Transylvania"** p. 52-53) warns here, that "Communism is nothing but State-Capitalism, where the State uses its executive power to arbitrarily determine the labor relations between itself and the citizens... The other Soviet precept prescribes the ...formula: 'first socialization, then self-government.' This means, that the nationality groups receive their autonomy only after... they are completely socialized... The history of communism is full of examples that show what happens to nationality groups who refuse to obey. They are either exterminated or deported."

On February 10, 1947, the Rumanian Peace Treaty was signed in Paris. It called for reparations reduction of armaments, and declared the official return of Transylvania to Rumania. At the Conference, a very interesting detail appeared. If anybody from the Western Delegations hesitated about the "right to belong" of Northern Transylvania (with its basically Magyar population) to Rumania, his skepticism had to be resolved, when he saw and heard, that the Hungarian relegation of Northern Transylvania itself requested the Conference about their desired return to "good, old Rumania" again!

What happened? Did the Transylvanian Magyars really wished their return to be the subject of Wallachian nationalism again? Did they really believ that Bucharest had any historical right to Transylvania?

Actually, what happened here, was, that the "Hungarian delegation was nothing else, but a group of Hungarian speaking Muscovites (educated, or even born in Soviet Russia). They never had any emotional associations with Transylvania, or with any other part of Hungary. Most of them were never inhabitants of any part Transylvania, or any other part of Hungary. These faithful "comrades" simply received the order from their Party in Moscow. According to this order, they had to act in Paris, as Northern Transylvanian Magyars, who were not only "good socialists", but also "good Hungarian patriots", and both their socialistic and patriotic feelings suggested to them, that Transylvania should belong to Rumania, and nowhere else in this world.

"At the Peace Conference of 1947" — notes Zathureczky — "the members of the Hungarian delegation, in the name of 'Socialist Brotherhood' prevented the official presentation of the Hungarian plans concerning the status of Transylvania. Thus the conference could do nothing but confirm Stalin's decision and give Transylvania officially to the Roumanians." (#853).

We may add several remarks to this. (a) Some of the individuals (appearing as "Transylvanian Magyars") never saw Transylvania in their life, some of them saw it for a few weeks or months, since arriving from Moscow, to organize "the new order" in this long-suffered conutry. (b) Zathureczky was making a slight mistake, mentioning the return of Transylvania to Rumania only as "Stalin's decision", because the Russian dictator received the (sometimes plain, sometimes only tacit) consent of the other Big Powers at the previous international Conferences, to do anything he liked to do, in the "sphere of his future regional interest." (c) If any of the "not well informed" western delegates hesitated about the political morality of the "new organization" of Eastern Europe, surely some "better informed" American, French or British diplomat gave him the discrete information. (d) Stalin did not expect any unpleasant surprise in Paris, but he had two important reasons to send the "Socialist Brotherhood" of "Hungarians": 1.) to create a formality, according which the people of the area" "agree" with the Big Power decisions, thus to associate "national selfretermination" with the "new internationalism" dictated by the victorious powers, and 2.) to test the suspected (and many times experienced) naivity and ignorance of his western "allies" again. (#854).

#853: Zathureczky: **"Transylvania"**. p. 53.

#854: Many years which passed since the Bolshevik Revolution, gave an important experience to the Russian Dictatorship. The Rumanian "Peace Conference" of 1947 was not the first, and not the last "experiment", in which the Russians could satisfy themselves about the unchanged Western naivity, and ignorance. They were "testing" this, year after year, and every repeated "evidence" encouraged Moscow for new political adventures.

By the "Peace Treaty" (ratified on Sept. 15, 1947), the cession of Bessarabia and northern Bukovina to the U.S.S.R., and of Southern Dobrudja to Bulgaria (#855) was confirmed; in exchange the Vienna Award was cancelled and Northern Transylvania restored by Hungary to Rumania.

In December, 1947, it was clear, that Moscow did not wish to co-operate with King Michael; and the fact, that in 1944, Rumania changed so surprisingly her sides was due to the Coup of the young king, became nothing else, but an insignificant historical detail. King Michael was forced to abdicate. In February 1948, the remnants o fthe Social Democrats (#856) merged with the Communists to form the Rumanian Workers Party. (#857), which together with the Ploughmen's Front (#858), and the "Hungarian People's Union" (#859), presented a single list as a "People's Democratic Front" in the ensuing elections. (#860). The "Front" claimed 405 out of 414 seats (91%) in the grand national assembly. Petru Groza continued as Premier. A Constitution of Soviet type was adopted in Apr. 13, and the "Rumanian People's Republic" proclaimed, with Constantin Parhon as first "President".

Simultaneously, Bucharest (which hoped to renew its former good connections with Paris) lost every opportunity for any independent foreign policy. A "treaty of friendship", collaboration, and mutual assistance was signed with the U.S.S.R., on February 4, 1948, and later, Rumania, gradually received more and more permission from Russia to enter into the network of alliances with different other "People's Republics" „instruced" also by Soviet "advisers".

While Rumania became a "people's democracy" immediately, almost without any popular hesitation, Hungary showed great resistance against the introduction of Soviet styled communism. A provisional Hungarian government was established under General Miklos already in 1944, which concluded an armistice with the United Nations on January 20, 1945, and benceforth co-operated in the war against Germany. (#861). It was a general hope among Hungarians, that "the West knows", that Hungary was an enslaved, and unwilling satellite of Nazi Germany, and "the West knows", that in the time when General Antonescu, the Rumanian fascist dictator fought side-by-side with Hitler, for common goals, Hungary was occupied by the German army, because Hitler was informed about the Hungarian effort for a separate peace. The Hungarians hoped, that "the West knows',' that Northern Transylvania became part of Hungary proper again, not only because Mussolini "proposed", and Hitler "permitted", but because it was unjustly cut off from Hungary in 1920, and because its population was traditionaly Hungarian. It took a few months, unitil the naive Hungarians understood, that "the West does not know anything", and if any of the western diplomats "seemed to know", he was instructed without delay, that its better if he tries to act as others, who "did not know, and does not know" anything about the past and present problems of Transylvania.

#855: Simultaneously, Bulgaria also became one of the Soviet satellites. She formally capitulated on Oct. 28, 1944, Georgiev formed the first Communist government on March, 1946, Tsar Symeon II went into exile, and on Sept. 15, Bulgaria was also a "People's Republic". They received the (mainly Bulgarian populated Dobrudja) as a "present" from Russia.

#856: Those, who were not murdered, or imprisoned before 1947.

#857: "Partidul Muncitorese Roman".

#858: It was actually the communistic transformation of the old Peasants' Party, after the extermination of its former leaders, who were bold enough to propose democracy for postwar Rumania.

#859: Hungarian Muscovites arriving with the Russian Army.

#860: March 28, 1948.

#861: The last German troop was pushed out from Hungary on Apr. 4, 1945.

The Russian Army occupied Hungary, and he soldiers settled down, seemingly for many years. Neverthless, the Hungarians, (even the Hungarian Socialists), refused to adopt Russian styled Communism. The first Gerenal Election (#862) gave an absolute majority to the anti-Communist Smallholders' Party, whose leader, Zoltán Tildy, formed a coalition cabinet. (#863).

The economic situation of the country was desperate as a result of the war, with serious food shortages and an unprecedented currency inflation. Large-scale Soviet requisitions further aggravated the situation. On February 1, 1946, a republic was proclaimed with Zoltán Tildy as President, and Ferenc Nagy of the Smallholders' Party became the Premier on February 4.

Some Hungarians, who were convinced, that the Russians came as "liberatiors", and both Russia and the West knows the real background of Transylvania, were shocked, when, on February 10 (#864), 1947, the „Hungarian Peace Treaty" was signed in Paris. It was sure now, that the Russian "liberator" brought actually a new type of totalitarian dictatorship to Hungary, and "good, old Uncle Stalin" was a ruthless Macchiavellian despot, who unified in his personality the internal methods of Hitler, with the external methods of Clemenceau.

The Hungarians (Socialists, and non-Socialists alike) did not have time yet to recover themselves from the schocking surprise, that Northern Transylvania became part of Rumania again, (and that the West did nothing only noded with its head again), when the Muscovites (led by Matthias Rákosi, "first secretary of the newly formed "Hungarian Communist Party"), began their "work", according to the carefully prepared schedule of Moscow. Being the Ministry of Interior, as the most important key position in the hand of the Communists (#865) this work was quite easy. The series of arrests began with the "disappearance" of Béla Kovács, the secr. of the Smallholders' Party. (#866). On May 31, Premier Nagy was accused of "conspiracy" by the Muscovites. He resigned, and was replaced by Lajos Dinnyés. The next step was, that the Socialdemocrats (#867) were forced to run together with the, relatively small, Communist Party (#868) in tre Elections of August 31, 1947. This trick worked very well. The "Socialist union" won at the elections. Premier Dinnyés continued in office, (#869) "leading" a coalition Cabinet of 15 members, including 5 Communists. The next step of this, so-called, "Salami-policy", was the arrests of those Socialdemocrat leaders, who did not wish to join the Communists. (#870). After this „foreplay", on Jan. 12, 1948, the Communist Party "fusioned" with the rest of the Socialdemocrats into the "United Workers' Party". On July 30, 1948, President Tildv was forced to resign, and was replaced by the chairman of the United Workers' Party, ex-Socialdemocrat, pro-Communist, Árpád Szakasits.

#862: November 3, 1945.

#863: The Smallholders' Party was always in sharp opposition both against semi-feudalism, and against Fascism in the interwar years. Its leader, Tibor Eckhardt (mentioned many times in my Ch. XVI.) is still the "great old man" of the Hungarian immigration in the U.S.A. in 1972.

#864: On the same day, when the "Rumanian Peace Treaty" was signed.

#865: Headed first by Ferenc Erdei, pro-Communist peasant leader, later by László Rajk of the Communist Party (later executed at the order of Rákosi.)

#866: His "crime" was, that, he kept the Party organization very sternly in hand, and did not let it "reorganize" in a way, as the Muscovites managed it, with the "National Peasants' Party in Rumania." (See: p. 164), and p. 166, #858, again).

#867: They were the second largest party after the Smallholders' Party.

#868: Which was only the fifth in order, since the Elections of 1945.

#869: He was only a puppet of Matthias Rákosi, the Communist leader.

#870: Including Anna Kéthly. (Still one of the leading emigrants in 1972).

Completing the "reorganization" of the anti-Communist Smallholders' Party into pro-Communist Smallholders' Party, by the long series of arrests, (#871), the "renewed" party called for the "resignation" of Premier Dinnyés and put pro-communist István Dobi in his place. (#872). The real power, however, was in the hands of Deputy Premier Rákosi, who received (day after day, since 1945) his orders from Moscow, and who declared himself as "the best student of the great teacher, Stalin."

On December 27, 1948, the refusal of the Catholic Church to make concessinos to the government led to the arrest of Cardinal Joseph Mindszenty, and other dignitaries. The charge was, once again, as was in all the previous cases in this "Salami policy", "conspiracy to overthrow the government, in the service of the capitalistic, imperialistic West". The Cardinal was "found quilty" and sentenced to life imprisonment on February 8, 1949. In May of the same year a "General Election" with "open voting" gave complete victory to the Communist-controlled "National Independence Front." (#873).

The peoples of Transylvania witnessed the Stalinistic terror both in Rumania proper and Hungary proper, just as they witnessed the terror of Fascism not many years before in both countries. The big differences were that (a) Fascism was especially extreme in Rumania proper, where the Iron Guard attempted to overshadow even German Nazism, and it was much more moderate in Hungary, where the government always tried its best to save the savable and ti find connections with the West, (b) the partial return of Transylvania represented some oasis in the desert of hopelessness. Now the situation was even worse for the Transylvanians, because (a) after the fast "Stalinization" of Rumania, the Hungarian resistance was also crushed, and Transylvania was surrounded by enslaved, Stalinized, Russian satellites, and (b) the Transylvanian Magyars realized that they were enslaved in a double way. First: they became subjects of the Wallachian, nationalist avengement, and secondly, under their own Muscovite "Hungarian" leaders, they adapted themselves to the humiliated, frigthened, beggarly life of the "new regime". Although Hungary itself was forced to be one of the "Peoples' Republic", Transylvanian Magyars, who seemed to sympathize with Hungary, were treated as "Hnugarian Fascists", sometimes by newly emerged Communist leaders, who, it was well known, not so long ago changed from the uniform of the Iron Guard into the uniform of the "new democratic Police Guard".

The Transylvanians (and not only the Magyars, but the Wallachians and the Saxons too) became gradually quite lethargic in these unfortunate circumstances. News from Hungary, or from Rumania was not interesting anymore, they could not bring any hope into their lives. On June 16, Lászlo Rajk, the Communist minister (#874) was arrested. The formerly glorified "hero" was suspected of not wishing to follow the Stalinist line, as it was dictated by Stalin, and followed by Rákosi. He was dreaming about the adoptation of some sort of "national communism" following the example of his friend Marchall Tito of Yugoslavia. (#875). Consequently, he was also accused as an "imperialist agent of the West", and hung.

#871: The Hungarian prisons were filled with Socialdemocrats and Smallholders' Ministers, politicians. In a Communist country the Secret Police always has the opportunity to arrest any member of the Parliament.

#872: Dobi was the Communist agent in the Smallholders' Party for years.

#873: The Hungarian citizens had to go to "vote" (under police supervision), declaring their "feeling" openly to the election "committees".

#874: He was Minister of External Affairs at this time. Rákosi never liked him, because he proved to be a Hungarian first of all, and only after it, a communist. (The name of Béla Kun was not permitted to be mentioned, because Kun was murdered on Stalin's order in Russia in the 1940-s.)

#875: Tito was a communist, and he signed a treaty of friendship with Rumania too (Dec. 19, 1947), but it was clear at this time, that Tito did not wish to turn Yugoslavia into a Russian satellite.

On August 7, a new "constitution" was proclaimed, following very closely that of the Soviet Union, on December 28, the government decreed the "nationalization" of all major industries, announcing the start of the first "Five-Years Plan." Simultaneously, in Rumania, the transformation into a full-fledged Soviet satellite made further progress. An uninterrupted series of trials purged the country of all political opponents and the Communist Party of "deviates". All religious organizations were subjected to state control, and if the Greek Orthodox organizations were treated in Transylvania somehow in a more moderate way, it was, because the Greek Orthodox Church was suspected only as "anti-Communist", but the Hungarian Catholic Church, the Hungarian Calvinist Church, and the Saxon Lutheran Church were also suspected as "nationalist" and even as "Fascist". "Nationalism" was identified with "Fascism" in Transylvania, and in other provinces of Communist Rumania, — if the "nationalist-fascist" was incidentally not a Wallachian. Wallachian nationalism was not identified with Fascism, — even if the suspected individual was a former member of the Iron Guard. — because Rumanian nationalism was officially associated with the "wonderful, new order" of Communism.

Catholic opposition led to the arrest of the remaining bishops and the dissolution of all Roman Catholic organizations, while the Muscovites, following the experiments of the Bolshevik Party on Russia, successfully organized some sort of "peaceful-coexistence" between the Communist Government and the Orthodox National Church.

The Muscovites also "collectivized" the agriculture, and "nationalized" the industry, just like in Hungary, and the death penalty was imposed for even minor offenses against the Communist state. Relations with the Western Powers were further deteriorated and several Western diplomats were accused of espionage. When Stalin called Tito, as "the chained dog of the Western Imperialists", Rumania denounced the treaty of "friendship" with Yugoslavia. (#876).

The official ethnic composition of Rumania was this: (#877).

Language Group	Total Number	%	Urban Number	%	Rural Number	%
Romanian	13,597,613	85.7	2,971,456	80.0	10,626,157	87.4
Hungarian	1,499,851	9.4	448,222	12.1	1,051,629	8.6
German	343,913	2.2	89,571	2.4	254,342	2.1
Yiddish	138,795	0.9	129,208	3.5	9,587	0.1
Gypsy	53,425	0.3	7,530	0.2	45,895	0.4
Serb-Croatian	45,447	0.3	5,783	0.2	39,664	0.3
Russian	39,332	0.2	14,105	0.4	25,227	0.2
Ukrainian	37,582	0.2	3,528	0.2	34,054	0.3
Czech-Slovak	35,143	0.2	4,409	0.1	30,734	0.3
Turk-Tatar	28,782	0.2	9,344	0.3	19,438	0.2
Bulgarian	13,408	0.1	1,567	0.0	11,846	0.1
Greek	8,696	0.1	8,491	0.2	205	0.0
Armenian	6,987	0.0	6,872	0.0	115	0.0
Polish	6,753	0.0	3,777	0.1	2,976	0.0
Albanian	735	0.0	701	0.0	34	0.0
Others	15,639	0.1	8,255	0.2	7,384	0.1
Not declared	523	0.0	325	0.0	198	0.0
Rumania total	15,872,624	100.0	3,713,139	100.0	12,159,485	100.0

#876: On October 21, 1949.

#877: Figures from Fred Pisky: "The People." (From Stephen Fisher-Galati ed.: "Romania", "East-Central Europe Under the Communists" series; Mid-European Studies Center, Free Europe Committee, Inc., Frederick A. Praeger, New York, 1957, p. 54.) The Rumanian census of 1848.

We have to make some important remarks in connection with this ethnography, which is based on the "distribution of population by Mother Tongue" in 1948.

(a) "East European ethnic statistics have seldom been reliable, for an unfortunate extremist nationalism created an atmosphere where members of an ethnic minority group often found it difficult to declare their nationality without fear af unfavourable economic, social, and political consequences . . . These figures of ethnic composition should accordingly be viewed with a degree of caution." (#878), (b) The largest ethnic minority group, the Hungarian, mainly concentrated in Transylvania, Crisana-Maramures (Hung: Mármaros), and the Bánát (all these territories were former provinces of traditional Hungary). (c) The Hungarians were still mainly city and town dwellers. This statistics shows in absolute numbers, but did not express in Per Cent, that only 22% of the Rumanians were living in urban areas, and almost 30% of the Hungarians populated the cities and towns, (d) The number of the Germans in Southern Bukovina and Northern Dobrudja sharply decreased due to the extensive repatriation program of 1940. Large ethnic German groups (Swabians) were removed from the Banat, and transferred to the Danubian Plain east of the Trianon frontier) by the Communists. The Transylvanian Saxon settlements were affected less by these changes. The reason that the number of Germans decreased from 700,000 (in 1930) to less than 350,000, was, that the rest was deported to Sibiria by the Russians.

On the cultural level, Bucharest seemed to fulfill, for a time the demands of Stalin, who warned the Rumanians to be over nationalistic at the expense of the minority groups. Hungarian education was authorized in the lower and higher levels. The Hungarian University of Kolozsvár (Rum: Cluj) was allowed to continue its functions. with a Hungarian Medical School in Marosvásárhely (Rum: Targu Mures). Stalin's "only" condition was, that an ethnic group may preserve its national traditions, if it places itself "unconditionally" under the direction of the Communist Party (#879). Consequently, all the Hungarian schools, all Hungarian cultural institutions, newspapers, publishing houses, theaters, etc. became "voluntarily" Party-directed institutions, because the ethnic minority groups could choose only this alternative, and they hoped, that preservation of ethnic identity would be relativelly easier under the "protection" of the Party, than under the oppressive domination of Rumanian nationalism. "The Hungarian cultural life became "nationalistic in form, socialistic in substance' " (#880). Everythingw as subordinated to the indoctrination and the de-nationalization of the Central Communist Party's plans.

The life of an individual was usually hard, and even dangeraus in any Communist country, but in Rumania. where the Hungarian and Saxon citizens could be easily "suspected" as "nationalists-fasists", consequently, as "imperialists" too (#881); an "ethnic citizen" really learned "to live dangerosly". According to the figures, not completely evaluated as yet, about 200,000 Hungarians were killed, imprisoned and deported, partly as "war criminals", later mostly as "imperialistic conspiratiors", or simply as "unwanted elements". "Urban Hungarians were evacuated with only one suitcase, and their homes, together with all their belongings were

---

#878: Warning of Fred S. Pisky in his work: **"The People"** p. 53.

#879: This was his "magic formula" in the Soviet Union too. Any ethnic group, which was ready to serve the Communist doctrines, could preserve its nationality for a while. "Rebellious" ethnic groups were Russified, or completely exterminated. (Stalin is still called in Russia as the "great teacher" of how to solve ethnic minority problems . . .)

#880: Zathureczky: **"Transylvania."** p. 55.

#881: According to the Soviet terminology, "nationalism," if not pro-Russian, is nothing else but agency of the Western "imperialism."

given to Roumanian colonists, mostly refugees from Russian occupied Bessarabia." (#882).

In 1949—50, the leaders, priests, ministers of the Roman Catholic, Presbyterian, Lutheran, and Unitarian Churches were all imprisoned, or sent to forced labor camps. The Greek-Catholic Church (#883) was liquidated by law. (#884).

While all these persecutions against the Hungarians in Transylvania went on, the Hungarian and Rumanian Muscovite "governments" assured each other with enthusiastic words of the "Socialist Brotherhood", and the "indivisible unity of the Socialist Camp, led by the great Soviet Union, and its great leader, Stalin."

In 1950 came a further step in both countries. In Hungary the remaining ex-Socialists, among them Árpád Szakasits, were dismissed from the government and from every important political, social, and economic position. The Communists wished to monopolize the term "Socialist", and the Socialdemocrats, and "national communists" were called "traitors", imperialist agents", even "fascists". In Rumania, the Communist Party announced the expulsion of 192,000 members over the previous two years. Former faithful communists, even leaders, were arrested (#885), if they were Rumanian nationalists, (not exactly in the Russian line), or nationalists from various ethnic groups, without the obligatory adoption of the Stalinistic methods, and doctrines.

In 1950, following the "advice" of the Soviet "advisers", the Government of Bucharest created an "Autonomous Magyar Region" from territory inhabited by the compact Székely population, and appointed as "capital" Marosvásárhely (Rum: Targu Mures). "This new autonomous region" — explained Wolff —" ended the brief linkage of the Szekler (Székely) counties with Brasov (Hung: Brasso, new Communist name: Stalin). It was modeled on the Soviet autonomous regions within the individual Soviet Republics . . . Though subject to the laws of the Republic of which it formed a part, its own administrative organs took responsibility for public order, the enforcement of the laws, local economic and cultural activities, and the approval of a regional budget and economic plan." (#886).

The population of the "Autonom Hungarian Province "included (#887) 731,361 people, of which 79.38% were Hungarians and 20.62% were Rumanians. The new creation obviously represented a Russian-sponsored Rumanian Communist attempt to deal with a long-standing Rumanian problem, and to remove one of the ancient sources of friction in Rumania: Szekler discontent with rule from Bucharest. Moscow hoped, that other Hungarians, who were not living in the "Autonomous Region", will desire also for similar "autonomy", and they will look for Russian aid against any "extremism" of Rumanian nationalism. This Muscovite step was a warning against some Hungarians, who did not adopt Communism, that they will be victimized by Rumanian nationalism. It was a warning against Rumanian nationalism, that all the nationalities could rebel against Bucharest, if the Rumanians wish to follow "Titoism". It was also a warning for Transylvanian Wallachians, that they may find themselves in a "Magyar Autonom Region", under the hated Hungarian administration, if they do not follow the Soviet orders with the expected "comradeship".

#882: Zathureczky: **"Transylvania."** p. 54.

#883: Common foundation of the Habsburgs and the Wallachians. (XVIII. C.)

#884: With this step, the Muscovites wished to "present a gift" to the Orthodox Church, hoping for "co-operations". All the former Greek Catholics "automatically" became Greek Orhodoxes!

#885: Among hem, wartime Communist leader Lucretiu Patrascanu. He was dismissed as Min. of Justice, arrested in Feb. 1948, was tried and executed in 1954.

#886: R. L. Wolff: **"The Balkans in Our Time."** p. 453.

#887: According to the 1956 Rumanian census.

Of course, Moscow was careful not to insult the Wallachians with the new creation. The "Autonomous Hungarian Province" was not autonomous at all. "Autonomy" had the same meaningless role in the Soviet system, as "Socialism", "democracy", "independency", etc. The "Autonom Province" was also labelled as the province of the "Unified and Indivisble National State af Great-Roumania." Nevertheless, it was clear now, that the Russians were good students of history, and placing themselves into the comfortable position of the Habsburgs, they began to play the interesting game of the "Divide et Impera" in their new, East-European Empire, where every ethnic minority group could represent an important figure on the chess-board.

The "Autonom Province" was not autonom at all in the traditional sense of this term, but Moscow, and the Muscovites of Bucharest, fulfilled their promises this time. The individuals in the "Autonom Province" did not have to serve Bucharest (in the "old nationalistic" sense anymore,) — if they were ready to serve Moscow directly. The individuals in this province did not have to learn Rumanian nationalistic literature in Rumanian language, — if they were ready to choose Russian, as "second language", and if they were ready to produce literature, and culture only in the Communist forms, including only the glorification of the Communist life, and the glorification of the great Stalin, of course. Székelyland received "cultural autonomy too", which was actually nothing else, but the fact, that Communists from Bucharest, Moscow and Budapest often visited the "autonomous" Magyar region using the various forms of literature, and music in the common glarification of Russian Communism, or "learning" together the great teachings of Marx, Lenin and Stalin — in Hungarian language. (#888). Life in the Autonom Province was easier economically, but it was not easy politically for any conscientious individual or, for anybody, who could not act in this large theater, with the necessary talent of imitating. Many peasants, techers, students, etc. were arrested, deported, even executed in the "Autonom Province", because it was proved in their case, that they "did not like" the regime, or "they did not like "Stalin, (who made possible for them to preserve their nationality,) and they still remained 'revisionists", or "dreamers" of a capitalistic type of freedom. (What ingratitude! — meditated in these cases Moscow, — Those Hungarians were always incorrigible rebels! Small wonder that both the Habsburgs and the Rumanians had always so much troble with them.)

The Muscovites had a recipe in their deep container of their "experiences" to deal with the Transylvanian Catholics. The Government allowed a session to meet in Cluj in February 1951, which called an extraordinary meeting for March to vote the acceptance of the new regulations prepared by the Catholic Action Committee, to adopt a schedule of pensions for teachers, and to plan for the renovation of the Cathedrals of Kolozsvár and Gyulafehérvár, (Cluj and Alba Iulia). The Roman Catholic laymen of Transylvania saw nothing unusual about this agenda, since it was the sort which had traditionally lain within the competence of a "Status Catholicus". On March 15, 1951, it became clear, that behind the hypocritical sentences about the formation of a new, enlarged "Status Catholicus" about "better relations" between Church and State, was the arrests of many "disloyal priests" again, almost all the Catholic bishops among them. The new "Status Catholicus" attempted to do nothing else, but the "nationalization" of the Catholic Church itself, property and spirit alike! (#889).

#888: The Székelys did not like the Communist visitors. In their agglutinative way, they called the visitors "a-stinker-from-Bucharest-from-Budapest-from Moscow." (Inf.: Wolff: **"The Balkans in Our Time."** p. 562).

#889: This event coincided with the arrest of Archbishop Grösz in Hungary. He was sentenced to life-imprisonment, as an "imperialist". (Simultaneously colossal Stalin statues were erected both in Budapest and Bucharest.)

In May, 1952, three leading communist ministers, among them Ana Pauker, were purged. Cheorghe Gheorghiu-Dej then became premier, Groza retiring to the presidency vacated by Parhon. A revised constitution, still closer to that of the U.S.S.R., was adopted on Sept. 24, and a new assembly elected on November 30, 1952.

It seemed that 1952 was some sort of "Year of Change" to the better — for a change — in Hungary. In August, the "National Assembly" still "elected" Matthias Rákosi, as Prime Minister (#890), but the miserable economic conditions gave opportunity for more and more professionals to replace the members of the arrogant, but (economically, socially, even politically) useless "labour aristocracy". The "great Stalin" died on March 4, 1953, and "his best student", Rákosi, continued to rule, but without the protection of his former "teacher", surrounded by jealous, other communist leaders, ideologists of "national communism" (of the Titoist type,) and, first of all, by Hungarian patriots, who were hoping for the creation of a Hungarian social-democracy, following the example of Sweden. On March 8, the "National Assembly" passed a law on "preservation of Stalin's memory", and Rákosi, with other Hungarian Stalinists stood guard around Stalin's bier in Moscow, — but Matthias Rákosi knew, that a new era was coming, — and this new era did not need him anymore.

On July 4, Imre Nagy, the new Prime Minister delivered his program to the Assembly in Budapest, and observers — first time since 1945, — recognized in this program the presence of the Hungarian political, social and economic interests. At the end of the month, the political prisoners received amnesty; in August, Government decree increased the size of househould lots in the collective farms, new trade licenses were granted and the tax was reduced for peasants. In the following months, the private handycraftsmen received special creadits, price cuts were introduced, delivery quotas lowered, etc.

There were rumours about "Destalinization" even in the Soviet Union. Hungary tried to hope again.

In Rumania Georghiu-Dei, (another "good student of the great, but passed-away — teacher",) still ruled the political scene. Hungary was lucky enough at this time, to witness the appearance of a great leader, Imre Nagy, who was able to associate his feelings about true Socialism with his Hungarian patriotism. Rumania did not have a Rumanian Imre Nagy. The other trouble of Rumania was that she was not a national State, as was Hungary. Bucharest still dominated an artificial, multinational State, shameful product of Trianon. The Rumanian Dictatorship of Bucharest really did not have any alternative, exept "to rule and change nothing" (#891). The death of Stalin could cause temporary destalinization" in Hungary, — even in Russia itself. Bucharest did not have a choice. Many of the Rumanian communists were probably quite happy, that from now on, they have a chance to be communists in their own ways. But to rule, to dominate a restless multinational territory, Bucharest could not find any other way in its history only the ways of Fascism, or the ways of Stalinism.

Was "Stalinism" over with the death of Stalin? Hungary belived it in 1953, even Nikita Khruschew belived it for a few months. Not much after the death of the Russian Monster, Khruscsev found out, that Stalinism was the only way, which was able to preserve the rule of the "New Class" (# 892) in the Communist World. The Hungarians learned in 1956, that the ghost of Stalin was still above Europe. For Transylvania, the situation became even worse after 1953. Going on their own ways, the Rumanian "national-communists" became free to complete their original plan: the "linguicide" of the Magyars of Transylvania.

#890: With many of his Stalinist-Muscovite friends, in complete power.
#891: Famous sentence of Francis I of Habsburg.
#892: From the terminology of Milovan Dylas. ("The New Class.").

XIX

THE HUNGARIAN REVOLUTION AND TRANSYLVANIA.

After the death of Stalin, the whole World observed, with growing interest, the exciting happenings in the Soviet Union, but "the news from Russia", — which were only "quite interesting", or maybe "quite important" for the West, — were, — or seemed to be, — answers for Life or Death for the enslaved peoples of Eastern Europe.

Did the death of Stalin represent the end of "Stalinism"? Could the successors turn to the road of democratic Socialism? Will the West use the extraordinary psychological opportunity to end the Cold War, and to stop the undermining communist propaganda everywhere? Will the great change give an opportunity to the Eastern European nations — sold by the West, and dominated by the Asiatic Despotism, — to became parts of Europe again? What will "Maoist" China say? Etc. etc. — these were the main questions asked by the individuals behind the Iron Curtain, who were Europeans, — with all the good and not so good characteristics of this term, — and who hoped, that the death of the "Red Tsar" will open a new opportunity to become Europeans again.

The peoples of Hungary and Rumania felt similar things. Probably the Hungarians' feeling was rather similar to their classical, traditional emotions, and the death of the tyrant reminded them not only of the chance to become part of the West again, but it recalled the memories of great freedomfights in their mind. Maybe another Bocskay, another Bethlen, another Rákoczy, another Thököly, another Kossuth should step on the historical scene now, to lead the Hungarians to freedom again?

The feelings in Bucharest were not exactly the same. They were happy too, — who were not happy in March 1953 in Europe?, — but they were slightly confused and worried. The special problem of any multinational, artificial state came up again. Will the next dictator protect Rumania? What will happen, if the next dictator will like Hungary, and will decide another solution for Transylvania? Will Bucharest receive a better opportunity to have free foreign policy? Could Rumania receive now a special situation. which still offers Russian "protection" in internal affairs, but offers the exercise of "national communism", as far as external affairs are concerned?

Feelings in Transylvania were quite similar in 1953—1954, as in 1943—44, — ten years ago. In the last years of the war, Hungary attempted to resist Fascism, and all the monarchic, liberal, peasant, socialist elements co-operated in this resistance. Rumania Proper became the most obliging servant of Hitler, and Rumanian Fascism tried to be even more extreme, than Nazism itself. (The weak resistance of the Wallachian peasants let itself down almost voluntarily, because the time of the royal semi-fascism already proved, that only dictatorship will be able to keep the rebellious ethnic minorities together in East Europe.) First time in their history in the Transylvanian Basin, the Magyars. Wallachians and Saxons had a common idea. Between the fires of the resisting but dominated Hungary, and the extremely fascist Rumania, even the Wallachians began to dream about an independent Transylvania, some sort of new Switzerland in the wreath of the Carpathians! The Magyars in Transylvania were disappointed about the growing fascist movement and the impotence of the government. The Wallachians, (the peasants of Maniu, the leader of the political opposition), felt, that Transylvania should separate herself from the Fascism of Bucharest. Even the Saxons (especially the older generation) felt, that surrounded by the storm of political immorality, the various peoples of this geographical unit schould fight hand in hand for a common goal.

Now, ten years later, the situation was somehow the same. Peoples of Transylvania, Wallachians, Magyars and Saxons alike, realized once again, that, as usual, in any turning point of history, the "mother counries", Hungary and Rumania, were both looking at Transylvania with the desire, or worry of the "rightful" owner, and nobody, ever wishes to ask, what was really the hope, the desire, the choice of the people themselves? Transylvanians (from various ethnic minority groups) became sick and tired of experiencing that the problem of Transylvania was some sort of "borderline problem" between Rumania and Hungary. They did not feel so. They felt themselves, more and more in the passing years, "Transylvanians". They knew, that the Transylvanian Magyar was not the same, as the Hungarian in Hungary; the Wallachian in Transylvania was politically very different, sometimes even directly opposing to the "official" "Regatul" in the last fifty years. The Transylvanian Saxons were separated from Germany Proper for six hundred years. They were still Germans in their language, but their social character, according to their feelings, was rather "Transylvanian", that German. Yes, Transylvania became, during these bloody centuries, from a geographical term a real social, political, even psychological term, and the Transylvanians, from all the ethnic minority groups, began to believe, that the "Transylvanian problem" was not only the problem of the "mother countries", not the problem of certain interfering Big Powers, but the problem of the Transylvanians themselves. To solve their own problem was their task, their responsibility, and — their only hope to create peace in Transylvania. Interferences "from outside" usually provoked even more hatred among the ethnic groups in Transylvania. Perhaps, without interference, they will be able to associate themselves, to work together? Maybe, the great changes in Moscow will offer this type of new opportunity?

These were the main ideas after 1953 in Transylvania, where the intellectuals watched the period of "melting" from Hungary (#893), and the period of growing, aggressive "national-communism" from Rumania proper, (#894), hoping to "balance" between them for the interest of Transylvania.

In the Soviet Union itself, the hope of Socialism turned into a new disappointment. Malenkov succeeded Stalin, but resingned in February 1955. He was not able to rule Russia, where original Marxism turned into a strange mixture of "Leninism", and of some sort of oriental despotism, a long time ago. His tendencies toward "Democratization" were undermined by powerful elements of the "Labour Aristocracy", who were realists enough to recognize, that only Stalinism was able, and will be able, to keep this giant structure together, and to preserve the privileges of the "New Class". Khruscsev, (who was the First Secretary of the Communist Party, a post which was held by Stalin himself for thirty years), took

---

#893: The meaning of "melting" in Hungary was, that, from now on, not only "imperialists" were imprisoned, but also "Stalinists", charging them with "criminal activities against the State and the people." Former victims of the Rákosi-terror, (János Kádár, for example) became free again. Even Anna Kéthly, the leader of the Socialdemocrats was released from prison. (Nov. 21, 1954). The "Stalinists" resisted. They were able to remove Imre Nagy again, but the new breezes of a hoped freedom produced a courageous, pro-western literary Renaissance in Hungary.

#894: On Oct. 3, 1955, Gheorghiu-Dei abandoned the premiership to Chivu Stoica, reverting the first secretaryship of the "Rumanian Workers' party. "Old Stalinism" was prepared to replace itself with a "Stalinistic type of National Communism."

the power into his own hands. Being the faithful servant of Stalin for so many years, receiving practice, — among other things, in the destruction, and almost extermination of his own ethnic minority, — the shrewd Ukrainian peasant really believed, that he held the "magic formula", which could preserve the power of the ruling class without continuing Stalinism. At a secret session of the Communist Party Congress in February 1956 he said that Stalin abused his powers, had permitted loyal communists to be falsely accused and punished, had failed to prepare for the German invasion, had made blunders in strategy, and had been responsible for the break with Yugoslavia in 1948.

Probably, this was a time, when Khruschev really hoped, that building popularity by the condemnation of the hated Stalin, introducing slight "democratizations" in the party-structure, "soft" diplomacy internally and externally (the "peaceful-co-existencia") will preserve the rule of the Labour Aristocracy; will calm down the restless millions; will keep together the Eastern European colonies of Russia, and will result in a bloodless victory above the "rotten West", which will probably "disintegrate" without spending as sacrifice one single Russian soldier.

Already in 1956, he found out, (probably already in 1955), that his plan did not work. Stalin could be easily condemned, but only Stalinistic terror could keep together the gigantic tower. which was built by Stalinism. Only dictatorship could oppress the subjected and restless millions, only dictatorship could close the mouth of the rising Soviet intelligentsia, only dictatorship could stop the movements of the overruled ethnic minorities, only dictatorship could crush natsionalistic uprisings in Eastern Europe, only military dictatorship could face "the rotten Western inmperialism" and the "aggressive Chinese Maoism" at the same time.

Djengiz Khan did not have any other way. He became the man, that he was only by the way of tyranny. Without tyranny, he could not be, and he was not anymore a tyrant. Attila, Charlemagne, Bonaparte, Hitler could not do it any other way. Turning soft, meant the end of power, disintegration, political suicide, death. Khruchev found out too, that dictatorship was not only a way of ruling, but a way, — the only way! — of selfpreservation, of defence. He could not solve his dilemma only by the continuation of "melting", because giving up terror, giving up aggressivity, meant no less, but to open the door for the destruction of the Soviet-Russian structure. The "rotten West" did not prove itself so rotten, as he believed, and in the middle of his "Destalinization", — he shockingly realized, that the Soviet system was so rotten itself, that only returning to Stalinistic methods could preserve power over oppressed millions of labourers, peasants, minority groups and enslaved European colonies.

But, let me leave Comrade Khruschev in the middle of his unsolvable dilemma. Let us go to hopeful Transylvania again, where "wishful thinking" replaced logical speculation a long time ago, because logic led only to disappointing realizations; — and it was so nice to dream! Although both Hungary and Rumania were forced to become members of the, Moscow directed , Warsaw Pact (May, 14, 1955), a counterpart of the NATO (#895), (and it was clear to every enslaved European nation, that this new military alliance was built up, not necessarily as a defensive force, but a preparative force to run down the rest of Europe); peoples of Transylvania were still dreaming about national freedom and "democratic socialism".

#895: Set up already on Apr. 4, 1949.

The Transylvanians were glad to hear, and read (the severed Rumanian censorship could not prevent the coming direct informations from the neighbouring "Comrade-countries"), that Cardinal Mindszenthy was released from prison and placed only under "house arrest" in Hungary. The Hungarian government permitted free marketing of grain. Archbishop Joseph Grosz was also released from prison, and many religious and political personalities received amnesty from the Hungarian Muscovites, who were under the heavy pressure of the restless, disappointed, impatient public opinion. On December 14, Hungary received admission to the United Nations. The Muscovites tried to declare this, as another great result of their effort, but Hungarians began to talk about the U.N. as a new source of hope. (#896). The Hungarian Stalinists, of course, understood the Siviet intention about the United Nations, and taking their chairs in the Assembly, they knew, that their task was to serve the interest of Moscow on this new stage of the Balance of Power. (#897). Rákosi was intelligent enough to realize, that since his "great teacher" died, he was not under the same "protection". He also understood the "Khruschevian Dilemma", simultaneously realizing, that only immediate return to military dictatorship will be able to preserve Communist dictatorship in Hungary, and in all other Russian colonies, including the giant "States" of the Soviet Union itself. He tried to make contact with Khruschev, but the contact was not the same, as in the "god old times. "His confusion was even greater, when he was humiliated by Moscow, receiving the instruction, that Hungary had to re-establish "good relations with Tito, who was not a "chained dog of imparialism" anymore, and became "comrade" again.

More and more exciting news came to Transylvania by coming Hungarian visitors, since the Hungarian citizens were not required to have passports for travel into Rumania (#898). One of the exciting news was, that the association of the anti-Stalinist, Socialist, and even Liberal new intellectuals and literary personalities, the "Petöfi Circle" sharply attacked the Central Committee of the Party, and the Muscovites could not use any means against this, (and against the demonstrations in the streets,) because the members of the army and police also, gradually turned against them. The general desire for democratic socialism was associated with a growing desire for political freedom. On July 18, Matthias Rákosi was simply pushed out from his position and from Hungary by the general disgust of millions, non-Socialists, and Socialists alike. Ernö Gerö, the other Muscovite, took over the power, who pretended, that he supported the "rehabilitation" of Lászlo Rajk (#899), and who tried to find solutions for the storming problems, in a special meeting between himself, Khruschev and Joseph Broz Tito, on October 1, in Crimea.

#896: It did not take a long time, until the Hungarians (and every oppressed small nations with them) found out, that he U.N. was not an international "parliament" at all, but the ridiculous reincarnation of the League, a stage for the Balance of Power, too impotent, and often even unwilling to fulfill its original obligations.

#897: In the time of the Hungarian Revolution, the Imre Nagy Government found out, that the "Hungarian" delegate in the U.N. was not even Hungarian, did not even speak Hungarian. He was a Russian, sent directly from Moscow, under a Hungarian name: Péter Kos.

#898: Since June 13, 1956.

#899: Former communist Minister of Interior and External Affairs, sentenced and hung under Rákosi. (Mentioned many times in the previous chapter. On March 29, 1956, already, Rákosi was forced to announce his "rehabilitation". On Oct. 6, a crowd of 200,000 demonstrated at the re-burial of Rajk and other "rehabilitated" martyrs of Stalinism.)

In Transylvania, the terror did not decrease, it was even more extreme, since the death of Stalin represented the end of Stalinist ethnic-system too. Acting as a good communist was not enough anymore. No Hungarian, or Saxon could save himself from ethnic discrimination, by simply trying to be better communist than the officials of Bucharest. Transylvanians found out, that Bucharest appeared since 1954, not only as the representative of Moscow, but the "old Bucharest" reappeared again, as center of Rumanian Chauvinism.

The total population of 17,489,450, according to the official census of 21 February 1956, was made up as follows:

Ethnic Rumanians	14,996,114
Hungarians	1,587,675
Germans	384,708
Gipsies	104,216
Jews	146,264
Ukrainians and Ruthenians	60,479
Serbs, Croats and Slovenes	46,517
Russians	38,731
Czechs and Slovaks	35,152
Tatars	20,469
Turks	14,329
Bulgarians	12,040
Unspecified	42,756 (#900).

Comparing these numbers with the Rumanian census of 1948 (#901), we may observe, that the total Rumanian population increased by 10.2% in the period of eight years, and the increase of both of the Rumanian population and of the Hungarian-speaking population was exactly the same. The "Divide et Impera" policy of Stalin forced the Magyars to act as communists, but, at least, they could preserve their national identity.

"The Hungarian minority is thus clearly by far the largest and most heavily concentrated", — realized Ghita Ionescu, — "more than a quarted of a million living in the Cluj area, almost the same number in the Oradea region, nearly 150,000 around Timisoara, over 100,000 around Brasov (#902), 37,000 in the Hunedoare region, and over a half million in the Magyar Autonomous Region in Eastern Transylvania. Here the proportion of Hungarians was 77.6 per cent, although in the country as a whole the Rumanian proportion was 65 per cent in 1956." (#903).

It was interesting, that the number of the Germans also grew by 10%. The deportations to Sibiria stopped, and the Saxons tried to live with the unsolvable facts. (#904).

One important change was (at the expense of the Hungarians, already in the Stalinist regime), that Bucharest pushed them out from the cities, towns, attempting to change the Magyar majority-situation into a Rumanian majority-situation. (In urban circumstances).

#900: Ghita Ionescu: "Communism in Rumania, 1944-1962." "The Opportunities for Coexistence." p. 294.

#901: See p. 169.

#902: Brasso, this ancient Hungarian town, which was called "Brasov" by Rumanians, which became "Stalin'" few years later — now became "Brasov" again. (Simultaneously the Hungarian Sztálinváros (Engl.: Stalintown), which was Dunapentele before the war, now became Dunaujváros (Engl.: Danube-new-town).

#903: Ionescu: "Communism in Rumania." p. 294.

#904: After 1956, the W. German Red Cross repatriated many families to West Germany (Until 1960 nearly 15,000 Germans were repatriated).

The following census-statistics indicate the shift brought about the forcible Rumanization practiced among the population of the twenty-five largest Transylvanian cities:

Hungarian sovereignty. Rumanian sovereignty. (#905).

Census:	1890	1910	1938	1948	1956
Hungarians	58.8%	65.3%	46.6%	41.0%	36.0%
Rumanians	15.8%	15.6%	32.0%	47.9%	51.9%

The replacement of the Hungarian population by Rumanian population was not simply an automatic process; it was not only the consequence of the fact, that Bucharest took over the domination and sent its officials to Transylvanian cities and towns; it was not only the natural consequence of the fact that after 1920, part of the illiterate Wallachian peasantry educated themselves, and appeared in the towns as some sort of new middle-class. Bucharest itself directed this process. The Rumanian officials were very unhappy to know, that twenty years after the Rumanian takeover, the majority of the large Transylvanian cities and towns were still Hungarians. Rumanization was very effective (the per cent of the Magyars dropped down from 65.3% to 46.6%), but still not satisfactory enough for the Rumanian Chauvinists. After 1945, the cities and towns became even more important for Bucharest, because rural life ment backwardness and poverty, urban life meant industrialization, labour class (which received new signaficance in the Communist regime), more culture and more comfort. Moscow did not let them go too far in the linguicide of the "alien" groups of Transylvania, but could not stop the effort of Bucharest to push the Hungarians out from the urban areas, replacing them by Rumanians from the Regat or Wallachians from rural Transylvania.

"The Rumanian authorities have been doing everything within their power to accelerate this development by refusing settling permits in these cities to the surrounding Hungarian population, while promoting the influx of ethnic Rumanians from the Regat, the Rumania of the pro-Trianon years." (#906).

Kolozsvár itself, was not an administrative, or political capital anymore, but still a cultural one. Its statistics over the last few decades were as follows:

Year	Total	Hungarian	Rumanian	German	Others	(#907).
1910	60,808	50,704	7,562	1,676	866	(#908).
1930	100,844	54,776	34,836	2,702	8,530	(#909).
1948	117,915	67,977	47,321	360	2,257	(#910).
1956	157,723	74,155	74,033	990	8,545	(#911).

#905: Osterhaven: "Transylvania" p. 12 ("Population").
#906: Ibid. p. 13.
#907: Ibid. p. 26. ("Kolozsvár, the Capital of Transylvania.")
#908: "Population Conditions of Transylvania "Journal de la Soc. Hongroise de Statistique, Budapest, 1939.
#909: "Recensamentul General al Papulatiei Romane din," 1930., Institutul Central de Statistics, Bucuresti, 1930.
#910: "Populatis Republicii Populara Romane le 25 Januarie 1948." Institutul Central de Statistics, Bucuresti, 1948.
#911: „Annarul Statistic al R.P.R." 1960., Bucuresti.

The loss of Kolozsvár was especially painful to Hungary in 1920, not only because its population was ethnically eighty-four percent Magyar, but because Kolozsvár was the most important cultural center in Transylvania and one of the most significant Hungarian centers in Hungary itself. "For centuries it has been a trustee of the Hungarian language, history, and other values which together determined its cultural heritage in the past and, in spite of present hardships, offered some hope for the future." (#912). In 1920, Kolozsvár was second only to Budapest in the total number of teachers and students, but a strong first in proportion to its population. ("In 1910 twenty-five parcent of its inhabitants were either educators or students in one of Kolozsvár's many schools. At the time of the transfer of Transylvania from Hungary to Rumania in 1920, there were eighty-nine educational institutions in the city." #913).

Kolozsvár, — as Cluj — was only the shadow of itself in 1956. The city became much bigger, but in a vulgarized way, the relative number of schools was much less, than forty years ago; industrialization appeared in the representation of large, smoky factories, and by the appearance of a large, semi-educated, mostly Wallachian labour-class; but

"it's twice as hard for Hungarians there, or, for that matter, for people of good will anywhere to witness the suppression of Hungarian culture in Kolozsvár today." (#914).

However, the cities were important for the Rumanian government. The Transylvanian cities were the largest cities in all of Rumania, if we would omit Bucharest, the capital itself. In 1956 this was the size of population of the five largest Rumanian cities: (#915).

City	Population	
1.) Bucharest	1,236,905	
2.) Kolozsvár (Cluj)	154,752	(#916)
3.) Temesvár (Timisoara)	142,251	
4.) Brasso (Brasov)	123,822	
5.) Ploesti	114,560	

Thus, from the five largest Rumanian cities, three were cities of Transylvania.

The increase of total population in the largest Transylvanian cities, shows the following picture:

City	1930	1941	1948	1956	(#917)
Cluj	100,844	110,956	117,915	154,752	(Hung:Kolozsvár)
Timisoara	91,580	110,840	111,987	142,251	(Hung:Temesvár)
Brasov	59,232	84,557	82,984	123,882	(Hung:Brasso)
Arad	77,181	86,674	87,291	106,457	(Hung:Arad)
Oradea	82,687	92,943	82,282	99,007	(Hung:Nagyvárad)
Sibiu	49,345	63,765	60,602	90,478	(Hung:Nagyszeben)
Tragu-Mures	38,517	44,946	47,043	65.118	(Hung:Szatmárnémeti)
Satu-Mare	51,495	52,006	46,519	52,099	(Hung:Marosvásárhely)

#912: Osterhaven: "Transylvania" p. 25.

#913: Ibid. p. 27.

#914: Ibid. p. 28.

#915: Fred S. Pisky: "The People." (From Stephen Fischer-Galati, Editor: "Romania." p. 42.)

#916: For some reason the population of Kolozsvár is not identical with the figure, produced on my previous page. (The source of Pisky was: "Populatia Republicii Populare Romane la 25 Ianuarie 1948", p. 14, Scanteia, May 6, 1956. (It is interesting that both of the authors used Rumanian documents, and they were not always identical).

#917: Fred S. Pisky: "The People." p. 42.

Thus, Kolozsvár (in 1956) was still the 2nd, Tmesevar the 3rd, Brasso the 4th, largest city of Greater Rumania. Additionally, it will be interesting to mention that

Arad, the 4th largest Transylvanian city, was 7th in whole Rumania,
Nagyvárad the 5th   10th ” ” ” ,
Nagyszeben 6th   13th ” ” ” ,
Marosvásárhely, the 7th largest   14th ” ” ” ,
and Szatmárnémeti, 8th   16th ” ” ” .

Of the sixteen largest cities of Greater Rumania, eight were actually Transylvanian cities, and built by Huingarians already in the Medieval Ages. (#918).

Taking a look at the absolute numbers of the largest Transylvanian cities (p. 180, #917), and remembering that from 1910 to 1956, the former 65.3% Magyar population was "transformed" into 36% Magyar population, we may have ideas about the aggressive Rumanization of Bucharest during this, historically quite short period, and the strong tendency, to "urbanize" Wallachians at the expense of the ethnic minority. (Evidence of Rumaniazation on p. 179, #905). (See also next page, with the map of Transylvania of today.

On October 23, 1956, the desire of the Hungarians for democratic Socialism and for national independency exploded in a revolution, and continued as freedomfight in the following days.

> "The 1956 Hungarian uprising" — remembers Zathureczky, — "which caused a great loss of prestige to the Soviet Union and disrupted the unity of the communist world movement, had its direct effect on Transylvania. We know positively today, that not only the Eastern European nations, but the youth of the Soviet Union itself, were sympathetic toward the Hungarians in their fight for freedom and were greatly influenced by this sponteneous outburst. However, due to the procrastination of the West, the Soviet Union, after having pulled out its troops once from Hungary, was able to return, and localize the outburst by crushing the uprising. Roumania stood on the side of the Soviet Union in those feverish days and immediately used the Hungarian uprising as a pretext for large scale actions of terror against the Transylvanian Hungarians." (#919).

Unquestionably, almost simultaneously with the beginning of the Hungarian Revolution, mass arrests, executions, and deportations were carried out in Transylvania. The prisons and forced labor camps were overcrowded again with thousands of Hungarians. When the Soviet tanks began to move against the people of Budapest, simultaneously the Rumanian Government received a free hand from the Kremlin in regard to its policy of terror against the Transylvanian Magyars. Khruschev had a general and a practical reason for this. (1) The general reason was, that he realised by this time already, that, (even after the death of Stalin,) only the system of Stalinism was able to preserve the power for the ruling class, both against other classes and against nationalities, or enslaved nations. (2) The practical reason was, as far as the "free hand" to Bucharest was concerned, that in Carpatho-Ukraine (#920), there was still a population of 200,000 "unreliable" Magyars, whose intimidation was in the interest of the Kremlin, and these activities had to be associated with activities in Transylvania.

#918: Figures from Fred S. Pisky: "The People." p. 42.

#919: Zathureczky: "Transylvania". pp. 54-55. "Transylvania under the Roumanian People's Republic."

#920: Originally part of Great Hungary, as "Ruthenia". Between 1920 and 1945, part of Czechoslovakia (Slovakia) as "Rusinko". The Soviet annexed it after World War II, as "Carpatho-Ukraine."

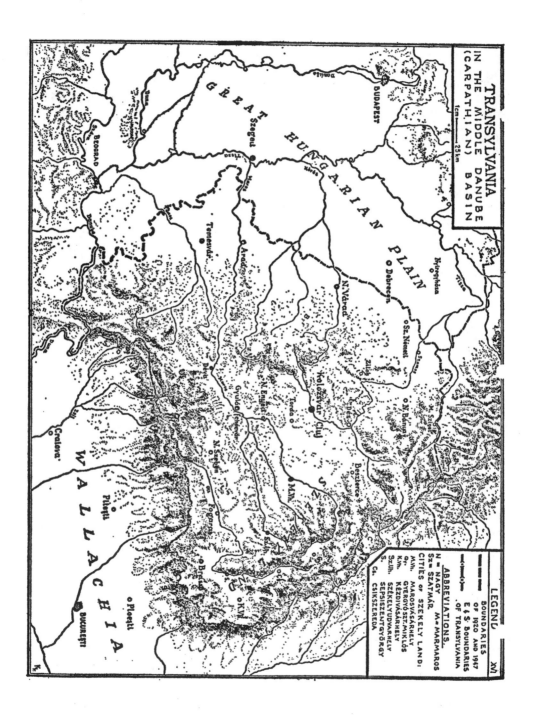

How did Rumanian officials, and the Stalinist press try to inform the people of Rumania about the Hungarian Revolution, in the first days?

"On 26 October" — answers Ghita Ionescu, — they were stigmatized as the work of capitalist agents. It is still a moot point whether Dej was not acting as Khruschev's emissary to discuss with Tito the deteriorating situation in Hungary and its possible repercussions on neighbournig countries such as Yugoslavia and Rumania, which might be faced with a free, anti-Communist and western-integrated Hungary." (#921).

However, the Transylvanians did not believe, that Budapest tried to start an "imperialist, capitalist, fascist", etc. revolution against "Socialism". They were too well informed. They realized this revolution as the struggle of the Hungarian Socialist, and Liberal elements against the terror of Stalinism, and against the colonial policy of Russia. The anxiety of the Rumanian Muscovites even increased, when, on Oct. 27, there were demonstrations even in Bucharest and Iasi. Disappointed Rumanians attempted to demonstrate their sympathy, — first time in Rumanian history! — with the fighting Hungarians! On the same day, Kolozsvár and Temesvár also reported to Bucharest, that the people on the streets, Magyors, and Wallachians alike, were demonstrating for freedom, cheering the "heroic" intellectuals, labourers, and soldiers of Hungary. Mostly the students in Transylvania and the Regat, were enthusiastic, and in their demonstrations, they demanded the abolition of the teaching of Russian in schools and universities.

"But especially in Bucharest, Iasi, and Timisoara, the workers were also active. Unrest was particularly marked at the headquarters of the railwaymen in Bucharest, and in Iasi, near the Soviet frontier, where many Soviet troops were stationed, street demonstrations took a defiant form." (#922).

Actually, Gheorghiu-Dei, as the First Secretary of the Party, was much more powerful, than Chivu Stoica, the Premier. Not the head of the Caminet, but he as the head of the Party, participated in the important discussion wih he Yugoslavs. On Oct. 23, he was still in Belgrade, when the news about the Hungarian Revolution arrived to him. The Rumanian Delegation hurriedly left Yugoslavia, and returning to Bucharest, the first thing that Gheorghiu-Dei did, was, to order the preparation of the Rumanian armed forces for a possible transfer into Hungary, in co-operation with the Soviet units, which were massed in Rumenia already, especially at the Hungarian-Transylvanian frontier.

"At the same time the increase of Soviet strength in Rumania was a source of strength to the Rumanian government, which was bending all its efforts to stemming rising unrest in that country too." (#923).

The effects of the Hungarian Revolution represented one more evidence, that the system of Stalinism was not only a system of domination, but also a system of preservation, of "self-defence". The panic of the Muscovites in Bucharest, and in Moscow, was closely connected to the fact, that the free radios, the newly published free press, all forms of the liberated mass communications openly called the other colonised nations, nationalities of Eastern Europe (a) to follow the Hungarian example, and (b) for the creation of a democratic Danubian Confederation!

#921: Ghita Ionescu: **"Communism in Rumania."** Ch. 12: "The Impact of Poland and Hungary." p. 267.

#922: **Ibid.** pp. 266-267.

#923: **Ibid.** p. 267.

Let me mention a few examples:

"Our country should become a member of the Danubian Federation as proposed by Kossuth." (#924) (#925), "The Hungarian Government should turn more attention to Hungarians living outside the Hungarian borders and should get in contact with these minorities. The foreign Policy Commitee of the Parliament should initiate a reconsideration of the Warsaw Pact and should propose the formation of a Danubian Confederation. (#926). "Slovaks! Rumanians! Serbians! Blood is flowing from our wounds and you are silent. We are fighting for liberty and you call us Fascist (#927), . . . We see that you too are groaning under the yoke we wish to throw off, . . . We are fighting for you too, for peace, for Socialist truth, for the guarantee of free development of our peoples. Help us in our fight!" (#928). "Yes, Hungary, from now on, has to work for the establishment of Kossuth's great legacy, the confederation of the Danubian people. This must be the most important demand of our foreign policy because only in this way can the small nations, living in this area, permanently safeguard their independence." (#929) "As of today we are no longer the tool of a colonialism disguised as socialism, nor a figure on the chess-board of some conqueror or other . . . (#930). We are extending a friendly hand towards all people, — to our neighbors, neutral Austria, and to free Yugoslavia which remains outside any blocks, towards Rumania, Czechoslovakia and the people of the Soviet Unon, we hope that their Governments will understand our little nation's thirst for freedom and national life . . ." (#931). The desire to live in friendship and in mutual respect, . . . in good neighborly relationship with Prague, Bucharest, Warsaw and Belgrad. (#932). "Rumanian and Slovak Brothers! We are bleeding and you are silent? We are fighting for freedom and you call us Fascists? . . . When we are talking about a confederation, we want friendship! . . . For us, brotherly nations, we want free development in a neutral political system . . ." (#933). Etc. etc. (#934).

One of the West-German newspaper, "THE SPIEGEL" gave probably the best information on the free world about the Hungarian Revolution and Freedomfight. (#935). One of its articles, under the title "The Hungarians are coming!", describes, how Moscow worked, in co-operation with the Rumanian secret police ("Securitate") in Transylvania, to stop demonstrations, and to turn the Transylvanian Wallachians against the Hungarian Revolution. They had a copy of the "14 Points" of the Hungarian students of Budapest re-published this pamphlet (which did not include of course, any revisionist, or anti-Rumanian centence), adding to it a "Point 15", according to which, the rebels "demanded the immediate reqonquest of Transylvania." The trick worked very well. Moscow, and the Muscovites always knew, when, in what cases, will Chauvinism aid their "internationalism". Simultaneously, their agents appeared among

#924: Kossuth became the greatest advocat of a Danubian Federation in his older years in Turin.

#925: Oct. 26, 1956. "Student Parliament Miskolc." Broadcasted Radio Free Kossuth.

#926: "Revolutionary National Council, Veszprém County."

#927: Of course, the "Fascist"-nomination appeared in the Muscovite-directed Czech, Slovak, Rumanian, Bulgarian newspapers, already beginning with Oct. 24, to mislead the public opinion in the satellite system.

#928: October 30, 1956. Radio Free Miskolc.

#929: Nov. 1, 1956. "Magyar Szabadság", newly publ. newspaper. (First page).

#930: This sentence was especially a message to the people of Transylvania, to all the three ethno-linguistic groups.

#931: "The Council of Free Trade Unions", in their official paper.

#932: Cardinal Mindszenthy's broadcast in the Radio Free Kossuth, Budapest.

#933: Radios Miskolc and Nyiregyháza (in Slovak and Rumanian language!)

#934: Quotations from the Study of Edmund I. Lázár: "Federalist Aspirations in East-Central Europe." ("Studies for a New Central Europe." 1964. p. 44.)

#935: The report of the "Anatomy of Revolution." Washington, Public Affairs Press, 1957. based largely on the direct reports of he Spiegel and others.

the Transylvanian Magyar university and high-school students, and at the meetings of the Transylvanian Magyar labour, hinting, that "The Hungarians are coming!" It was a good step to provoke irresbonsible extremism, and to have excuses for arrests in large number. With this trick, the Muscovites were able to separate the Transylvanian Wallachians from the Magyars again. Simultaneously, Bucharest" placed the Oradea, Timisoara. Iasi regions under special military jurisdiction, and "no foreigners were alowed to enter either Moldavia or Transylvania." (#936). In spite of this, the demonstrations did not stop. The Muscovite Press criticised the "unhealthy attitude of students", and of course, continued to charge the Transylvanian Magyar professors, and scholars with "Fascism." (Most of these, were actually Liberals, middle class-Jews, even Socialdemocrats, or "Titoists". Unquestionably, the national feeling of solidarity appeared in the circles of the Hungarian intelligentsia, but, understandig the call for a Danubian Federation, they demonstrated on the streets not only with Hungarian, but with Rumanian flags. They welcomed the Hungarian Revolution, not only as Hungarians by origin, but as citizens of Rumania, desiring freedom, and political independence. from Russia.)

The Transylvanian demonstrators were much more cautious than the Hungarians. The Wallachians did not associate their demonstrations with historical traditions. The Transylvanian Magyars, were hoping for rather an independent Transylvania, than re-unification with Hungary. According to Stephen Fischer-Galati ". . . the most striking phenomenon in the few demonstrations . . . reflected dissatisfaction with economic conditions and anti-Russian grievances. No calls for the overthrow of the Communist regime per se voiced at any time." (#937). The author, I feel, underestimated the significance of these demonstrations. However, even in the Hungarian demonstrations, the demonstrators advocated against Russian interference in internal affairs, and the workers demands for more favorable working conditions The general attitude of the demonstrations, both in Hungary and Rumania, were rather pro-Socialist, that anti-Socialist. The naive demonstrators did not even suspect, that their movement, their anti-Stalinist demands will be "considered", "interpreted", falsified, publicized, and propagated, as "anti -Socialism", "Fascism", "provocation of the Western Imperialists", etc. Gheorghiu-Dei realized, just like the Muscovites in Budapest, or the Kreml itself, that the apperance of true Socialist demands, connected with Liberalism, democratizations, national selfdetermination, etc., could result not only in the disintegration of the East-European empire, but the disintegration of the Soviet Union itself. To condemn any "counter-revolution" as "Fascism", "Capitalism" etc., was the only way of "self-defence" for the Muscovites in Moscow, and in all the satellite capitals.

Gheorghiu-Dei knew, that Rákosi and Gerö could not return to Hungary anymore. He also knew, that János Kádár, who appeared among the new "democratic Socialist" in the Imre Nagy Revolutionary Government, was actually the filtered agent of Khruschev. He suspected that the West will only "glorify" the "heroes of Budapest", but will not take any positive step. He suspected, that the United Nations will be paralyzed by various Muscovite tricks. Knowing, and suspecting all these, he concentrated only on "consolidation" in Transylvania, and in the rest of Rumania. When Moscow began the deportations from Hungary to Sibiria, Bucharest used the opportunity to deport thousands of Transylvanian Magyars and Saxons with these shipments, and the prisons, labor camps of Rumania were filled with Hungarians again.

#936: Ghita Ionescu: **"Communism in Rumania, 1944-1962."** p. 268.

#937: Stephen Fischer-Galati: **"The New Rumania". "From People's Democracy to Socialist Republic."** The M.I.T. Press, Cambridge, Massachusetts, and London (England), 1967. p. 63. ("Recular Our Mieux Sauter", 1952-1960).

XX

THE RUMANIAN "NATIONAL COMMUNISM" AND TRANSYLVANIA.

The events in Hungary, following the massive Soviet military interference, do not belong in the framework of this essay. The system of the Muscovite revenge, using the irresolute and opportunist semi-Stalinist Kádár Government, will be studies and analyzed by professional "Kremlinologists" for many more years. Let us return to Rumania.

Although János Kádár faced many more problems in Hungary, than Gheorghiu-Dei in Rumania, it was unquestionable, that (even many months and years after the series of excutions, deportations, imprisonments), in all satellite conutries "Fascism" received a new interpretation. It was associated with Hitler, Mussolini, Francisco Franco and with the Japanese dictators until 1956. Since 1956, every revolutionary feeling, any emotion, which attempted to immagine "Socialism" without Muscovite "patronage',' was labeled as "Fascism", stimulated by the "Western Imperialists".

However, the Muscovite propagandists had to re-interpret, even rewrite the works of Karl Marx, and of Lenin too! The works of Stalin disappeared from the bookshelves, but the "Ruling Class", from now on, had more and more troubles with curious communist students too, who seemed to be puzzled with statements, of Lenin, like this:

> "Some people belive, that revolution in a country could be prepared by order, or by agreement. We know that it would not be possible to make a revolution in any country by order, or by agreement. Revolutions will break out, when Tenmillions reach the the conclusion, that they could not live like this anymore." (#938).

George Bailey, an American journalist, decribed the oppression of the Hungarians in Transylvania. (#939). According to him, after the crushing of the Hungarian Revolution of 1956,

> ". . . thousands of Hungarians were arrested, perhaps hundreds put to death. In one trial alone in Cluj, thirteen out of fifty-seven accused were executed. This year some eight thousand political prisoners were released with considerable fanfare by the Rumanian government in a general amnesty. (#940). But as far as I could ascertain in my recent travels through Transylvania, not one of the Hungarians arrested during the revolt has yet been released." (#941).

Bucharest, of course, reestablished the diplomatic relations with the semi-Stalinist Government of János Kádár. "Gheorghiu-Dei, and Stoica led two delegations to Hungary in November 1956 already, and January, 1957. The object of these visits seems to have been to persuade the new Hungarian leaders to renounce any claims to Transylvania, and to denounce those, who had taken part in the revolution as chauvinists and nationalists with irredentist aims. This Kadar did when he visited Rumania in February 1958." (#942). Following this, Bucharest continued the executions with more ambitions. The Hungarian Revolution was identified with "bourgeois chauvinism" in smaller cases, and with "criminal-minded Fascism" in more serious cases.

#938: "Lenin Művei." (Engl.: "The Works of Lenin.") Vol. 27. p. 491. Szikra, Budapest, 1952.

#939: In the "The Reporter" of November, 1964.

#940: In 1964, the satellite countries released many political prisoners.

#941: M. Eugene Osterhaven: "Transylvania." "The Present Situation of Hungarians in Transylvania." p. 34.

#942: Ghita Ionescu: "Communism in Rumania. 1944-1962." p. 294.

Bucharest had a very important role in the "Imre Nagy case." On November 14, Kádár promised not to take reprisals against freedom fighters and pledged to abolish the secret police. He promised to hold free elections, and include non-Communist parties in the government. He asserted, that Imre Nagy was not under arrest, because Imre Nagy was a "good communist", who did not deliberately aid the "counter revolution". Consequently Imre Nagy, — said Kádár, — has the choice of participating in Hungarian political life.

Until November 23, everybody knew, that Imre Nagy was kidnapped when he left the Yugoslav Embassy (#943) by a Soviet military motorized unit, waiting for him at the fron of the Embassy. On Nov. 23, an official comunique stated, that Imre Nagy "has asked and been granted permission to go to Rumania".

The Prime Minister never saw his beloved Hungary again!

Who killed him? We still do not know. Did he die in Rumania, or in Russia? Historians could not find out yet.

On November 25, Kádár delivered a speech in which he called Nagy's departure for Rumania "correct", because his presence would stir up trouble. He insisted, however, that Nagy was free, and he was not exiled. The next day, Kádár, surprisingly changed his tone, calling Imre Nagy a "counterrevolutionary", an "Imperialist agent", etc. On June 17, Moscow and the Kádár Government simultaneously announced, that Imre Nagy, and all leaders of the "Fascist Counterrevolution" were executed. and some minor leaders were imprisoned for life. We know now, that János Kádár was informed about the "executions" only, when Moscow felt that the time was right to inform him, but we still do not know anything about the "legal process", and the place of the excutions. We know, that Bucharest co-operated with Moscow, and after 1958, the Soviet troons left Rumania, declaring that, Rumania proved her "political maturity" in the previous years. (#944). Beginning with 1959, Bucharest, under the leadership of the "new star", Nicolae Ceausescu, began the final closing of all Hungarian educational institutions, including universities, high-schools, and elementary schools. Unquestionably, Rumania received a free hand from now on from Russia. Terroristic Rumanization was associated with the military terror in the minority-towns and villages. Rumania received special permission to exercise some sort of "National Communism" under the supervision of Russia. Russia realized, that extreme nationalism was one of the main characteristics of the politicians in Rumania Proper. Russia also realized, that Bucharest was tending to imitate the system of Tito in Yugoslavia. "Paying" to the Muscovites of Bucharest for the "co-operation" since 1956, Muscow did not mind to begin this new experiment.

Simultaneously the Soviet policy toward Hungary could be defined in these points: (a) To make the Magyars realize, that the West had given up Eastern Europe completely, and there could be no hope for aid against a Russian type of communism. (b) The World should learn now from the Hungarian example, that there can be no revolt against the Kremlin. (c) To create through small concessions (which could be revoked at any time), an atmosphere which would take the wind out of the sail of future revolutions. (#945).

Gheorghiu-Dej, returning from Moscow, on February 19, 1959, said: „The basic principles of our great Party recognizes the equal rights of the ethnic minorities." Following this phrase, Ceausescu (mentioned al-

---

#943: He received there some sort of temporary refuge for few days.

#944: All these troops, and many others, concentrated from now on in Hungary, especially around the industrial centers, and at the Austrian border.

#945: Khruschev's tactic worked well for years. In 1968, the "melting" in Prague began, but Dubcek learnt from the fate of the Hungarians, and opposed armed resistance. Nevertheless, the "Czechoslovak Spring" became, in many of its characteristics, similar to the Hungarian Revolution.

ready in this Chapter),launched the last period of the Rumanian "denationalization" program against the Transylvanian Hungarians. On that very day, when Ghearghiu-Dej, arrived and declared his hypocritical sentence, a special meeting was called at the Hungarian University of Kolozsvár, where "the speakers of the Party declared that 'the higher interests of socialism demand that the ethnic minorities learn the Roumanian language and learn to appreciate the Roumanian culture of the homeland'." (#946).

> "Two weeks later, it was pointed out that 'the maintenance of a bilingual university is in opposition to the interests of socialism, and national isolationism in culture and science, just like any other manifestation of nationalism, is a poisoned weapon in the hands of the enemies of the people'." (#947).

This was the end of Hungarian opportunities to learn anything in the Hungarian language. The Hungarian and Rumanian universities, the Hungarian and Rumanian high schools 'fusioned'. To be a Hungarian, it became a very shameful thing in Rumania from now on. Around 1960, it was still possible to find undergraduate courses, where the teaching-languange was Hungarian. After 1960, the Hungarian language disappeared from all the schools. The young Magyars learned to realize very fast, that to find a wider field for their talent, they had to abandon their Hungarian identity.

The persecutions appered, of course, in other fields too.

> "The peasants found themselves without farms and were herded into the kolkhozes, a national workers' organization was labelled 'forign to the classes', i.e. to the proletariat. . . . A merciless persecution of the Church followed. Hordes of Rumanians from the old kingdom were imported into the frontier regions populated by Hungarians, in an attempt to recast the ethnic make-up. The Rumanian country-proletariat descended upon the towns. The prisons overflowed with Hungarians, and they were deported by tens of thousands as forced laborers into the swamps of the Danube delta." (#948).

On December 24, 1960, the Rumanian Parliament passed a resolution in which two districts were removed from the "Autonom Hungarian Province" and attached to a Rumanian populated territorial district. The population of these two (replaced) districts was 92% Hungarian. At the same time, another large area was added to the "Autonom Hungarian Province" on the other side, with an 88% Wallachian population. The name was changed from "Autonom Hungarian Province" to "Autonom Hungarian-Mures Territory". The population, by these administrative changes, changed too; the Magyar population was reduced from 79.38% to 63. 97% and the Rumanian increased from 20.62% to 36.03%.

> "Rumanian has effectively replaced Hungarian at every level as the language of official and public life." — wrote George Bailey. (#949). Then he described, that Hungarians are scared to use their native language, if a "stranger" was at present, suspecting that the "stranger" might be from the secret police. Then he continued this way: "The Rumanian authorities have adopted a wide variety of measures to isolate the Hungarian minority from contact with . . . their homeland. Foreign tourists in Rumania are allowed the run of the country, unless the tourist happens to be a Hungarian citizen." (#950).

#946: Zathureczky: "Transylvania". p. 55.
#947: Ibid. pp. 55-56.
#948: Gyula Zathureczky: "National Minorities, Step-Children in Communist Lands." (In "Studies for a New Central Europe." 1964. Vol. 1. No. 2. p. 37.)
#949: In "The Reporter". Nov. 1964. Quoted by Osterhaven: "Transylvanja."
#950: Osterhaven: "Transylvania." pp. 34-35.

The Rumaniazatsion of Transylvania, especially on political fields, was so "successful", that, when, in Sept. 1963, Gheorghiu-Dej visited the "Autonom Territory", the newspapers reported the names of those leading officials who were responsible for the "well-being" of the people of that territory. There was not one Hungarian name among them.

Did Transylvania become a totally Wallachian populated territory? Was the anxiety of Bucharest over about the Hungarian problem? Absolutely not! Moscow itself did not wish the complete annihilation of the Magyars in Transylvania. From the point of view of the Kremlin, it was much better, if Rumania was a troubled, multinational state, than a unified, Nation. The "Divide et Impera" — policy could be played only with an emotionally, culturally-divided country. And, since Maoist China turned against the Soviet Union, the Kremlin needed very much to use the "Divide et Impera" — policy again!

Tito became very independent since about 1958, thus Moscow could not use the traditional Serbian-Croatian hostility against Belgrade. Bulgaria did not mean so much. With her nearly eight million population, she was a national state, especially, since the Bulgarian Muscovites expelled the Turkish minority. (1950). However, Bulgaria played a relatively minor role in the satellite system of the Kremlin. Moscow kept the traditional Czech — Slovakian hostility alive. Novotny, and the other Muscovites in Prague were in absolute power, and the Czechs voluntarily joined Moscow in 1945, but the Kremlin knew, that Czech nationalism was seriously insulted by the liquidation of Ian Masaryok and the other national-democrats, and — it was so good to have a few ambitious young communists in the "storage", especially, because those Slovak communists hated the Czech communists, and believed that they would do better . . . Moscow did not believe, that "the most dangerous nationality", the Hungarians, would try anything in the coming decades. They lost too much in their revolution; among other things, they lost their faith in the West. However, Hungary was the only national State among the satellites (93% Magyars, according to the final figure). The Kremlin checked the Hungarians by stationing so many divisions in Hungary, which was almost enough for the conquest of the rest of Europe. Secondly: the Kremlin checked Hungary, by permitting unlimited increase of the population in Slovakia and Rumania Proper, without any artificial, medical limitation, and simultaneously, the Muscovites permitted free abortion in Hungary. The average abortion-cases in the 1960's, in Hungary exceeded 200,000 annually! Moscow hoped, that the Magyars could not revolt anymore, simply, because, around 1990, the country could not send enough people to the streets. (#951). The Muscovite calculation was very logical, and the hope of the Kremlin was realistic, for other reasons: (a) Hungary was the leading nation of the world as far as the number of suicides are concerned. (b) Hungary lost 200,000 emigrants after 1956, and (c) In October, 1956, 25,000 Magyars died on the bloody streets of Budapest, and elsewhere, and beginning with 1957 many thousands died in prisons, on the gallows, or in the labor-camps of the Russian empire. Yes, Moscow had many reasons to be optimistic about the Hungarians!

The Kreml could check Poland with East-Germany of Walter Ulbricht, and with the fact, that Poland was a multinational state too, with her many millions of German inhabitants. ("Wasserpolacks").

The Kreml could check Rumania, — blackmailing her with Transylvania!

#951: István Sisa mentioned in the **"Qou Vadis Hungaria?"** (Apr. 11, 1964, "Magyar Élet"-"Hungarian Life", Toronto) that in Hungary 21 (per thousand) was the rate of natural increase. (In Rumania 80 and in the Soviet Union 160 per thousand!)

In 1964, he Russo-Chinese relations turned to hostility between the two Communist Giants. Khrushchev determined to seek the expulsion of the Chinese from the international Communist movement. Simultaneously, and surprisingly, Rumania, — which was in search of a more independent foreign policy, — self-appointed herself as "mediator" and maverick in the Communist block. The Kremlin realized, that Bucharest was actually looking for the role of "balancer" in this new "Balance of Power", inside the Communist World.

"But whereas Peking sought to encourage the Rumanians' independent course despite the inadmissibility of their proposals, Moscow sought to force the unsuccessful Rumanians back into line. Upon the Rumanians' admission of failure it is reported that Khrushchev formally (but not publicly) raised the disturbing question of territorial revisionism in Transylvania." (#952).

The Russian dictator went so far, that, he suggested the holding of plebiscites in all areas of the Communist world where territorial questions could be raised. In Rumania's case, he specifically indicated his readiness to allow such plebiscites in Bessarabia as well as in Transylvania. It is not known whether the threat of reviving the territorial questions related to Bessarabia and Transylvania was used by Moscow to secure Rumanian adherence to the Kremlin's formula for Russo-Rumanian reconciliation; but it was sure, that Bucharest knew, that the Kremlin (even after the era of Khrushchev, in the Brechnev-Kossygin regime), could use Transylvania, any time, as a means of blackmail, against Rumanian politicians, who did not stop dreaming about "natonal communism" and political semi-independence, since 1964. The Russian dictatorship proved that they knew, and they were able to make better use of the great experiences of history, that the ignorant West. The Kremlin could operate so well with the "Divide et Impera" system, that the Habsburgs, and Adolf Hitler did not do better. Transylvania was always, and it is now more than ever before, an important card in the hand of the authoritarian (later: totalitarian) dictatorships in the great poker-game of international diplomacy.

If the United Nations Organization was not able, or if it was not willing, to serve the purpose of its original foundation anymore, if it — instead of being an international parliament in the defence of the smaller nations against the aggression of some Big Powers, — became a stage for the new Balance of Power; who, or what social, or political force could fight for Transylvania? What political force could prevent the final genocide of the Transylvanian Magyars?

In a Communist dictatorship political opposition does not exist, thus the Transylvanian Magyars could not hope for internal political aid. They could not hope for any aid from Hungary either, because the Kremlin put János Kádár into power, after 1956, on the condition of quiet obedience, and faithful service to the Russian interest, if necessary at the expense of the Hungarian interest itself. The Hungarian public was very well informed about the political, social and economic conditions of the Transylvanians, (#953), but the Kádárist government remained dead silent. (#954)

#952: Stephen Fischer-Galati: "The New Rumania." p. 101.

#953: The Rumanian average yearly salary was very low, even relating it to Iron Curtain countries. (Yearly income in the U.S.A.: $2,893. — In Canada: $1,825. Yearly income in the U.S.S.R. $1,195 — in Hungary: $1031 — in Czechoslovakia before 1968: $1,482 — in Poland: $904 — both in Bulgaria and Rumania: $691 per year. (Datas from 1967.)

#954: János Kádár occupied "only" the position of the First Secretary of the Paryt for years. Since 1965 Eugen (Jenö) Fock took the premiership over, but it did not make any significant difference: in Hungary both the Government and the Party were puppets of Moscow.

Russia knew, that neither Kádár's Hungary, nor Walter Ulbricht's East Germany will protest about the Transylvania situation. The Kremlin also knew, that since West Germany was not in the political position to protest; De Gaulle's France and Wilson's Britain did not wish to protest, the Transylvanian question remained a figure on the chessboard in the Russo-Rumanian game. The United States and Mao's China observed the Transylvanian situation; these two world powers expressed opinions of displeasure, from time to time, but these powers postponed any plan of international action for the far future, in this question.

But political activity in genocide cases should not be postponed! The only social and political force of the world, which did not postpone, and did not give up dealing with the Transylvanian problem, was the Hungarians living in free countries.

If we do not count the scattered Jews of this world, if we ignore the fact, that — due to the previous colonizations — Englishmen were populating actually all the Continents; the Hungarians were the only people, of whom only 68.2 per cent lived in, their motherland.

Here are the details (1968):

Hungary:	9,900,000
Neighbouring states:	3,350,000 (From this: 1,850,000 in Rumania)
Other states of Europe:	200,000
American Continent:	990,000 (From this: 800,00 in the U.S.A.)
Australia:	35,000
Africa and Asia:	25,000
Hungarians (total No.):	14,500.000 (#955).

Since Hungarians on the American Continent represent a considerably high number, and since many of these immigrant are in high political, or social positions, the "American Hungarian Federation" and in its frame, the "Transylvanian Institute of Philadelphia" attempted to introduce the Transylvanian problem to the American public, and to influence Washington to prevent the Transylvanian minorities from final annihilation. Since Hungarians in emigration celebrated the anniversaries of the fateful Treaty of Trianon (which was never ratified by Washington), the Transylvanian problem reappeared in the American Senate, time after time.

Of course, many western newspapers reminded the public about the terror in Transylvania, since 1962. Gearge Bailley wrote (#956), that "By the end of 1962 there was no longer a single wholly separate Hungarian school in Rumania." The NEUE ZÜRICHER ZEITUNG mentioned (#957), that "the presence of the secret police is still strong. Political opponents and troublesome intellectuals are put behind bars without delay". The Transylvanian Institute of Philadelphia, annaunced in a separate pamphelt, that "A few courageous Hungarians (of Transylvania) have addressed a memorandum to the United Nation protesting against these actions. They have been arrested and excuted. Others have organized a movement to annex Transylvania to the Soviet Union, Their names have been given out by Moscow to the Rumanian authorities who condemned them to 25 years in prison." (#958). Many Transylvanians left their homeland, and migrated to Bucharest, in search of more humane conditions. "Bucharest has about 250,000 Magyar inhabitants." — wrote the "LE MONDE" in 1964. (#959).

#955: Official datas from the United Nations ethnographical figures. (1968).

#956: In "The Reporter." (Nov. 1964). Quoted from Osterhaven's "Transylvania." p. 34.

#957: Quotation from Osterhaven's "Transylvania." p. 32.

#958: Pamphlet of the Transylvanian Institute of Philadelphia, 1968.: "The Problem of Transylvania."

#959: "Le Monde", July 4-5, Paris. Quotation from the "Irodalmi Ujság" ("Literary News") of Paris. 1968. (Tamás Schreiber: The Situation of the Hungarian Minority in Rumania.")

The "International Commission of Jurists" examined the Transylvanian minority problem in 1962—63. The results of this examination was published already in 1963, and in various politcal periodicals only in 1964.

"In a Communist State" — wrote the report — the denial of freedom to any particular group must be examined in the context of the entire social and political outlook of the State, since many rights and freedoms as understood in liberal democracies are denied to the whole population." (#960).

Knowing this, and pointing this out in the very beginning, the Commission found a situation in Transylvania, which was unusual even in a communist dictatorship. The Commission included in its Report the fact, that the Peace Treaty between the Allied Powers and Rumania in 1947, stipulated in Part II (Political Clauses), Section I, Art. 3, that

(1) Rumania shal take the steps necessary to secure to all persons nder Rumanian jurisdiction, without distinction as to race, sex, language or religion, the enjoyment of human rights and fundamental freedoms, including freedom of expression, of press and publication, of religious worship, of political opinion and of public meeting.

(2) Rumania further undertakes that the laws in force in Rumania shall not, either in their content or in their application, discriminate or entail any discrimination between persons of Rumanian nationality on the ground of their race, sex, language or religion, whether in reference to their persons, property, business, professional, or financial interests, status, political or civil rights or any other matter." (#961).

The Commission found, that Rumania ignored the Political Clauses of the Peace Treaty, and ignored its own Constitution, in which Article 82. provides that "all the national groups are entitled to use their respective languages and to have at all levels establishments of public education in which instruction is given in their mother tongue, and further that the spoken and written language used by administrative and judicial authorities in disctricts where a national group other than Rumanian is in the majority should be the language of this national group. Civil servants in such areas should be appointed from among members of this majority group, or if from other groups, it is necessary that they speak the language of the majority," etc. (#962).

The Commission found, that Bucharest ignored the Rumanian Constitution, which also promised to protect national minorities, and especially their culture, their equality before the law, and against any kind of chauvinistic persecution. The Commission found, that Rumanian administrative measures, and discrimination in the cultural field, is actually leading to the final genocide of minorities in Transylvania.

This genocide is going on, using the system of linguicide.

". . . the whole pattern of cutting down Hungarian-language instruction in an area which is or was so Hungarian that it was a part of Hungary for almost 900 years cannot be reconciled with respect to the constitutional rights of the Hungarian minority and is by no means explicable as part of the normal process of shaping a Communist society. For centuries Hungarian culture and tradition have taken deep root and susvived the vicissitudes of fortune, both kindly and outrageous. It is diffecult to conceive that a people so deeply rooted in its culture would itself clamour for the destruction of that culture by absorption into the Rumanian mainstream." (#963).

#960: Intern. Com. of Jurists: "The Hungarian Minority Problem in Rumania."
#961: Ibid.
#962: Ibid.
#963: Ibid.

The Report ends with this conclusion:

"Too many individual items which could be capable of other explanations than discrimination if taken singly point unmistakably when viwed as a whole towards a pattern of conduct. In short, as far as the Hungarian people in Rumania are concerned, they appear in the give and take of living together to lose on both the swings and the roundabouts. When this happens to a minority group it is rifficult to resist the conclusion that they are being subjected to discrimination." (#964).

The Situation in Transylvania turned to the worse after this Report, which was ignored both by Bucharest and Moscow. The "collectivization" into agricultural cooperatives was managed by terror. The Rumanian "militia" (#965) coerced the Székelys in the "Autonomus" territory by beating them up or by torturing them to make them join the agricultural cooperative farms, known as "Kolchos"—s. They had to hand over, without compensation, their lands, animals, and equipment.

"People, without exception, including clergymen, are forced to work in the collectives and even then it took beating and torture to subdue the Székelys. In Gyergyo people fled to the forests or mountains but the Rumanian militia hunted them down and shot them." (#966).

Bucharest also proved that it adopted the "experience" of Lenin-Stalinism very well. In order to make it seem that the Hungarians are on their side, they listed the handful of Hungarian collaborators and traitors who, motivated by personal ambition and often using Rumanianized names, follow the orders issued by the Rumanian overlords.

"Authorities . . . mention that there is a Hungarian language press and there are Hungarian theaters in Rumania, but they do not mention that they have been made instruments of subtle Rumanian Communist propoganda in order to nip in the bud any Hungarian nationalist sentiment, any historical consciousness, or memory." ,#967).

The Hungarian churches are exposed to a considerable duress and Catholic priests and Protestant ministers are exposed to constant harassment. According to the latest informations, a number of priests and ministers were released in the amnesties, but they were not allowed to resume their work or return to their residences. The police institution known as the "Office of Church Affairs," maintains strong control over all functions of the churches, especially of the Hungarian churches.

The Protestant and Roman Catholic high schools were either liquidated or transformed into Rumanian state institutions, with the aim of spreading the spirit of Communism and Rumanian national chauvinism. One of the most tragic milestones of forceful Rumanization was the merger of the Hungarian and Rumanian universities of Kolozsvár into one Rumanian institution. (#968). Following the merger, many of the Magyar professors committed suicide as a sign of protest and despair.

#964: Bulletin of the "International Commission of Jurists", No. 17: "The Hungarian Minority Problem in Rumania." (From the "Studies for a New Central Europe." Vol. 1, 1964. Editor: Alexander Gallus. pp. 72-77.)

#965: Gendarmes, police, political police, and investigators.

#966: Osterhaven: "Transylvania." p. 35.

#967: Ibid. p. 36.

#968: It was carried out by the Secretary General of the Communist Party, and President of Rumania, Ceausescu.

On October 12, 1967, the Executive Committee of the Rumanian Communist Party decided to abolish all administrative districts, including the "Mures-Magyar Autonomous Territory" and return to the prewar county system. This spells the end of the hitherto nominal autonomy of this Hungarian area.

"The chauvinistic policy of Communist Rumania in its Stalinist anti-Hungarianism disregards all human rights and international obligations solemnly agreed upon and promised in peace treaties." (#969).

"Rumania of 1970" was not similar to "Rumania of 1945" anymore. In 1945, Bucharest, already ruled by pro-Russians, and partly by Muscovites, receiving Transylvania from the Kreml, tried to prove its loyalty, with selfhumiliating complaisance. In 1956, Bucharest, still under Muscovite, Stalinist rule, learned, that serving Russia in the destruction of the Hungarian uprising, helps not only "proletar-internationalism", (#970), but, simultaneously aids Rumanian nationalist ambitions. After 1956, the Kreml tried to use Transylvania as a means of blackmail against Rumania, which changed her previous attitude, and from servile statellite, attempted to become a semi-independent, "national-communist" state. Rumania knows, that, as a multi-national state, she could be easily the victim of the "Divide et Impera" policy. Consequently, the Rumanian Government, (Stalinist in internal affairs, but not Muscovite in international relations anymore!) — exercises the most forceful extermination of the natinal minorities, — to become a "national state", as soon as possible.

Will this effort be successful?

The answer for this question will be written in another Chapter. This other Chapter will be part of another essay, written by another author — in the future.

Transylvania, this East-European citadel of the Western European culture, includes still three main ethno-linguistic nationalities today. The cultural traditions of the national minorities are still essential parts of the every-day life in this land. Linguicide, in 1970, was still quite far away from final, and complete success.

In the beginning of 1970, — when I arrived to the final conclusion of this essay, — it seems, that Rumanian "national communism" tries to continue its dangerous game, attempting to play the role of the "balancer" between the two Communist Giants, Russia and China. Simultaneously, Rumania tries to renew her former Western connections too. (#971). Bucharest realizes that the continuation of this game is very dangerous in the neighbourhood of Soviet Russia. They may face the "Brezhnev Doctrine" in the representation of the endless line of Russian tanks any time. Rumanian nationalism takes this risk anyway.

Changes in the international situation could offer a new chapter, — better or worse, — in the history of Transylvania.

#969: Osterhaven: **"Transylvania."** p. 40.

#970: Or using "other words": the Russian imperial interests. (The fact, that the phrase of "proletar-internationalism" was actually a cover term for the Russian imperialistic ambitions, became quite clear following the destruction of the "Czechoslovak Spring" by the Russian tank-divisions, when Brezhnev, with his famous "Doctrine" attempted to associate the interests of "proletar-internationalism" with the interest of Soviet-Russia. 1968-1969.)

#971: Diplomatic connections between France and Rumania, President Nixon's visit to Bucharest in 1969, were clear evidence of this policy.

XXI.

CONCLUSION.

In this essay I attempted to discuss one of the most complex minority problems, that the history of mankind ever produced; the minority problems of Trasylvania.

I am using the term "problems", and not simply "problem", on purpose. My study of Transylvania gave me, and supposedly to the readers of this essay too, the recognition, that we were dealing here, not with one problem, but with a chain of many problems, both in chronological, and in territorial sense.

We were dealing with the series of problems in chronological sense, because Transylvania's geographical location was, in the time of the Great Migration, exactly at the frontier line of the Roman Empire facing the coming waves of various Asiatic hordes; because Transylvania represented the crossroad for the newcomers to move westward, or southward; Transylvania, with its mountains and deep river valleys, became the hiding palce of many ethnic fragments in the middle of the migratory storms. Following these centuries, Transylvania preserved these curious ethnic characteristics, because the one thousand year long Hungarian domination was tolerant enough, and the various ethno-linguistic minorities could not only fit into the multinational system of the Holy Crown, but they were also protected to preserve their national culture. However, ethnolinguistic minority problems — in a chronological sence — appeared beginning with the thirteenth century, and the chain of these problems represented more and more difficulty, when the Wallachian infiltration from the Balkans, did not represent anymore only the humble request of the poor newcomer, asking for help, homes, protection, but it gradually transformed itself, and became the aggressive representation of a growing ethnic group, (minority in Hungary, but already majority in Transylvania), demanding political domination and — in order to achive the desired final goal, — producing a historical theory, which attempted to prove, that they, the immigrants from the Balkans, were the actual, legal owners of this land.

The minority problems of Transylvania, showing the characteristics of the chemical change-reactions, followed in a chronological sense, when the Hungarian majority became an ethno-linguistic minority, in an even larger multinatinal complexity: the Habsburg Empire. Beginning with this, the ethnic picture shows various levels or authority, where the minority could perhaps find solution in co-operation with the political power, which dominated the ethnic majority above. This hope and attempt always promised success, because the authority at the top of this complex multinational structure, was usualy willing to use the "Divide et impera"-system, which proved to be the only successful system in a multinational empire. To protect the weaker minorities, or even to incite them against the nationality, which seemed to be the most dangerous against the top-authority, was used, as a system, by the Habsburgs, very well. It was a difficult, and dangerous game, but the Habsburgs were good gamblers.

World War I proved that a multinational empire, where only the "Divide et impera" represented the main support of balance, fell down as a castle in the air, because it was not able to stand in the storms of nationalism.

Than minority change-reactions continued in Transylvania, and this land, after one thousand years, changed its master. The former ethnic majority became a minority, and the ethnic minority, together, and in co-operation with ist Balkanic relatives, became an overwhelming majority.

No reason to discuss details in this Conclusion, the changes, — which resulted that, for instance the present Transylvanian generation was forced to change its citizenship three times, without even leaving the town or village of its birthplace, — were introduced in the previous chapters. This incomplete, and oversimplified summary tries only to remind the reader, that the Transylvanian minority problems always represented series of connecting problems, in a chronological sense.

I mentioned in the beginning of this Conclusion, that the complexity of problems appeared not only in a chronological sense, but in a territorial sense as well.

What do I mean by this term: "territorial sense"?

If any sort of historical, political effect appears, in connection with the territorial location of a historical or political unit, we tend to draw together the words of "geography" and "politics", and we talk about "geopolitics". Well, Transylvania, with its complex minority problems, represents a good example in this "geopolitical" sense too. Transylvania is unquestionably a geographical unit, but unfortunately, this geographical unit existed always, throughout its entire history, at the frontiers, in the close neighbourhood, or even in the focus or crossroads of opposing, even larger geographical units, or more powerful political units. Transylvania was the place where the Romans faced the Great Migrations; Transylvania was the land where Huns and Avars could centralize themselves to meet the powers of Rome, Byzantium and the pressure of Asia; Transylvania was the area, which represented a natural citadel of the "pagan" Magyars against Roman-Europeanism; Transylvania was the borderland between Roman and Byzantine Christianity; Transylvania became the citadel of Europe against the terrible waves of the Mongols; Transylvanian became the citadel of Protestantism against the revenging hatred of the Counterreformation. Transylvania could biuld its own golden age, surrounded by the opposing imperialism of the Habsburgs and the Moslems, etc.

But could a multinational land, like Transylvania separate itself from the influencing, interfering ideas, propositions, intrigues of the international environment? Of course, it could not, and the interference of the international environment caused its repeated tragedies. Multinational atmosphere could cause hostility in a domestic sense, even without the provocations of some outside-power, but when ethno-linguistic cultural, or political ambitions were aided by the promises, or by the practical support of some outside powers, this unfortunate land usually became the battle-field, where the local ethnic groups were engaged in life-or-death battles, encouraged, or supported by one, or the other. neighbouring state, or empire. Did the Turks, the Wallachians of the Regat, the Habsburgs, the White or Red Tsars of Russia, really care about the future and happiness of Transylvania? Did Vienna, Moscow, Constantinople, Berlin, -- playing well, or not so well the "Divide et Impera"-game, — really associate themselves with the interests of the Transylvanian Magyars, Székelys, Wallachians, or Saxons? We learned from the lessons of history, detailed in this essay, that these outside powers did not care at all about the interest of Transylvania itself. Transylvania was nothing else in the great games of the East-European "Balance of Power", buth one minor weight on one or the other side of the scale, or it was nothing else, but one small figure on the chess-board.

In the twentieth century the World became smaller, and smaller again. Transylvania, one minor figure on the chessboard of Eastern-Europe, became evene a smalles, even less significant figure on the chessboard of Europe. If the sultans, the Habsburgs, or the Tsars did not care about the actual ethno-linguistic rights of some minor nationalities, so the new representatives of the "newly created political democracies" cared even less. "National selfdetermination" remained a "useless" slogan of the Wilsonian terminology. Who could care about national selfdetermination, when "Great Power interest" promised itself to become the magic solution for world-peace? Versailles and Trianon helped to disintegrate the "old and useless" Dual Montrchy. It was "immoral", because it was multinational. Consequently the mentioned peace treaties constructed three other artificial and multinational states in the Danubian Basin. The new states could not preserve their promised political democratic systems, — because in the circumstances of multinationality, political democracy gradually transformed itself into oppressive authoritarianism, or fascist dictatorship of the dominating nationality, — and the vacuum of power in East-Central Europe opened the door first to Pangermanism (appeared as Nazism), and later to Russian imperialism (appeared as Panslavism, Stalinism, and in our days as a penetrating action in the sense of the "Brezhnev Doctrine".)

The unfortunate geopolitical position of Transylvania appeared not only in the fact, that it became a figure on the chessboards of the Habsbugs, Clemenceau, Hitler, Stalin and the Red Tsars following him, but also in the fact, that the outside powers always used the special opportunity offered by the multinational conditions of Transylvania. Opportunist leaders studied the ethnic frontiers of Transylvania very carefully before international actions, because operating with these frontiers, using the nationalistic emotions of certain ethnic minorities against some other minorities, fit into the 'great plan" of the game. The provocation of ethnic hostility in Transylvania was associated with the plans of Great Powers, of the Habsburgs, the Nazis, or the Kremlin, so the very existence of the ethno-linguistic minority received a special significance — before, or during the international action. And following the action? Interestingly enough, the same Macchiavellism of Great Power-diplomacy, which studied and used the ethno-linguistic minorities of Transylvania in international conflicts, — seemed to "forget" their existence, when the time came to sign "peace"-treaties. The delegates cut the Carpathian Basin into pieces, and Transylvania was considered as a homogeneously Rumanian populated province, where the Magyar, Székely, and Saxon native population somhow "disappeared". When international diplomacy demonstrated in Yalta, that it did not learn anything from the dangerous consequences of Versailles, Transylvania again, together with many other unfortunate East-European lands, was simply sold by the West. Transylvania was dominated from now on by the double yoke of Russian imperialism and Rumanian nationalism, and the Kreml, — since then, — used Transylvania as a means of international blackmail again, as an area of the "Divide et Impera"-policy again, as a simple weight in the European "Balance of Power" again.

And, once again, I have to raise the main question: did anyone of the Great Powers, or any of the neighbouring states care about the actual interest of Transylvania itself? Do the peoples of this unfortunate land have any opportunity to express their own national interests? Did these people ever have an opportunity to prove, that — if outsiders would leave them alone, — they would be able to live in peace, to build their own political, social, economic life according to their own ideas?

Let me remind the reader now of my basic assumptions, which represented the role of some sort of opening thesis in may Introduction. My two assumptions were these:

a.) The Transylvanian problem represents not a border-dispute, but mainly the problem of co-existence among three ethno-linguistic nationalities in the frame of a geopolitical unit, which is Transylvania itself.

b). A just solution could be imagined only in a case when outside power-interest is not involved and the approach to final settlement is concerned with only the interests of the three Transylvanian nationalities. (#972).

My thesis guestion, in close connection with my two assumptions, was this:

How can the undisturbed and productive co-existence of the three Transylvanian nationalities best be achieved? (#973).

I mentioned many times in this essay, that political democracy in itself, could never represent a solution in multinational circumstances, because political remocracy in a practical sense is nothing else, but "the rule of the majority", consequently the minority will find itself in a constitutionally unfair position. We saw, that even in interwar-Czechoslovakia, where one of the "prophets" of Political democracy, Masaryk organized the political life of his artificial, newly created state, he, and his successors could not prevent, that Czechoslovakia became a dictatorship of the Czechs at the expense of the oppressed other nationalities. On the Balkans, where liberalization and democratization was not among the traditions and not among the national ambitions of the dominative nationality either, the interwar years produced royal dictatorships, later fascists dictatorships, where the major nationalities were protected, and the opporessed nationalities were ruthlessly dominated by the centralized, fascist state. In the case of Transylvania, the extreme nationalistic centralism of Bucharest, which associated itself so successfully with fascism in the interwar years, transformed itself into a "national communism", without losing its essential characteristic: extreme, oppressive nationalism. If this extreme nationalism is able to be "clever enough" to use "Big Power interest" for its nationalistic purpose, and to use the usual ignorance of "Big Powers" about ethnic minority problems, then nobody and nothing will stop Bucharest from completing the original plan: the genocide of ethnic minorities, other than Wallachians, in Transylvania.

> "It is obvious" — wrote Zathureczky, — "that the main reason for apparent insolvability of the Transylvanian problem can be found in the political system of our age and its practices. The rejecting attitude of the big powers, which they evidence in connection with this problem, exhibits a great measure of hypocrisy and is in complete opposition to the substantial interests of Europe." (#974).

Before proposing some sort of solution for the Transylvanian problem, let me speculate first, what was behind the ignorance of the West, which made Western politicians almost incapable to approach or to solve ethno-linguistic minority problems?

#972: See: Chapter I. p. 4.
#973: **Ibid.**
#974: Zathureczky: **Transylvania.** p. 6.

In Europe there were always peoples of different races, different languages, different religious beliefs and different cultures living together in the same organized framework of statehood. From the beginning of its history clear up to the 19th century, Europe recognized only two political and social units as absolute essentials: the State and the family. The relationship between these two units, State and family, was coordinated by the social system which grew out from the masses and which alone practiced politics: the nobility. In their hands lay the right and the possibility for organized action. They were the representatives of the State, and were called the Nation.

This situation began to change everywhere with the French Revolution. Everywhere where the peoples were affected by the new nationalism suggested by the French Revolution. "Nation" received a double meaning beginning with the nineteenth century. In one sense, it was recognized, that the nation, or nationality represents people with one language, with common historical and cultural traditions, but on the other hand and sense, and especially in multinational circumstances, the sovereign personality of the "absolute monarch", or the "major nationality", or simply the political structure of the State was associated with the term "nation". Consequently, philosophically, and theoretically, everybody agreed, that nation, and nationality has something to do with common language and customs, and historical and cultural traditions, — every encyclopeedia, and dictionary wrote this very clearly; but "practically", the word "Nation" was associated with the "State", because leading nationalities of certain "Big" and "Middle" Powers felt very uneasy about the original, philosophical meaning. After all, — they felt, — if we associate the "nationality" and the "nation" with some people speaking one common language, feeling togetherness because of common descent, or tradition; if we agree with the idea of "National selfdetermination", — then what will happen with our State? Consequently, it will fall into pieces.

It was much more "practical" to associate "nation" with the "State". Thus 'national selfdetermination" could represent the legality of the State in the international system.

We have many states in this World were the State is based on the people as an ethnic, linguistic and cultural unit. But, if we take a closer look at the Big Powers which represented extraordinary authority in the various peace-treaties after World War I and II, it will be easy to recognize, that these Big Powers, and their semi-colonies, and "dominions", were, and are mostly multinational complexes themselves, and not national states. In multinational complexes, strong central government, organized, and ruled by the "majority nationality", the term "State" is usually identified with the term "Nation". These types of States, and their delegates usually used the words "national selfdetermination" as a meaningless phrase, and East-Central Europe could never really hope just treaties from these delegates. After all, if the delegates would declare "nation" and "national selfdetermination" in its orginal and fair sense, who would prevent that some of the "restless" nationalities would demand the same recognition of "nation" and "national selfdetermination", — in their home?

Thus, Transylvania suffered not only the effects of the Macchiavellian Big Power neighbourhood, but also the Macchiavellian "ignorance" of some Western Powers, whose domestic interest suggested remaining-ignorant.

At this point, I have to mention again the great mistake of some Western politicians, who really believed, that political democracy will solve the ethnic problems. I discussed this in many parts of my essay, but here, in my Conclusion, (as an addition,) I quote one of the great experts on the Transylvanian problems, Zathureczky, again:

"The law and practice of democracy does not recognize ethnic autonomies. All it can do at best is to grant equal human rights. It does not
recognize ethnic groups as independent legal units, but it still demands
from them absolute loyalty. Therefore, the ethnic minorities, even in the
most tolerant States, must accept the status of second grade citizens."
(#975).

Law, Constitution usually underlines the fact, that the member of the
ethnic minority group is "equal" with any member of the major nationality. Here again, I have to underline the fact, that the real value of any
law bases itself on the actual opportunity. Without this opportunity, the
law remans empty phraseology. The uniforunate tact is, that members of
national minorities do not have the same opportunities as do the members
of the dominating nationality. In countries, where some ethnic nationalities are allowed to form their own political parties, their influence on the
policy of the State is very weak, if felt at all, because of their permanent
minority status. "Therefore, they feel that the country in which they live
is only their homeland in a regional and not in a political sense, and while
they try to find a modus vivendi in order to survive, they always nourish
the secret dreams of one day joining their own National State, by moving
the borders in order to fit heir own geographical location." (#976).

After this speculation, — which hopefully gives some ideas in ethnolinguistic problems, and also explains the behaviour of some Great Power
delegates in postwar "peace-treaties", let me return to Transylvania again.

There are two opposing political and philosophical views in connection
with the problems of Transylvania. Hungary (#977) claims Transylvania
on the basis of historic rights. In opposition to this point of view ,Ruma-
nia claims the land on the basis of the simple mathematical fact that the
majority of the population is Rumanian.

> "Hungarian rule over all Transylvania, Roumanian rule over all
> Transylvania, and partition having all proved unsatisfactory,
> how can the problem be dealt with?" — a question raised by Hugh
> Seton-Watson, — "The atitude of the nationalists on each side is
> irreconcilable. The Roumanians rightly insist, that they form the
> majority of the population, and have a much greater rate of in-
> crease . . . The Hungarians point out with equal truth that it is
> they who have given Transylvania its peculiar character, that for
> a thousand years the culture of Transylvania has been essentially
> Hungarian." (#978).

It is difficult to believe, that the restitution of the whole of Transylvania either to Rumania or to Hungary could bring a solution, as long as
either country remained organised as a nationalist State. (#979). The
Transylvanian problem cannot be solved permanently bv the dictatorial
assertion of "Rumanian Transylvania" or "Hungarian Transylvania."

There were always various "schools" of the "Transylvanian solution".
There were always politicians, history professors, or columnists, who believed and advocated, that "regional autonomy", "exchange of population",
or a "just federation" could be the "magic formula" for solution. Let us
examine these "magic formulas".

Both Hungarians and Rumanians advocated "regional autonomy" time,
after time. But the Hungarian "autonomists" insisted that autonomous
Transylvania should form part of Hungary, and the Rumanian "autonomists", that it should belong to a "national" Rumanian state.

#975: Zathureczky: **Transylvania**, p. 37.
#976: **Ibid.** pp. 37-38.
#977: Not "Hungarian Govt. of today", but Hungary in a traditional sense.
#978: Hugh Seton-Watson: **Eastern Europe Between the Wars.** pp. 303-304.
#979: Being communist countries formally Hungary and Rumania are not "national-
ists", but essentially, and emotionally, they certainly are.

"In fact" — felt H. Seton-Watson, — "past experience suggests that it is unlikely that any Roumanian or Hungarian Government which received Transylvania on condition that should be autonomous would execute its promise, or if it did so that it would maintain it for long." (#980, #981).

The supposed grant of "egional autonomy" would present other difficulties. Let us suppose, that Transylvania belongs to Hungary. Let us also suppose, that the Wallachians received regional autonomy in Transylvania. The Roumanian population of an autonomous Transylvania, or outonomous Rumanian population in the province of Transylvania, however free and happy it might be, could never forget that across the mountains lies a Rumanian "national" State, in which its kinsmen were not only free and happy, but were the dominant nation. The same would be true of the Hungarian population of the autonomous Transylvania belonged to nationalist Rumania, or the Magyars received autonomy in the national Rumanian State. However honourable the intentions of the central Government of Bucharest, or Budapest, there would be a "dominant nation" and a "secondary nation", and the latter would feel it had two countries, "its own" native homeland and "the other country" beyond the mountains. The original feeling of ethnic-nationalism would not be limited by the grant of "regional autonomy". It would only be encouraged.

I feel, that the grant of "regional autonomy" is not the right solution to the Transylvanian minority problem, even if we suppose the most generous, most democratic, most helpful attitude from the central Government or by the dominant ethno-linguistic nationality. The grant of "regional autonomy" could work only in some cases, when the kinsmen of the ethnic minority are not in the close neighbourhood, forming an independent national State. In Transylvania's case Hungary Proper, and Rumania Proper are at the frontiers of the country, and the nearness of the "homelands" could represent encouragment for the people of the "regionally autonomous" area, even if the homeland does not provoke this encouragement.

Let us examine now an other formula, promising solution in the Transylvanian ethnic problem. This is: the exchange of populations.

At this point, we have to remember again, that, curiously enough, the bulk of the Magyar and Székely population are living mostly at the eastern side of Transylvania, and the bulk of the Wallachians population is living rather in the western and central side. If we suppose the exchange of the Magyar populations with the Wallachian population, this activity could only mean and result in the partition of Transylvania. This land is a natural unit, a plateau, surrounded by very high mountains, and almost all the rivers are flowing from the inner side of these high mountains into the center of this plateau, or into the big rivers of the Carpathian Basin. (#982). Any partition of Transylvania represents a disruption which can only cause dislocation in the economic, social and cultural fields.

I have another argument against exchange of population, and against partition. Ignorance about the suffering of the population, ignorance about the social effect of artificial and superficial, "new", political frontiers, was always very characteristic, and typical, as the attitude of the delegates of certain multinational, or cosmopolitan powers, collaborating with extreme nationalist opportunists. Hugh Seton-Watson probably rea-

#980: H. Seton-Watson: **Eastern Europe Between the Wars.** p. 304.

#981: The "autonomy" of the Székelys in Communist Rumania in the time of Stalin and Khruschev was a formal autonomy only, actually subjected both to Moscow and Bucharest.

#982: Introduced and eplained in details in my Chapter II (pp. 5-7).

lized, that turning against the "peace-treaty"-systems of ingnorant Big Powers, and of extreme nationalist collaborators, actually, he criticized his father's (R.W. Seton-Watson) emotions, and the emotions of certain Versailles-Trainon-opportunists, (supported by the books, articles of his father.) He realized this, and he proved to be a courageous, abjective historian enough to introduce superficial treaties, artificial political frontiers, as sources of endless suffering and as sources of new wars. His comment on "exchange of population" and "partition of a natural unit" was this:

"This solution is essentially that of an arm-chair expert and of a nationalist intellectual at that. It takes no account of the devotion of the peasant to his home and his land as such, things much more important to him than the theories of elegant intellectual speculators." (#983).

To exchange the population would be inhuman, and would result in only the artificial division of a natural geopolitical unit. However, it would be definitely unfair against one of the interests. It would be entirely favourable to Rumania, because Wallachian population represents a majority in Transylvania, and the result of this supposed exchange would appear in a division in which Bucharest would receive a much larger part. The Hungarian claim on Transylvania was based on the fact, that this land was part of Hungary for one thousand years, and its culture is mainly Central-European and Hungarian culture. The Rumanian claim was based mainly on the fact that Transylvania is populated by more Wallachians than Magyars. (#984). Thus, any exchange of population and any partition following this population-exchange, would support only the Rumanian claim, which was connected with population and not with historical rights or culture.

One absurd result of the population-exchange would be, that the Székely monutaineers, populating the Eastern Carpathians for more than one thousand years, possibly even for a longer time (#985), would be draged away from their ancient home, and the Wallachian peasants of the Maros, or the Banat would be uprooted from the land they have enriched, shipping them to the slopes of the Székelyland, of whose problems they have neither experience nor understanding.

Well, it seems to me, that we have to throw out not only the idea and proposal of "regional autonomy", but also any ideas, or propositions, which would advocate "population-exchange" or "territorial partition". We have rejected these proposals, because they are unjust solutions, inhuman interferences, — or they do not represent any solution at all.

In order to find a suitable solution, we have to realize, that (a) Transylvania is an individual part of South-Eastern Europe, with well determined specific geopolitical and economic functions. Therefore, it must rejoin this geographical and cultural unit. (b) There can be no lasting peace in South-Eastern Europe until the unity of the Danubian Basin is restored.

The problem of the national minorities, not only in Transylvania, but in almost all multinational states of Europe, can be solved only in an all-European framework.

Zathureczky quotes Professor Ermacora, in connection with this question. Professor Ermacora summed up the activities of the United Nations, in the following words:

#983: H. Seton-Watson: **Eastern Europe Between the Wars.** p. 305.

#984: At this point, I do not take the "Dako-Roman theory" into consideration, because this theory could not be proved by Bucharest, and was not generally recognized by most of the historians of the world. The main basis of the Rumanian claim is unquestionably the Wallachian majority.

#985: The Székelys were only "in worst case" members of the conquering Magyars (9th C.). Much more probable that they are Hun or Avar descendants (from the 5th, or 8th centuries). (See Chs. IV and V).

"The attempts to include directives and regulations concerning the protection of ethnic minorities into the Declaration of Human Rights, failed. However, it was possible to include some such regulations into a draft dealing with civil and political rights. The United Nations prepared a whole series of studies and textcollections on this question. Finally, the General Assembly effectuated some concrete measures in the protection of some ethnic minorities." (#986).

The main sentence here was, that international attempts to include the protection of ethnic minorities into he Declaration of Human rights, failed. The problem of ethnic minorities, in most of the multinational states, was such a complex problem, that not yet has an international formula been found for its solution. Neither the Charter of the United Nations, nor the 1948 Declaration of Human rights contains clear provisions for the protection of ethnic minorities. International law, — which was usually not respected by powerful nations, and multinational empires, — international agreements and treaties, — which were also not respected by most of the states in a given time, — treated ethnic minorities in the spirit, and within the framework of the general and individual human rights, but these paragraphs of international law, or these sections of treaties became usually only useless pieces of papers, when the interest of some ruling group, or when the interest of some government, wished so. History has proven, that the value of those obligations, which are included in the international law, into peace treaties, or mutual agreements, depends always and everywhere upon the good will of the majority nationality in a multinational state. The "protection" of ethnic minorities could be included in multiliteral, or biliteral agreements, or could be included in the constitution of a state. The "practical" method is usually uniliteral, and this unliliterality is nothing else, but the activity of a government, influenced by the interest of a nationality, which is forming the majority in a particular multinational state.

If international law often becomes a piece paper, if international organizations (like the League of Nations and the United Nations) are losing the power of interference, and international respect; if multi-, and biliteral agrements, if obligations included in "national" constitutions, are losing their credits, — who, what possible political, or social force will be able to protect ethnic minorities from discrimination, or against various forms of genocide?

The answer must be connected with internationalism, even after the disappointing experiences with the League. with the United Nation; even after the disappointing experiences, caused by inhuman peace-treaties, infringed multiliteral and biliteral agreements, constitutions, ignored by governments. But, the solution should be connected with a very different type of "internationalism," with a very different type of "humanism", in the future.

"To solve this problem," — reminds Zathureczky, — „the evolution of international law and in the same time, the evolution of public opinion must reach the point where the ruling nation does not see any more 'foreign elements' in the minorities, and on the other hand, the ethnic groups take full responsibility for the well-being of the country and do not isolate themselves as minorities." (#987)

#986: Zathureczky here — in his **Transylvania**, pp. 57-58, — quoted from Felix Ermacora: **"Der Minderheitenschutz vor der Vereinigten Nationen."** Europa Ethnica, 1961, No. 3.

#987: **Ibid:** p. 58.

Zathureczky, of course, does not mean here the complete abandonment of isolation. Some kind of linguistic- cultural isolation is very necessary for the ethno-linguistic minority, surrounded by a different ethno-linguistic majority, because this is the only way to preserve the ethnolinguistic identity. However, this tendency toward isolation should not go into extremes. The member of the ethno-linguistic minority should not feel, that he is surrounded by some sort of "hostile" majority. Hostility should not be the main characteristic of the minortity and the individual in it. "Separatism" is obvious, and instinctive in cultural and linguistic fields, but not so obvious in social and political fields, so the ethnic minority should participate very actively in political-social life, aiding the majority in the creation of such conditions, which seem to satisfactory for the citizens of the given country, majority and minority alike.

But, let me return to the expected new ways of internationalism, which could bring new guarantees to the existence of ethnic minority groups, defending them against discriminations, or linguicide.

Today the integrationist movements of Europe seem to point in this direction. History shows that where ethnic minorities were treated without discrimination, a slow and steady assimilation has taken place. Persecution draws resistance and increases extreme nationalism.

> "However, the thought of assimilation should not even enter the
> question", — warns Zathureczky "It should be recognized as
> man's inalienable right to speak the language he wishes to speak,
> to worship God in the manner he wishes to worship, and to belong
> to any cultural circle to which he wishes to belong in his pursuit
> of happiness" (#988).

I mentioned in my Chapter XIX (pp. 183—184), that the Hungarian Revolution of 1956 was much more than a national resistance against Russian imperialism, and much more than the appearance of national-communism against Stalinism. The idea of the Danubian Confederation appeared again, not for the first time, and probably not for the last time in connection with Central or Eastern European problems, and in connection with the desire to solve those problems in the framework of a general solution. The idea of the Danubian Confederation should be, of course, only part of a general European Confederation. In the Western part af Europe, — not overshadowed by Russian imperialism and by the "Brezhnev Doctrine", — European integration, as a slow, but gradual movement exists. Probably, this movement is really too slow, and facing many difficulties, This slowness and the large number of difficulties creates bitterness and impatience. This slowness is natural, because we are living, basically, still in the age of nationalism. Nationalist tendencies are restraining factors. However, the time is coming, when the nationalist forces in Europe will realize, that European unification does not mean amalgamation, and national interest could fit into the framework of a general European interest. The historical fact, that Europe is under the unpleasant influence, both on her Western and Eastern side of alien spirits of other Continents (#989), and European unification is the only way to face this domination, will hopefully accelerate, even this natural integration.

The United Nations, as an international organization, proved to be impotent to solve ethno-linguistic minority problems. It became a new batt-

---

#988: Zathureczky: Transylvania. p. 58.

#989: At this point, I consider the Soviet Union as a basically Asiatic power, because its territory is mostly Asiatic, and in a smaller extent European; and secondly because its spirit and system is more characteristic in Asia, than in Europe.

leground for the new "Balance of Power"; it concetrates more on other Continents, than on Europe; it tends to adopt the Macchiavellist doctrine of "the Might is right", and it identifies the term "Nation" with the term "State", consequently the national minorities are considered as some sort of "social groups" in the framework of the State. The State, — which is identified as a "Naion" in the U.N., (even if it is a multinational complex, ruled over by one of its majorities or even minorities,) — sensitively defends its "national sovereignty" in the United Nations, consequently, this international organization is not authorized to "interfere" in the "domestic policy" of the meber State. In these circumstances, no international institution is able to protect national minorities, or defend them against final genocide, because it would be"interference" into the "domestic policy", insulting the "national sovereignty" of the State, which appears in the Assembly as a "Nation". Additionally to this; it would be a great mistake to feel, that the United Nations could be identified with the world-wide "representations" of nations and nationalities, because multinational States are "represented" only by the major nationality, thus the problems of the national minorities could not appear in the U.N. by the cries of the minorities themselves. (#990).

If the United Nations represent a failure, (among other things,) in the solution of the ethno-linguistic minority problems; the rising other internationalism, European integration represent a much more positive hope. "National sovereignty" will appear as a problem in a United Europe too, but the fact that the member nation, or nationality could be checked by the economic aid, or economic pressure of the centralized Common Market, would soften nationalistic extremism. Consequently, the centralized European Assembly could effectively protect ethnic minorities against the extremism of the national majority; definitely much more effectively, than the League, or the U.N. ever did.

Eastern Europe, colonised by an ahen Big Power for many years, will certainly take the first historical opportunity to join the European Confederation, and, as a matter of fact, the cry for a European integration comes from the enslaved Eastern Europe, pear after year.

The solution, — and probably the only solution — of the Transylvanian problem could happen only in the wider framework of a general European integration. This integration should and will be associated with the series of mutual, biliteral and multiliteral agreements among nations, facing each other with hostility many times in the past, but now, recognizing that co-operation leads to much more success in the long run, than hostility; realizing that a European alliance is the only way against alien dominatons, they wll be certainly ready to search for security by these multiliteral agreements. Hungary and Rumania will certainly participate, and the Transylvanian problem will be much less a borderline problem, then ever before.

If a Danubian Federation, — and around it even a Great European Confederation — guarantees the existence of Transylvania as a geopolitical unit, it will be unquestionable, that for Transylvania itself, the only solution is the federal solution. This would recognise that Transylvania is neither Rumanian nor Hungarian, but has a peculiar character and unity of its own, to which both nations have contributed and can contribute in the future.

„Transylvania would form an autonomous unit within a larger federation," — proposed H. Seton-Watson too, — "which would include not only Roumania and Hungary but several other neigh-

---

#990: Soviet Russia "solved" this problem in a very curious way, "representing" the nationalities of the Soviet Union and even the satellites in Eastern Europe by Muscovite agents.

bouring States. Within Transylvania the Roumanian and Hungarian languages would have absolute equality, posts in the civil service would be allotted as far as possible in accordance with the numerical proportions of the two nationalities, and the new generation of civil servants and intellectuals would be brought up to be bilingual." (#991).

What to do with the Germans in Transylvania? The descendants of the Transylvanian Saxons and Swabians do not represent a high percentage, since Rumanian communism, in co-operation with the Kremlin, deported, or exterminated them. Their remainders could find security, could receive grant for the free use of their language in their offices, schools, political and public lives, in the framework of an independent Transylvania, where political tendencies are not influenced, or pushed by neighbouring nationalisms, or by interfering Big Powers; and where ethnic minorities are protected not only by the Transylvanian Constitution, but by the patronising influences of the Danubian Confederation, and possibly by the European Confederation, which higher political levels should always serve, as opportunities for legal appeal, in case of unsolved differences between the ethnic minority and the national majority.

In the previous chapters of my essay you have often read, that Transylvanians often felt themselves nothing else but Transylvanians, or as "Transylvanians first of all," and only secondly as Magyars, or Wallachians or Saxons. During the centuries, the idea and dream of Transylvanian independence there grew up among Transylvanian Magyars, and also among Transylvanian Wallachians, as a sense of being different from the Hungarians in Hungary Proper, or from the Wallachians in the Regat. It was a special kind of Transylvanian patriotism.

> „The intellectual and political life of the Transylvanian Hungarians . . . has followed different lines from those of Trianon Hungary. The differences of mentality are not less profound between the Roumanians of Transylvania and the Old Kingdom. The combination of Turco-Byzantine practice and French theory which characterises the intellectuals of the Old Kingdom is alien to those Transylvanian Roumanians who can remember clearly Habsburg times. The introduction of Balkan standards of administration and justice, and the centralising tendencies of Bucharest, were bitterly resented in Transylvania." (#922).

The visitor in Transylvania could meet with many different peoples, and could communicate in many different languages. The time, when I am concluding this essay, is January, the first month of the year, when peoples of the world are wishing usually "happy new year" to others. The visitor will see Rumanians, who will wish him "Anul Nou Cu Fericirea!" He will mees with Magyars, who will wish him the same thing, but with these words: "Boldog Ujévet!" He will be invited perhaps into a friendly Saxon family, and he will hear: "Got sejen det noa joor!", or to Schwabians, where to wish "Ein frohes neues Jahr" is the usual way of good wishes at this time of the year. The visitor will be certanly impressed by the fact, that these various peoples speaking different languages, having different traditions, remembering historical periods, when they faced each other with hostility; — these ethnic groups are Transylvanians first of all, recognisably different from the peoples of Hungary and of Rumania Proper. After so many years of common suffering, after so many

---

#991: Hugh Seton-Watson: **Eastern Europe Between the Wars.** p. 306.
#992: **Ibid.** p. 307.

years of common, (or nearly common) environmental circumstances, Transylvanians became mainly Transylvanians, and nothing else, or only secondly anything else. If history would offer an opportunity for Transylvanian political independence, for a Transylvanian federation of nationalities, in the framework of a larger Danubian Federation, most of the Transylvanian population would happily vote for it, understanding simultaneously, that an independent Transylvanian State, — as a second „Switzerland" in the Carpathian Alps, — could maintain itself only by good association, and co-operation with its neighbours.

I mentioned before the necessity, that co-operative understanding around Transylvania, the larger Federation of the Danubian States, represent an important condition for the survival of Transylvania, as a Confederative State. At this point, it will be understandable, that the peaceful understanding and co-operation between Hungary and Rumania would be essentially important.

Is it possible to immagine it, after so many centuries of hostility?

We have to presuppose it, because without this basic condition the security of Transylvania would be very questionable. In spite of the disappointing past, we have many historical reasons to presuppose this friendship. (#993).

"... the two nations have much in common. They are the only non-Slav nations in Eastern Europe, surrounded by Slavs to north and south and threatened by the ever-recurring thrust of the Germans into the Danube Basin. The Hungarians and Roumanians are the two essentially Danubian nations, occupying the space between the Alps and the Black Sea, a space distinct from the Baltic region or the Balkan peninsule. These two nations know each other perhaps better than any other pair of nations in Eastern Europe." (#994).

The author of this quotation wrote about common Hungarian-Rumanian interest, facing the Slav international environment, or facing the modern versions of the "Drang nach Ostern". Additionally to this, we have to remember, that both Hungary and Rumania were German satellites, and a large majority of their population was very unhappy about it (#995), then they both became unwilling satellites of Soviet Russia, and again the large majority of their population would resist against this enforced situation, — if they would have an opportunity to resist. (#996). It is true, that after the hoped liberation of Eastern Europe, when the Transylvanian problem could openly reappear as a theme of discussion and negotiation at the round tables of international forums, or at the tables of Hungarian and Rumanian delegations, some Hungarian, or Rumanian extreme nationalists would certainly reappear to continue their eternal struggle for Transylvania. Hopefully, international forums, and the moderate Hungarian and Rumanian majorities will be able to appease, or caldm down extreme emotions. Both Hungarian and Rumanian nationalists have shown themselves incompetent to deal with the Transylvanian problem. They would never agree with a federal solution. They would never help to build a second Switzerland on the Carpathian Alps. They should not have any voice in discussions leading to the final solution. Fortunate-

---

#993: Here, at this point, we should not consider the colaboration of Hungarian and Rumanian Muscovites as friendship of these nations.

#994: H. Seton-Watson: **Eastern Europe Between the Wars.** p. 308.

#995: The Transylvanian Peasants' Party was the main force of the resistance.

#996: The Transylvanian Wallachians were again the main force of the resistance against Stalinism, and also against the new waves of the "national-communism" of Bucharest. (Discussed in my Chs. XVII-XX).

ly, in spite of opposing factiors, there are on both sdes a considerable number of able and intelligent people, who wish to solve the problem on the basis of moderate emotions and mutual understanding.

"Thoughtful Hungarians realise that their nation is in the minority, and that population trends are such that it is not likely ever to became a majority. If, despite this, Hungary were to seize Transylvania, using some temporary favorable opportunity, she could never feel secure in possession, perpetually threatened by a Roumania growing in population and in economic and military power. But within an autonomous Transylvania, member of a larger Federation, the Hungarians could use their superior education and skill to ensure an influence greater than their numbers would suggest." (#997).

On the Rumanian side desire for friendship is not lacking. (#998). Not all the Rumanians accepted the aggressive fascism, and extravagant nationalism of the Iron Guardists, or the extreme nationalism of the national-communists since 1953.

Unquestionably, the preliminary condition of the suggested solution is, that peoples of East-, and East-Central Europe have to be liberated from Russian domination, receiving the opportunity for national selfdetermination. Hopefully, nations of the Danubian region learned their lesson from previous bitter experiences, and they are ready to realize, that nationalistic quarells among themselves represent historical suicide for all the small nations here, sooner, or later; representing advantage only for alien Big Powers. Only mutual understanding and common willingness to create a federal solution will give security to nations, and national minorities alike. Nationalism and partition have failed. There remain — friendship and political-economic cooperation.

Today, under the given conditions, political independency and federalism represent the only possible, and sensible solution for Transylvania. This "independency" should not be associated with hostile separatism against any direction around her political frontiers. Transylvanian political independency and federalism could be successful only, if the newly created political unit (which was actually always a geopolitical unit) is surrounded by friendly and co-operating nations, if it is part of a larger, Danubian Federation, — which will be, hopefully, sooner or later, part of the United European Confederation.

The Transylvanian independency should be guaranteed on international, multiliteral level, but the Transylvanian Confederation should be based on sensible, and moderate internal conditions.

"Today, . . . this cannot be done successfully in any other way, than through national autonomies given to all three existing nations", — feels Zathureczky too, — "the Hungarian, the Roumanian, and the German. Finally, to avoid any further territorial discussions, through the union of these three autonom nations, the plan of a federated autonom Transylvania must be worked out with extreme care." (#999), (#1000).

#997: H. Seton-Watson: Eastern Europe Between the Wars. pp. 309-310.

#998: At this point, of course, I am not thinking about "official" friendship" of Muscovite, or any Communist-, or Nationalist Government, but the good will of the Rumanian people.

#999: Quotation from Zathureczky: Transylvania p. 59.

#1000: Zathureczky here, agrees with many other historians, desiring actually not bilingualism, but the acceptance of all the three main languages, as official, and working languages. This type of Constitution would fit not only the practice of Transylvanian federalism, but it would be the modernized version of the Transylvanian "Three Nation" tradition.

Supposedly, many readers of this essay will feel, that I subjected the solution of the Transylvanian ethno-linguistic minority problem under too many pre-conditions. (Liberation from the Russian domination; Hungarian-Rumanian mutual understanding and co-aperation; Transylvanian autonomy and federalism in the fremework of a Danubian Confederation; even in the possible framework of a Greater European integration, etc.). If anyone feels, that these, mentioned, preconditions are too utopistic, if anyone is too sceptical, or too pessimistic about the possibility of these preconditions, I do not have too much evidence in 1970, which seem to prove, that those necessary pre-conditions, as suppositions will appear very soon. Thus, I can not argue with sceptics, cynics and with pessimists.

(Sceptics, and pessimists have many reasons to be sceptics and pessimists. However, the connected trouble is, that radicals, Macchiavellists, aggressors were always seriously aided by sceptics and pessimists. As a matter of fact, those sceptics and pessimists usually became accidental, or unwilling supporters of the radicals, extremists, Macchiavellists, and aggressors. The hesitation of the Habsburgs aided Napoleon, the „appeasement" aided Hitler, the "Better to be red than dead" -philosophy of Bertrand Russel, — and other, "little bertrand russells", — aided and is aiding Stalin, Khrushchev and Brezhnew. Thus, western scepticism and pessimism usually appeared as a decadent, even paralysing force, and, it is very much a fact, that scepticism and pessimism are not necessarily realistic factors, but rather factors, which are preparing the atmosphere for the aggressors, and dictators. Aggressors and dictators are often strong enough to break windows and doors. Pacifism, (and its two "cousins," scepticism and poitical pessimism) are very helpful, opening windows and doors, which would propably resist against the penetration of the aggressive force. Old western philosophers, and the "flower children" of the West; they are closer "relatives", than they really think, and they represent this strange circulus viciosis, which encouraged many Soviet and Maoist leaders of our days to believe: the West will lose the Third World War, without taking the life of one Russian or Chinese soldier in the battlefield.)

I had to mention those preconditions, because without them, the solution of the Transylvanian minority problems, and the solution of other European minority problems, are just not possible.

Of course, the Transylvanian ethnic-minorities do not have too much time to wait Gepocide in the form of linguicide, or more drastic forms) is a very fast "solution" to every minority problem. We are witnessing in these years a life-and-death "race" between the extreme activities of dominating nationalisms over ethnic minorities, and the natural forces of historical development. If the natural historical devalopment is too slow, — there will be no more minority problems in Transylvania. Few more decades and Great Rumania will become a purely "national State." In 1970, we may speculate, and stil hope for a humanistic solution, asking: "Quo vadis Transylvania?"

In my Preface, I described my personal sad experiences about the ignorance of the West about East-Central Europe. I described, that many interviewed individual mentioned that according to his knowledge, Transylvania was Count Dracula's land. In most of the cases, this was the maximum information of the interviewed people. Unfortunately, it is a fact, that a detailed reference book about Transylvanian history is, more or less, unknown in the West. (I used 112 references for this study, but from these only two, short pamphlets were direct studies about Transylvania.) Hopefully, the reader of this essay, (agrees or disagrees with me, this is another question,) received a considerable amount of information, which makes him one of those, who now realizes: Transylvania was much more in history, than the home of the mysterious vampire, Count Dracula.

BIBLIOGRAPHY

1.) Andrews, Marshall edit.: *Anatomy of Revolution.* A Condensation of the United Nations Report on the Hungarian Uprising. Publ. in co-operation with Coordinated Hungarian Relief, Washington. Public Affairs Press, Washington, 1957. (This source was used for Ch. XIX. only.).

2). Apponyi, Albert: *The Historic Mission of Hungary.* (In the *Justice for Hungary.* ed. Apponyi and others. Longmans, Green and Co. Ltd. London, 1928. (Review and criticism. The effect of the Treaty of Trianon. Used for Chs XV. and XVI. only).

3.) Asztalos, Miklós & Pethő, Sándor: *A Magyar Nemzet Története.* Lantos Publ. Co, 1953. (A gen. history of the Hungarian nation.)

4.) Bailey, Thomas, A: *Woodrow Wilson and the Lost Peace.* Quadrangle Books, Chicago, 1944. (Source for Chs. XV. & XVI.)

5.) Balla, Antal: *A Legújabb Kor Világtörténete.* Könyvbarátok Szövetsége, Kir. Magyar Egyetemi Nyomda, Budapest, 1932. (This source contains the affairs of Worldpolitics from 1870 to 1930. It was useful for the Chs. XIV, XV, and XVI.)

6.) Balla, Antal: *Magyarország Története az 1790-91-iki Országgyűléstöl a Világháborúig.* Singer and Wolfner, Budapest, 1940. (This source discusses Hungarian history from 1790 to 1914.)

7.) Baráth, Tibor: *Erdély Geopolitikája.* (This short article appeared in the *Magyar Élet* (Hungarian Life), Toronto, April, 1968. It introduces Transylvania as a geopolitical unit. I used for my Ch. II.).

8.) Bátky, Sigismund: *The Ethnography of Hungary.* (In *View of Trianons' Hungary.* Gabriel Bethlen Press, Budapest, 1912. This source was very useful for the discussion of ethnographic situation in Transylvania before the World War I; Ch. XV.)

9.) Berzy, József: *Európa felszabaditása.* Publ. by the author, Argentina, 1966. (Ideas and principles about the Paneuropean movement. I used as a source to my Conclusion).

10.) Birsdall, Paul: *Versailles Twenty Years After.* Reynal & Hitchkock, New York, 1941. (This source proved to be useful to the Ch. XVI: "Transylvania, as Province of the Rumanian Kingdom.")

11.) Bobula, Ida: *Origin of the Hungarian Nation.* Problems Behind the Iron Curtain Series, No. 3., Publ. by the Danubian Research and Information Center, Florida, 1966. (This source was used for my prehistoric, ancient and medieval approaches; Chs. III-VII. It is a very brief pamphlet, but contains the newest prehistoric findings and speculations.)

12.) Brown, Francis: *Nationalism.* In F. J. Brown, and Others ed: *Contemporary World Politics.* John Willet & Sons, London, 1939. (An introduction to the problems of intrenational relations, discussing the theory and practice of modern nationalism.)

13.) Buell, Raymond, Leslie: *Europe, A History of Ten Years.* The Macmillan Co., 1930. (Discusses the postwar years, 1920-30. I used for my Ch. XVI.)

14.) Cholnoky, Eugene: *The Geographical Unity of Transylvania.* In the *Hungarian Quarterly,* 1940-41. (It was very useful for the Ch. II.)

15. Csabai, Stephen: *The Real Dracula.* The *Hungarian Quarterly,* Autumn, 1941. Vol. VII. No. 2. (I included the essence of this essay in my Ch. X; "The Zenith of the Hungarian Power.")

16.) Csato, Tamás, and Others, ed: *Egyetemes Történelmi Kronologia.* Tankönyvkiadó, Budapest, 1967 (Chronology of important dates.)

17.) Csatári, Mária and Others: *Történelmi Atlasz,* Kartográfiai Vállalat, Budapest, 1967. (It was useful source for my maps, introduced in this essay).

18.) Csiknémasági, N.: *Dák Régészeti Leletek a Székelyföldön.* Article from the *Kanadai Magyar Ujság (Canadain Hungarian News;)* December 10, 1965. (Detailed description of the Dak archeological findings in Transylvania. It was a useful source for Ch. IV: "Ancient Transylvania.)

19.) Deák, Francis: *The Hungarian-Rumanian Land Dispute.* A Study of Hungarian Property Rights in Transylvania under the Treaty of Trianon. Columbia University Press, New York, 1928. (Used for Ch. XVI: Transylvania as Province of the Rumanian Kingdom.)

20.) Dominian, Leon: *The Frontiers of Language and Nationality of Europe.* American Geographical Society of New York, Henry Holt and Co., 1917. (An excellent source for the analysis of European ethnolinguistic groups. In this essay it was used for Ch. VI: The Problem of Wallachian Origin and Early Migration.)

21.) Donald, Robert: *The Tragedy of Trianon.* Thornton Butternorth Ltd., London, 1928. (Some ideas were used in Chs. XV. and XVI.)

22.) Eckhardt, Tibor: *Regicide at Marseille.* American Hungarian Library and Historical Society, New York, 1964. (The recollections of the leader of the anti-fascist resistance in Hungary. Mainly, the book discusses the circumstances of the assassination of King Alexander of Yugoslavia, but many other parts of it was very useful for Ch. XVI: Tr. as Province of the Rum. Kingdom.)

2f.) Elekes, Louis: *The Development of the Rumanian People.* Article of *The Hungarian Quarterly.* 1941. Vol. VII.) (Important source for the investigation of the Wallachian origin and migration, discussed in Chs. VI., VII, & VIII.)

24.) Ernyei, Caspar: *The Spirit of Transylvania.* Article in *The Hungarian Quarterly,* Vol. VI. No. 2. Summer, 1940. (It deals with the spirit of Hungarian art and literature in Rumanian dominated Transylvania, in the Interwar Years. Used for Ch. XVI.)

25.) Fall, Andrew: *Hungarian Culture — Rumanian Culture. (Danubian Review;* 1940, Vol. VIII. No. 6. November). Brief article, used for the analysis of the schooling system in Hung. dominated Transylvania following the "Ausgleich". Ch. XIV.)

26.) Fall, Andrew: *Re-Incorporated Areas Welcome Hungarian Soldiers with Indescribable Enthusiasm.* Brief editorial introduction in the *Danubian Review,* Vol. VIII. No. 5. October, 1940. (Used for Ch. XVII. The Dismemberment of Transylvania.)

27.) Featherstone, H. L.: *A Century of Nationalism.* Thomas Nelson and Sons, Ltd., London, 1939. (Good source, which describes very well the revolutionary atmosphere of liberalism and nationalism in the first half of the XIX. Century. Used for Chs. XII and XIII.).

28.) Fischer-Galati, Stephen: *The New Rumania. From People's Democracy to Socialist Republic.* The M.I.T. Press, Cambridge, Massachussetts, and London. (England), 1967. (Very important source for the investigation of Transylvanian minority problems since the World War II.)

29.) Fischer-Galati, Stephen: *Romania.* (East Central Europe under the Communists-Series. Robert F. Byrness edition, publ. for the Mid. European Studies Center of the Free Europe Committee Inc., Frederick Praeger, New York, 1957. (Fischer-Galati is the gen. editor, and author of many useful articles for Chs. XVII-XX.)

30.) Fritz, Ladislas: *Feverstricken Rumania.* Article in the *Danubian Review,* Vol. VIII, No. 6, November, 1940. Used for Ch. XVII: The Dismemberment of Transylvania.)

31.) Galántai, József: *Az 1867-es Kiegyezés.* Kossuth Könyvkiadó, Budapest, 1967. (The book discusses historical problems before, under and after the "Ausgleich". Used for Chs. XIII and XIV.)

32.) Gathorne-Hardy, G. M.: *The Fourteen Points and the Treaty of Versailles.* At the Clarendon Press, 1939. (Excellent analysis comparing the Wilsonian idealism with the sorrowful realism of Versailles. Used for Chs. XV. and XVI.)

33.) Ghyka, Matila: *A Documented Chronology of Roumanian History.* B. H. Blackwell, Ltd. Oxford, 1941. Translated from the French by Fernand G. Renier, and Anne Cliff. (This extremely pro-Rumanian source was used for almost all Chapters from phe-historic times to the World War II.)

34.) Goldwin, Robert A., — Stourzh, Gerald, — Zetterbaum Marvin, editors: *Reading in Russian Foreign Policy.* Oxford University Press, New York, 1959. (The main source is not connected directly with the topic of this essay, but many of the Chapters are discussing the Soviet methods in the interference into the domestic life of E. European countries. Used for Chs. XVI-XX.)

35.) Halecki, Oscar: *Borderlands of Western Civilization.* A History of East Central Europe. The Ronald Press Company, New York, 1952. (The book of the great Polish historian could be used for almost all of my chapters. He discusses everything very briefly, but his short indications were helpful for investigations for more details.)

36.) Hammond's *Historical Atlas.* Published by C. S. Hammond & Co., Maplewood, New York, 1957. (Its maps were used for map-drawings.)

37.) Horthy, Miklós *Titkos Iratai.* Magyar Országos Levéltár, Kossuth Könyvkiadó, 1965, Budapest. (Studying the private correspondence of Regent Horthy helped to write Chs. XVI and XVII.)

38.) Horváth, Eugene: *Responsibility of Hungary for the War.* Publication of the Hungarian Frontier Readjustment League, Budapest, 1933. (Pamphlet. Used for Chs. XV, and XVI.)

39.) Ionescu, Ghita: *Communism in Rumania.* Oxford University Press, London, 1964. (Excellent source, written by the immigrant Rumanian historian. His attitude is pro-Rumanian in many chapters, but anti-communist. Used for Chs. XVI-XX.)

40.) Iorga, Nicholas: *A History of Roumania. Land, People, Civilization.* Translated from Rumanian by Joseph McCabe. Dodd, Mead, and Co., New York. He is the classical Rumanian historian of the post-Trianon years, the champion of the Dako-Roman theory, who appeared personally in Rum. politics. Pro-Rumanian source. Used in almost all my chapters.)

41.) Jászi, Oscar: *The Dissolution of the Habsburg Monarchy.* The University of Chicago Press, Chicago, 1929. (The authors speculations were used in Ch. XIII (Compromise), Ch. XIV: (Magyarization) and Ch. XV: (Trianon.))

42.) Jókai, Mór: *Erdély Aranykora.* Akadémiai Kiadó, Budapest, 1962. (The classic historical novel of the great XIX. C. romantic author discusses the critical age of Transylvania. Useful for the nalysis of the Independent Transylvanian Principality. Ch. XI.)

43.) Kann, Robert, A: *The Multinational Empire. Nationalism and National Reform in the Habsburg Monarchy. 1848-1918.* Ruthers University. New York, Columbia University Press, 1950. (Used for Chs. XIII, XIV, XV.)

44.) Karsa, Tamás: *Hozzászólás a Dákó-Román Elmélet Jogosultságához.* Article appeared in the *Magyar Szabadság,* Hung. emigrant paper, June 17, 1964. It discusses the Hungarian view in the Dako-Roman theory, the Wallachian origin, and the role of the Wallachians in 1848.)

45.) Kassay, John: *New Situation in South Eastern Europe.* Article in the *Danubian Review.* Vol. VIII. No. 5. Oct. 1940. Pro-Hungarian. Used in Ch. XVII. The Dismemberment of Transylvania.

46.) Kerekes, Lajos: *Bánffy Miklós Politikai Küldetése Romániába 1943-ban.* Article in the *Történelmi Szemle,* VI-2, 1963. Budapest. (The short article describes the political mission of Nicholas Bánffy to Bucharest in 1943, trying to find connection with Maniu. The source was used in Ch. XVII., discussing the dismemberment of Transylvania.).

47.) Kirkconnel, Watson: *The Magyar Muse.* (Kanadai Magyar Ujság Press, Winipeg, 1933). (A selection of Hungarian poetry translated by the author, with excellent, brief biographies. It was used for the description of the Transylvanian spirit, especially in the XIX. century.)

48.) Kirkconnel, Watson: *A Little Treasury of Hungarian Verse.* American-Hungarian Federation, Washington. (Another selection of Hungarian poetry, selected and translated by Kirkconnell, Reményi's poem, demonstrating Hungarian emotions in Transylvania in the Interwar Year, was chosen from this selection.)

49.) Kovács, Imre: *Facts about Hungary.* Hungarian Committee, New York, 1950. (Brief outline history, with important chronological events, detailing events since 1945.)

50.) Kölcsey, Ferenc: *Historiai Vázolatok a Két Magyar Haza Egyesülése és Magyarországnak a Részekhez való Joga Felett.* Article in the framework of *Kölcsei Ferenc Összes Művei,* Szépirodalmi Könyvkiadó, Budapest, 1960. (The article was written by Kölcsey, famous 19th cent. Hung. poet and historian, the author of the Hung. national Anthem. The article was discussing the possibilities of the reunification of Transylvania with Hungary Proper in 1836. Used for Ch. XII.)

51.) Langer, William, L.: *An Encyclopedia of World History.* Houghton, Mifflin Co., The Riverside Press Cambridge, 1968. (It was useful to note important events in footnotes.)

52.) Langsam, Walter, Consuelo: *The World Since 1914.* The Macmillan Co., 1933. New York. (Used Chs.: IV: The Making of Peace, V; The Famous Treaties, XVI: Two Heirs of the Habsburgs, XIX: Southeastern Europe.)

53.) Lázár, Edmund, I.: *Federalist Aspirations in East-Central Europe.* Article in the *Studies for a New Central Europe,* Publ. by the Mid-European Research Institute, New York, 1964, Vol. I, No. 2. (The article documented the federalist ideas appeared in the Hungarian Revolution of 1956. Speculation about its effect on Transylvania was included in my Ch. XIX.)

54.) Lengyel, Emil: *1,000 Years of Hungary.* The John Day Company, New York, 1958. (Outline Hungarian history, mentioning problems of Transylvania on many pages).

55.) Lipson, E.: *Europe in the Nineteenth Century.* New York, 1928. (The Vol. II, Ch. IX: "Racial and Constitutional Problems in Austria-Hungary; 1815-1867." was useful in the analysis of the early XIX. C. period.)

56.) Macartney, C. A.: *Hungary.* Edinburgh, University Press, 1962. (A short historical outline, mentioning the problems of Transylvania on many of its pages.)

57.) Macartney, C. A.: *Hungary and Her Successors. The Treaty of Trianon and Its Consequences. 1919-1937.* Oxford University Press, London, New York, Toronto, Issued under the auspices of the Royal Institute of International Affairs, 1937. (The most excellent source of the main topic. Especially the following chapters were useful: Introduction, Transylvania (pp. 251-348) and Conclusions. The Ethnographical Map of Hungary (from Count Paul Teleki) was analyzed and reproduced in the present essay.)

58.) Macartney, C. A.; and Palmer, A. W.: *Independent Eastern Europe.* Macmillan & Co. Ltd., New York, 1962. (Useful Chapters were III: The Peace Settlement, X: Democracy and Humanity, IV: The Anatomy of the New Europe.)

59.) Macartney, C. A.: *Minorities: A Problem of Eastern Europe.* Article in the *Foreign Affairs,* American Quarterly Review, Vol. I., 1922. (The article discusses the fact that the transformation from feudalism ti liberal democracy represent many difficulties in E. Europe, because the multinational nature of the area.)

60.) Macartney, C. A.: *National States and National Minorities.* Oxford University Press, London, 1934. (Excellent source, discussing the nature of the minority problems in East-Central Europe.)

61.) Macartney, C. A.: *October Fifteenth. A History of Modern Hungary. 1929-1945.* At the University Press; Edinburgh, 1957. (A very carefully detailed description, with many documents. It was especially useful, because its many explanations about Hungarian-Rumanian relationship before World War I, and the circumstances of the dismemberment of Transylvania. (Chs. XVI and XVII in my essay.)

62.) Macartney, C. A.: *Studies on the Early Hungarian Sources.* Sárkány Printing Co., Budapest, 1940. Vol. III. (Its speculations about the problems and circumstances of the Hungarian Conquest of 895-896 were used in this essay, in Chs. IV and V.)

63.) Macartney, C. A.: *The Danubian Basin.* Oxford Pamphlets of World Affairs. N. 10. At the Clarendon Press. 1939. (A very short pamphlet, with a clear, well organized introduction of the geographical and geopolitical problems of the Danubian Basin.)

64.) Macartney, C. A.: *The Magyars in the Ninth Century.* Cambridge, University Press, 1930. (A very extraordinary source about the Hungarian migration and the conquest of the Carpathian Basin, dealing with the problem of early Transylvania on many of its pages.)

65.) MacKay, R. A. and Sounders, S. A.: *The Modern World. Political and Economic.* The Ryerson Press, Toronto and Halifax, 1935. (The Ch. XVI: "The Modern State System" and Ch. XVII: "Nationalism" represented some use.)

66. Marzali, Henrik: *Hungary in the Lighteenth Century.* Cambridge University Press, 1910. (It was a good source, because it mentioned Transylvanian problems, which could be used in my Ch. XII: "Transylvania, as the Province of the Habsburg Empire", and in my Ch. XIII: "Revolution, Reaction, Compromise.")

67.) Marczali, Henrik: *Magyarország Története.* Athenaeum, Budapest, 1912. (A general history of Hungary, written by the classical historian of Hungary. It discusses Transylvanian events in many of its chapters, up to the end of the XIX. Century.)

68.) Masaryk, T. G.: *The Making of a State. Memories and Observations, 1914-18.* London, 1927. (This source was used only for the Ch. XVI., when the example of the Szechoslovakian State was used, discussing the problem of minorities in a multinational political democracy.)

69.) Maskin, N. A.: *Az Okori Róma Története.* Tankönyvkiadó, Budapest, 1951. (The author is one of the most respected Rusisan historian. The used source is the Hung. translation of his work. The age of certain Roman emperors, beginning with Augustus, were studied in connection with the Roman conquest of Dacia. The book has an excellent map-collection too, introducing East-Central Europe in Roman times.)

70.) May, Arthur, J.: *The Age of Metternich. 1814-1848.* Austin, University of Texas Press, 1957. (This source was used for the study of the Habsburg policy in Transylvania in the first half of the XIX. Century.)

71.) Maurice, C. Edmund: *The Revolutionary Movement of 1848-49 in Italy, Austria-Hungary and Germany*. George Bell and Sons, London, 1887. (This source was useful for the investigation of the emotional and military aspects in 1848-49, in Hungary proper and Transylvania.)

72.) Mayo, H. B.: *An Introduction to Democratic Theory*. Oxford University Press, New York, 1960. (Used only for discussing the problem of political democracy in multinational circumstances. Ch. XVI.)

73.) McCormick; T. C. T.; (and Others): *Problems of the Postwar World. A Symposium of Postwar Problems*. McGraw-Hill Book Company, Inc. New York, and London, 1945. (I used Ch. XII only: "The New Nationalism.")

74.) Miskolczi, Gyula: *A Magyar Nép Történelme*. Anonymus, Roma, 1956. (The excellent source discusses the history of the Hungarian people from the Tragedy of Mohács, 1526, to the First World War. Many of the chapters are discussing Transylvanian minority problems.)

75.) Montgomery, John, Flournoy: *Hungary, the Unwilling Satellite*. The Devin Adair Company, New York, 1947. (A detailed description of the Hungarian problems under the shadow of Hitler. I used for my Chs. XVI and XVII. It has many indications in connection with the Transylvanian problems.)

76.) Móricz, Zsigmond: *"Erdély."* Szépirodalmi Könyvkiadó, Budapest, 1942. (It is one of the Hungarian classics. A series of historical scenes, describing the problems in Transylvania in the age of the Independent Principality, in the time of Gabriel Bethlen).

77.) Nagy, László and Molnár, Miklós: *Két Világ Között. Nagy Imre Utja*. Nagy Imre Politikai és Társadalomtudományi Intézet, Brüsszel. 1960. (This book deals with Imre Nagy only. Some of its chapters was used, discussing the Imre Nagy problem, and his possible execution in Rumania. Ch. XX.)

78.) Ottlik, László: *Democracy and the Multi-National State*. Essay in *The Hungarian Quarterly*. Vol. IV., Winter, 1938-39, No. 4. Budapest, London, New York. (Very useful essay for the speculation about the problem of democracy in multinational circumstances. The author is one of the East-European expert of ethnic problems. I used in my Ch. XVI.)

79.) Ottlik, László: *The Minority Problem Yesterday and Today*. Budapest. Szemle. (It deals also with the problem of democracy in connection with ethno-linguistic problems.)

80.) Osterhaven, M. Eugene: *Transylvania. The Pathos of a Reformation Tradition*. A Reformed Review Occasional Paper. Published by *The Reformed Review* of the Western Theological Seminary, Holland, Michigan, 1968. (This excellent brief pamphlet contains many important descriptions and statistics used in this essay. It contains some useful maps too.)

81.) Padányi, Viktor: *Dentumagyaria*. Editorial Transylvania. Magyar Történelmi Tanulmánysorozat. Buenos Aires, Argentina, 1956. (Excellent source, which was used in the speculation of the Magyar-Hun-Avar, etc. relationship. Ch. IV: Ancient Transylvania.)

82.) Palmer, R. R. ed.: *Atlas of World History*. Rand McNally Company, New York, Chicago, San Francisco; 1965. (I used many of its maps for the map-speculations about Transylvanian transformations.)

83.) Pisky, Fred: *The People*. Essay in Stephen Fisher-Galati ed. *Romania. East-Central Europe under the Communists*. Mid-European Studies Center, Free Europe Committee, Inc. Frederick A. Praeger, New York, 1957. (Very useful source for the analysis of the ethnographic situation in Rumania since the Wolrd War II).

84.) Rath, R. John: *The Vienese Revolution of 1848.* Austin, Univ. of Texas Press, 1957. (This book was important for my speculation about the revolutionary atmosphere in East-Central Europe in 1848.)

85.) Roucek, J. S.: *Central Europe. Crucible of World Wars.* Prentice-Hall, Inc., New York, 1946. (excellent source for the analysis of the Rumanian domestic situation in the interwar years. I used Ch. XII "Romania, 1918-1945" for my Chs. XVI & XVII.)

86.) Seton-Watson, Hugh: *Eastern Europe Between the Wars; 1918-1941.* Archon Books, Hamden and Conneticut, 1962. (One of the best sources which were used for my essay. The author is the son of R. W. Seton-Watson, with unquestionably better historical technique and with more objectivity than his father's.)

87.) Seton-Watson, R. W.: *A History of the Roumanians. From Roman Times to the Completion of Unity.* Archon Books, Hamden and Contennicut, 1963. (The author, using the name of "Scotus Viator" was member of a group of pro-Little Entente, postwar western historians, who usually adopted the subjective, sometimes even falsified, introductions of Czech, Rumanian, Serbian historians, without individual investigations, or without even the attempt of objective approach. I read, and used this work as a stimulative source.)

88.) Simonds, Frank, H., and Emeny, Brooks: *The Great Powers in World Politics.* American Book Company, New York, 1939. (Ch. XVI: "The Smaller States", and Ch. XVII. "The Problem of European Peace." were used for my Ch. XVI: Transylvania, as Province of the Rumanian Kingdom.)

89.) Sinor, Denis: *History of Hungary.* Allen and Unwin, London, 1959. (An outline history of Hungary, useful only for very beginners in my main, and related topics.)

90.) Sisa, István: *Quo Vadis Hungaria?* Hungarian Life — Magyar Élet, Toronto, 1964. (Series of articles, dealing with contemporary Hungarian problems and Transylvanian problems.)

91.) Schreiber Tamás: *A Magyar Kisebbség Helyzete Romániában.* Article in the *Irodalmi Ujság,* Paris, 1964. (This article discusses the problems of the Hungarian minority in Transylvania in 1964, using, as reference the article of the *Le Monde,* Paris, July 4-5, 1964.)

92.) Stein, Werner: *Kulturfahrplan. Die Wichtingsten Daten Der Kulturgeschichte Van Annbeginn Bis Heute.* Berlin-Grünwald, F. A. Herbig Berlagsbuchhandlung, 1946. (Excellent chronology of dates in German language.)

93.) *Der Spiegel.* Series of articles in the West German newspaper from 1957 to 1959, about the tragedy of the Transylvanian Magyars following the Hungarian Revolution of 1956. I used the article, which was translated as *Jönnek a Magyarok* (The Hungarians are coming), and appeared in the *Magyar Elet,* Toronto, 1966. See p. 175.)

94.) Szakonyi, István: *Az Oláhokról Szóló Első Történelmi Feljegyzések és a 'Dákó-Román Elmélet' Történelmi Alapjai.* Article, appeared in the *Kanadai Magyarság,* Sept. 10, 1966. — Nov. 12, 1966. (The author discusses the Dako-Roman theory with criticism, describes the Wallachian migration into Transylvania, and describes episodes from Rumanian history.)

95.) Szalay, Jeromos: *Románok Erdélyben.* Article in the *Magyar Elet* (Hungarian Life, Toronto), 1964. It discusses the Horia-Kloska rebellion in Transylvania, and the connection of the rebels with Joseph II of Habsburg. It also discusses the previous peasant-rebellions, and the foundation of the "Unio Trium Nationum". Used for my Ch. XII (Tr. as the Province of the Habsburg Empire.)

96.) Szász, Zsombor: *Hungarians — Rumanians.* Article in *The Hungarian Quarterly.* 1941. Winter; It analyzes the infiltration of the Wallachians beginning with the 12th century. It deals with the problem of the "Dako-Roman continuity", and with the "Nationalities Law" after the "Ausgleich".)

97.) Szász, Zsombor: *Rumanian History.* Article in *The Hungarian Quarterly,* 1941. It discusses special aspects of Rumanian history, especially in connection with the Rumanian demand for Transylvania. It criticises Prof. Giurescu's extremism in the evaluation of the Wallachian race.)

98.) Szász, Zsombor: *Rumania at the Paris Peace Conference.* Article in the *Danubian Review.* Oct. 1940. Vol. VIII. No. 5. It discusses Bucharest's special attitude before, under and after the Peace Conferences in Paris.)

99.) Szegfű, Gyula: *Állam és Nemzet.* Magyar Szemle Társaság, Budapest, 1942. (The author is one of the classics of Hungarian historiography. This book was especially useful with his analysis about the structures of the "state" and of the "nation." Its chapter "Tanulmányok a Nemzetiségi Kérdésről" (Studies about the nationality question.) was very useful in many speculations of this essay.)

100.) Tamás, András: *Délkeleteurópa a Diplomáciai Törekvések Sodrában. (1939-44 Között).* Az "Északi Fény", Montreal, 1961. Printed in the Printing Press of the Kanadai Magyar Ujság, Winnipeg. (This pamphlet discusses in details the attempt of the Hung. Govt. in the late 1930-es to find diplomatic connections with the Western powers. It also explains the breakdown of the Little Entente, esp. the alienation of Bucharest and Belgrade.)

101.) Tápay-Szabó, László: *Az Emberiség Története.* Publ. by the Pesti Napló Rt. Athenaeum, Budapest, 1933. (It is a brief outline book of World History, but it includes especially useful chapters about the ethno-linguistic history of Transylvania before the Hungarian Conquest. Used for my Ch. V.)

102.) Teleki, Paul Count: *The Evolution of Hungary and Its Place in European History.* The Macmillan Co. New York, 1923. (One of the Hungarian classics. The author was identical with the prime-minister, who commited suicide in 1941. He deals with the Transylvanian minority problem in many chapters of his book and his ethnographical map was one of the best of its kind.)

103.) *The International Comission of Jurists. A Bulletin.* (The Bulletin itself appeared in many articles of political science. I found and used it from the *Studies for a New Central Europe.* Ed. Alexander Gallus, Publ. by Mid-European Research Institute, New York, 1964. Vol. 1. No. 2. It was a report written by the International Institute of Jurists about the oppression of national minorities in Transylvania since the World War II).

104.) Tiltman, H. Hessel: *The Terror in Europe.* Frederick A. Stokes Company, New York, 1932. (For the main topic especially Chs. XXII and XXIII: "The White Terror" and "Hungarian Justice", and Ch. XXIV. "Roumania" were useful. These chapters are discussing political, economic, social circumstances in Hungary and Rumania in the first decade following the World War I).

105.) Torjai-Szabo: *Centuries of Transylvania.* Münich, 1956. (An outline history of Transylvania. I used only for Ch. XI, discussing the problems of the independent Transylvanian Principality.)

106.) *Transylvanian Institute Pamphlets.* (The Transylvanian Research Institute resides in Ardmore, Pa. USA. It publishes pamphlets ocassionally. One of the used pamphlets: *"The Problem of Transylvania"* was used as a gen. source for this essay.)

107.) Vaugham Williams, E. L.: *The Hungarian Question in the British Parliament.* Speeches, Quotations and Answers thereto in the House of Lords and the House of Commons from 1919 to 1930. Grant Richards London, 1933. (Many of the questions and answers are connected with the problem of Trianon and Transylvania.)

108.) Wanklyn, H. G.: *The Eastern Marshland of Europe.* George Philip and Sons, Ltd., Liverpool, 1941. (Az excellent general source, including introduction about the geography and outline history of East Europe. It could be very useful especially for beginners, who are not too familiar with E. Europe. For this essay the Part III: "The Danube Lands." was useful as a general source.)

109.) Wolff, Robert Lee: *The Balkans in Our Time.* Harvard University Press, Cambridge, Massachussetts, 1956. (One of the most useful sources and aids for the writing this essay. I could use especially its speculations about the Dako-Roman Theory, and its descriptions about the gradual expansion of Rumania at the expense of her neighbours.)

110.) Yolland, Arthur, B.: *The History of Hungary.* Part of the edition of *One View of Trianon's Hungary.* Turul Association, Bethlen Gábor Press, Budapest, 1928. (The author was one of the Hungarian classics in historical writing. From his approach, especially the chapter about the independent Transylvanian Principality was useful.)

111.) Zathureczky, Gyula: *National Minorities, Step-Children in Communist Lands.* The author is one of the experts of Transylvanian minority questions. This article appeared in *Studies for a New Central Europe.* Ed. A. Gallus, The Mid-European Research Institute, New York, 1964. It was very useful for the analysis of the minority problem in Transylvania since the death of Stalin.)

112.) Zathureczky, Gyula: *Transylvania. Citadel of the West.* Problems behind the Iron Curtain Series. No. 1. Publ. by the Historical Research Centre of Florida. Translated and edited by Albert Wass de Czege, University of Florida. (This pamphlet is a condensed edition of the *Transylvanian Dispute* by the same author. It was very useful for this essay, and many parts of it were quoted in this essay.)